JOHN W. F. DULLES is University Professor of
Latin American Studies at The University of
Texas at Austin. During spring semesters he
holds a professorship of history at The University of Arizona. His volume *Yesterday in
Mexico: A Chronicle of the Revolution, 1919–
1936* (University of Texas Press, 1961) was described by the *Hispanic American Historical
Review* as "an absorbing, objective, yet sympathetic and frequently witty account of this era
of the Revolution" and one which "deserves a
place in the library of everyone concerned with
the history of Mexico." Professor Dulles is
presently engaged in extensive research for a
forthcoming study of Communism in Brazil, and
he has previously published *Vargas of Brazil:
A Political Biography* (University of Texas
Press, 1967).

UNREST IN BRAZIL

UNREST

UNIVERSITY OF TEXAS PRESS · AUSTIN & LONDON

IN BRAZIL

Political-Military Crises 1955–1964

By JOHN W. F. DULLES

67914

Standard Book Number 292–70006–7
Library of Congress Catalog Card Number 75–101519
Copyright © 1970 by John W. F. Dulles
Printed by The University of Texas Printing Division, Austin
Bound by Universal Bookbindery, Inc., San Antonio

CONTENTS

ILLUSTRATIONS

MAPS

INTRODUCTION

"Seldom has a major nation come closer to the brink of disaster and yet recovered than did Brazil in its recent triumph over Red subversion." Thus *The Reader's Digest* commented on the overthrow of President João ("Jango") Goulart in 1964. Lincoln Gordon, who was American ambassador to Brazil at the time, referred to the event in glowing terms when he said: "Future historians may well record the Brazilian revolution as the single most decisive victory for freedom in the mid-20th century."[1]

Reflecting a contrary point of view, Goulart's Justice Minister, Abelardo Jurema, would have us recall the words of Madame Roland before she was guillotined in 1793: "O Liberty! Liberty! What crimes are committed in thy name!"[2]

This book proposes to tell of Goulart's overthrow and of the events that led up to it.

Goulart, deposed by the decisions of Army officers in 1964, was known as the political heir of Getúlio Vargas. Vargas, the most important personality in Brazilian politics from 1930 to 1954, committed suicide in 1954 when military leaders demanded that he leave the presidency.

The post-Vargas political crises began as struggles said to have been between Getulistas (followers of Getúlio Vargas) and anti-Getulistas. Participating in these struggles were thirteen political parties. Only three of them had a sufficiently wide geographic distribution of strength to be really national. Two of these had been founded in 1945 at the

---

[1] Both quotations appear in Clarence W. Hall, "The Country That Saved Itself," *The Reader's Digest*, November 1964, pp. 135–158.

[2] Abelardo Jurema, *Sexta-Feira, 13: Os Últimos Dias do Govêrno João Goulart*, p. 240. Jurema incorrectly attributes these words to Marat.

suggestion of Vargas: the Partido Social Democrático (PSD—Social Democratic Party) and the Partido Trabalhista Brasileiro (PTB—Brazilian Labor Party). At the same time Vargas' foes had founded the third national party, the União Democrática Nacional (UDN—National Democratic Union), and many smaller parties. During the 1950's and early 1960's the parties entered into all sorts of alliances. The electorate, interested in personalities, did not worry when these alliances violated the traditions and programs of the parties.

Long-time Vargas adversaries were active in giving a Getulista–anti-Getulista interpretation to the events. The term Getulista may for a while have been somewhat useful, but it is difficult to attribute to it any particular views (including any views Getúlio Vargas might have had). The term has been used with reference to a group of men who had worked with Vargas and who, like Vargas, were accustomed to power. The Getulistas liked to associate themselves with accomplishments. PSD leaders pointed to achievements in the field of economic development; PTB leaders spoke of advances in social justice. Leaders of the anti-Getulista UDN—for the most part in the position of "outs" —concentrated on criticizing; they were particularly critical of the morals of the "ins."

Military officers were often ready to step in "to save Brazil from its politicians." The military had played leading roles in doing away with the constitutions of 1824, 1891, 1934, and 1937. During the crises of 1955–1964 the military, frequently divided, was closely watched by politicians. The "in" group and the "out" group each felt concern lest the other gain military support in favor of a coup that would violate the 1946 constitution with the explanation that the violation was necessary for preserving or achieving the noblest of ideals.

During 1955 such reasoning persuaded well-placed Army officers that it was necessary to depose Carlos Luz and João Café Filho from the presidency. Juscelino Kubitschek, who succeeded in completing a constitutional five-year term (1956–1961), observed that: "In Brazil one is elected by the people, but one governs with one's eyes turned to the armed forces."[3]

[3] *Ibid.*, p. 200.

Neither Jânio Quadros nor Jango Goulart, elected President and Vice-President in 1960, completed the five-year term that began in 1961. Quadros, who resigned, and Goulart, his successor, saw Congress as a roadblock to their aims. They convinced many that the prevailing political system should be blamed for Brazil's ills. Goulart and far leftists encouraged manifestations of popular support for a radical agrarian reform that Congress did not favor.

Those who worried about the Far Left and about Goulart's intentions organized demonstrations at which they proclaimed that the 1946 constitution was sacred. But the military leaders who assumed control after Goulart's downfall decided that it was not to be so sacred after all. They maintained that the condition in which they found the country made it necessary for them to modify the 1946 constitution.[4]

Whenever the military intervened in political matters, opinions differed as to whether the step was justified. It is hoped that this book's account of political-military crises during the ten-year period will throw some light on the role played by the military while civilians governed Brazil and will be of help to readers who seek to appraise that role.

J.W.F.D.

[4] The 1946 constitution was modified by "Institutional Acts" issued in April 1964 and October 1965. The regime of Marshal Humberto Castelo Branco, which took over soon after Goulart's fall, gave Brazil a new constitution in 1967. This, in turn, was modified late in 1968 by another "Institutional Act," issued by Castelo Branco's successor after a conference with the National Security Council.

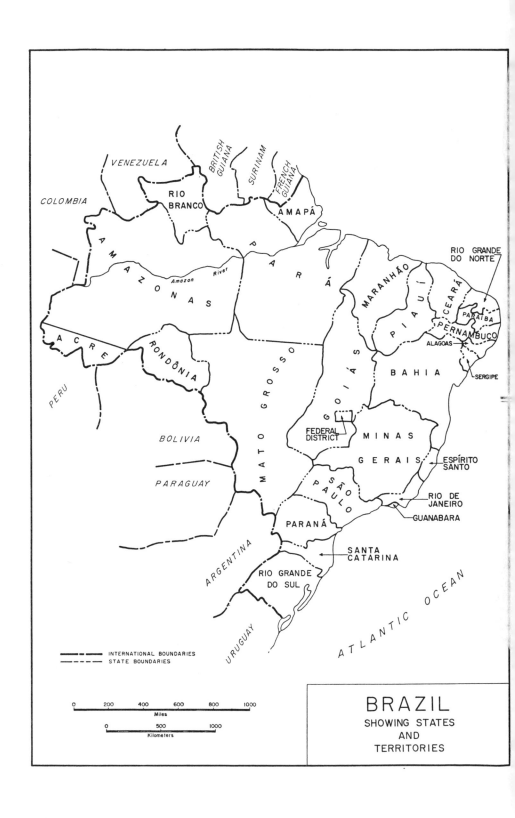

COLOMBIA

VENEZUELA

BRITISH GUIANA

SURINAM

FRENCH GUIANA

RIO BRANCO

AMAPÁ

A M A Z O N A S

P A R Á

MARANHÃO

RIO GRANDE DO NORTE

CEARÁ

PIAUÍ

PARAIBA

PERNAMBUCO

ALAGOAS

SERGIPE

Amazon River

ACRE

RONDÔNIA

PERU

BOLIVIA

PARAGUAY

M A T O   G R O S S O

G O I Á S

BAHIA

FEDERAL DISTRICT

MINAS GERAIS

ESPÍRITO SANTO

SÃO PAULO

RIO DE JANEIRO

GUANABARA

PARANÁ

SANTA CATARINA

ARGENTINA

RIO GRANDE DO SUL

URUGUAY

ATLANTIC OCEAN

INTERNATIONAL BOUNDARIES
STATE BOUNDARIES

| 0 | 200 | 400 | 600 | 800 | 1000 |
Miles

| 0 | 500 | 1000 |
Kilometers

BRAZIL
SHOWING STATES AND TERRITORIES

BOOK I: *The Election of 1955*

"We have no illusions: legality will only be pre-served with your blood and with the arms which the people have furnished you. I feel that the desperation of a reckless minority converts itself into a grave threat."

Army Inspector-General Zenóbio da Costa
manifesto to Army men, October 17, 1955

"In my government the one who speaks in the name of the Army is my War Minister. At 4:00 P.M. bring me here to Catete Palace, for my signature, the decree dis-missing General Zenóbio da Costa."

President Café Filho to War Minister Lott
October 17, 1955

1. "I Offer My Life in a Holocaust"
(August 24, 1954)

IN 1954 THE VIEW of Army officers belonging to the anti-Communist Democratic Crusade prevailed in the Brazilian Military Club. Two years earlier, by a vote of 8,288 to 4,489, the anti-Communist wing had captured the Club's presidency from "nationalist" Army officers who opposed the United States and its position in the cold war.[1]

Democratic Crusaders stressed that the armed forces were the protectors of the 1946 constitution, and they forever reminded themselves that "the price of liberty is eternal vigilance." This vigilance was practiced not alone against "Communist infiltration." The "Crusaders" —who would have made poor politicians—shook their heads at the ways of "the populists" and "the demagogues." They were particularly vigilant against any who attracted the masses by complaining that the constitution favored an old-fashioned type of liberalism, "rooted in inequality." Long opposed to Getúlio Vargas, the astute politician who was President of Brazil, the Democratic Crusaders suspected from

[1] *A Razão*, São Paulo, May 25, 1952. During 1952 this weekly presented the campaign of the Democratic Crusade against what it called the "Communist conspiracies" of its opponents.

his past behavior that he might be guilty of favoring reforms (and his own tenure of office) at the expense of the constitution.

These Army officers were particularly upset by the attitude of the thirty-seven-year-old Labor Minister, João ("Jango") Goulart. Goulart had, in the course of strengthening his position, been helpful to a group of labor leaders, a small fraction of whom were members of the Communist Party of Brazil. He was friendly with Argentina's Juan Perón, who was working to have Brazil join Argentina and Chile in an anti-United States bloc. The Democratic Crusaders of Brazil's Military Club feared that Perón would influence Goulart to turn Brazil into what they called a "República Sindicalista." (This, they explained, was a nation run by labor unions.) Nor were these Army officers at all happy about Goulart's proposed 100 per cent increase in the minimum wage; it would bring this minimum for urban workers in the Federal District up to the scale being received by Army second lieutenants.

President Getúlio Vargas, whose ranch in the southern state of Rio Grande do Sul adjoined that of cattle raiser Goulart, was about to become seventy-one. At times he seemed tired after his long and successful role on the political stage. This role, poorly regarded by lovers of electoral democracy, had been interrupted in 1945 when the military, quick to fear that Vargas might want to remain in office instead of preside over elections, had ousted him. But he had returned to the presidency "on the arms of the people" by winning the 1950 election as candidate of the Partido Trabalhista Brasileira (PTB—Brazilian Labor Party).

Vargas, a short, stocky, affable cigar smoker, knew how to bend with the wind. Early in 1954 he sought to placate Army officers by accepting the resignation of neighbor Goulart. But Jango continued to live at Catete Palace, the presidential residence in Rio, and he remained the chief power in the Labor Ministry. The 100 per cent wage increase was made effective May 1, 1954.

What particularly shook Brazil in 1954 was the evidence uncovered in August after shots wounded anti-Vargas newspaper owner Carlos Lacerda and killed his companion, Air Force Major Rubens Vaz. It was found that the attack, which had been designed to murder Lacerda, had been ordered by the head of Vargas' personal guard. The evidence

EAST AND SOUTH
BRAZIL

also disclosed corruption by members of the guard and by others connected with the regime. Getúlio, dismayed by the crime and distressed
by the revelations, reportedly remarked that he had the impression of
being "upon a sea of mud."

Lacerda, who was running for Congress, stormed against Vargas in
newspaper editorials and nightly radio broadcasts. Military men, cry-
ing about "the degraded state of the nation," resolved to "save democracy"—as they had done nine years earlier—from the threats of
"would-be imitators of Perón." Thus Air Force *brigadeiros* and Navy
admirals called for the resignation of the President. A manifesto, bearing the same sentiment, began circulating among Army generals.

Because the Army was vastly more powerful than the other two
branches of the military, much attention was given to the words of War
Minister Euclides Zenóbio da Costa. Speaking to Vargas and his
cabinet at 3:00 A.M. on August 24, he asserted that any effort to save
the regime by military force would result in much bloodshed and be
uncertain of success. Vargas agreed to withdraw from his post provided the military ministers would maintain order. If order were not
maintained, Vargas said, then "the rebels will find my dead body
here."[2]

Younger brother Benjamim Vargas, speaking with Getúlio at 7:00
A.M., said: "'I know that this is the end. It was the easiest way to remove you from office."[3] Benjamim was describing a meeting of generals at which the War Minister had just given assurances that Vargas'
withdrawal was definite.

An hour later Getúlio Vargas shot himself. Radios were soon carrying his farewell message, which opened saying, "Once more, the forces
and interests which work against the people have organized themselves
afresh and break out against me." In one emotional sentence after
another the message pictured its signer as having fought constantly for
the people and against the spoliation of Brazil. "The underground
campaign of international groups joined that of the national groups
which were working against the regime of workers' guarantees. . . .

    [2] Alzira Vargas do Amaral Peixoto, "A Vida de Getúlio Conforme Narração ao
Jornalista Raul Giudicelli," *Fatos & Fotos*, ch. 12, September 28, 1963.
    [3] F. Zenha Machado, *Os Últimos Dias do Govêrno de Vargas*, p. 123.

There is nothing more I can give you except my blood. If the birds of prey want someone's blood, if they want to go on draining the Brazilian people, I offer my life in a holocaust. I choose this means of being always with you. . . . This people whose slave I was will no longer be slave of anyone. My sacrifice will remain forever in their souls and my blood will be the price of their ransom."[4]

[4] Amaral Peixoto, "A Vida de Getúlio," *Fatos & Fotos*, ch. 13, October 5, 1963.

2. Café Filho in the Presidency

GUSTAVO CAPANEMA, Vargas' leader in the Chamber of Deputies, observed that the anti-Getulistas had triumphed at 3:00 A.M. but been beaten at 8:00 A.M.[1]

With the news of the tragedy and the broadcasts of Vargas' last message, mobs shouted against Air Force Brigadeiro Eduardo Gomes, who in 1950 had been candidate of the União Democrática Nacional (UDN—National Democratic Union) to oppose Vargas for the presidency. Delivery trucks of *O Globo,* the prominent afternoon paper that had been attacking Vargas, were set afire. Hard-pressed authorities had difficulty defending the plant of Carlos Lacerda's *Tribuna da Imprensa*; and they were particularly busy preventing rioters, led by Communist troublemakers, from moving against the Air Ministry building and the American Embassy.

But those not inclined to be violent made up the vast majority. One hundred thousand mourners, sorrowing, waited to file past the body of the former President as it lay in state until 8:15 A.M. on August 25. Many waited all night but could not get into Catete Palace. They jammed the streets as the coffin was taken to Santos Dumont Airport in downtown Rio, and they broke through lines of police to help carry

[1] Victor Nunes Leal, interview, Brasília, October 22, 1965.

it to the airplane that was to take it south to São Borja, Rio Grande do Sul, for burial.

In this tense setting Vice-President João Café Filho took over the presidency and prepared to complete the seventeen months of Vargas' five-year term. At Laranjeiras Palace, which until then had been used to accommodate distinguished guests of the government, he carried out the task of selecting fellow administrators. Between conferences he underwent medical treatments lest the strain aggravate his poor heart condition.

Café Filho had not been one of Brazil's leading political figures. As a newspaperman and a socialist in a small northeastern state, he had earnestly opposed the Vargas dictatorship (1937–1945). Those who had heard of him before 1950 recalled that he had said: "Remember 1937!" For this reason he had seemed a suitable running mate to Vargas, who liked to show that old wounds were healed. Also, he belonged to one of the larger minor parties, the Partido Social Progressista (PSP—Social Progressive Party), with whose dominant figure, Ademar de Barros, Vargas had made a deal for support in 1950.

When Café Filho found himself thrust into the presidency, the Vargas family and many others who had been close to Getúlio were in no mood to cooperate with him. He had annoyed them during the crisis by suggesting that Vargas and he resign jointly and by defending this idea in an anti-administration Senate speech describing conditions as critical. Therefore, Ernâni do Amaral Peixoto, son-in-law of Vargas, declined the new President's invitation to come to Laranjeiras Palace.[2] He was head of the Partido Social Democrático (PSD—Social Democratic Party), the largest of Brazil's twelve political parties. Practically all Vargas' cabinet ministers preferred not to stay on.

Café Filho had shaken himself of socialist concepts three years earlier. Now he brought into his cabinet, as Finance Minister, conservative Economics Professor Eugênio Gudin, who had called the large May 1 wage increase "a disaster." Café Filho's Labor Minister, Napoleão Alencastro Guimarães, a foe of Goulart, started trying to eliminate Communists from labor union posts.

[2] João Café Filho, *Do Sindicato ao Catete,* II, 365.

The same break with the recent past was clearly apparent in the military appointments. Café Filho appreciated that it would be difficult to govern without the support of military leaders who had opposed Vargas during the crisis. The first man appointed to the new cabinet was Eduardo Gomes, who became Air Minister. The austere and unsmiling *brigadeiro*, UDN standard-bearer in 1945 and 1950, was the embodiment of anti-Getulismo.

The new President was well impressed with the Escola Superior de Guerra (National War College), whose intellectual "Grupo da Sorbonne" had been filled with misgivings about Goulart. His esteem for the Escola led Café Filho to put the Navy Ministry in the hands of Admiral Edmundo Jordão Amorim do Vale and to select General Juarez Távora to be head of the presidential Casa Militar (Military Household).[3]

For a few days the key post of War Minister continued to be held by General Zenóbio da Costa. While Getulistas in the Army (and elsewhere) were suggesting that Zenóbio was still in his post because "disloyally" he had favored the retirement of Vargas, Zenóbio sought to dispel this image. Café Filho felt it best to find a new War Minister about whom there was no controversy. This idea so upset Zenóbio that he made threatening declarations against the new regime which were transmitted on the radio.

Café Filho consulted the general with the greatest prestige—Military Club President Canrobert Pereira da Costa, who had served as War Minister in the rather anti-Getulista presidential administration (1946–1951) of Marshal Eurico Gaspar Dutra. Canrobert agreed with Café Filho that, in the interest of Army unity, Zenóbio should be succeeded by a nonpolitical general.

Casa Militar head Juarez Távora then turned to the Army Almanac and drew up a list of generals whose years of service gave them high seniority. When he and Café Filho reached the name of Henrique Batista Duffles Teixeira Lott, Távora could find no objection. Lott, who was unknown to the public, was a hard-working, methodical disciplinarian. Like Távora, he had been one of the twenty-seven generals

[3] *Ibid.,* pp. 375, 382.

who had signed the manifesto of August 22 calling on Vargas to resign; but he was described by his colleagues as revering *legalidade* and
as having kept away from political matters. He did not belong to the
"Grupo da Sorbonne."

It was 9:00 P.M., and Lott had retired for the night. But he answered
the telephone summons and decided to make an exception of his habit
of going to bed early. He took over from Zenóbio at once, as Café
Filho wished.

3. The Military Memorandum of January 1955

SOME POLITICIANS MAINTAINED that the emotion resulting from
Vargas' suicide had so affected the nation that it would be best to postpone the gubernatorial and congressional elections of October 1954.
But neither Café Filho nor the constitution-loving military leaders
shared this view, and the elections were carried out on schedule. For
the most part they confirmed the strength of the populist political
forces with which Getúlio had identified himself. There were exceptions. In the Federal District (the city of Rio), the UDN's hard-hitting
Carlos Lacerda was elected federal congressman. And, in the far south,
Goulart, head of the Vargas-founded PTB (Brazilian Labor Party),
lost his race for a Senate seat from Rio Grande do Sul.

After the returns were reported, Juscelino Kubitschek, Getulista
governor of the large southeastern state of Minas Gerais, started campaigning to win the presidency on October 3, 1955. Exuberant and
optimistic, Kubitschek declared himself well-pleased with the 1954
election results. He explained to Café Filho that he would use the
strategy that had helped him to win the governorship in 1950: by
taking his campaign to the people ahead of anyone else, he would get
the PSD (founded, like the PTB, by Vargas) to nominate him.

In January 1955, while Kubitschek was strenuously addressing
crowds, the military leaders became worried. They offered their opinion

in a secret memorandum (*memorial*) delivered to Café Filho by the Navy Minister. Largely the work of Juarez Távora,[1] it was signed by him, by the three military ministers, and by the chiefs of staff of the armed forces and of each military branch. Military Club President Canrobert Pereira da Costa signed as Army chief of staff. The signature of João Batista Mascarenhas de Morais, who had headed Brazil's World War II troops in Italy and had become Brazil's only active marshal, gave the *memorial* even greater weight.

Four among this group (Canrobert, Lott, Távora, and Eduardo Gomes) were being mentioned as possible presidential candidates, but the *memorial* stated that its signers had no desire to see any military man a candidate. With this show of disinterested patriotism, the *memorial* also expressed a warning. The signers were "profoundly preoccupied about the dangers" that would result from "a violent electoral campaign in the midst of the serious economic and social crisis which affects the nation." They urged the leaders of the nation's political forces to solve "the problem of the presidential succession on a level of understanding and with a spirit of interparty collaboration, without the incitement of hates and dissensions which have seriously upset the nation's life."[2]

Because the military leaders called on the President to work for a candidate "of national unity," Café Filho spoke with a few politicians. Soon the press was producing passages from the *memorial*. Therefore, with the approval of its signers,[3] Café Filho made it public in one of his frequent, undemagogic radio addresses.

Transportation Minister Lucas Lopes, Kubitschek's representative in the cabinet, resigned after Café Filho told Kubitschek that the *memorial* would be broadcast.[4] His reaction made it clear that Kubitschek shared the impression of some of his friends that the *memorial* was the voice of the military against his candidacy. However, this interpretation did more to promote than to block popular support for

[1] Joffre Gomes da Costa, *Marechal Henrique Lott,* pp. 231–232; Juarez Távora, interview, Rio de Janeiro, October 20, 1967.

[2] Gomes da Costa, *Marechal Henrique Lott,* pp. 231–232.

[3] João Café Filho, *Do Sindicato ao Catete,* II, 498.

[4] Lucas Lopes, interview, Rio de Janeiro, October 30, 1965.

Kubitschek, a man who had no intention of slowing down his drive while the administration looked for a civilian acceptable to all. At the PSD convention in Rio, Kubitschek dramatically defended his right to be a candidate regardless of the opinion of the military.

Aided by this interpretation and by PSD President Amaral Peixoto, Kubitschek won his party's nomination.

4. The Café Filho–Quadros Agreement (April 2, 1955)

WHILE PRESIDENT CAFÉ FILHO vainly sought a name that would conciliate all political currents, Brazil wondered whether "charismatic" Jânio Quadros would run for the presidency.

In October 1954, at thirty-seven, Quadros had continued his unbroken streak of election victories. As the nominee of some small political parties for the São Paulo governorship, he had defeated candidates representing past São Paulo regimes, including the PSP's formidable Ademar de Barros. Disheveled, thin, and indignant, Quadros had shouted against "corrupt politicians" and shown a remarkable ability to attract a large following among the poor.

To be eligible to be a presidential candidate, Quadros would have to resign his recently won gubernatorial post before April 3, 1955. As the deadline approached, Café Filho received emissaries from São Paulo. Some, like the vice-governor, said that Quadros would certainly run for President. Others, including Senator Auro de Moura Andrade, advised that Quadros would desist if the federal government would put some "acceptable" Paulistas in the cabinet and renegotiate large debts owed by the state.

Quadros let the President know that, in case of such an arrangement, he would support General Juarez Távora, whom the small Partido Democrata Cristão (PDC—Christian Democratic Party) had been encouraging to run for the presidency. For Vice-President,

Quadros would support Café Filho's warm friend, Paraná Governor Bento Munhoz da Rocha Neto.

Since Ademar de Barros had advised the President that he would not be a candidate,[1] Café Filho saw the possibility of uniting important forces around the ticket suggested by Quadros. The UDN and the dissident wing of the PSD, both backers of the Café Filho administration, turned to Távora. But when Távora was visited by Quadros' emissaries, he explained that, under the circumstances, he was in no moral position to urge the President to accept the arrangements being proposed by Quadros. Távora also said that selection of a running mate should be left up to the political parties that supported the Távora candidacy.[2]

On April 2 the signers of the military *memorial* reinforced Quadros' proposal by deciding that, as no "national unity candidate" could be found, the signers were free to seek the presidency.

Late that day, not long before the April 3 deadline, Café Filho approved a two-page document in which Quadros listed the conditions under which São Paulo would support the Távora-Munhoz da Rocha ticket.[3] Ten minutes later Jânio addressed an excited multitude at São Paulo's Campos Elísios Palace. He promised to remain at his post and fulfill his campaign pledge of bringing administrative, economic, and moral "recovery" to the state. He explained that São Paulo, which contributed the most to the national treasury, would no longer be "abandoned" by the federal government.[4]

When Távora learned of the agreement, he was dismayed. He expressed some of his sentiments in letters to Café Filho and Quadros. "I feel that I have no connection whatever with any arrangement made up to now, and I refuse to allow my name to be advanced as a candidate for the presidency as part of commitments tied to such an arrangement." In his letter to the President, Távora made it clear that he had always considered an understanding between the São Paulo and federal governments indispensable, but he added that it had been

[1] João Café Filho, *Do Sindicato ao Catete*, II, 515.

[2] Juarez Távora, "Porque Desisti de Ser Candidato em 4 de Abril Findo," (type-written memorandum), p. 3.

[3] Café Filho, *Do Sindicato ao Catete*, II, 518.

[4] Viriato de Castro, *O Fenômeno Jânio Quadros*, p. 131.

unwise to include mention of his name as a candidate. "The document could be interpreted as being something indispensable for the backing of my candidacy, and this might hurt the prestige of your government."[5]

The *Tribuna da Imprensa* attacked the "shady deal" and assailed Quadros so bitterly that the São Paulo Governor consulted lawyers about the possibility of suing Lacerda.

Quadros, wondering whether he had made himself unavailable for the presidential race and then been double-crossed, came to Rio on April 4. He found Café Filho vexed with Távora. But the President made it clear that, in spite of Távora's attitude, the administration would fulfill its part of the bargain. Thus the federal ministries of transportation and finance were placed in the hands of two eminent Paulistas suggested by Quadros: Otávio Marcondes Ferraz and José Maria Whitaker. Whitaker named a new head of the Bank of Brazil.

Other changes were made in the cabinet. Munhoz da Rocha, who had resigned the Paraná governorship to become the administration's candidate for the vice-presidency, became, instead, Minister of Agriculture. The Justice Minister, a Paulista unacceptable to Quadros, resigned. To this post—considered to be of particular importance during an election—Café Filho appointed a former president of the UDN, José Eduardo do Prado Kelly. Air Minister Eduardo Gomes, the former UDN standard-bearer, was delighted.

[5] Copies of Távora's letters of April 3, 1955, to Café Filho, Quadros, and PDC President Arruda Câmara are in Távora's files. Excerpts from his letter to Café Filho are given in Café Filho, *Do Sindicato ao Catete*, II, 519–520.

5. Candidates for the Presidency

WHILE QUADROS AND THE PRESIDENT conversed on April 4, General Távora advised leaders of the UDN, the PDC, the Partido Libertador (PL), and the PSD's dissident wing that, having rejected the deal of April 2, he might be willing to run for office. But on the next evening, as these leaders gathered to launch his candidacy, Távora telephoned them to say that he preferred to have a clear conscience and therefore was not authorizing that he be considered.[1]

This decision left the UDN leaders in an awkward position. In seeking support for Távora they had entered into an alliance with the PSD dissidents. This they decided to respect, and so they accepted as their candidate the politician being urged by their allies: Etelvino Lins, former governor of the northeastern state of Pernambuco and a PSD dissident. Although Eduardo Gomes and General Osvaldo Cordeiro de Farias (governor-elect of Pernambuco) saw merit in the selection, it was not hailed by others in the UDN.

The electorate, far from getting a "national unity" candidate, was given four presidential hopefuls to choose from. For a while there were five.

While Kubitschek campaigned, big, gruff, ambitious Ademar de Barros, still smarting from his recent defeat in São Paulo, got himself nominated by the PSP. At the same time he conferred much with lawyers because the Quadros state government was reopening the case concerning the accusation that he had committed financial irregularities as governor in 1949.

Former "Green Shirt" leader Plínio Salgado was nominated by the Partido de Representação Popular (PRP). This minor party, an offspring of Plínio's Integralista marchers of the 1930's, opposed "fascism, Communism, and Nazism." Finding few self-declared Fascists or Nazis, it worked principally against Communism.

Távora, soul-searching in seclusion in the interior of Paraná, was assisted by the visit of a representative of Quadros. Surely, Távora was told, he could now seek the presidency with a clear conscience, that is to say without Café Filho's support. And if he did not give Quadros this chance to secure a split in São Paulo's vote, Távora would be responsible for a "national disaster": the election of Ademar de Barros.

Agreeing that Ademar was "even worse than Kubitschek," Távora resolved, without enthusiasm, to do his duty. He held a press confer-

---

[1] Afonso Arinos de Melo Franco, *A Escalada: Memórias*, pp. 364–365.

ence in Rio on May 18. The tall, handsome military figure, whose career as a revolutionary had begun in 1922, agreed to be the presidential candidate of the PDC. But his candidacy was to be clearly recognized as one that involved no commitments or agreements with any people, groups, or interests. The *tenente* (revolutionary lieutenant) of the 1920's was now the *tenente de cabelos brancos* (*tenente* with white hair), and this time the revolution was to be made by means of the polls. "I have nothing to offer or request except sacrifices," he announced.

With the renowned Távora a candidate again, the UDN lost interest in the faltering campaign of Etelvino Lins. The Pernambucano withdrew to run for the Senate, but he and other PSD dissidents let it be known that they were joining the Christian Democrats (PDC), the UDN, the small Partido Socialista Brasileiro (PSB), and the tiny Partido Libertador in backing Távora. The UDN sought to run Távora's campaign (evoking some complaints by the candidate), and it supplied his running mate: UDN President Milton Campos, the serious, eminent lawyer who had once governed Minas Gerais.

At the suggestion of Osvaldo Aranha, Vargas' long-time associate, the two Vargas-founded parties, the PSD and PTB, cooperated to support Kubitschek for President and Goulart for Vice-President. Since these were two of the three major parties, it was a strong combination. Jango, if he achieved the vice-presidency, was to be in charge of labor matters—an attractive prospect for far leftist union leaders, who were unhappy with what they had been receiving from the Labor Ministry since Vargas' death.

Ademar sought to split the PTB by choosing Danton Coelho as his running mate. Coelho maintained that in 1950 Vargas had committed himself to back Ademar as his successor.[2]

---

[2] *Correio da Manhã*, July 9, 1955.

6. Electioneering Gets Under Way

AFTER HIS NEGOTIATIONS HAD FAILED, Café Filho assumed a position of strict neutrality.[1] Meanwhile, the election campaign went forward, bringing all the agitation the military had feared in January.

Goulart was accused of misusing union funds. *O Globo* printed the facsimile of a card that had made Goulart an honorary member of the ill-famed Vargas personal guard.

Carlos Lacerda wrote and spoke in a threatening tone. The galleries of Congress were packed when he declared that with Goulart a candidate there would not be any elections, and that, if they were held, no inauguration would follow. "We are," he said, "headed for an election which all Brazilians know will not be fair. The dead and the illiterate are going to vote."[2] He called for a temporary revision of the constitutional regime so that the Executive might reform electoral legislation at once.

When Lacerda insisted on the immediate establishment of a two-year dictatorship he did not reflect the views of a majority of his fellow UDN congressmen. Rather, his position made things uncomfortable for the UDN leadership. Lacerda's "tirades, his proposals, almost always senseless but almost always brilliant, had greater repercussions than my explanations," writes Afonso Arinos de Melo Franco, who was UDN congressional leader.[3]

Former War Minister Zenóbio da Costa wrote Café Filho to advise that, if necessary, the armed forces would act to guarantee the inauguration of those elected.[4] The President would not consider any Army matter unless it were presented to him by Lott and in all such cases he relied entirely on Lott's judgment. "This letter should have come to me

---

[1] Carlos Castilho Cabral, *Tempos de Jânio e Outros Tempos,* p. 80.
[2] *Correio da Manhã,* July 5, 1955.
[3] Afonso Arinos de Melo Franco, *A Escalada: Memórias,* pp. 366–367.
[4] *O Estado de S. Paulo,* July 26, 1955.

through you," he told his War Minister, who noted Zenóbio's message without comment.[5]

While Kubitschek spoke of great development goals and tried to present himself as a harmonizing influence ("I have no personal enemies"), UDN congressmen and writers described him as corrupt and controlled by Communists.

The candidates listed their assets as Congress told them to do. Ademar declared he had a vast fortune, whereas Távora and Plínio Salgado revealed they had little.[6] Kubitschek, the main target, listed some valuable real-estate holdings in Minas. UDN congressmen, suspicious of how these had been acquired, then insisted that the candidates explain the origins of their assets.

Kubitschek felt that the objective of the UDN congressmen was to injure his image by getting him into a chair, pointing fingers at him, and submitting him to long questioning. For a while his supporters in Congress, working against the investigation, were not sure of their strength. They appreciated that the Café Filho administration, which they regarded as unfriendly, could count on the UDN, the dissidents of the PSD, and all of São Paulo (including Ademar's PSP). But it turned out that the PSD-PTB combination—aided by the little Partido Republicano (PR—Republican Party)—had the upper hand. PSD floor leader José Maria Alkmim, astute congressman from Minas, gained the presidency of the Commission Investigating the Origin of the Assets of the Candidates. With that, the commission did no investigating.[7] The matter, said Alkmim, was one for the normal procedures of justice.

Charges of Communist support for the PSD-PTB ticket were made by Ari Campista, non-Communist head of a fast-growing Communist-dominated labor movement, the Movimento Nacional Popular Trabalhista (MNPT). Facing a crowd of thirty thousand at an MNPT Congress in São Paulo, Campista refused to play the role of "useful innocent" of the Communist labor leaders; instead, he dramatically accused them (Roberto Morena, in particular) of betraying the workers

[5] João Café Filho, Do Sindicato ao Catete, II, 537, 599.
[6] Adauto Lúcio Cardoso, interview, Rio de Janeiro, December 15, 1965.
[7] Ibid.

by selling the political position of the MNPT to the PSD-PTB leaders.[8] He then resigned from his post.

Soon after, Campista announced that the MNPT had built up a membership that was 80 per cent Communist and had decided to obtain funds by offering to support Kubitschek and Goulart and to help provide good turnouts at rallies held in their behalf. This offer, he said, had been accepted by prominent backers of the PSD-PTB ticket.[9] The news was not surprising to those conversant with the money-raising methods used by the illegal Communist Party of Brazil during election campaigns. It got what money it could from candidates and was known in one local election to have sold its services to three men who opposed each other for the same office.[10]

The Communists hoped to get Kubitschek to agree that their party would be legalized if he were elected. Kubitschek refused, pointing out to the Communist representative, Pedro Pomar, that as a congressman he had voted against such a project. Pomar could only get Kubitschek to agree that Petrobrás, the government petroleum-extracting monopoly, was sacred and "untouchable."[11]

[8] Ari Campista, interview, Rio de Janeiro, October 9, 1968. The MNPT meeting in São Paulo is described in Paulo Henrique Amorim, "Sua Exelência, O Pelego," *Realidade*, II, no. 24 (March 1968).

[9] *O Estado de S. Paulo*, August 11, 1955.

[10] Osvaldo Peralva, *O Retrato*, p. 213; and interview, Rio de Janeiro, September 14, 1963.

[11] Osvaldo M. Penido, interviews, Rio de Janeiro, September 6, 1963; October 10, 1967. Mário Schenberg, interviewed in São Paulo on November 14, 1966, said that he arranged for Kubitschek to meet with Communist leader Pedro Pomar, who did the talking on behalf of the Communist Party of Brazil.

7. Canrobert Speaks (August 5, 1955)

ON AUGUST 5 the Air Force Club held a session in memory of Rubens Vaz, killed a year earlier when Gregório Fortunato, head of the Vargas personal guard, had sought to have Lacerda assassinated. The main speaker, Military Club President Canrobert Pereira da Costa, had become Chief of Staff of the Armed Forces. For two months he had been confined to his home by the illness that was soon to kill him. He was in a pessimistic mood.

"Once again," he said, "new threats loom and expand against the unity of the military classes, against which, as always, there is a conspiracy led by the maleficent, embittered forces of passions, of parties, and of all the uncontrolled ambitions of individuals and diverse groups." Canrobert spoke of "the multiple scandals of the clamorous mismanagement of public money," and of the failure of Brazilian justice to punish the guilty. The phrase of the general which created the greatest furor was: "the democratic falsehood in which we insist on living." He also made a reference to "pseudo-legality." Canrobert forecast that after the election "large, dissatisfied interest groups, and old, repressed hates" would "resort to denouncing frauds and lawlessness, imaginary or real," and that the result would be to ignite the furnace of "intranquility and disorder in our unhappy Brazilian land."[1]

Kubitschek was quick to state that he could not agree that "we live in a democratic falsehood," and some congressmen expressed the thought that the President should arrest the renowned general. Café Filho had already reached his decision about the matter. When War Minister Lott had discussed the speech with him before it had been delivered, Café Filho had objected to it. But Lott had defended Canrobert's right to give the speech. Canrobert, Lott had pointed out, would be speaking not as Chief of Staff but in the name of an association, the Military Club. After the speech was delivered, Canrobert submitted his resignation, but the President, following Lott's recommendation, refused to accept it.[2]

When Lott made a public statement it was to "express the preoccupation which we all have about recent facts, such as the Communist Party's support" of Kubitschek and Goulart and "their acceptance of that support."[3] Kubitschek denied having made any hidden agreements and observed that "the Communists can back me or oppose me without that altering my ideas in the slightest."

[1] *Correio da Manhã*, August 6, 1955.
[2] João Café Filho, *Do Sindicato ao Catete*, II, 545–546.
[3] *Correio da Manhã*, August 18, 1955.

8. Final Months: The *Cédula Única* and the Brandi Letter

Jânio Quadros took a leave of absence from the São Paulo governorship to campaign for Távora and Milton Campos, who became known as the candidates of the National Renovation Front (Frente de Renovação Nacional). Ademar tried to attract the Paulistas to the idea of having, for the first time since 1930, a man from their state in the presidency. But Quadros cried out, in São Paulo and elsewhere, that "No thief will wear the sash of the presidency of the Republic." Távora promised that, if he were elected, the tax that was supposed to support the labor unions (*impôsto sindical*) would no longer be what he called a fund for fattening parasites.[1]

Air Minister Eduardo Gomes, highly irritated by Communist manifestos that supported Kubitschek and Goulart and attacked the military, kept repeating that the 1946 constitution made an absolute majority necessary for election. Almost five years earlier, however, the Superior Electoral Tribunal had rejected this interpretation; and in 1955 not enough federal congressmen favored Gomes' thesis to make it the law of the land. Nor did the many supporters of a parliamentary form of government, described as a European system, muster quite enough votes for their desired alteration of the Brazilian political system.

The chief debate in Congress centered around a project to alter the method of voting in elections. Many members of the UDN felt that fraud in elections helped the PSD-PTB majority. They proposed, therefore, that an officially printed ballot (*cédula oficial*), bearing the names of all the candidates for an office, be given each voter at the time he entered the booth. Justice Minister José Eduardo do Prado Kelly argued that the customary ballots, being handed out ahead of time by party bosses and being of different sizes and typography (depending on the candidate), were hardly secret and promoted intimida-

---

[1] *O Estado de S. Paulo,* August 9, 1955.

tion. In some areas it was felt that the PSD largely dominated the distribution of ballots.[2]

Although the Senate favored the *cédula oficial,* PSD leaders in the Chamber of Deputies felt that its adoption would be a political defeat.[3] They argued that there was no time to effect the change and that its implementation on the eve of balloting would disconcert the voters. They asserted that the electoral justice system was not extensive enough to carry out the required distribution, and that, for political reasons, local election officials might refuse to pass out ballots.

UDN leaders pointed out that the *cédula oficial* would reduce the tension produced by Canrobert's speech. They accused the PSD of favoring fraud. Kubitschek's friends retorted that in Congress the UDN disregarded important reform measures in order to confuse matters with talk about the *cédula oficial* and the wealth of the candidates.

Eduardo Gomes persuaded Cardinal Jaime de Barros Câmara to express himself in favor of the *cédula oficial.* War Minister Lott, with misgivings about past electoral practices, spoke with Chamber of Deputies President Carlos Luz. A part of the press then complained of interference by the War Minister.

Late in August a compromise emerged, largely the result of work by the PSD's José Maria Alkmim. All the candidates for one post would be listed on one ballot (*cédula única*), which was to be printed and distributed by the government. But such ballots could also be printed and distributed by the political parties. "A partial victory," thought the UDN's Afonso Arinos. But Lacerda described the outcome as "a total defeat."[4]

Lacerda, although a director of the UDN, long refused to support Távora. He claimed that his was a losing candidacy, which only served to "legitimize" the election of October 3.[5] Not until September 18 did Lacerda yield to a plea of vice-presidential candidate Milton Campos and announce his "unconditional" support for the UDN ticket. Then

[2] José Eduardo do Prado Kelly, interview, Rio de Janeiro, October 8, 1965; Afonso Arinos de Melo Franco, interview, Brasília, October 16, 1965.

[3] José Maria Alkmim, interview, Brasília, October 15, 1965.

[4] Afonso Arinos de Melo Franco, *A Escalada: Memórias,* p. 374.

[5] *Correio da Manhã,* July 14, 1955.

he unsuccessfully appealed to former "Green Shirt" Plínio Salgado to withdraw in favor of Távora.

At the same time, Lacerda's *Tribuna da Imprensa* published what it asserted was the facsimile of a letter written in August 1953 by an Argentine Peronista congressman, Antonio Brandi, to then-Labor Minister Goulart. According to this letter, Perón had approved the sale of arms from an Argentine weapons factory for what were described as Goulart's "worker shock brigades." The arms, disguised as foodstuff, were said to have crossed the border at Uruguaiana, Rio Grande do Sul, and to have been delivered to the mayor there. The letter further indicated that Goulart had been seeking instructions on how best to form workers' militias.[6]

Admiral Carlos Pena Bôto, commander-in-chief of the naval squadron and president of the Brazilian Anti-Communist Crusade, said that the contents of the Brandi letter did not surprise him. Like *O Globo* and *Tribuna da Imprensa* his Crusade had been denouncing the smuggling of arms from Argentina.

With only thirteen days remaining before the election, the PTB bloc in Congress asked Lott to head an immediate investigation of the Brandi letter, described by Goulart as a forgery. But Lott felt that his position made this impossible.

Lacerda, who had received the letter from two Argentines, turned it over to the Navy Minister. The military ministers met with Café Filho and decided that the job of investigating should be assigned to General Emílio Maurel Filho, who had been studying the loss of weapons from Army depots.

Maurel reached Argentina just as Perón was falling and cabled Lott about the Brandi letter on October 2. Accordingly, on election day the press reported that the Argentine police chief felt it "highly probable" that the signature was authentic.

By then the campaigning had ended with mass meetings for the candidates. At the most costly of these, Ademaristas provided a two and one-half hour display of fireworks and rockets. The great closing Juscelino-Jango rally in São Paulo was heavily sprinkled with placards

[6] *Jornal do Commercio*, Rio de Janeiro, October 1, 3, 4, 1955; Joffre Gomes da Costa, *Marechal Henrique Lott*, p. 261.

calling for the legalization of the Partido Comunista do Brasil (PCB—Communist Party of Brazil).

Luís Carlos Prestes, head of the PCB, had been underground for over seven years due to a warrant for his arrest. From his place of hiding he issued a last-minute manifesto advising that "the victory of Kubitschek and Goulart will be the defeat of the *golpista* generals."[7] Quadros issued a different last-minute appeal. Stating that his eyes were "brimming with tears," he described the campaign as one against "vice in all its repellent forms." "Reject, all of you, in the ballot boxes, the swindlers of democracy; let us expel them from the temple of the regime. Turn the regime over to Juarez do Nascimento Fernandes Távora."[8]

[7] *Golpista* generals: generals favoring a *golpe*, or coup d'état.
[8] *Jornal do Commercio*, Rio de Janeiro, October 2, 1955.

9. Aftermath of the Election

IN SPITE OF QUADROS, São Paulo supported "favorite son" Ademar. But Minas backed Kubitschek more heavily. A week after the election it appeared that the results would favor the PSD-PTB ticket, and this was confirmed later.

For President

Kubitschek	3,077,411
Távora	2,610,462
Ademar de Barros	2,222,725
Plínio Salgado	714,379

For Vice-President

Goulart	3,591,409
Milton Campos	3,384,739
Danton Coelho	1,140,261

Kubitschek asked the nation to put aside personal rancor and ambitions: "I need peace in order to work and to let all of Brazil work." PSD congressional leader Alkmim negotiated alliances with Ademar de Barros (PSP) and Plínio Salgado (PRP). Plínio's price was Kubitschek's promise that the forthcoming administration would not recognize the Soviet Union or grant legality to the Communist Party of Brazil.[1]

Supporters of Távora speculated on what the results would have been had Salgado withdrawn from the race. A few anti-Getulistas kept insisting that the Superior Electoral Tribunal had been in error in January 1951 when it had declared that an absolute majority was unnecessary for election. Others, agreeing with the *Tribuna da Imprensa*, maintained that Communist voters had tipped the scales in favor of Kubitschek and Goulart, and they demanded that the Electoral Tribunal rule whether the votes of known Communists were legal. (The Communist Party of Brazil, outlawed in 1947, had about 55,000 members, but, on the basis of elections held in 1945 and 1947, it could claim almost 600,000 votes.) Foreign Minister Raul Fernandes wrote a memorandum arguing that the Communist Party had organized PSD-PTB rallies and, "acting as a body," had provided enough votes to give the lead to Kubitschek and Goulart. He concluded that this had been illegal and that victory should be "given to Juarez Távora and Milton Campos."[2]

The charge most frequently hurled at the apparent victory of Juscelino and Jango was that it had been achieved by means of fraudulent votes, particularly in Minas. This was the complaint of the Frente de Renovação Nacional. In the presence of leading representatives of the UDN, PDC, and PL, Juarez Távora and Milton Campos released a manifesto to the nation. "We have trustworthy information that in some states, including the one which gave the most votes to those in the lead, intimidation and fraud reigned, often vehemently. Therefore the justified suspicion that the congressional rejection of the *cédula oficial* was part of a deliberate plan to falsify the public will. . . . We have only one hope for the peaceful correction of the electoral vices:

---

[1] Plínio Salgado, interview, Brasília, October 14, 1965.
[2] Afonso Arinos de Melo Franco, *A Escalada: Memórias*, pp. 375–376.

popular remonstrance, and drastic, courageous and impartial action by the Superior Electoral Tribunal."[3]

The military ministers discussed the situation quietly, often at the home of Henrique Lott. Gomes suggested that Lott speak, in the name of the three of them, to Luís Gallotti, president of the Superior Electoral Tribunal, and recommend the need of an absolute majority.[4] But Lott told his two colleagues that he opposed having the military interfere with justice. Lott, who had voted for Távora but who did not favor annulling the election results, noted that Gomes and Amorim do Vale had a poor impression of these results. Admiral Amorim do Vale spoke of a financial transaction, which he said had been carried out by Goulart and Communists at the home of Aranha.

Lacerda and Admiral Pena Bôto made the most noise. On October 14 *O Globo* published Pena Bôto's message to "Brazilian Patriots." "What is to be done now? It is indispensable to prevent Juscelino and Jango from taking over posts to which they were improperly elected." He stressed that their inauguration would doom the nation, and he emphasized that, even with Communist assistance, the J-J combination had received only about one-third of the vote.[5] "The Gregórios shall not return to office," Lacerda declared in a reference to the man who had been responsible for wounding him and killing Major Vaz. In the Chamber of Deputies Lacerda stubbornly defended the thesis that the electoral justice system had not functioned and needed to be revamped immediately.[6]

War Minister Lott, determined to uphold his reputation as a rigorous defender of the constitution, listened with sympathy to the arguments of influential Juscelinistas, among them businessman-poet Augusto Frederico Schmidt and politicians José Maria Alkmim and Armando Falcão.[7] Café Filho, unworried about a possible coup, kept repeating

[3] *Jornal do Commercio,* Rio de Janeiro, November 6, 1955.

[4] Henrique Baptista Duffles Teixeira Lott, "Depoimento Prestado ao Juiz da 11ª Vara Criminal Respeito do 11 de Novembro de 1955," in Joffre Gomes da Costa, *Marechal Henrique Lott,* pp. 501–518; see especially, p. 508.

[5] Gomes da Costa, *Marechal Henrique Lott,* p. 264.

[6] José Loureiro Júnior, *O Golpe de Novembro, e Outros Discursos,* pp. 13–36.

[7] Carlos Lacerda, "Rosas e Pedras do Meu Caminho," *Manchete,* ch. 11, June 24, 1967, p. 106.

that his administration would turn the government over to those who were declared victors by the Electoral Tribunal.

Zenóbio da Costa seemed more concerned. Vargas' last War Minister issued a manifesto that appeared in the press on October 18. Speaking as Army inspector-general, he addressed Army men: "We have no illusions. Legality will be preserved only with your blood and with the arms which the people have furnished you. . . . I feel that the desperation of a reckless minority converts itself into a grave threat."[8]

Although Zenóbio's manifesto praised Lott, the War Minister maintained that it was improper for Army officers to speak out on political matters. He also saw the manifesto as part of a maneuver that might give the President a reason to dismiss both Zenóbio and himself.[9] Lott, however, need not have been worried about himself. Café Filho told him to dismiss Zenóbio: "In my government the one who speaks in the name of the Army is my War Minister."[10]

Taking advantage of the situation, Lott received Café Filho's approval also to dismiss coastal artillery inspector Alcides Etchegoyen, a general who opposed the inauguration of Kubitschek and Goulart. After that, Gomes imposed ten days of imprisonment on an Air Force officer who had given a press interview stating that military men should back the authorities elected under the constitution.

In the latter part of October, General Maurel Filho concluded his investigations about the Brandi letter. He had flown to Argentina's Corrientes district to speak with Brandi and had gone on to Rio Grande do Sul, where the two Argentines who had forged the letter were arrested. Having confirmed their confessions by other evidence,[11] Maurel arrived in Rio and announced that the letter was a forgery.

But Lacerda turned this development into a further opportunity to strike at Goulart. Testifying before Maurel, Lacerda presented a pile of documents. They included a radiogram from the Brazilian naval attaché in Buenos Aires to Navy Minister Amorim do Vale affirming

[8] *Jornal do Commercio*, Rio de Janeiro, October 17–18, 1955.

[9] "Depoimento de Lott" in *Manchete*, November 19, 1955. (See first page of the *depoimento*.)

[10] João Café Filho, *Do Sindicato ao Catete*, II, 537.

[11] Emílio Maurel Filho, interview, Rio de Janeiro, October 11, 1965.

that contraband arms had been shipped from Argentina to Brazil. Also disclosed was a letter of October 3, 1951, in which José Segadas Viana, Goulart's predecessor in the Labor Ministry, had advised Vargas that Perón, "basing his Government on the organized working mass, can, without delay, paralyze all transportation and means of communication, blocking the action of rebels." Segadas had wanted Vargas to authorize that steps be taken so that the Brazilian proletariat could be "spiritually and materially" mobilized to act on behalf of the government in any emergency.[12]

At the same time Lacerda continued to advocate a coup. A successful coup remained most unlikely, however. General Juarez Távora rejected the use of violence and counseled against it. Of greater importance, War Minister Lott, who opposed a coup, could count on those he had placed in command of troops. Nor did the UDN leadership agree with Lacerda, and it limited itself to seeking legal reasons for nullifying the reported election returns.

[12] *Jornal do Commercio,* Rio de Janeiro, October 29, 1955.

BOOK II: *The Coups of November 1955*

"Discipline is learned only through serving, commanding, and suffering in the Army."

General Lott, November 1955

"Insurrection is a political crime, but, when it is victorious, it becomes a right to glory. . . . Against an armed insurrection, crowned with success, the only thing of value is a counter-insurrection with a stronger force. And this, positively, cannot be carried out by the Supreme Court."

Supreme Court Justice Nelson Hungria
opinion, December 1955

1. Canrobert's Funeral (November 1, 1955)

ON OCTOBER 31, 1955, Brazilians learned of the death of General Canrobert Pereira da Costa. A few of them had hoped that Canrobert, pessimistic president of the Military Club, would lead a coup designed to revamp the constitution and prevent the inauguration of Kubitschek and Goulart.

Late on the afternoon of November 1, thousands stood in the streets in a torrential rain to pay their respects as the funeral procession moved from the Military Club to the cemetery. At the side of the grave Lott spoke first, on behalf of the Army. Then, after orations had been delivered in the names of the Air Force and the Navy, Lott was surprised to find one of the "Grupo da Sorbonne," Colonel Jurandir Mamede, reading a speech on behalf of the Military Club. Mamede, who had a brilliant Army record, was a leader of the Army's anti-Communist Democratic Crusade.

The War Minister restrained—for the moment—the anger that filled him as he heard Mamede's words. Mamede, using some controversial expressions Canrobert had uttered in August, emphasized how right Canrobert had been. "Will it not be clearly a 'democratic falsehood' to have a presidential regime which . . . comes to sanction a victory of the minority . . . ? Will it not also be obvious 'pseudo-legality' to have that which seeks to legitimize itself in order to defend intransigently a mechanism prepared to assure voting by the illiterates, prohibited by law?" To Lott's annoyance, Chamber of Deputies President Carlos Luz gave Mamede an especially enthusiastic handshake.[1] Luz, like Canrobert, had served in Dutra's anti-Getulista cabinet.

Although the speech had been approved by the directors of the Military Club, Lott was determined to discipline Mamede. Air Minister Gomes told Lott that he did not feel discipline was necessary; but, he added, the matter was one for Lott to solve.[2]

To solve it Lott needed Café Filho's help because Mamede was not under the authority of the War Minister. The bespectacled Colonel taught at the Escola Superior de Guerra, which reported to the Estado Maior das Forças Armadas (EMFA—the Armed Forces General Staff), which, in turn, reported to the presidency. On November 3, following All Soul's Day, Lott telephoned the chief of the President's Casa Militar. He learned that Café Filho had suffered a heart disturbance that morning and had gone to the Government Hospital for Public Servants.

Café Filho had been shaken by a demand of the military ministers, who had unsuccessfully been trying to get Justice Minister Prado Kelly to close down the Communist press. Newspapers like *Imprensa Popular*, which followed the Moscow line, were fiercely attacking Brigadeiro Eduardo Gomes and Admiral Edmundo Jordão Amorim do Vale.[3] On the morning of November 2 the President had received a long *memorial,* signed by Lott, Amorim do Vale, and Gomes. In conclusion it said "we judge it our duty to request of your Excellency the immediate closing of the above-mentioned newspapers and magazines to save our institutions and for the good of the Nation."[4] After study-

---

[1] Henrique Lott, interview, Rio de Janeiro, August 27, 1963.

[2] *Ibid.*

[3] Edmundo Jordão Amorim do Vale, interview, Rio de Janeiro, September 7, 1963.

[4] *Memorial* of November 2, 1955, in Appendix 20 of Bento Munhoz da Rocha, *Radiografia de Novembro,* pp. 132–133.

ing this pronouncement and contemplating resisting the military, Café Filho had fallen ill late on November 2.

Café Filho's illness, described as a "slight" cardiovascular disturbance, was said not to be serious, but it was recalled that he had suffered a heart attack three years earlier.

With Café Filho in an oxygen tent, Lott telephoned an Air Force *brigadeiro* who, on Canrobert's death, had become acting head of the EMFA. The *brigadeiro* refused to punish Mamede. On November 5, therefore, Lott asked the head of the presidential Casa Militar to release Mamede from the War College.

2. Luz's Decision (November 10, 1955)

On November 8 Café Filho learned from his doctors that he would have to remain inactive a few more days. Therefore he addressed a letter to Carlos Luz, who was next in line for the presidency and who had taken over earlier in the year during Café Filho's trip to Portugal. By this letter Café Filho again transferred the presidency to Luz, "as long as the impediment lasts." José Antônio Flôres da Cunha thereupon succeeded Luz as head of the Chamber of Deputies.

Luz, a Mineiro, was not well regarded by the Kubitschek people because he belonged to the PSD dissident wing and had reached the presidency of the Chamber of Deputies as the result of UDN support. In the case of Chamber Vice-President Flôres da Cunha, a sentimental Gaúcho with a long career of fighting, politics, and gambling, the situation was the reverse. Nominally a member of the UDN, he owed his post to his many friends in the PSD's large orthodox wing.[1]

Lacerda hailed the advent of Luz to the presidency in a signed editorial in the *Tribuna da Imprensa* on the ninth. "It is important that it be clearly—very clearly—understood that the president of the Cham-

[1] Afonso Arinos de Melo Franco, interview, Brasília, October 14, 1965.

ber did not take over the government in order to prepare the inauguration of Juscelino Kubitschek and João Goulart. These men cannot take
over, should not take over, and will not take over. It is important to
tell everything truthfully. The government inaugurated yesterday,
under the aspect of a routine succession, is a government that was born
and will continue only by means of the consensus of the military leaders responsible for August 24 [1954]."[2]

At a cabinet meeting on November 9, Luz invited the ministers to remain, explaining that he expected to be Acting Chief Executive only
a short while. After the meeting Lott told Luz that a decision about the
Mamede case—one of military discipline—should not be allowed to
drag on. Luz offered to obtain the opinion of the legal consultant to
the presidency, but Lott insisted that it was an Army matter, not one for
juridical people.[3] Four days earlier Lott had suggested to Luz three
ways in which it would be technically possible to punish Mamede, and
he had added that, if none of these courses were followed, he would
resign as War Minister.[4] Some officers argued that Mamede's actions
had been no different from Canrobert's behavior on August 5, and
others discussed legal intricacies. The feeling of a great many generals as well as colonels reflected their long-inculcated reverence for
discipline: the War Minister should not be thwarted if he had made up
his mind to punish Mamede.

Top Army officers gathered at the Rio home of the governor-elect
of Minas. There they persuaded PSD Senator Benedito Valadares,
long a power in Minas, to warn President Luz. But when Valadares
spoke with Luz on the morning of the tenth, Luz replied with one of
his favorite expressions: "I think they are bluffing and shall pay to
see their cards."[5]

That afternoon radios proclaimed developments to gatherings in
the streets and to groups in apartments. The War Minister had been
called from his residence to Catete Palace at about 5 P.M. and was

[2] Joffre Gomes da Costa, *Marechal Henrique Lott,* p. 287.

[3] Henrique Lott, interview, Rio de Janeiro, August 27, 1963.

[4] *Ibid.* Carlos Luz's speech in Congress, November 14, 1955 (see Appendix 21
of Bento Munhoz da Rocha, *Radiografia de Novembro,* pp. 133–153).

[5] Lucas Lopes, interview, Rio de Janeiro, October 30, 1965.

described as sitting stiffly in the waiting room outside the President's office. Congressional officers, having already made an appointment to extend their good wishes to Luz, passed Lott in his chair as they went in to see the President.

Lott, the broadcasts revealed, had been kept waiting ten minutes—then fifteen. So it went while the legislators, beyond the reach of radio coverage, asked Luz whether he had handled the "Mamede affair." The Acting President said that he had done so, "faithful to my duty," in spite of a warning that the troops would march if he opposed Lott.[6] After the legislators left, Luz called in the Finance Minister and the Bank of Brazil president, who had been waiting to take up an urgent matter. Finally, irritated by a forty-five minute wait, Lott was admitted to see Luz.

Luz produced a legal opinion, which he had received that day from consultant Temístocles Brandão Cavalcanti. The opinion stated that the War Minister could not punish Mamede.[7] Lott argued that this civilian opinion was beside the point, for the President could have Mamede transferred to the regular Army. Lott thought that such a transfer, without any other step against Mamede, would have the effect of preserving discipline. "Discipline," he told Luz, "is learned only through serving, commanding, and suffering in the Army."[8]

Luz refused to transfer or punish Mamede.

To whom, Lott asked, should he turn over the War Ministry? The new minister, Luz advised, would be General Álvaro Fiuza de Castro, who had retired from service earlier in the year.

Lott said that Café Filho had decided against naming Fiuza War Minister because Fiuza, as Army chief of staff during the August 1954 crisis, had played an active part in the events that had resulted in Vargas' suicide.[9] Fiuza continued to lead one wing in the Army, and the opponents of that wing would become doubly upset if Fiuza started his

---

[6] Rui Santos, interview, Brasília, October 15, 1965.

[7] Themistocles Brandão Cavalcanti, *Pareceres do Consultor Geral da República,* II: (*Julho a Novembro de 1955*), 364–368.

[8] Joffre Gomes da Costa, *Marechal Henrique Lott,* p. 288.

[9] General Fiuza de Castro had been the first to sign the generals' manifesto of August 22, 1954, calling for the resignation of Vargas.

turn in the ministry by making sure that Mamede not be punished. Finally, the sixty-year-old Lott pointed out that "Fiuza is older than I am, and is left with" the problem created by the Mamede incident. "Fiuza deserves more consideration and better luck."[10]

Fiuza was called in. Both Luz and Fiuza wanted the transfer of office to take place at once, as when Lott had replaced Zenóbio. But Lott spoke of some matters he wanted to take care of before leaving the ministry. "Tomorrow at 3:00 P.M." said Lott. "Perfect, very good," replied Fiuza. The generals shook hands, and then Lott left.

When Luz objected to Fiuza about the delay, Fiuza explained: "I have Lott's word of honor. . . . That is enough for me."[11]

[10] Lott, interview, August 27, 1963; Gomes da Costa, *Marechal Henrique Lott*, p. 289.
[11] Otávio Marcondes Ferraz, interview, São Paulo, August 9, 1963.

3. Lott's Decision (1:00 A.M., November 11, 1955)

LOTT WAS DISCONCERTED to learn that, before he had spoken with Luz, the *Diário Oficial* had already published the news of Fiuza's appointment.

He reached his home at 9:00 on the evening of the tenth, and received a visit from General Odílio Denys, commander of the troops of the Eastern Military Zone (which included Rio). Denys was concerned lest he and other troop commanders, who considered themselves to be great respecters of Army discipline and the constitution, be replaced by men who would create a crisis. He urged Lott to head a military movement, and he suggested that the troops be put on the alert. But Lott rejected these ideas.[1] Denys, a large man who preferred action to words, left.

Those who were upset by Lott's dismissal had gathered at various residences. General Zenóbio da Costa's home was filled with officers

[1] Viriato de Castro, *Espada x Vassoura: Marechal Lott*, p. 30.

who called themselves the "Central Command" of the Movimento Militar Constitucionalista (MMC). They disagreed with the anti-Getulistas and opposed the anti-Communist Democratic Crusade and the "Grupo da Sorbonne."[2] Now they spoke of following the impetuous Zenóbio in a rebellion on behalf of the inauguration of Kubitschek and Goulart.

Congressman Alkmim had seen another of his political prognostications fulfilled when Lott lost his job, and he had immediately sent word advising Lott that he would serve the nation well if he would not withdraw in favor of Fiuza.[3] There was such a mob around Alkmim's Hotel California apartment that the shrewd little Mineiro sent word to his congressional associates to meet that evening in an apartment at the Copacabana Palace Hotel Annex. Before joining them, and between telephone calls to Kubitschek in Minas, Alkmim sounded out Army sentiment.

The gathering at the home of Denys, near that of Lott, was by far the most important. Ten of the generals there controlled the Army power in the Federal District. Also present was General Olímpio Falconieri da Cunha, in charge of the Central Military Zone, which included São Paulo. Falconieri, some thought, might side with his close friend, Brigadeiro Eduardo Gomes. Falconieri was also a friend of Kubitschek. But what motivated him and the other indignant generals who reviewed the "fourth class burial" of Lott[4] was the prospect of Fiuza in the War Ministry.

Denys joined the group in his home after learning from Fiuza that Mamede was not to be punished and that the War Ministry would cooperate fully with Luz. Denys was pleased neither with this prospect of command changes, nor with the idea that the MMC might take the leadership in the military on behalf of the scheduled inauguration of Kubitschek and Goulart. He felt that Zenóbio's group was full of ambitious officers who had connections with Communists, and he did not want Kubitschek to take office on its wings.[5]

[2] Joffre Gomes da Costa, *Marechal Henrique Lott*, p. 237.
[3] José Maria Alkmim, interview, Brasília, October 15, 1965.
[4] Joaquim Justino Alves Bastos, *Encontro com o Tempo*, p. 297.
[5] Odílio Denys, interview, Rio de Janeiro, December 14, 1965.

Denys' generals voted down a suggestion that they all resign as a protest to Lott's fate. Instead, they agreed to take over key points in the city and force the government to show respect for military discipline.[6] Denys proposed that Marshal João Batista Mascarenhas de Morais head the movement, but the generals chose Denys. Denys accepted and told them to get their men ready to follow orders, which would soon be issued.

Lott had been trying to sleep, but his heart "pounded" as he reviewed recent events and foresaw worse ones. At about 1:00 A.M. he picked up his military "field" telephone and spoke with Denys: "I'll head the movement. It's impossible to accept the present situation. You are right. Time is running short. We must act."[7] He learned about the plans that had been made. Denys and Falconieri soon arrived and drove him in the rain to the War Ministry.

Troops were ordered to come from Vila Militar to take over Catete Palace, the police headquarters, the telephone company, and the telegraph operations; troops also seized the *Tribuna da Imprensa* and the Clube da Lanterna (Lantern Club), which had close ties with Lacerda's newspaper.

Lott wired commanders of the military zones and regions: "As the presidential solution of the case of Colonel Mamede is considered, by the Army chiefs here and by the Commander of the Central Military Zone (who is here), to be an act of positive provocation, I decided to try to re-establish the application of disciplinary precepts in order to prevent the breakdown of unity in the Army."[8]

[6] Bastos, *Encontro com o Tempo,* p. 298.

[7] Salomão Jorge, *A Vida do Marechal Lott: Com a Visão Panorâmica da Obra Monumental do Presidente Juscelino Kubitschek de Oliveira,* p. 93.

[8] Gomes da Costa, *Marechal Henrique Lott,* p. 303.

4. The Army Seizes Catete Palace
(November 11, 1955)

W<small>HILE</small> D<small>ENYS HAD BEEN CONSPIRING</small>, President Luz and close associates had dined and watched a movie at Catete Palace and then gone to their homes. Thus Justice Minister Prado Kelly was at his apartment by midnight when Police Chief Geraldo Menezes Côrtes telephoned him to report that Army leaders were meeting at the home of Denys. Prado Kelly instructed the Federal District police force to protect communications, such as radio stations, which he felt might be among the first to be attacked by "the Communists."[1]

Admiral Pena Bôto, warned by worried members of his Brazilian Anti-Communist Crusade, had already ordered "readiness" on the part of all available ships—nine destroyers, and the Navy's two twelve-thousand-ton cruisers, the *Barroso* and the *Tamandaré*. The *Barroso* was about to enter the Navy yard and had no ammunition or fuel. The boilers of the *Tamandaré* were being cleaned and had been disconnected from the turbines. Pena Bôto told Captain Sílvio Heck, the new commander of the *Tamandaré*, to get on with the work quickly.

At 2:00 A.M. the Police Chief called Prado Kelly again. This time it was to say that lights were on at the War Ministry and that he felt a coup was being planned.

Luz was advised, and he sped with a few members of his administration to Catete Palace. Among those who joined him there was General Fiuza de Castro, the bearer of good news: Lott had advised him that all he was doing at the War Ministry was handling papers in preparation for his departure from his post.

But the news that followed was more disturbing. Police Chief Menezes Côrtes had been ordered to the War Ministry and was on his way there, surrounded by an unfriendly escort provided by Zenóbio da Costa. The police headquarters were being invaded by troops.

At about 4:00 A.M., before Lott's soldiers reached Catete Palace,

---

[1] José Eduardo do Prado Kelly, interview, Rio de Janeiro, October 8, 1965.

Transportation Minister Marcondes Ferraz took Luz and Prado Kelly to the Navy Ministry. There Eduardo Gomes and Amorim do Vale issued a manifesto that was hardly brief although it consisted of one sentence; it declared the Navy and Air Force to be at the side of Luz. Gomes then left to get an air squadron moving to São Paulo.

Lott's soldiers, headed by General Floriano Lima Brayner and Emílio Maurel Filho, reached Catete Palace in time to seize Generals Fiuza de Castro and Alcides Etchegoyen. These two anti-Getulistas were taken to the War Ministry, where Marshal Mascarenhas de Morais pronounced them prisoners. Etchegoyen was so furious that he collapsed while he was expostulating and had to be sent to an Army hospital. When Lott said to Fiuza, "Excuse me, but I had to fool you for four hours," Fiuza replied: "No, Lott, you fooled me for forty years."[2]

Admiral Pena Bôto left his *Barroso* bunk to go to the Navy Ministry, where he was surprised to find "people all over the place, like cockroaches." Introduced to President Luz, he suggested that the presidential party board the *Tamandaré*. "Your position in Rio is untenable; let's go to São Paulo," the anti-Communist crusader said.[3] Thanks to Pena Bôto's earlier order for "readiness" on the part of the fleet, calls had gone out instructing the one thousand crew members of the *Tamandaré* to come aboard. Many of them were busy hauling ammunition up to the cruiser's turrets.

Luz consulted his cabinet ministers, and they agreed to go by sea to Santos, São Paulo's port city. Marcondes Ferraz telephoned Governor Quadros to advise of the government's plan to resist Lott, and he learned that all was quiet in the great industrial state.

At 8:30 A.M. on November 11 the presidential party boarded the *Tamandaré*. Among the twenty-seven passengers were Carlos Luz, Prado Kelly, Marcondes Ferraz, Munhoz da Rocha, Carlos Lacerda, Jurandir Mamede, José Monteiro de Castro (head of the presidential Casa Civil), and Colonel José Canavarro Pereira (head of the Casa Militar). Navy Minister Amorim do Vale remained behind to lead the whole fleet out of Guanabara Bay that evening.

Before the cruiser pulled away from the Ilha das Cobras wharf at

---

[2] Otávio Marcondes Ferraz, interview, São Paulo, August 9, 1963.
[3] Carlos Pena Bôto, interview, Rio de Janeiro, October 27, 1965.

9:20 A.M., Luz signed several copies of a statement, typed by Prado Kelly, which messengers were to make sure reached the presiding officer of the Chamber of Deputies. This statement advised that Luz, considering the serious occurrences that had violated the constitution, was remaining at the post of President on board a naval vessel in territorial waters.

5. Falconieri Reaches São Paulo (November 11, 1955)

GENERAL OLÍMPIO FALCONIERI DA CUNHA, after participating with Lott and Denys in the outbreak of the coup in the federal capital, set out by car at 4:30 A.M. to take charge of things in his Central Military Zone. This zone included the Second Military Region (São Paulo) and the Fifth Military Region (Mato Grosso), whose commanders decided to adhere to Falconieri's position. Falconieri planned to make some stops along the highway between Rio and São Paulo to give orders to regiments.

He was just starting his drive when an airplane from Rio headed for São Paulo with two pro-Luz officers. One of these, General Tasso Tinoco, was a close friend of Eduardo Gomes and commanded an infantry division in São Paulo City. Tasso Tinoco's fellow passenger, Brigadeiro Antônio Guedes Muniz, left the airplane when it landed at the Guaratinguetá Air Force School near the Rio–São Paulo highway. Tasso Tinoco, before flying on to São Paulo, asked Guedes Muniz to arrest Falconieri when he passed through in his car.[1]

In São Paulo Tasso Tinoco failed to persuade the most important Army officers, such as Second Military Region Commander Stênio Caio de Albuquerque Lima, that they should take a stand against Falconieri. The head of the Fôrça Pública (São Paulo state police), which had 7,800 men in the state capital and several thousand more in the interior,

---

[1] Antônio Guedes Muniz, interview, Rio de Janeiro, December 7, 1965.

wanted to have this elite militia go into action on behalf of Luz. But other Fôrça officers preferred to await the outcome[2] before inviting a clash with the Army, which was vastly better equipped. Governor Quadros, who had final say about use of the Fôrça Pública, had to be cautious. His secretary of public safety closed the banks and schools and devoted himself to the maintenance of order.

On the Rio–São Paulo highway, near Guaratinguetá, Falconieri was stopped and taken to see Guedes Muniz at the Air Force School. He asked if he might speak by telephone to Eduardo Gomes, who was still in Rio. Guedes Muniz hesitated to arrest a senior officer unless it was clear that he was a rebel, and Falconieri was saying nothing rebellious. The least Guedes Muniz wanted to do was to make Falconieri lose time. He agreed to the call, thinking that the lines must be out of order.

But the call went through. Falconieri assured Eduardo Gomes that he was seeking to defend "our cause" and would help maintain "legality."[3] Guedes Muniz took the receiver and was told by the Air Minister to stop delaying Falconieri and to put an airplane at his disposal.

Falconieri preferred to continue by car. At the Caçapava barracks at 11:30 A.M. he broadcast a pro-Lott manifesto, thus dispelling rumors that he had been made prisoner at Guaratinguetá. He sent a regiment, five-hundred-strong, from Caçapava to Santos, and he ordered additional troops to descend on Santos from São Paulo. He also had Army units take control of the airfields and allowed no gasoline for flyers.[4]

Eduardo Gomes alighted at São Paulo's Cumbica Air Force Base early in the afternoon. There was little to encourage him at his 3:00 P.M. conference with Quadros. In the state of Paraná, to the south, the

---

[2] Statement of José Canavó Filho to José Stacchini in *O Estado de S. Paulo,* June 13, 1965.

[3] Guedes Muniz, interview, December 7, 1965. Falconieri, explaining the incident to Carlos Castilho Cabral, said: "I knew very well that I had been taken prisoner, but in order not to upset things all I could do was hope that the telephone call to Eduardo would go through, for without orders from him Guedes would not let me go. I did not lie to Eduardo, because in truth I was going to defend the Constitution and the Law against the coup of Luz with Lacerda and Pena Bôto" (see Castilho Cabral, *Tempos de Jânio e Outros Tempos,* p. 92).

[4] Olímpio Falconieri da Cunha, interview, Rio de Janeiro, November 10, 1965.

Army commander was General Nelson de Melo, who had earlier agreed with Lott that the election results should not be annulled.[5] Now Nelson de Melo began moving troops to São Paulo. The military game, whereby the outcome is decided by a study of the strength of each side —rather than by an actual clash—was going badly for Luz. Tasso Tinoco could count on one mechanized squadron, one artillery division, and a battalion of engineers. These units, together with the Fôrça Pública and the Air Force, were no match for the contingents loyal to Lott and Falconieri.

[5] Afonso Arinos de Melo Franco, *A Escalada: Memórias*, p. 376.

6. The *Tamandaré* Sets Forth[1]
(November 11, 1955)

ON THE MORNING OF NOVEMBER 11 the *Tamandaré* started out of Guanabara Bay in the rain with only two of its four boilers working. It could move at only eight knots instead of its top speed of thirty.

Below, the presidential party had crowded into the *praça d'armas,* the ship's most ornate room. From a wall, a portrait of Admiral Tamandaré, with all his whiskers and decorations, looked down on the passengers. The portholes had been closed so that no light would show in the gloom outside. Naval officers and sailors were above, at the battle stations.

At 10:14 A.M. the cruiser, moving south, reached the *barra,* or passage between Guanabara Bay and the ocean. Fort Lage, one of the three

[1] The *Tamandaré* had once been the *St. Louis,* famous for having survived the Pearl Harbor attack. Carlos Pena Bôto has given an account of its November 1955 voyage in *Manchete* (November 26, 1955), and Carlos Luz has given an account in *O Cruzeiro* (December 3, 1955). Statistics and other information about the cruiser may be found in a Brazilian Navy booklet, *Cruzador Tamandaré*.

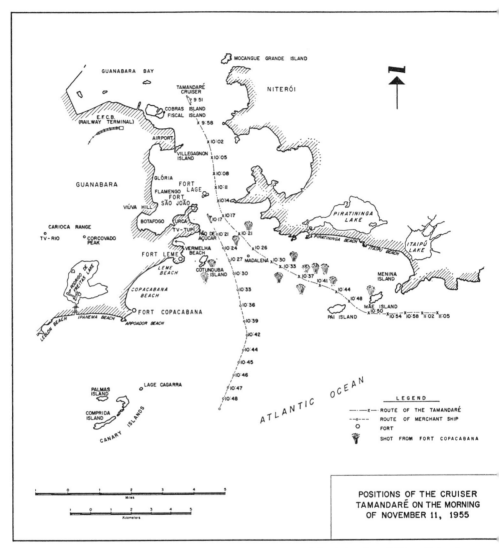

On board the *Tamandaré*: President Carlos Luz, Chief of the Casa Militar Colonel José Canavarro Pereira, Chief of the Casa Civil José Monteiro de Castro, Justice Minister José Eduardo do Prado Kelly, Agriculture Minister Bento Munhoz da Rocha Neto, Transportation Minister Otávio Marcondes Ferraz, Carlos Lacerda, Colonel Jurandir Mamede, Vice-Admiral Carlos Pena Bôto, Sílvio Heck, Sílvio Monteiro Mountinho, and other officers.

forts guarding the *barra,* displayed naval flags to signal that transit was forbidden to warships. Admiral Pena Bôto ignored the order and told Captain Sílvio Heck to sail on.

Fort São João, near Fort Lage, then issued a blank shot, to serve as a warning. In the *praça d'armas* Luz asked whether the *Tamandaré* was firing, or whether the presidential party was being saluted.[2] Prado Kelly found a telephone in the adjoining room (which was being used as Luz's cabin) and learned about the situation from Heck.

A few minutes later serious firing in the general direction of the *Tamandaré* was started at Fort Leme. This fort, otherwise known as Fort Duque de Caxias, lies south of Forts Lage and São João and like them was to the cruiser's starboard.

The *Tamandaré* had shells ready in its fifteen six-inch guns and eight five-inch guns. But Pena Bôto refrained from firing because crowded civilian districts lay in the same direction as the fort.[3] Entering the *praça d'armas,* he advised Luz of developments. "The mission," said Luz, "must be fulfilled."

In the face of more shots from Leme, the *Tamandaré* sought to keep under the protection of an Italian cargo ship that was leaving Rio.

Soon Cotunduba Island lay between the *Tamandaré* and Fort Leme. But by then it was within range of Fort Copacabana, about nine thousand yards to the west. Copacabana sent twelve shots in as many minutes, some going short and others long. The great splashes shook the ship, and the shells came close enough to fill the men aboard with apprehension and indignation. Officers under Pena Bôto wanted to fire back.

Lott did not want the Navy to leave Guanabara Bay, and had ordered the shooting. When he had been told that one cruiser was beginning to move, he had instructed that the cruiser be advised by signals not to go out of the bay. If the signals were not obeyed, Lott had said that blank shots should be fired. If these proved ineffective, then the forts were to shoot in front of the cruiser. And if even this

[2] José Eduardo do Prado Kelly, interview, Rio de Janeiro, October 8, 1965; Gualter Maria Menezes de Magalhães and Telmo Becker Reifschneider, interview, aboard *Tamandaré,* December 6, 1965.

[3] Carlos Pena Bôto, interview, Rio de Janeiro, October 27, 1965.

step did not bring obedience, then, Lott had said, the forts should shoot directly on the ship.[4]

On Copacabana beach and on the neighboring streets a great crowd braved the wet weather to watch the firing by the well-known fort. The fort did not live up to its fame for accuracy in hitting targets. Lieutenants, it is said, arranged to have the shots miss the ship, while a superior officer fumed at their apparent inability.

The *Tamandaré,* moving eastward away from Copacabana, was approaching two small rocky islands known as Pai (Father) and Mãe (Mother). Visibility was very bad. One of the last shots from Copacabana hit Mãe, illuminating the scenery. ("A beautiful sight," thought Pena Bôto.) Then the cruiser passed between Pai and Mãe and sailed to the east with the islands protecting it from further gunfire. Safely out at sea, it turned west to go to Santos. After five hours, its speed reached sixteen knots.

Most of the ship's passengers were tired. They ate *bacalhau,* the dried salt codfish customarily used in the Navy. There was nothing cheering about the news reports carried on the radio, but Luz appeared in a good mood until 5:00 P.M., when the radio announced that the Chamber of Deputies had deposed him.

[4] Henrique Lott, interview, Rio de Janeiro, August 27, 1963.

7. Congress Declares Luz Deposed
(November 11, 1955)

AFTER LOTT AND DENYS started their coup, a petition was addressed to Chamber of Deputies Acting President Flôres da Cunha by Alkmim of the PSD and by the leaders of other political parties that had joined the PSD-PTB coalition. It advised that more than half the congressmen wanted a special session at 10:00 A.M.

At 4:00 A.M. Alkmim was called to the War Ministry. So were Flôres da Cunha and Nereu Ramos, the presiding officers of the Chamber and the Senate. Lott told them that a quick solution to the political problem was necessary.[1]

At 11:00 A.M. the Chamber of Deputies met to vote on a motion that, "in view of the serious events which began yesterday, and considering the de facto situation created by them, it recognize the existence of the impediment mentioned in Constitutional Article 79, Paragraph 1," and, in accordance with that same article, have the presiding officer of the Senate take over the office of President of the Republic.

Flôres da Cunha read the message Luz had sent him before the *Tamandaré* put to sea. Majority leader Capanema expressed a hope that the minority might be heard without hostile demonstrations. Flôres da Cunha, supporting the majority's motion, was bitterly attacked by fellow members of the UDN. Asked about soldiers who had received the congressmen when they arrived, and who were in the corridors of the Chamber, he explained that he had requested troops from Lott to provide security.[2]

João Agripino (UDN, Paraíba) wanted to know whether it was proper for the presiding officer to be supporting an illegal government. "We, who until yesterday were being accused of a coup, are now witnessing a coup by the accusers."[3]

Each side interjected news items. Herbert Levy (UDN, São Paulo) provided information said to have originated in Quadros' office: "All the military forces of the state of São Paulo, under the direction of General Tasso Tinoco, and including the Air Force, declare themselves loyal to President Carlos Luz."[4] Opposition leader Afonso Arinos de Melo Franco, pale and weary, said that at that very moment the *Tamandaré* might be reaching shore to install the legal federal government in São Paulo.

Capanema, handling things for the PSD-PTB-PSP-PRP-PTN-PR majority, kept repeating that Congress should recognize that Carlos

---

[1] Henrique Lott, interview, Rio de Janeiro, August 27, 1963.

[2] *Ibid.*; José Loureiro Júnior, *O Golpe de Novembro e Outros Discursos*, p. 249. Appendix III in Loureiro's book gives full text of the Chamber of Deputies session of November 11, 1955.

[3] Loureiro Júnior, *O Golpo de Novembro*, p. 245.

[4] *Ibid.*, p. 297.

Luz was materially impeded from governing. "If the Army forces, which caused the President to leave the seat of government at Catete Palace, do not permit his return to his post, there is no legality. It is not up to us to judge now the merits of the armed movement. The nation cannot continue without a government." Capanema suggested that if Congress did not act there was an unacceptable alternative: the Army might "organize a *junta militar* to take over."[5]

The majority brought the issue to a vote at 3:00 P.M. With few *deputados* breaking away from party leadership, the motion carried, 185 to 72, and was forwarded to the Senate. There, after a two-hour debate, the Chamber's resolution was approved, 43 to 9.

Thus Nereu Ramos, a man steeped in constitutional law, prepared—a little reluctantly—to take over the presidency of Brazil until Café Filho returned from the hospital. General Lott, presiding over the ceremony at Catete Palace, read a document recording the decision made by the legislative houses, and he was the first to sign it. It was also signed by Nereu Ramos and Flôres da Cunha and by some of the military figures who had played a role in deposing Luz: Marshal Mascarenhas de Morais and Generals Zenóbio da Costa and Ângelo Mendes de Morais.

Then Nereu Ramos named cabinet ministers. The group aboard the *Tamandaré* and their friends were dropped. Lott again became War Minister. Kubitschek's friend Lucas Lopes reassumed the transportation post, which he had left in January when Café Filho had broadcast the military ministers' request for a candidate of "national unity."

Foes of the new order described the presidency as having become a subsection of the War Ministry.

[5] *Ibid.*, p. 256.

8. The Return of the *Tamandaré*
(November 12–13, 1955)

I N THE *praça d'armas* of the *Tamandaré* Carlos Luz consulted the men around him. Although Mamede felt that the situation was quite hopeless and although most of the others agreed, they resolved to follow Pena Bôto's suggestion that they carry on with the slow voyage to Santos. Some favorable development might occur. But Luz decided that a radio message should be sent to Amorim do Vale to cancel the arrangement whereby the fleet was to leave Guanabara Bay for Santos. Pena Bôto objected to signing because he felt that "such a message would prove very disconcerting to the crews." He suggested that Luz sign. "You are President."[1]

So Amorim do Vale received the message from Luz: "Do not leave the port." The admiral had moved with his staff to the *Barroso* at midday after noting that soldiers were beginning to surround his ministry.[2] Upon receipt of Luz's message, he canceled the preparations being made for the great exodus. Lott, noting that the fleet remained in Guanabara Bay, concluded that the shots fired in the general direction of the *Tamandaré* had had a good effect.[3]

Later in the night Luz conferred further with his companions and sent messages to Eduardo Gomes and Amorim do Vale recommending no further resistance. This, Luz said, was to avoid bloodshed and prevent a combat within the armed forces.

After more dried salt codfish, the passengers on the *Tamandaré* slept. Some used the sofas in the *praça d'armas,* and Prado Kelly climbed up to a cabin by a tower to find a bunk. The accommodations were generally good because the warrant officer's mess was transformed into a dormitory with twelve cots and because officers made room, giving up cabins or sharing them.[4]

[1] Carlos Pena Bôto, interview, Rio de Janeiro, October 27, 1965.
[2] Edmundo Jordão Amorim do Vale, interview, Rio de Janeiro, November 10, 1965.
[3] Henrique Lott, interview, Rio de Janeiro, August 27, 1963.
[4] Bento Munhoz da Rocha Neto, interview, Curitiba, November 28, 1965; Telmo

At 4:30 A.M. on the twelfth the *Tamandaré* was within one hundred miles of Santos. Pena Bôto received a message advising that airplanes from the Santos air base might be used to bomb the cruiser. He took the ship south, but, as no attack materialized, he veered toward Santos again. By then, however, it was perfectly clear from messages that no development was going to remove Falconieri's troops from the port city and that these troops were not going to allow a landing.

Santos was never even sighted by those aboard the *Tamandaré*. Pena Bôto wanted to go to Salvador, Bahia, which he felt was "loyal" and where there was a large naval base. But Luz ordered the return to Rio. On the afternoon of the twelfth the *Tamandaré's* guns were emptied of their shells in the easiest and safest way. Far out at sea they were fired into the ocean.

The *Tamandaré* reached Rio on the morning of Sunday, November 13. Unlike the preceding days, it was sunny. The beaches were crowded with bathers, and the *Tamandaré* provided them with an interesting show. To demonstrate the anger of the cruiser's officers and men against Fort Copacabana, Pena Bôto brought the ship as closely as he could to it (until he had but fifty centimeters beneath his keel).[5] At the same time the *Tamandaré's* band was playing. A loudspeaker, trained on Fort Copacabana, blared the old Navy song, "Cisne Branco" (White Swan).

For those aboard the *Tamandaré* a surprise was in store as it made its way into Guanabara Bay. A banner on Fort São João proclaimed: "Long Live the Navy" (*Viva a Marinha*).

Shortly before noon the *Tamandaré* anchored in the bay, and launches from Rio brought prominent politicians on board. Ovídio de Abreu, PSD *deputado*, represented the Nereu Ramos government. He came to ask Luz to resign the presidency of the Chamber of Deputies (and thus eliminate himself from the presidency of the Republic) in return for being allowed to disembark.[6] Luz said that he

---

Becker Reifschneider, interview, aboard *Tamandaré*, Rio de Janeiro, December 6, 1965.

[5] Pena Bôto, interview, October 27, 1965.

[6] Carlos Luz, speech to Chamber of Deputies, November 14, 1955, in Bento Munhoz da Rocha, *Radiografia de Novembro*, Appendix 21.

planned to resign but would not sign a resignation statement aboard the *Tamandaré*. His word should be respected or he should be locked in a fortress, he said.

The new government was consulted. Nereu Ramos was satisfied. But Lott observed: "The Army will in no manner retreat. We have taken a step forward and will not step backward. Although I have never broken an Army regulation, now I shall have to scratch a page of the constitution. But we cannot vacillate any more."[7] He and some of the other cabinet ministers were concerned lest Luz take legal action against the vote of Congress. Only after Luz denied having this intention was he allowed to go ashore.

Upon reaching land, two colonels were arrested. One was Mamede, who was later sent to a recruitment post in the interior of São Paulo. The other, Colonel José Canavarro Pereira, was the head of the Casa Militar under Café Filho and Luz. Lacerda was advised by Afonso Arinos de Melo Franco and Juraci Magalhães to go into exile. As a first step he found asylum in the Cuban Embassy after the chargé at the Peruvian Embassy hesitated to welcome him.

Late at night Ovídeo de Abreu called at Luz's apartment and asked for the resignation statement. Luz wrote one out and said: "You can go and soothe the head of the government, for he can show this to the military ministers and sleep peacefully."[8]

After midnight Luz received another visitor, Cardinal Jaime de Barros Câmara. On behalf of the government the Cardinal appealed to Luz to give up his plan of appearing in Congress on November 14. "Your presence might provoke adverse manifestations. The Communists might attack you. The government guarantees your life and assures you your rights, but it cannot do it in the Chamber."[9] Luz, a brave man, was determined to defend his actions before a hostile Congress, and he told the Cardinal that, if he could not do so, it would be best to have Congress closed down. It took him two hours to persuade the Cardinal.

Afonso Arinos has written that Luz in giving his speech—courageously and firmly, but not defiantly—reached "without doubt, the su-

[7] Armando Falcão, interview, Rio de Janeiro, November 30, 1966.
[8] Carlos Luz, speech to Chamber of Deputies, November 14, 1955.
[9] *Ibid.*

preme moment of his long public life."[10] It was a long speech, giving a full account of Luz's activities starting with his decision about Mamede and ending with his resignation as president of the Chamber of Deputies. No interruptions were supposed to be made. But at one point rash Leonel Brizola (PTB, Rio Grande do Sul) broke in to say that the speaker was "making statements which we do not wish to leave uninterrupted, because that would represent our agreement with what is untrue."[11]

While Luz spoke, orderliness and a show of respect generally prevailed. But soon after the Chamber was bedlam. UDN leader Afonso Arinos could hardly be heard when he exclaimed that "the War Ministry has transformed itself into a fortress of treason" and when he protested against the press censorship that was being exerted, without the existence of a "state of siege," against anti-Lott publications. In the course of one bitter exchange of words on the fifteenth, Flôres da Cunha rushed from the presiding officer's table to the door of the Chamber, accompanied by his son, who pulled out a revolver and flourished it in the air.[12]

[10] Afonso Arinos de Melo Franco, *A Escalada: Memórias*, p. 390.
[11] Carlos Luz, speech to Chamber of Deputies, November 14, 1955.
[12] Melo Franco, *A Escalada*, p. 393.

9. The Army's Ultimatum to Café Filho
(November 20, 1955)

IN THE HOSPITAL, Café Filho was shocked when he learned how Luz had handled the Mamede case. He prepared a letter to tell Lott how sorry he was about the development, which, without his having been consulted, was depriving him of the services of so useful a War Minister. But he never sent it because, when he was about to sign it, he learned of the coup of November 11 which again made Lott War Minister.

News of the *Tamandaré*'s trip set Café Filho's blood pressure to the highest point of his illness. Learning about the new cabinet, which was chosen without his advice, Café Filho came to see the coup of November 11 as something hostile to him as well as to Luz. His friend, Dr. Felix Pacheco Raimundo de Brito, left the presidency of the Hospital for Public Servants during a dispute with the new Labor Minister, whereupon Café Filho moved to a private clinic.[1]

Alkmim sought out Munhoz da Rocha to learn whether Café Filho would agree to certain conditions if he were allowed to return to the presidency. These concerned the cabinet, particularly the War Minister, who had suddenly become the hero of the Getulistas. Munhoz da Rocha told Alkmim that Café Filho would agree to no conditions.[2]

Nereu Ramos made it clear that he would step aside as soon as Café Filho's health allowed his return. But many in the new government were saying that, under the circumstances, it was Café Filho's patriotic duty to resign.

Café Filho was contemplating resigning, and he had his secretary draw up an appropriate letter. But he held it aside, awaiting developments and not wanting to use it without consulting his principal collaborators. He prepared to have a group of eight medical specialists examine him on November 21 to see whether he was in condition to reassume the presidency if he wanted to.

Before the checkup took place, Lott presided at a meeting of generals. A majority of them resolved that it was to the best interest of the nation that Café Filho not return. Some feared that he might retain his former ministers, in which case Lott would feel "uncomfortable" in the presence of Eduardo Gomes and Amorim do Vale.[3]

When Lott visited the São Vicente Clinic on Sunday afternoon, November 20, Café Filho expected to receive an overdue account of the recent coup. The patient remarked that he had learned in *Manchete* magazine about steps that had been taken without his having been consulted.[4] Luz's resignation, Café Filho said, had been such a step. Lott

---

[1] João Café Filho, *Do Sindicato ao Catete,* II, 560–564.
[2] Bento Munhoz da Rocha Neto, interview, Curitiba, November 28, 1965.
[3] Café Filho, *Do Sindicato ao Catete,* II, 570.
[4] Henrique Lott, interview, Rio de Janeiro, August 27, 1963.

replied that he had to say something he found "very disagreeable."
With things the way they were in Brazil and considering Café Filho's
poor health, it would not be wise for him to return to the presidency.
"Mr. President, the generals consider your return inconvenient."

Café Filho gave up the idea of resigning. "If that's the way it's going
to be, I prefer to be deposed. . . . You speak in the name of generals
who exercise the principal commands. These were conferred by me on
the recommendations you made as minister. It is impossible for me to
accept, without sacrificing my personal dignity and the decorum of the
post, an insistence by insubordinate military people."[5] He went on to
say that if the medical checkup showed that he was not up to the job,
he would step out; this, he added, might be the "easiest" solution. But
he let Lott know that he could not refuse to assume the presidency if
the doctors felt that he was physically able. "You can put me out, but it
is my duty to take over."[6]

Before leaving the clinic, Lott stopped to speak with Dr. Raimundo
de Brito, Café Filho's personal physician. From Lott's remarks, the
doctor concluded that the War Minister was asking for a medical report showing that Café Filho's health would not allow him to be President again. "He wants to turn a professional examination into a farce,"
thought Raimundo de Brito.[7] Lott observed that he was a General of
the Army, whereupon Raimundo de Brito described himself as a "General of Medicine."

Again Lott and Denys met with their comrades. Resolving to stand
by their earlier decision, they awaited the findings of the physicians.

Before the examination began, the doctors asked Café Filho about
his "psychological state." He replied that the ultimatum by "a group
of generals to whom I conferred the principal commands" made him
want to assume the presidency at once.[8] Late on the morning of November 21, all eight specialists found that he was in condition to do
so. Café Filho then signed an official statement, drawn up by Prado

[5] Café Filho, *Do Sindicato ao Catete*, II, 573.

[6] Lott, interview, August 27, 1963.

[7] Felix Pacheco Raimundo de Brito, interview, Rio de Janeiro, December 14, 1965.

[8] Café Filho, *Do Sindicato ao Catete*, II, 575.

Kelly, advising Nereu Ramos and the heads of the Senate, the Chamber of Deputies, and the Supreme Court that "as of this moment I reassume" the presidential post.

10. Congress Declares Café Filho Deposed
(November 22, 1955)

AFTER CAFÉ FILHO'S STATEMENT reached the Chamber of Deputies, congressmen turned their attention from the budget to the new crisis. Word came that Lott wanted Congress to vote Café Filho out of office. The War Minister reasoned that the Luz administration had not wanted to see Kubitschek inaugurated and that a new Café Filho administration would feel the same way. Majority leader Capanema maintained that Congress could not vote an *impedimento* (the existence of an impediment) against Café Filho. Members of the majority who agreed with Lott then turned to majority vice-leader Tarcilo Vieira de Melo, and he prepared the speech that Capanema refused to deliver.[1]

Some senators questioned the medical report and discussed the possibility of creating a legislative commission "to examine Sr. Café Filho's state of health."[2]

Lott and his generals tried to convince President Nereu Ramos that he should not step aside for Café Filho. But Nereu Ramos consulted the 1946 constitution, which he had played an important role in writing. He could find no legal ground for accepting Lott's reasoning.

At the clinic that afternoon (November 21), Café Filho discussed the situation with Eduardo Gomes, Amorim do Vale, Munhoz da Rocha, Prado Kelly, and Napoleão Alencastro Guimarães, who had been his Labor Minister. He learned that his secretary, bearing his official notification to Nereu Ramos, had been unable to enter Catete

---

[1] Gustavo Capanema, interview, Brasília, October 23, 1965.

[2] Bill proposed by Senator Reginaldo Cavalcanti (see *Correio da Manhã*, November 22, 1955).

Palace because of the tanks and troops with which Lott had surrounded it. The heart patient also heard rumors that soldiers might surround the clinic. Friends used strong words to express their anger and their determination to see their President back at his Catete desk. Since he had decided first to spend the night at his home, they drove with him there.

They found the Copacabana apartment building surrounded by troops and tanks. With the arrival of Café Filho, mobs filled the streets and balconies to watch, and occasionally to jeer at, the troops. Soldiers snatched cameras from newspaper photographers. Café Filho was allowed to enter his residence, but visitors were not permitted to accompany him. Trying to get in, Alencastro Guimarães insisted on his rights as a senator, but to no avail.

Within well-guarded Catete Palace, Nereu Ramos, Lott, and other officials of the Army and government listened to a tape recording of the conversation that had taken place at the São Vicente Clinic before Café Filho had left with his friends for his home. Lott heard words that infuriated him.

By then the War Minister had deployed enough troops to convince Capanema that a virtual "state of war" existed in Rio. Catete Palace was surrounded by tanks, trucks, and other "combat vehicles." They filled the streets in the vicinity. To the trucks and troops around Café Filho's apartment were added members of the tough Polícia Especial (Special Police Force).[3] "Almost the whole stretch of Posto 6," Café Filho has written, "gave the impression of a battlefield, where a clash was imminent."[4] Lott put all local Army units on the alert.

Congress, Capanema was now willing to admit, could recognize, as it had done in the Luz case, a condition it had not created which effectively prevented Café Filho from taking office. This appeared particularly true after lawyers argued that Café Filho should do his "reassuming" at Catete Palace in a proper ceremony.[5]

Among his friends Café Filho had said that he wanted to preside over an administration that would allow the electoral tribunals to

[3] Henrique Lott, interview, Rio de Janeiro, August 27, 1963.

[4] João Café Filho, *Do Sindicato ao Catete*, II, 581.

[5] Lott, interview, August 27, 1963. One of these lawyers was Francisco Brochado da Rocha.

study the October returns without pressure. He argued that the "*juscelinista* and *janguista* forces, backed by the Communists,"[6] must have feared an impartial inquiry if they had to turn to illegal means to prevent the return of the constitutional President. But the Kubitschek people were not sure how impartial the study would be if their foes, now gathering around Café Filho, took over the administration. They shuddered to think what changes in Army commands Fiuza de Castro might have made.

When Congress met for its lively night session, one representative of the majority called Café Filho a *golpista*. Another tried to maintain that Café Filho was displaying a lack of honor in failing to follow the policy established by the PSP, on whose ticket he had been elected in 1950. Still another—a PTB man—suggested that a study be made of Café Filho's letter from the clinic; it might, like the Brandi letter, be one of those "false letters" that the UDN "likes to produce."

Interrupting a speech by a member of the PSD, Afonso Arinos de Melo Franco declared that a minority congressman was absent because he was being prevented by the police from leaving Café Filho's apartment. The vote, said Afonso Arinos, should not take place until the absent lawmaker appeared. The majority hooted down this suggestion. A Partido Libertador congressman then proclaimed it significant that Capanema had stayed away in order not to participate in the act that his colleagues were about to "perpetrate." But at that moment Capanema made a dramatic entrance and was loudly cheered by the majority.

Shortly after midnight Afonso Arinos delivered his speech. The majority jeered loudly and frequently when he protested press and radio censorship and when a colleague joined in to criticize Rádio Nacional for having announced the decision of Congress before a vote had been taken. The decision, Afonso Arinos said, was going to be made under the threat of troops, armed to the teeth. In an interruption he was called a liar, but he went on to declare that a crime "was about to be committed against the constitution."

Other UDN speakers maintained that the Chamber was abdicating

---

[6] Café Filho, *Do Sindicato ao Catete*, II, 582.

its sovereignty and lending itself "to illegal and ignominious maneuvers." One described Congress as becoming a rubber stamp for approving unconstitutional acts. Two congressmen declared that Nereu Ramos and Lott were dictators.[7]

A spokesman of the Partido Socialista Brasileiro arose to point out that the PSB had opposed Café Filho's "unpopular" administration, and that it favored the inauguration of the candidates who had been elected. But, this speaker said, the PSB could not vote for a clearly unconstitutional resolution. If Congress wanted to throw anyone out of the presidency, it should follow the regular and lengthy procedure of "impeachment."[8]

In spite of the majority's habit of booing and hooting, other minority speakers wanted to be heard. The majority decided, however, to end the debate shortly after 2:00 A.M. in order to send the *votação de impedimento* to the Senate for an early morning session. By a vote of 179 to 94 the resolution carried in the Chamber.

In the Senate some argued brilliantly that the Chamber had acted unconstitutionally, but before 9:00 A.M. the Senate approved the resolution, 35 to 16.

The admirals met and issued a statement saying they would accept the situation of force created by the Army because they were not in a position to resist; but they added that the Navy was manifesting "its complete disapproval of, and its repulsion for, an act which is illegal in spite of being approved by Congress."[9]

Jânio Quadros, too, issued a manifesto declaring his disagreement with the step taken by Congress. "The Governor," the statement said, "believes that that decision will receive a terrible judgment from the voice of History."[10] The manifesto went on to say that the Governor would, however, abide by the resolution until it was found illegal by the courts.

[7] *Correio da Manhã,* November 22, 1955.
[8] *O Estado de S. Paulo,* November 22, 1955.
[9] *Correio da Manhã,* November 23, 1955.
[10] *Ibid.,* November 25, 1955.

11. No Insurrection by the Supreme Court

SOON AFTER THE SENATE reached its decision about Café Filho, Nereu Ramos asked Congress to declare Brazil in a "state of siege" for thirty days, the maximum period allowed by the constitution. He based his request on a petition of the military ministers which was forwarded to Congress. It explained that

the movement to return to constitutional ways, initiated and concluded on the morning of November 11, was not dictated simply to re-establish fully the principle of discipline, essential for the life and honor of the military institutions, but also and principally for the need of stopping the imminent consummation of subversion of the constitutional order, openly threatened by bad Brazilians in the legislature, in the press, on the radio and television, and made possible by some military leaders and the holders of some high posts in the executive branch of the government. . . . Whoever reads the subversive newspapers and the parliamentary speeches of the last few weeks will find plenty of material demonstrating the outrageous advocation of crises against the safety of the State.

The three ministers spoke of "foci of subversion, apparently dormant, but still endowed with dangerous potential."[1]

To consider the matter the Chamber of Deputies met in an extraordinary session early on the afternoon of November 23. With Flôres da Cunha presiding and Capanema leading the majority, congressmen debated into the night the many amendments proposed by the UDN. Among those passed was one providing that civilians accused of crimes against the state were to be tried by civil courts and not by military tribunals. Afonso Arinos failed with his controversial suggestion that censorship not be applied to any parliamentary speech or document.

The "state of siege" passed the Chamber 178 to 91, and on November 24 it was approved by the Senate 35 to 16.

This, the first "state of siege" enacted under the 1946 constitution, was not used to interfere with the life of the average citizen. Besides providing a measure of protection which Lott felt useful, it adversely

[1] *Correio da Manhã,* November 23, 1955.

affected the legal steps being taken on Café Filho's behalf. The congressional majority, therefore, kept extending it every thirty days as long as Nereu Ramos was in office.

The legal battle began on the afternoon of November 22 when Prado Kelly and another lawyer took habeas corpus and *mandado de segurança* petitions to the Supreme Court. The habeas corpus was filed against Nereu Ramos and requested the withdrawal of the "military and political force which is posted" in front of Café Filho's residence, "impeding his movement and that of his family." The *mandado de segurança* argued that Café Filho was President. It recalled that in 1896, when President Prudente de Morais had taken a similar absence and had handled the notifications as Café Filho had, Congress had not interfered with his return.[2]

The two petitions were dealt with quickly. On December 14 the Supreme Court ministers gave their decision about the *mandado de segurança*. A majority of those participating declined to make a judgment until the state of siege was ended. Only one, Álvaro Moutinho Ribeiro da Costa, voted in favor of granting Café Filho's request.

The most discussed decision was handed down by Nelson Hungria when he refused to recognize the request for the *mandado*.

Congress did nothing more than acknowledge the material impossibility of Sr. Café Filho reassuming the presidency in the face of tanks and bayonets of the Army. . . . It is a situation of fact created and maintained by the force of arms, against which, obviously, any decision of the Supreme Court would be impractical. Insurrection is a political crime, but, when it is victorious, it becomes a right to glory. . . . Against an armed insurrection, crowned with success, the only thing of value is a counter-insurrection with a stronger force. And this, positively, cannot be carried out by the Supreme Court.

Against "an imposition by insurrectional Army forces," Hungria said "there is no remedy in juridical pharmacology."[3]

With regard to the habeas corpus petition, the government said that

---

[2] The petitions are summarized in an article in *Correio da Manhã*, November 23, 1955. They are given in more detail in Chapter XLV of Edgard Costa, *Os Grandes Julgamentos do Supremo Tribunal Federal*, III.

[3] Costa, *Os Grandes Julgamentos*, III, 396–398.

Café Filho and those dwelling with him could move freely. Café Filho, seeing some nonuniformed members of the Polícia Especial on the street outside, did not agree; nor did he stir out of his apartment. When the Supreme Court dealt with the request for the habeas corpus on December 21, it refused to grant it because Brazil was in a "state of siege."

On January 7, 1956, during Kubitschek's five-day visit to the United States, the Superior Electoral Tribunal issued "official" election returns that hardly differed from those the press had reported; they confirmed the election of Kubitschek and Goulart.

BOOK III: *Expressions of Discontent, 1956–1959*

Reporter (in 1960): *"What was the most important moment of your government?"*

President Kubitschek: *"It was the twenty-third of November, 1956. On that day I took office a second time. I had the impression that an August 24 was being prepared. But in a few hours everyone realized that I was unwilling to commit suicide."*

1. Major Veloso Starts a Rebellion (February 1956)

ON JANUARY 31, 1956, Kubitschek and Goulart took office. Outgoing President Nereu Ramos became Justice Minister, and Alkmim took over the Finance portfolio. Lott and the other two military ministers, who had been installed on November 11, continued at their posts. So did Eastern Military Zone Commander Odílio Denys. Kubitschek called for peace so that he could govern and work on behalf of the economic development goals he had stressed as a candidate.

Within the military, the greatest dislike for the new regime existed among officers of the Navy and Air Force. A few of these officers spent the five-year period making their displeasure as evident as possible. Despite these strong feelings regarding the events that had begun with the assassination of Major Vaz in 1954, peace did prevail during Kubitschek's five-year term.

This peace was maintained largely because top military commands were controlled by the victors of 1955. Furthermore, although the strength of Democratic Crusaders in the Military Club almost equaled that of the supporters of the November coups,[1] this did not mean that many Democratic Crusaders favored a new coup. Some of them were

---

[1] Joffre Gomes da Costa, *Marechal Henrique Lott*, pp. 344–345 (see also footnote, p. 345).

influenced by Juarez Távora, who had, since Vargas' suicide, opposed all coups and who did not believe that two "bad" coups in 1955 justified a third—this one against what he called Kubitschek's *de facto* regime. While many Democratic Crusaders considered that much was wrong, they could not agree with die-hards who liked to think that a new coup would be a popular move. A cursory look at the political scene showed that Kubitschek had good alliances with most parties and that hardly anyone in the opposition UDN and PL favored an armed move against the government.

Several armed rebellions were planned, however. The two uprisings that did take place, one in 1956 and the other in 1959, were minor, and few conspirators actually carried out their schemes.

The first outbreak occurred soon after the inauguration, when Brazil was preparing for its annual Carnaval merry-making. The nation was still nominally under a state of siege, scheduled to end shortly before Kubitschek completed his first month in office. Those who were emotionally resentful of the new regime felt that it was by no means certain that Lott had achieved a position of dominance. The test was undertaken by some young Air Force officers who strenuously objected to the continuation of Brigadeiro Vasco Alves Seco in the post of Air Minister.

Before daybreak on February 11, 1956, two Air Force officers, Major Haroldo Veloso and Captain José Chaves Lameirão, used an Air Force five-passenger Beechcraft to leave the military airfield of Campo dos Afonsos, on the outskirts of Rio. Veloso's rebellious mission was to take control of the Brazilian interior and thus force an attack from the coastal regions by the troops under pro-Kubitschek commanders. Conditions along the coast, it was felt by the conspirators, would then become favorable for those who wanted to take up arms to bring about "an investigation of voting practices carried out in October 1955."[2]

Major Veloso, who had served in the office of Air Minister Eduardo Gomes in 1955, was perfectly suited to his task. A short, trim, active, thirty-five–year-old engineer, he knew the interior intimately and the natives there were disposed to follow him. In the early 1950's he had been in charge of installing airstrips so that airplanes coming from

---

[2] Haroldo Veloso, interviews, Marietta, Georgia, January 6–7, 1966.

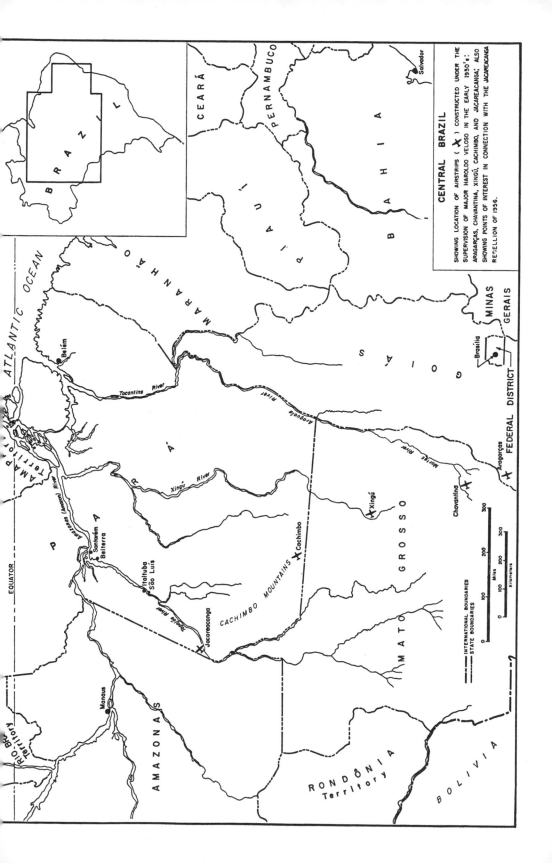

CENTRAL BRAZIL

SHOWING LOCATION OF AIRSTRIPS (✈) CONSTRUCTED UNDER THE
SUPERVISION OF MAJOR HAROLDO VELOSO IN THE EARLY 1950's:
ARAGARÇAS, CHAVANTINA, XINGÚ, CACHIMBO, AND JACAREACANGA; ALSO
SHOWING POINTS OF INTEREST IN CONNECTION WITH THE JACAREACANGA
REBELLION OF 1956.

INTERNATIONAL BOUNDARIES
STATE BOUNDARIES

Miles

Kilometers

ATLANTIC OCEAN

EQUATOR

BRAZIL

CEARÁ

PERNAMBUCO

PIAUÍ

BAHIA

Salvador

MARANHÃO

Belém

Tocantins River

Araguaia River

GOIÁS

Brasília

FEDERAL DISTRICT

MINAS GERAIS

Aragarças

Chavantina

Mortes River

Xingú

MATO GROSSO

Cachimbo

CACHIMBO MOUNTAINS

Xingú River

PARÁ

AMAPÁ Territory

Amazonas (Amazon) River

Santarém
Belterra

Itaituba
São Luis

Jacareacanga

Tapajós River

Manaus

AMAZONAS

RIO BRANCO Territory

RONDÔNIA Territory

BOLIVIA

the north of Brazil might reach Rio without going out of their way to refuel at Belém in the east. Over a period of four years Veloso, working his way northward, had installed airfields at Aragarças, Chavantina, Xingú, Cachimbo, and Jacareacanga. He had also established schools to teach reading; he felt that the people in the interior were always being exploited by traders and were otherwise forgotten by the rest of Brazil.[3]

Flying rebelliously into the interior in January 1956, Veloso reflected that the key city for the uprising was Santarém, to the north of Jacareacanga. It lies where the Tapajós River, flowing northward, joins the Amazon and was the refueling point for airplanes traveling between Manaus and Belém. Being also a center for trade in rubber, vegetables, fruits, and nuts, it had a population of thirty thousand. Veloso, who appreciated that most of these people would follow him, calculated that whoever controlled Santarém would be master of two-thirds of Brazil's territory.

Upon reaching Jacareacanga on their way to Santarém, Veloso and Lameirão placed gasoline drums all over the airstrip to prevent pursuers from landing.

In Rio, Air Minister Vasco Alves Seco issued a note to the press explaining that there had been no rebellion; it was merely "an act of personal indiscipline by two officers who will be vigorously punished."[4] Airplanes sent from Belém to capture the rebels were unable to land at Jacareacanga. They dropped messages advising the two officers that drastic measures would be taken if they did not surrender within two days.

These two days had passed by February 16, when Brazilians, in the midst of Carnaval, learned that a DC-3 had left Belém, taking Air Force Major Paulo Vítor and twenty men, armed with machine guns, to capture Veloso. After flying over Jacareacanga for twenty minutes, the DC-3 was permitted to land. Some of the sergeants who alighted were surprised when Paulo Vítor joined Veloso in rebellion.

This act of Paulo Vítor, a friend of Veloso, provided the rebels with

[3] Luís Werneck, Flávio Galvão, Roberto Brandini, Luís Maciel Júnior, and Heber Perillo Fleury, interview, São Paulo, November 24, 1965.

[4] *Correio da Manhã,* February 16, 1956.

machine guns. But it was not regarded by Veloso as an unmixed blessing; according to earlier arrangements, Paulo Vítor was to have worked for the rebellion in Rio after government troops had left for the interior.[5] Paulo Vítor explained to Veloso that Brigadeiro Alves Cabral, commander of the First Air Zone, with headquarters in Belém, had ordered him either to persuade Veloso to desist or else to capture him.

The three rebel officers used the DC-3 to take natives, many of them Indians, from Jacareacanga to Itaituba and Belterra, villages on the Tapajós River south of Santarém. Sergeants who had come with Paulo Vítor noted that the people of Santarém ("ruffians" they called them) were faithful to Veloso and had that airfield under control.[6] The few sergeants who refused to adhere to the revolt were made prisoners.

By January 19, Santarém, Jacareacanga, Belterra, Itaituba, and Cachimbo were all in rebel control. Regular airline flights in the Brazilian interior had been canceled.

[5] Veloso, interviews, January 6–7, 1966.
[6] Statement of three sergeants, in *Correio da Manhã*, February 24, 1956.

2. The End of Veloso's Jacareacanga Revolt

LOTT AND THE OTHER MILITARY MINISTERS examined the situation with Kubitschek in Rio and decided on February 18 that the Army, Navy and Air Force would carry out a joint operation. The soldiers being flown to Belém were to be taken up the Amazon by the Navy. The Army would be in charge of occupying Santarém, and the Air Force would have the responsibility of taking over the airport there.

At Campo dos Afonsos the forty Air Force officers belonging to the Second Air Transport Group refused to help put down Veloso's rebellion; all of them, including their commander, were arrested. Then in Salvador, Bahia, the head of the air squadron and fifteen officers were imprisoned for insubordination. The commander of the Fortaleza air base and his assistant were likewise made prisoners for refusing to send airplanes to bomb rebel strongholds. Some commercial airline pilots resolved not to participate in military action.

The vessel selected to carry the soldiers up the Amazon was the *Presidente Vargas*, a ship belonging to the government-owned Serviço de Navegação Amazônica e Administração do Pôrto do Pará (SNAPP). Inaugurated the previous September, the *Presidente Vargas* had a capacity for 1,500 passengers and was described as "ultra-modern and air-conditioned." Hearing of this decision, Navy Captain Edir Rocha indignantly resigned the directorship of SNAPP, a post he had held for ten years. Objecting to the "odious mission" assigned to the *Presidente Vargas*, he sent Kubitschek a telegram for which he was sentenced to prison.

Rocha's telegram criticized the arrest of "illustrious" military officers who were not sympathetic to the government. It suggested that serious armed conflict be avoided by dismissing War Minister Lott, a man described as a traitor to his military companions and one who would be known in history for having brought disunity to the armed forces. Rocha found it "repugnant" to cooperate with the joint military action or to arrange to transport troops whose objective was "to silence the call of profound sentiment and rebellion against the present situation, a call by a group of brave men who, in a gesture of rare heroism, show the nation the need of a complete change in the political-military situation."[1]

Nevertheless, on the evening of February 21 the *Presidente Vargas* set out from Belém with 450 men, 150 of them Marines.

While the ship made its way up the Amazon, a few loyal airplanes made trips to fire on the rebel positions. The rebels were usually forewarned by sympathetic Air Force sergeants who handled radio messages from the ground or sometimes by radio operators who were in the attacking airplanes.[2]

No one was killed in these shootings from the air. But after a large amphibious Air Force airplane had shot at the Santarém airport building, Veloso sent a message to Brigadeiro Alves Cabral in Belém ad-

[1] *Correio da Manhã*, February 21, 1956.
[2] Haroldo Veloso, interviews, Marietta, Georgia, January 6–7, 1966.

vising that civilians, including women, had been in the building. "From this moment on we shall react to any threat. We make you responsible."[3] Veloso was described by reporters as nervous and continually smoking cigarettes and drinking coffee.[4] What most dismayed him was the failure of fellow conspirators to do anything in Rio.

From Rio, Antônio Guedes Muniz, the *brigadeiro* who had tried to delay General Falconieri's November 11 automobile trip to São Paulo, telegraphed Brigadeiro Alves Cabral: "The newspapers advise of your 'ultimatum' to bombard our brethren in the forest of Jacareacanga. You, false legalists of last November, are now going to demonstrate to the entire world the type of bloody legality you want to implant in our Brazil. The bombardment that you promise will kill Indians, civilian workers and their families in the ridiculous and cowardly hope of murdering three of our own comrades. . . . If you murder them you will transform them into new heroes, such as those made sacred by the legalists of 1922."[5]

Kubitschek ordered Guedes Muniz imprisoned for ten days. Admiral Pena Bôto, whose bombastic anti-Kubitschek position made him a prominent candidate for the presidency of the Navy Club, was sentenced to ten days of "rigorous" imprisonment for his attack on the Kubitschek administration during Veloso's revolt. Former Navy Minister Amorim do Vale was put under house arrest for a statement intended to cast doubt on the right of Kubitschek and Goulart to be in their posts. Self-exiled Carlos Lacerda made his declaration in Norwalk, Connecticut: "The present regime of Brazil is based on force. The Supreme Court decided that a regime of force prevails in Brazil when it refused President Café Filho the right to be heard as the legitimate President."[6]

In Congress the PSD-PTB majority insisted that the uprising, and some of the recent antigovernment statements, showed that the opposition had intended to use force to prevent Kubitschek's inauguration. Therefore, the majority said, Lott had had to act as he did in Novem-

[3] *O Estado de S. Paulo*, February 22, 1956.
[4] *Correio da Manhã*, February 24, 1956.
[5] Glauco Carneiro, *História das Revoluções Brasileiras*, II, 513.
[6] *O Estado de S. Paulo*, February 24, 1956.

ber. UDN congressmen were careful. Adauto Lúcio Cardoso said that
he had always opposed "extra-legal solutions."[7]

The Santarém airfield received more machine-gunning on February
23, and on the morning of the twenty-fourth, the *Presidente Vargas*
reached its destination. Veloso withdrew to the south, up the Tapajós
River, while the government forces at Santarém were transferred to
smaller boats to try to capture him and to regain control of the villages
on the river. By the twenty-sixth Itaituba had been occupied by 350
government men, some of these brought by airplane.

In Itaituba Colonel Hugo Delaite, in charge of the government operation, used threats on a native to learn of Veloso's whereabouts.
Then the colonel, familiar with the region, set forth in a heavy down-
pour with thirty-four well-armed soldiers for the island village of São
Luís. Veloso, evacuating men from São Luís, expected to hold out for a
long time among the natives at Jacareacanga still further south. Paulo
Vítor and Lameirão were at Jacareacanga; but since they were un-
familiar with the country, Veloso had agreed that they might leave for
Bolivia in the DC-3 in the event that he did not join them soon.

On the island of São Luís, Delaite's men came upon a group of
rebels, and in the ensuing scuffle the rebellion's only fatality occurred.
The victim, a civilian known as "Capitão Casusa," was one of Veloso's
many devoted admirers. He had malaria and was among the men Veloso wanted to take back with him to Jacareacanga. An Air Force sergeant, already involved in a personal feud with "Casusa," shot him
down.[8]

Veloso left the island for a nearby settlement, where he hoped to
get his first sleep in forty-eight hours. But the shelter he used belonged
to the native who had been giving Colonel Delaite helpful information, and he was arrested there. Colonel Delaite, considering himself fortunate, admitted that it would have been difficult to capture
Veloso in Jacareacanga.[9]

At Santarém on February 29 the residents, particularly the women,
greeted the prisoner by waving handkerchiefs and shouting "Viva Ve-

[7] *Correio da Manhã,* February 21, 1956.

[8] Veloso, interviews, January 6–7, 1966.

[9] *Folha do Norte,* Belém, March 4, 1956.

loso!" Before Veloso was placed aboard the *Presidente Vargas*, he sent
a message for Paulo Vítor in Jacareacanga: "There is nothing more I
can do except leave you and Lameirão free of any commitment to me."
But Paulo Vítor, Lameirão, and a rebel sergeant had left Jacareacanga
a few hours before the capture of their leader. Faced with a full-scale
invasion, they had removed the bushes and branches that camouflaged
the DC-3 and had departed for Bolivia.[10]

Answering questions, Veloso asserted that neither Eduardo Gomes
nor Juarez Távora had been involved in the revolt. Unwilling to im-
plicate those who were to have started uprisings at coastal centers, Veloso described the affair as a personal one for which he assumed full
responsibility. By this time some UDN congressmen were agreeing
that "the rebels deserve at least our respect, for they have sacrificed
themselves for a respectable sentiment and a respectable cause."[11]

With prisoner Veloso aboard, the *Presidente Vargas* reached Belém
on the night of March 3. In the meantime his three recent companions
who had flown to Bolivia had been granted asylum by the government
of that country.

But the fate of all the rebels was decided by Kubitschek, who was
seeking an atmosphere of good will. The President called for "full and
unrestricted" amnesty for all civilians and military people who had
been charged with "revolutionary acts" between November 10, 1955,
and March 1, 1956. Congress approved.

[10] Carneiro, *História das Revoluções Brasileiras*, II, 515.
[11] *O Estado de S. Paulo*, March 2, 1956, quoting João Batista Vasconcelos Torres
and Herbert Levy.

3. Távora Resumes Active Military Service

THE JACAREACANGA REBELLION convinced Juarez Távora of the
likelihood of a new cycle of military uprisings similar to those in which
he had participated in the 1920's. In order to work against such a disaster, he resolved to return to active military service. On February 23,

before the Jacareacanga rebellion had been subdued, Távora made his decision known to Lott. Relations between the two men had become strained because of the November coups and because Távora, on the War Minister's instructions, had been held prisoner "by mistake" on November 22.

Távora now explained, in the February conversation and in a memorandum delivered to Lott in March, that he was returning to military service to work for changes that might save Brazil. These changes included the dismissal of the military ministers and the granting of important commands to officers who had objected to the November coups.

Lott was hardly pleased to be told that these changes might forestall a series of uprisings by providing much-needed moral authority to the government. Kubitschek's lack of authority and prestige, Távora said, stemmed from the November coups, the election deal with the Communists, and the past refusal of Kubitschek's congressional supporters to favor a proper election law or a full investigation of his wealth. In Távora's opinion the resulting division in the armed forces was so serious that uprisings would probably occur until ended either by a Goulart-populist-Communist takeover or else by a dictatorship established by those who "opposed the Bolshevization of the nation."[1]

Lott had nothing good to say about this interesting forecast when Távora again spoke with him in April. Because the tone of Távora's expressions was so antiadministration, in May the "*tenente* with white hair" found his name placed with the names of some Navy and Air Force officers on the War Ministry's list of those who were working to assassinate Lott. A few months later, government investigators, military and civilian, implied that Távora, as head of Café Filho's Casa Militar, had sought to adopt an unpatriotic atomic energy policy. Concluding that, within the Army, he had little opportunity to promote harmony or reduce the likelihood of future revolts, Távora terminated his short renewal of active military service in August 1956.

Lott was increasingly considered to be in a position of "absolute predominance." Cheering to him and the administration was the out-

[1] Juarez Távora, "Esquema de Ação para Tentar Dirimir a Atual Crise Político-Militar," March 1956, p. 3. (Typewritten memorandum.)

come of the biennial election for the presidency of the Military Club. In the closest of elections, the candidate of the Democratic Crusade was defeated by General João Segadas Viana.

UDN legislators liked to describe Lott as a "Prussian" type of military officer who did not hesitate to have the government use force "illegally" even though the state of siege had expired early in 1956. While it is true that the government occasionally used force in mid-1956, the instances revealed a determination to curb the agitation of extremists who were poles apart. Late in May 1956 the Rio police acted against mobs that had been encouraged by Communists to demonstrate against a streetcar fare increase decreed by the foreign-owned Light and Power Company.[2] On August 24, 1956, the same police apprehended that day's issue of *Tribuna da Imprensa* because it commemorated Vargas' death by publishing a violent manifesto in which the absent Lacerda branded the Kubitschek administration as subservient to Communists and dominated by "traitors."[3]

[2] Afonso Arinos de Melo Franco, *A Escalada: Memórias*, p. 405.

[3] Thomas E. Skidmore, *Politics in Brazil, 1930–1964: An Experiment in Democracy*, p. 172.

4. A Jail Sentence for Gregório Fortunato

WITH ITS DECLARATION of amnesty in March 1956, the administration dropped its legal case against Lacerda and other directors of the Clube da Lanterna who were charged with having incited a conspiracy against the democratic regime in October and November 1955. Lacerda's cry that "the Gregórios shall not return to office" had been declared subversive.[1]

This reference to Vargas' personal guardsman, who had perpetrated the crime of August 1954, continued to be used by opponents of the Kubitschek regime. "Generals of the return" was a label they applied

[1] *Tribuna da Imprensa*, February 25–26, 1956.

to those who had taken control in November 1955. They made somewhat similar remarks about others who seemed to them to impede their
work of discrediting Vargas and his political heirs.[2]

Air Minister Alves Seco was accused of putting difficulties in the
way of Colonel João Adil de Oliveira, head of the Air Force commission that had installed itself at the Galeão Air Base to investigate the
case against Gregório Fortunato. Colonel Adil, an avid anti-Getulista,
became a controversial figure—all the more so when he blasted General
Emílio Maurel Filho for finally concluding that the Brandi letter, published in the *Tribuna da Imprensa* before the 1955 election, had been a
forgery. Adil maintained that the general, after spending a few days at
São Borja and speaking there with Goulart, had done some document
switching.[3] For holding this view, Adil was sued by Maurel. Adil's
lawyer retorted that "to bring about the new return, they want to make
another Colonel Mamede out of Colonel Adil."[4]

Adil's lawyer and the UDN's Adauto Lúcio Cardoso pushed the
case against Gregório in a civil criminal court. Gregório, fifty-six, repeated that Colonel Adil had tried to kill him at the Galeão Air Base
and had only been prevented from doing so by another colonel. As for
his crime, Gregório maintained that General Ângelo Mendes de Morais had asked him to act against Lacerda in order to save the life of
Vargas and free the nation from a civil war. The defendant added that
Deputado Euvaldo Lodi, who had since died, had also spoken of the
need to end Lacerda's life.[5]

In October 1956 a tribunal of judges sentenced Gregório to twenty-
five years in prison. The two men who had carried out the assault were
each given a thirty-three-year sentence. The greater the responsibility,
the smaller the sentence, Lacerda observed.

Soon after the convictions, Colonel Adil received additional satisfaction. Air Minister Alves Seco, unpopular with Air Force officers,

[2] See article in *O Estado de S. Paulo*, dateline Rio de Janeiro, November 9, 1956.

[3] João Adil de Oliveira, interview, Rio de Janeiro, December 20, 1965; Emílio
Maurel Filho, interview, Rio de Janeiro, October 11, 1965.

[4] Letter of Hugo Baldessarini, in *O Estado de S. Paulo*, dateline Rio de Janeiro,
April 21, 1956.

[5] *Tribuna da Imprensa*, October 12, 1956.

was replaced by Brigadeiro Henrique Fleiuss, who promised to do all possible to :"bring about harmony in the Air Force." Moreover, the Supreme Military Tribunal decided, in a five to four decision, to forget about General Maurel's charge against the Air Force colonel.

5. Remembering November 11

WITH THE APPROACH of the first anniversary of November 11, 1955, the nation embarked on the program Kubitschek said would give it "fifty years of progress in five years." The optimistic Chief Executive ably drew the nation's attention to economic development and was successful in instilling a new spirit of confidence.

The Development Council had defined thirty specific and ambitious goals, both for the private and for the public sectors. These goals dealt with power, transportation, agriculture, and basic industries and included steps that would increase significantly Brazil's petroleum-refining capacity and her output of steel and electric energy. Among the projects was a new motor vehicle industry. In Washington the Export-Import Bank, heartened by the Brazilian administration's pledge to combat inflation, announced—"as an initial action in connection with the development program"—a 100 million dollar loan to finance equipment to rehabilitate Brazil's railroads. The Instituto Superior de Estudos Brasileiros (ISEB), a course-giving dependency of the Education Ministry which had been established during Café Filho's administration, emphasized studies dealing with development.

Kubitschek had persuaded Congress to approve the creation of NOVACAP, a company created to build a new national capital in the interior by April 1960. Unprecedented construction plans, including great road-building projects, stirred the imagination and offered the promise of jobs and business opportunities.

On November 11, 1956, the nation's attention was momentarily drawn from such vast programs to the upsetting episode of a year earlier. The ceremony at which Lott was presented with a magnificent sword of gold hardly promoted harmony in the armed forces. For this occasion thousands of workers gathered in front of the War Ministry to hear sixteen speakers eulogize in prose and verse the year-old coup and its "hero." The mayor of São Paulo was present to declare that Lott was clearly the man to take the place left vacant by Vargas' suicide. Vice-President Goulart, who handed the golden sword to the War Minister, reproached opponents of the November coup for their use of intrigue and slander.

In Congress and elsewhere the reaction was loud, and the military ministers spent the next days handing out punishments to officers for speaking on political matters. On November 19 the administration announced that the ruling against political pronouncements by military figures applied not only to those in active service but also to anyone who was in the reserve or retired. (The regulation, of course, did not affect Lott, who had declared the post of War Minister a "political" one and had then gone on to advise congressmen not to vote a parliamentary form of government for Brazil.)

The first to violate the order of November 19, 1956, was Juarez Távora. On the twenty-first he sent a lengthy "declaration" to seven newspapers. In this he explained that statements made about him during the "commemoration" of the "coups" required that he reveal the true facts. In doing so he made public the texts of documents in which he had denounced the President and the War Minister. Then on the twenty-second Távora appeared in a television-radio interview to discuss political matters and refer to his "declaration," already a press sensation.

On November 23 Távora was sentenced to forty-eight hours of house arrest (during which his home was filled with well-wishing admirers). On the same day the military ministers closed down the Clube da Lanterna.

Kubitschek, by declaring in 1960 that the most significant moment of his administration occurred on November 23, 1956, revealed his apprehension about the situation that had existed in the armed forces. "On that day I took office a second time. I had the impression that an August 24 was being prepared. But in a few hours everyone realized that I was unwilling to commit suicide."[1]

[1] *O Cruzeiro*, April 2, 1960, p. 91 (reproduced in Joffre Gomes da Costa, *Marechal Henrique Lott*, p. 376).

6. The Navy Salutes the President

ALTHOUGH IT WAS NOW CLEAR that Lott had the military situation well under control and that Kubitschek had turned the attention of many from petty politics to rapid economic development, early in 1957 a new plot was hatched for bringing down the regime.

Plans developed after it became known that Kubitschek was to leave Santos for Rio on the *Barroso*, and, in the course of the trip on the cruiser, was to be saluted by the men and ships of the Navy. Some irked naval officers turned to Admiral Pena Bôto to lead them in making Kubitschek prisoner after he boarded the *Barroso*. They were supported by retired Colonel José Canavó Filho, who, as head of the São Paulo Fôrça Pública in November 1955, had been disappointed when Governor Quadros had not allowed him to lead an attack on Lott's soldiers. The scheduled homage to Kubitschek on the *Barroso*, Canavó has written, "was considered not only a humiliation, but also an affront, for the recollection of the bombardment of the *Tamandaré* continued to upset most of the Navy."[1]

Pena Bôto felt that he could count on "the entire Navy" to blockade the Santos harbor in support of the seizure of the President. But he wanted the help of 10 per cent of the Army and 10 per cent of the Air Force and found that he could get nothing from either. Air Force friends had available only a few airplanes without bombs. Five Army generals could offer only sabotage and recommended that the plot be

[1] José Canavó Filho, statement to José Stacchini, *O Estado de S. Paulo*, June 20, 1965.

abandoned. The anti-Communist admiral agreed, not wanting a repetition of the Navy's unsuccessful rebellion of 1893 against President Floriano Peixoto.[2]

Sílvio Heck, the captain who—under Pena Bôto's orders—had piloted the *Tamandaré* during its famous voyage, was unwilling to abandon the rebellion. He went to Santos, but there he could not persuade the commander of the *Barroso* to act against Kubitschek.

As planned, Kubitschek was honored at sea on January 29, 1957. This "affront" Canavó blamed on security measures taken by the governor of São Paulo, Jânio Quadros.

Sílvio Heck then issued a manifesto in which he referred to "the humiliation imposed on the Nation on the afternoon of January 29." "The sad spectacle, which for a moment caused people to forget the exemplary attitude of the *Tamandaré* on the glorious trip of November 11, 1955, was due exclusively to a deplorable omission on the part of leaders in whom we had confidence. We cannot remain waiting indefinitely while leaders of proven inertia contribute, by this omission, to the perpetuation of a disgraceful situation which is contaminating our traditional and glorious organization and is poisoning our Nation."[3] Heck called for new naval leaders who would act to remove the "stain" of January 29, 1957.

One Paulista, inspired by these fighting words, wrote Heck that a conspiratorial staff was being organized "to prevent the continuation of a tradition splattered with mud." The government put Heck aboard a vessel as a prisoner.

Kubitschek, seeking to mollify the unhappy Navy, had purchased an aircraft carrier, H.M.S. *Vengeance*, from Great Britain in December 1956. Renamed the *Minas Gerais*, it had a capacity for twenty-one aircraft. Sometimes disrespectfully referred to as Brazil's "floating debt," its purchase price was nine million dollars, and the cost of its complete overhaul was twenty-seven million dollars. During and after this reconstruction work, carried out in Rotterdam between 1957 and 1960, Air Force officers insisted that authority over the carrier belonged

---

[2] Carlos Pena Bôto, interview, Rio de Janeiro, December 10, 1967.

[3] Heck's manifesto is given in the statement of José Canavó Filho to José Stacchini, *O Estado de S. Paulo*, June 20, 1965.

to their branch of the service. The Navy argued for a naval air force and pointed out that the carrier's chief function was to operate against submarines. Representatives of the Navy and the Air Force, theretofore well united in criticizing the administration, quarreled with each other heatedly about this new issue, and Kubitschek was credited with having made a clever move in purchasing the ship.

7. Defiant Air Force Officers

PROMOTIONS DID NOT COME QUICKLY to men like Sílvio Heck, particularly after he had spoken of the "stain" of January 29, 1957. Haroldo Veloso, leader of the Jacareacanga revolt, was always the last man in his group to be promoted.[1] And Colonel Adil, whose investigation of the Vaz assassination had made him known as the "President of the Republic of Galeão" (the Galeão Air Base having been the headquarters of the inquiry), was continually passed over. Instead of promotions, these men received manifestations of the support and admiration of their comrades.

A particularly impressive luncheon was planned for honoring Colonel Adil on July 27, 1957, after his name had been passed over in spite of the long time he had been top in seniority on the list for promotion to *brigadeiro*. The trouble with this scheduled homage at the Air Force Club was that Kubitschek opposed it and so advised Air Minister Henrique Fleiuss, who had given the President to understand that he had full control of the Air Force.[2]

Brigadeiro Gabriel Grün Moss, president of the Air Force Club, headed the Air Transport Command in Rio. He still hoped to persuade Kubitschek to give Adil his long-overdue promotion. He felt, however, that the lunch would make this difficult and would result in the replacement of Air Minister Fleiuss by a man less sympathetic to

---

[1] Haroldo Veloso, interviews, Marietta, Georgia, January 6–7, 1966.
[2] João Adil de Oliveira, interview, Rio de Janeiro, December 20, 1965.

the views predominating in the Air Force Club.[3] Therefore, Grün Moss passed along, to all who served under him, the recommendation of Fleiuss that they not attend.

When Adil's supporters insisted on holding the lunch, Grün Moss reversed his stand. Twenty-two *brigadeiros* and approximately four hundred Air Force officers were present in defiance of the President and the Air Minister.[4] Among them were Eduardo Gomes, Antônio Guedes Muniz, and the 1956 rebels, Haroldo Veloso, Paulo Vítor, and José Chaves Lameirão. Although most of the officers were not in uniform, and although the lunch was publicized as one without speeches, the results were as Grün Moss had foreseen. Air Minister Fleiuss fell and was succeeded by Brigadeiro Francisco Correia de Melo, who had been closely associated with Lott. Adil was not promoted. Grün Moss, resigning his Air Transport Command post, complained that Kubitschek preferred politics to justice.

By May 1958 Lieutenant-Colonel Haroldo Veloso and Captain José Chaves Lameirão considered their situations "intolerable." In letters to their commanders in São Paulo they criticized top Air Force officials and accused them of sending spies to report on their activities. Veloso, who said he was breaking a silence of two years, described an atmosphere of corruption.[5] Air Minister Correia de Melo dismissed him from his job, and the commander of the air zone imprisoned him for thirty days. When two hundred Air Force sergeants in São Paulo signed a statement supporting Veloso's charges, Army units in São Paulo were put on the alert.

In October 1958 discontented *brigadeiros* were given a splendid opportunity to irritate Lott. The War Minister became Acting Air Minister while Correia de Melo made a short trip abroad. Most of the *brigadeiros* refused to attend the ceremony at which Lott assumed his temporary post.[6] One of them made a public protest. As soon as he was disciplined, a long list of Air Force officers backed him in a published statement. Lott punished them all, including Grün Moss, and

---

[3] Gabriel Grün Moss, interview, Rio de Janeiro, December 12, 1965.

[4] *O Estado de S. Paulo*, July 28, 1957.

[5] *Ibid.*, June 6, 1958.

[6] Viriato de Castro, *Espada x Vassoura: Marechal Lott*, p. 59.

brought a legal charge against the *Diário de Notícias*, the Rio newspaper in which the statement appeared.[7]

By this time Lott himself was being sued for slander. This action resulted from a confidential memorandum issued by Lott's office in the middle of 1957 which stated that some military officers, including Brigadeiro Eduardo Gomes, were planning to assassinate the War Minister.[8]

Air Force Minister Correia de Melo, after returning to Brazil and taking back the Air Ministry from Lott, became involved in a squabble with Brigadeiro Guedes Muniz. The outspoken antiadministration *brigadeiro* charged that Air Force commands were being given to Communists, and he described the Air Minister as unable to discuss the charge because "he lacks the moral authority to be Air Minister." According to Guedes Muniz, the ministry was really being run by Francisco Teixeira, "a friend of Communists" who was administrative chief in the office of the ministry.

The charge that Lott and the administration were pro-Communist stemmed in part from the PCB's position in the 1955 election and its unrestrained praise of Lott after November 11, 1955. Communist baiters also took note that in March 1958 the courts dismissed a multitude of charges, which had been heaped against Luís Carlos Prestes and other leading Communists during prior regimes. Prestes emerged from ten years of hiding and became very active. In his first public interview he praised Lott's "patriotism" and stressed the PCB's new Far-Right position: cooperation with all Brazilian forces, including the bourgeoisie, to combat United States "imperialism."

[7] Joffre Gomes da Costa, *Marechal Henrique Lott*, p. 393.
[8] Afonso Arinos de Melo Franco, *A Escalada: Memórias*, p. 430.

8. Civilian Antigovernment Manifestations

LATE IN 1956 influential and conservative Cardinal Jaime de Barros Câmara bolstered Kubitschek's position by declaring, at long last, that his election should be acknowledged by all.

Nevertheless, in civilian circles struggles took place as a result of the same discontent that had caused a minority of military men to assail the regime. An intensification of these struggles was assured soon after the Cardinal made his declaration, for it became known that Carlos Lacerda was returning to Brazil. While in Lisbon Lacerda had been in touch with Buenos Aires, receiving information about Goulart's past relations with the recently deposed Perón.

To deal with Lacerda, the Kubitschek administration issued a regulation that would shut down for thirty days any radio station over which "subversive" speeches might be broadcast.[1] Aware of the financial loss such a close-down would entail, Rádio Globo canceled its arrangements featuring speeches in which the returning Lacerda was scheduled to give his impressions of Portugal. The regulation limited Lacerda's effectiveness during the Kubitschek regime.

Lacerda was prepared to wage war early in 1957 when he was named UDN congressional leader (Afonso Arinos having become leader of the combined UDN-PL opposition). In the Chamber of Deputies Lacerda accused Goulart of having been the "Brazilian legislator" who was said to have made arrangements with Perón in 1950 for the sale of Brazilian lumber to Argentina; the deal, Lacerda added, had helped finance the Vargas election campaign of 1950.[2] To support his charge, Lacerda created a sensation by "divulging" what he said were the contents of Telegram No. 293, sent in 1956 from the Brazilian ambassador in Buenos Aires to the Brazilian Foreign Ministry.

The administration retaliated by calling on its congressional majority to vote to allow the military justice system to judge Lacerda for

[1] Cleantho de Paiva Leite, interview, Santiago, Chile, June 28, 1967.
[2] Carlos Lacerda, *O Caminho da Liberdade*, p. 170.

having violated the National Security Law when he revealed the contents of the confidential Foreign Office message. Lacerda retorted that what the Kubitschek regime wished to keep from the public was the behavior of Goulart. "I consider it absolutely indispensable that the people know about the connections of certain demagogues with the dictator Perón, and the amount of protection which the Kubitschek Government dedicates to those international conspiracies."[3]

Lacerda, as he wanted, became the center of a fight that, in the words of Afonso Arinos, stirred "all corners of Brazil."[4] While Kubitschek and his team rushed Brazil into rapid industrial development, legislators argued about congressional immunities and the confidential nature of diplomatic messages. It became known that Goulart's name had not even been mentioned in Telegram 293; however, the UDN submitted evidence to show that he had, nevertheless, been the "cloaked Brazilian legislator" in Argentina. It insisted that he ought to collaborate with an impartial investigation of the details of the case.

Afonso Arinos (who once remarked that "Carlos attacks alone but defends himself in a group")[5] led the defense with oratorical support from the fiery central figure of the case and from men like Prado Kelly and old Otávio Mangabeira. The UDN's able José Bonifácio de Andrada worked more quietly to convince government supporters that they should protect the right of a fellow congressman to speak as he saw fit in the Chamber.

The secrecy of the voting hampered the government forces, led by Vieira de Melo. In the end the government bloc, although receiving more votes than Lacerda's supporters, could not muster a majority of Brazil's 326 federal *deputados*. It failed by thirteen votes, which was equal to the number of those who submitted blank votes.[6] The UDN was pleased with the result.

In the elections of October 1958 Lacerda was handsomely re-elected to the Chamber of Deputies, and Afonso Arinos, also running in the

[3] *Ibid.*, p. 108.
[4] Afonso Arinos de Melo Franco, *A Escalada: Memórias*, p. 421.
[5] *Ibid.*, p. 419.
[6] Armando Falcão, interview, Rio de Janeiro, October 6, 1968.

Federal District, defeated Lutero Vargas and others in gaining a seat in the Senate. But on an over-all basis the congressional elections represented no defeat for the Kubitschek-Goulart PSD-PTB alliance.

With the 1958 election over, the Kubitschek administration talked for a short while about implementing an anti-inflation program, prepared by Finance Minister Lucas Lopes and National Economic Development Bank President Roberto Campos.

Lucas Lopes had taken over the Finance Ministry in June 1958 after Alkmim had run into difficulties, occasioned in part by a fall in the world coffee price. Coffee growers in northern Paraná were incensed about the cruzeiro price that Lucas Lopes subsequently established for their commodity, which was then being produced in excessive amounts. Seeking a better price, they planned a great Marcha da Produção (Production March) to take them to Rio's Catete Palace in the latter part of October 1958. This march was to be undertaken in hundreds of trucks, automobiles, pickups, and jeeps and was to be joined in São Paulo by Paulista coffee growers who were equally eager to exert pressure on behalf of an "adequate coffee policy."

The Army prepared to impede the marchers. War Minister Lott, who left Brazil at this moment to be received by Pope Pius XII in the Vatican, was again assailed by the screams of opposition politicians. (A typical scream: "Tanks, General Lott, will not suffocate the cries of those who are wronged.") The *marcha* became the principal subject of congressional debates.

After federal soldiers blocked a few bridges and other points, preventing the marchers from reaching Rio, one congressman described the affair as "the strangest of all wars."[7] Finance Minister Lucas Lopes assumed the responsibility for the use of military force.

---

[7] Carlos Castilho Cabral, *Tempos de Jânio e Outros Tempos*, p. 133.

9. The Instituto Superior de Estudos Brasileiros

A CURRENCY STABILIZATION EFFORT, blessed by the International Monetary Fund (IMF), was a requirement for the additional loans the Export-Import Bank had earlier contemplated making to help Brazilian development. But such an effort ran counter to the liberal credits and currency printing, which were becoming a part of the program of massive construction. Measures of financial austerity, never popular, had in this instance the stigma of being sponsored by the IMF and Washington bankers. They aroused the ire of nationalists who, like the Communists, directed their fire at the United States.

An anti-United States nationalism was being effectively advanced by the intellectuals in the government-supported Instituto Superior de Estudos Brasileiros (ISEB), directed by Roland Corbisier, former Integralista. Some of the Brazilian military, connected with the Escola Superior de Guerra, became concerned about ideas being propounded by ISEB, and, to get a first-hand report about what was going on, they enrolled an officer in a class of eighty-three who were taking one of the Institute's one-year courses. He concluded his course work by presenting a thesis in which he wrote that Communist propaganda was harmful to the development of Brazil. The thesis was not accepted by ISEB's faculty, and he left, without graduating, to report to the Armed Forces General Staff (EMFA) that ISEB was trying to create a national fervor of hostility to the United States.[1]

The policy of ISEB (regarding courses, speakers, books, and translations) was supposed to be established by a *conselho* (board) of fifty prominent men. When the *conselho* met in 1958 to hear Corbisier and Álvaro Vieira Pinto attack ideas in a recent book of Hélio Jaguaribe, some of the *conselho* members used the opportunity to complain about Corbisier's selecting speakers and department heads without consulting the *conselho*. The session became a heated ideological debate about nationalism. *Conselho* member Roberto Campos suggested that Cor-

---

[1] Gerson de Pinna, interview, Rio de Janeiro, October 14, 1966.

bisier should resign his directorship because he had usurped the functions of the *conselho*.

After Education Minister Clóvis Salgado backed ISEB's director, the anti-Corbisier members left the Institute. In 1959 a government decree made it clear that ISEB's affairs were in the hands of Corbisier, assisted by the directors of the five departments into which the studies were divided. ISEB surged ahead, a sort of nucleus for a possible future ultranationalist political party. Outside of Rio it established affiliates and alumni groups.

Those who did not share ISEB's ideas lamented the use of government funds to support what they felt was "a hotbed of Marxist pseudo-scientific teaching and propaganda."[2] The Commercial Association of the city of Rio de Janeiro and the conservative press, in a strenuous anti-ISEB campaign, did not fail to call attention to the presence of Marxist Colonel Nelson Werneck Sodré as head of ISEB's History Department; nor did they overlook ISEB's sponsorship of lectures on Marxism by Communist theoretician Jacob Gorender.

ISEB's program for "emancipating" Brazil from "economic and cultural dependence on the United States" was the same program the PCB was advocating, but this coincidence of ideas did not mean that the advocates of ISEB's program were necessarily Communists, as their opponents were sometimes inclined to charge. Seldom were they.

Such was the program of the PCB that it was impossible to determine whether statements were "Communist" or "non-Communist." While Corbisier argued that ISEB's position was not Socialist or Communist because "nationalism can be defined as including a national bourgeoisie,"[3] Brazilian Communism was seeking to appeal to the "national bourgeoisie." The PCB's program even sought to attract large landowners, struggling against "imperialism" in the form of "high prices" of chemicals manufactured by du Pont. "A full united front, including large landowners," Prestes said, "will be possible if Communists will refrain from wanting a radical agrarian reform, and will limit themselves to steps of agrarian reform within the Constitution."[4]

---

[2] Memorandum from Estanislau Fischlowitz to J.W.F.D., August 1966.

[3] Roland Corbisier, interview, Rio de Janeiro, October 25, 1966.

[4] Luís Carlos Prestes quoted in *Correio Paulistano*, May 19, 1959.

Like the ultranationalists, the PCB attacked Finance Minister Lucas Lopes and National Economic Development Bank President Roberto Campos. Such currency-stabilization-minded men were called *entreguistas* (those who would turn Brazil over to foreign "imperialists"). In May 1959 the "Far-Left nationalists" found a hero: Rio Grande do Sul Governor Leonel Brizola expropriated a subsidiary of the Electric Bond and Share in his state.

10. The Break with the International Monetary Fund (June 1959)

THE UNPOPULAR STABILIZATION PLAN fell by the wayside. In its place came the great inflation, which was destined to triple the currency in circulation and the cost of living in the course of the Kubitschek administration. In part it was the price paid for "Fifty Years of Progress in Five Years." The progress, not noticeable in agriculture, provided ambitious industrial and hydroelectrical projects as well as the new capital and a start on the network of roads for connecting Brasília with distant points. Expenditures for the new capital exceeded the total amount of currency which had been in existence in Brazil when Kubitschek took office.

Funds spent on Brasília, Luís Carlos Prestes said, should have been spent, instead, to improve conditions in Brazil's long-neglected Northeast. The nation's financial policies were considered to have been more helpful to industrial development in the south-central sector than to development in the Northeast, where illiteracy was high and the per capita income, even before the 1958 drought struck, was less than half of Brazil's average. The 1958 drought created such misery that a great deal of attention, both in and out of Brazil, was given to alleviating the suffering and planning for rehabilitation. Starting in 1958 the Kubitschek administration had to earmark vast appropriations for the distressed area.

On the evening of June 17, 1959, Kubitschek spoke at Catete Palace to reply to the International Monetary Fund's censure of his administration's spending spree. To show support for the President, an audience of about two thousand, mostly organized workers and students, gathered outside the palace. Some carried placards calling for the reestablishment of diplomatic and commercial relations with the Soviet Union. Luís Carlos Prestes was present.

After the president of the UNE (National Union of Students) and some "nationalist" legislators had been heard from, Kubitschek spoke. He stressed that it was up to Brazil alone to decide whether to accept or reject opinions that financial experts rendered about Brazilian internal financial and economic affairs. More than such advice, "we need effective and dynamic cooperation. . . . We want to continue to believe that our friends are really our friends."[1]

"The break with the IMF," Prestes said in Recife in July 1959, "was the most important act of the government of Juscelino Kubitschek." He compared it with Brizola's expropriation of a utility owned by United States investors. Like other ultranationalists, the PCB experienced additional joy a month later: Lucas Lopes (who had been unwell) and Roberto Campos were dropped from their posts.

Washington officials cooperated with Operation Pan-America, launched by Kubitschek in 1958 so that hemispheric underdevelopment might be attacked jointly by the American nations. As the Eisenhower and Kubitschek administrations drew to a close, however, the Washington lending agencies were cold to Brazil, noting that earlier Kubitschek pledges to curb inflation had by no means been fulfilled.

Within Brazil, too, the inflation provided wide discontent. It was mentioned in the press as one of the reasons why the voters in São Paulo city, going to the polls in October 1959 to choose aldermen, gave the most votes to a rhinoceros, loaned to the São Paulo zoo by the Rio zoo. "The corruption of the politicians" was another reason cited.

In the federal Congress in 1959 and 1960 the opposition sought to bring about an investigation of what it liked to call "the corruption of Kubitschek in the construction of Brasília." The administration's con-

[1] *O Estado de S. Paulo,* June 20, 1959.

gressional majority agreed to the establishment of a parliamentary investigating commission provided that its purpose be limited to finding out how much it was costing to build Brasília. However, after the PSD, UDN, and PTB named accountants to check NOVACAP's books, no satisfactory NOVACAP books could be found to check.[2]

Those who in 1955 had sought to put Kubitschek in a chair where they could point accusing fingers at him had no more success than they had had earlier. But again they managed to stir up talk about corruption.

[2] Adauto Lúcio Cardoso, interview, Rio de Janeiro, December 15, 1965.

11. The Aragarças Revolt (December 1959)

THE UNSUCCESSFUL JACAREACANGA REVOLT of 1956, in which so few military officers had participated, continued to excite the imagination of plotters for a long time. Following its failure, adventuresome military men and civilians—full of anger at what they called the "corruption and subversion" of the Kubitschek regime—met constantly, working for a new and better rebellion. Top planning was in the hands of two officers from each branch of the military; they looked to a military junta to bring "purity" to Brazil and relieve it of "fictitious legality."

On several occasions between 1956 and 1959 some leading participants dropped out. Although as a rule their places would be taken by others (who resolutely declared that "if they won't make a revolution, we shall"), the number of conspirators tended to decline.[1]

Early in 1957 Lieutenant Colonel Haroldo Veloso, the protagonist of Jacareacanga and one of the new conspiracy's top planners, persuaded lawyer Luís Mendes de Morais Neto, a forty-six-year-old retired Air Force lieutenant, to draw up a series of pronouncements and decrees. These were to be issued when "The Revolutionary Com-

[1] Prudente de Morais Neto, interview, Rio de Janeiro, December 13, 1966.

mand," made up of three members of the armed forces (representing the Navy, Army, and Air Force), assumed power. Legislatures and judicial bodies would be closed down, Brazil's institutions would be revamped, and political rights would be taken from all who "directly or indirectly" had been involved in making the revolution "necessary."[2]

Late in 1958 Luís Mendes de Morais Neto became acquainted with another conspiring Air Force lieutenant colonel, João Paulo Moreira Burnier. Burnier, who had vexed the Kubitschek regime by refusing to use his military airplane to transport bricks for the construction of Brasília,[3] consulted Morais Neto about the situation of the Air Force officers who had been arrested following the incidents that occurred when Lott became Acting Air Minister. In mid-1959 Burnier was speaking enthusiastically about the forthcoming military uprising. He claimed that 324 persons were interested in it.[4] However, a split presently developed between those who wanted to take the offensive and those who saw their organization as a defensive one which was only to act if the government, on losing the 1960 presidential election, should try to engineer a coup. By early November 1959 misunderstandings had reduced the group of plotters to a small number of determined activists.

During that month these conspirators, led by Burnier, were excited by information concerning plans for another rebellion. This movement, which they described as "Communist," was said to have been fostered by Governor Brizola[5] and was scheduled to break out at the end of the year in order to create conditions that would bring about the cancellation of the October 1960 elections. A fellow conspirator of Burnier and Veloso, having been asked to join the so-called Com-

[2] Copies of proposed revolutionary decrees, in possession of Luís Mendes de Morais Neto in Rio de Janeiro.

[3] Glauco Carneiro, *História das Revoluções Brasileiras*, II, 521.

[4] *Ibid.*, pp. 521–522.

[5] Armando Falcão, interview, Rio de Janeiro, November 30, 1966. See Armando Falcão, *Denúncia ao Povo Brasileiro*. See also statement of Colonel Hugo Delaite given in testimony of José Chaves Lameirão (Declaration at 24th Criminal Court, Guanabara State, re Processo No. 9899 ["Movimento de Aragarças"], May 8, 1961 [typewritten]).

munist plot, accepted the invitation in order to keep the Burnier-Veloso group informed about it.

Late November 1959 brought another development. Jânio Quadros shocked the UDN leadership and disappointed much of Brazil by withdrawing as the antiadministration presidential candidate. This step, Burnier decided, justified starting his long-postponed rebellion, designed to allow a military rule to remake Brazil. The "prevailing political confusion," he said, gave it a chance of success, and he hoped that the example of a few would attract a majority of the military.

On December 2, at Burnier's request, Mendes de Morais Neto updated the draft of a manifesto he had prepared for Veloso earlier. In its revised form, this manifesto declared that force and corruption ruled the nation, which had reached an unparalleled state of disorder. Demagogic laws, the misuse of public funds, the depressed state of agriculture, the high cost of living, and the economic misery of the people were cited. "In the face of this state of deterioration, adepts of Communism, having infiltrated in all sorts of sectors, in and out of public administration, seek to gain the maximum out of the misery and hunger of the people, in order to implant their regime of human slavery." Quadros was mentioned in the manifesto as having demonstrated that revolution was the only way to liberate the nation from the group that was dominating and ruining it. Dated December 3, 1959, and signed by "The Revolutionary Command," the manifesto ended with "Vivas" for Brazil and the "Revolution."[6]

Before daybreak on December 3, as the rebels were departing in airplanes for the interior, copies of the manifesto were confidentially delivered by a conspirator to some of the opposition congressmen. Among them was Otávio Mangabeira, who had earlier told Veloso that it was his duty to go ahead with rebellion in spite of personal sacrifice.[7] Mangabeira, mentioned in the manifesto as having indicated what path should be followed, became the only politician to support the outbreak.

Carlos Lacerda also received a copy at 4:00 A.M. on December 3.

[6] *Correio da Manhã,* December 4, 1959.
[7] Haroldo Veloso, interviews, Marietta, Georgia, January 6–7, 1966.

Like most members of the political opposition, Lacerda felt that late 1959 was an unfortunate time for an armed outbreak. It might give the authorities an excuse for declaring a state of siege and calling off the elections of October 1960. The opposition parties were trying to persuade Quadros to re-enter the contest; with him as standard-bearer they expected to use the polls to rid the Executive Branch of PSD-PTB domination.

Lacerda contacted Eduardo Gomes, but the *brigadeiro* could do nothing; the rebelling Air Force officers were already flying into the interior. Lacerda expressed his misgivings to a few congressional leaders, making it clear that the political opposition was not involved. Deputado Bento Gonçalves, with whom Lacerda spoke, headed the Frente Parlamentar Nacionalista and supported the administration. Gonçalves telephoned Lott, who in turn advised Kubitschek.

The rebellion had begun when three Air Force C-47's (DC-3's) had left Rio's Galeão Air Base. At the same time, a few rebels at Belo Horizonte's Pampulha Airport had seized a private Beechcraft and also made for the interior. The common destination was Aragarças, a town of about ten thousand on the Goiás-Mato Grosso border, three hundred miles west of the tumultuous construction activity at Brasília. Veloso, one of those to leave Rio, was assigned the task of taking control of points he had dominated in February 1956.

An unusual experience awaited the thirty-five passengers who had left Rio for Belém at 11:30 P.M. December 2 on the regular commercial flight of Panair's Constellation. At 5:30 A.M. on the third, half an hour before the Constellation was due at Belém, passengers noted that the sun was rising on the wrong side of the airplane. An hour later they were told that the airplane, unable to land at Belém was proceeding to a field in Bahia. What they did not know was that with the outbreak of the rebellion, when the Constellation was over Maranhão, Air Force Major Eber Teixeira Pinto had invaded the pilot's cabin and used a revolver to force the commander to turn back and fly to Aragarças. The conspirators wanted a craft with a long flight range.

At 8:30 A.M. when the Constellation landed at Aragarças, the passengers were met by ten military men. Besides Burnier and Veloso, they found a rebel Army colonel, Luís Mendes da Silva, who had once instructed Veloso at military school. Supporting the rebels were some local civilians, employees of the Fundação Brasil Central, the government's organization for developing central Brazil.

Veloso, the passengers observed, spent his time looking intermittently at his watch and at the sky. But the only additional airplane to arrive was a Beechcraft from the Air Mail Service, and it brought two Air Force officers and one Army officer.

In the small airport building, Veloso told the Panair passengers that a revolution was under way and they should go to the local hotel. In the hotel they heard Luís Mendes de Morais Neto ask for the names of the most important travelers. He was told that among them was Remy Archer, president of the Banco da Amazônia. Archer was asked to come in a jeep to the revolutionary headquarters at the airport. "Is this an order?" he inquired. "It is a request, but if you refuse it is an order." Thereupon Archer instructed a sergeant, who was guarding the hotel, to carry his bags to the jeep. Archer was told that the revolutionary soldiers were not porters. Upset, Archer carried his own two bags.[8]

Veloso could do nothing at Jacareacanga or Santarém. Finding the government forces in control of the Jacareacanga airport, he had to land his C-47 on a football field.

The situation at Santarém was surprising and resulted from the decision of two Army captains, involved in the "leftist" plot attributed to Brizola, to try to lead a revolt in the far north. One of the captains was attempting an uprising in Belém; the other, Creso Coimbra, was momentarily running things at the Santarém airport. Veloso, returning to Aragarças, concluded that some of the "Communists" had acted on the assumption that the Aragarças uprising was their own.[9]

The two rebelling Army captains in the far north supposed that the Aragarças uprising would create a "climate" helpful to their own sub-

[8] "A Rebelião de Aragarças," *Mundo Ilustrado*, December 19, 1959.

[9] Veloso, interviews, January 6–7, 1966. This hypothesis is sustained by a statement of Colonel Hugo Delaite given in the testimony of José Chaves Lameirão (Declaration at 24th Criminal Court, State of Guanabara, May 8, 1961).

versive plans.[10] However, they were subdued on December 3, a few hours after they had tried to start a movement whose background differed substantially from that of the Aragarças revolt.

[10] Report (February 16, 1960) of General Humberto Castelo Branco (Military Commander of Amazônia and the Eighth Military Region) regarding the rebel Army captains.

12. No Amnesty

THE GOVERNMENT had paratroopers flown to the neighborhood of Aragarças. In Congress majority *deputados* suggested that Veloso was behaving unchivalrously in view of the 1956 amnesty, and they implied that Lacerda was involved in the uprising. Majority leader Abelardo Jurema (PSD, Paraíba), speaking "in the name of the government," blamed Lacerda directly.[1]

Lacerda stated that the 1956 amnesty had benefited, principally, those who, between November 11 and November 22, 1955, had acted improperly and unconstitutionally. He and opposition leader Afonso Arinos de Melo Franco asserted that, although the Aragarças rebellion should be condemned, it was understandable. The government was responsible for the desperation felt in the country. "Sincerely and honestly," said Afonso Arinos, "we cannot declare that the young military men are criminals who should be cursed and punished by those responsible for the nation's political life." Otávio Mangabeira, who had fought Vargas since 1930, arose to observe that Brazil needed men of character like Veloso. Quadros, about to withdraw his resignation as a candidate, declared that "even the greatest courage, even the purest ideals," could not justify "insurrection."[2]

The rebellion was brief. Early on December 4, as federal paratroopers moved on Aragarças, the rebels took to flight in their airplanes. The majority, including Veloso and Army Colonel Luís

[1] *Correio da Manhã*, December 4, 1959.   [2] *Ibid.*

Mendes da Silva, went in two C-47's to Paraguay. Burnier and two others went in a Beechcraft to Bolivia.

After these departures, the Panair Constellation left with its passengers, flying for half an hour in a northerly direction. But Major Eber Teixeira Pinto threatened the pilot again, forcing him this time to fly the Constellation directly to Buenos Aires. There the Frondizi government granted asylum to the few rebels aboard. Amazônia Bank President Remy Archer praised the pilot. The press quoted him as adding that he had been treated courteously by the rebels, but that he could not forgive them for the humiliation of having had to carry his own suitcases at the Aragarças hotel.[3]

The third rebel C-47 had been away from Aragarças at the time of the exodus. With its occupants not knowing that the Aragarças field had fallen under the control of forty federal paratroopers, it returned and landed. Before its engines had been cut, its pilot became aware of the true state of affairs and tried to get the airplane off the ground again. Government soldiers began placing gasoline drums on the airstrip and machine-gunning the airplane's wheels. A shot hit the airplane's gasoline tank causing an explosion and minor injuries.[4] The rebel pilot and one sergeant were made prisoner. Some of the natives who had been in the airplane were caught, but most of them, talented at moving unseen, escaped.

The rebellion, therefore, was over before Brazil learned that "The Revolutionary Command" had come out with a second manifesto, this one in São Paulo. It spoke of new adherents who were joining the movement against "corruption in the federal government."

Kubitschek, speaking on the radio, said that this time the rebels would be rigorously punished. Wives of the *brigadeiros* solicited funds to help the families of the exiled Air Force officers. Air Force Club President Grün Moss announced that "the statutes of the club do not rule out the furnishing of humane assistance, without any political character, to the club's associates."

On December 10 Justice Minister Armando Falcão addressed the

---

[3] "A Rebelião de Aragarças," *Mundo Ilustrado*, December 19, 1959.
[4] *Ibid.*

Chamber of Deputies to make sensational charges. They were, he said, based on papers such as those taken from Luís Mendes de Morais Neto after the lawyer, preferring arrest in Brazil to exile in Paraguay, had left one of the departing airplanes when it stopped in Pôrto Esperança, Mato Grosso.

Actually, the first document Falcão read to the excited *deputados* was a proclamation drawn up by the rebels in the far north; the Justice Minister's listeners mistakenly understood that it was related to the much-discussed Aragarças uprising. It called for using Fidel Castro's tactics for a movement that young officers, backed by laborers and peasants of the north and northeast, were to begin about December 31, 1959, in order to overthrow "the corrupt, the traitors and the *entreguistas*." The Jacareacanga pattern was to be followed. Listed for early seizure were the governor's palace in Belém, radio stations, banks, barracks, military bases, and all aircraft in Brazil. "The economic crisis and the general discontent of the people are to be the strong points for conquering the Power in a few months of struggle."[5]

Falcão next read an "ultimatum" that Luís Mendes de Morais Neto had prepared for issuance by "The Revolutionary Command." It spoke of the federal legislature's "disordered" issuance of demagogic laws and its mishandling of public money; it also mentioned the "corruption" of justice, and the disintegration of political parties "into factions." João Agripino, UDN *deputado* from the drought-stricken and impoverished Northeast, praised the objectives listed by the conspirators. "I only regret not having been invited to participate in such a movement," he told his fellow legislators.[6]

The "alarming" words of Falcão, the UDN felt, could have only one purpose: to prepare for a state of siege and possibly to close Congress and cancel the election. Lacerda recalled that a false document (the "Cohen Plan") had been used in 1937 to make a case for taking those steps. "We can," the *Tribuna da Imprensa* wrote, "advise with certainty that the documents read in the Chamber by Minister Armando

[5] *Diário do Congresso Nacional*, December 11, 1959.
[6] *Ibid.*

Falcão were not in the possession of lawyer Mendes de Morais." They were "forged," the newspaper said.[7]

War Minister Lott, about to become the presidential candidate of the PSD-PTB majority, declared that he opposed the steps feared by the UDN. "The salvation of Brazil can only be found within the scope of the democratic institutions," he added.[8]

From La Paz, Bolivia, came the words of Burnier: "Our movement attained its objective with the decision of Jânio Quadros, who has popular support, not to withdraw."[9]

A report from Asunción revealed that exiled rebels in Paraguay led by Luís Mendes da Silva and Veloso planned to remain in that country until Quadros was victorious. But soon they went to Buenos Aires, blaming Brazilian government pressure for their difficulties in Paraguay. Nor were conditions in Buenos Aires what they desired. The Argentine government would not grant them pilot licenses. Veloso, a good engineer, found work easily. But other prominent rebels had to accept employment in kitchens. Colonel Luís Mendes da Silva worked as a stevedore.[10]

In April 1960 the majority in the Brazilian Congress blocked suggestions of the minority that amnesty be voted for the participants in the Aragarças revolt. The exiles said they were uninterested. The groups in Argentina and Bolivia each signed a manifesto authorizing no one to support any amnesty project on their behalf. The ideals that had inspired them in December 1959, they stated, continued strong.[11]

At the same time they justified their rebellion as having been necessary to deflate a "leftist" or "Communist" revolt planned for late December 1959 by Brizola and his associates. Testifying in May 1961, Aviation Captain José Chaves Lameirão, who had flown to Jacareacanga with Veloso in 1956, quoted "leftist" revolutionaries as having said that the Aragarças affair had set back their plans for December

[7] *Tribuna da Imprensa,* December 15, 1959.
[8] *Diário de Notícias,* December 13, 1959.
[9] France Presse, La Paz, December 17, 1959.
[10] Haroldo Veloso, interviews, Marietta, Georgia, January 6–7, 1966.
[11] Manifesto dated Buenos Aires, April 12, 1960; regarding exiles in Bolivia, see *O Estado de S. Paulo,* April 26, 1960 (dateline Rio de Janeiro, April 25, 1960).

31, 1959. Lameirão declared that in January 1960 he was invited by Lieutenant Colonel Hugo Delaite, Veloso's 1956 captor, to participate in plans still being hatched by Brizola, who was said to be promising men and money.[12]

Leonel Brizola, a man who never hesitated to preach boldness, was to play a key role in the years immediately ahead. Born in circumstances of poverty in a small town in Rio Grande do Sul in January 1922, he had worked as a railroad station porter while getting his primary education. Later in Pôrto Alegre, the state capital, he became an elevator operator and took a university course in engineering. A tireless worker, he is said to average between four and five hours sleep per night.

While still a university student in 1946 and 1947 he was a leading organizer of the state PTB and became a state assemblyman. He married the sister of Jango Goulart. As in the case of the more intellectual Lacerda, dramatic speaking ability contributed to his political advances. He became state secretary of public works, federal congressman, mayor of Pôrto Alegre, and, in October 1958, was elected governor of Rio Grande do Sul.

Like Lacerda, he, too, could use the radio to attack with enormous impact and was inclined to make life difficult for whoever was in the presidency. As governor of Rio Grande do Sul, he did not receive the financial assistance he wanted from the Kubitschek administration. He then began to assail the President in weekly radio broadcasts.

[12] Testimony of José Chaves Lameirão at 24th Criminal Court, Guanabara State, May 8, 1961.

BOOK IV: *Jânio*

*"Organize a military junta and
run the country."*

Jânio Quadros to the Military
Ministers, August 25, 1961

1. O Fenômeno Jânio Quadros

JÂNIO QUADROS' FOUR-YEAR TERM as governor of São Paulo was characterized by his strongly personal method of administration. Newspapers published his *bilhetinhos*, severe, aggressive notes with instructions to subordinates.[1] From them people could see that the unusual governor was hard at work, often attending to minute details in an authoritarian manner.

When campaigning in the rough-and-tumble politics of São Paulo, Jânio was always dramatic. Associating himself with the poor and often appearing exhausted and unkempt, he emotionally—sometimes tearfully—put on "the campaign of the humble tostão" (ten centavos) against what he said were the "millions" being spent by the powerful. His propaganda posters showed his broom scaring away frightened, political "rats."

He liked to be known as temperamental and attracted multitudes rather than made friends.[2] He was reserved in office, suspicious of the

[1] See J. Pereira, *Bilhetinhos de Jânio*.
[2] Carlos Castilho Cabral, *Tempos de Jânio e Outros Tempos*, p. 143.

opinions of others, and sure of his own infallible touch. At times he seemed to regard opposition to his will as something bent on destroying the dignity he sought to give to the post in which the people had placed him.

Aided by his "beloved professor," Finance Secretary Carlos Alberto Carvalho Pinto, and by a good working relationship with the federal government, Quadros gave his state a successful four years. The Kubitschek industrialization program was particularly beneficial to São Paulo.

For Quadros the chief political setback was administered by veteran Ademar de Barros. This archrival returned from exile after lawyers had succeeded in having a prison sentence set aside, and in March 1957 he won the mayorship of the city of São Paulo.

But Quadros showed his strength in the elections of October 1958. Running for federal *deputado* from Paraná on the PTB (Labor Party) ticket, he was elected by more votes than any other Paraná victor. Simultaneously in São Paulo he campaigned against the PTB's official position, giving his support to the gubernatorial campaign of Carvalho Pinto, candidate of the PDC, UDN, PTN, PR, PL, and PSB. After Quadros promised his listeners that he would run for the Brazilian presidency in 1960 if his candidate won the governorship,[3] Carvalho Pinto was elected over Ademar de Barros and Auro de Moura Andrade.

Quadros, turning the governorship over to the professor at the end of January, 1959, declared that "on innumerable occasions I cried alone as though I were entirely abandoned, a prisoner of my adversaries. Nevertheless, thanks to God, who has always helped me, I maintained my faith."[4]

The new PTB congressman from Paraná spent little time in Tiradentes Palace. A man who liked to travel by sea with his mother, wife, and daughter, he left with them early in 1959 on a steamer, which went to Japan via the African coastline. In the course of this round-

---

[3] "A Eleição de Carvalho, o Fato do Ano em São Paulo," *O Estado de S. Paulo*, January 4, 1959; reproduced in Viriato de Castro, *O Fenômeno Jânio Quadros*, pp. 216–223 (see especially p. 221).

[4] Viriato de Castro, *O Fenômeno Jânio Quadros*, p. 224.

the-world trip he paid calls on Tito, Khrushchev, and Nasser. South America, he concluded, "needs another Nasser."[5]

In the meantime in Brazil many wanted to play a role in placing Quadros in the presidency. In April 1959, eighteen months before the election, one of the smaller labor parties, the Partido Trabalhista Nacional (PTN), made him its candidate; as the first presidential candidate to be registered, he would be the first listed on the official ballot.[6] Then two more of the smaller parties, the Partido Libertador (PL) and the Partido Democrata Cristão (PDC) nominated him. Janistas all over the republic began displaying miniature brooms, the Quadros symbol for doing away with corruption.

Oscar Pedroso d'Horta and Francisco Quintanilha Ribeiro, Jânio's closest São Paulo advisers, kept their distance from Carlos Castilho Cabral, who became head of a nonpartisan student-based Movimento Popular Jânio Quadros with headquarters in Rio. All of them corresponded with the world traveler. Occasionally agents of political groups made quick trips to talk with the great man in distant hotel rooms.

[5] Vladimir Reisky de Dubnic, *Political Trends in Brazil*, p. 132.
[6] Castilho Cabral, *Tempos de Jânio*, p. 149. This time the ballots would be handed out at voting time by the electoral justice system, as the UDN had wanted in 1955.

2. The Candidates in 1960

EARLY IN 1959 Lacerda felt convinced that although Quadros had never run on the UDN ticket, the PTB congressman could win the presidency for the UDN by attracting multitudes in a way that past UDN presidential candidates had been unable to do. Forgetting that in 1955 he had described Quadros as another Hitler, he came out in favor of him. His action was criticized by Juraci Montenegro de Magalhães, UDN president and governor of Bahia. Juraci, who had been

Lacerda's choice a few months earlier, said that Lacerda was guilty of speaking prematurely and of favoring a non-UDN man.[1]

Juraci had served in the last Vargas administration and had many friends outside the UDN. One of these was Kubitschek, and for a while there was talk about a possible PSD-UDN coalition around Juraci. "I have the support of Juscelino and Jango; if you will support me in the UDN, I shall win the election," Juraci is reported to have said to Lacerda.[2] But a large faction in the UDN wanted to win without Kubitschek and the PSD. There was, besides, the likelihood that Jânio would win without the backing of the UDN or any big party, for the allegiance of voters to parties was insignificant. The talk of a PSD-UDN coalition around Juraci only annoyed Jânio's supporters and sent Lacerda to Santos for a friendly discussion with Jânio.

Kubitschek, busy building Brasília, paid little attention to the presidential succession and gave the impression of believing that nobody in Brazil was prepared to be his successor. The constitution permitted him to run again but only after an intervening term. There was nothing he could do about that except set an example of impartial devotion to legality—an example that might be useful five years later. Among the President's friends, all one heard was "J.K. in '65."

As for 1960, no one connected with the Kubitschek regime was immune from the erosion of prestige which the great inflation brought. The so-called Getulistas—or traditional "ins"—were not optimistic about defeating the never-beaten Quadros. The PSD governor of Minas was interested in trying; but he was not popular with the PTB, and the Getulistas could see no chance at all unless the PSD and PTB remained united.

Unity, PTB leaders argued, should this time be achieved with a man of their party heading the slate. But the PSD rejected the proffered Goulart-Amaral Peixoto ticket. Finally the two parties agreed that the presidential nomination should go to Lott, the "legalist hero" of November 1955 who had refrained from involving himself in party

[1] Mário Victor, *Cinco Anos que Abalaram o Brasil: de Jânio Quadros ao Marechal Castelo Branco*, pp. 38–39.

[2] Carlos Lacerda, "Rosas e Pedras do Meu Caminho," *Manchete*, ch. XI, June 24, 1967.

bickering. For his running mate Getulistas hoped to interest Osvaldo Aranha, the long-time Vargas associate who was popular with the PTB. But Aranha died, and Goulart agreed to run for Vice-President again.

Quadros, advised in Rome that Lott would probably be his opponent, spoke highly of the Marshal's austerity and other qualifications. Quadros also indicated that his own running mate should be a northeasterner. This sent politicians scampering to Bahia to try to forge a Jânio-Juraci ticket.

Although a majority of the UDN's directive committee had favored Quadros since Lacerda had spoken in January 1959, Juraci Magalhães continued to hold out for his party's presidential nomination. At a meeting of UDN directors in Bahia, he asked São Paulo's Herbert Levy to speak of Jânio's "crazy behaviors"; but the several Paulistas present said that the crazy outbursts were for the good, because Jânio was really a great administrator.[3]

Before the UDN held its national convention in Tiradentes Palace on November 8, 1959, the capital was covered with posters explaining that the governor of Bahia was so clean that no broom was needed by the UDN.

At the convention Quadros received 205 votes to 83 for Juraci Magalhães. The new nominee, back from voyaging, made a dramatic entrance and was greeted by hundreds of waving brooms. UDN leaders, such as Eduardo Gomes, Prado Kelly, Lacerda, and Milton Campos, who so often had seen their party frustrated, could not contain their emotion. "In my hands," Quadros declared, "the flag of the UDN will not fail." He went on to describe himself as favoring good and opposing evil. Good included Petrobrás.

Late that month, at a small gathering in the São Paulo residence of Quintanilha Ribeiro, the easily irritated candidate decided to hold the flag no longer. Party leaders, planning a visit he was to make to the territory of Acre, were discussing the problem created by his having two running mates. After the PDC had nominated Fernando Ferrari, a Gaúcho, to run with Quadros, the UDN had nominated Leandro

[3] *Ibid.*

Maciel, former UDN governor of a small northeastern state. Maciel did not wish to go to Acre with Ferrari.[4]

Vexed, Quadros withdrew from the conversation and wrote a letter to José de Magalhães Pinto, new president of the UDN. "I resign my candidacy. . . . If in this phase it is difficult to coordinate the forces and unite the desires of the people of goodwill who operate in the various parties, it will be impossible to govern for the rights of the people and the Brazilian needs."[5]

Members of the Movimento Popular Jânio Quadros rushed around collecting signatures on petitions that beseeched Quadros to reconsider. Juraci Magalhães observed: "Like all Brazilians, I was not surprised to receive the news of the position taken by Jânio Quadros. . . . More episodes will take place."[6]

Leaders of the pro-Quadros parties conferred for a week, after which it was agreed that Quadros' official running mate would be the UDN candidate for the vice-presidency; Fernando Ferrari would campaign on his own. Quadros let himself be persuaded by Carvalho Pinto to withdraw his resignation.

Quadros had tried to give the image of one who would not be dominated by politicians. He preferred, as he made known, to be "a free citizen, rather than a prisoner in the presidency."[7]

Ferrari, who seemed likely to split the anti-Goulart vote, refused to withdraw from the vice-presidential race in spite of Lacerda's urging. It was Leandro Maciel who dropped out, after finding that his candidacy attracted little interest. But the UDN kept the vice-presidential race a three-cornered one. Having gone outside of the party to get Quadros, it wanted him to run with someone steeped in UDN tradition; besides, it could not see Ferrari, the labor politician from the far south, as a match for Goulart. UDN leaders called Rome and received an acceptance from the honorable Milton Campos, who had almost beaten Goulart in the three-cornered vice-presidential contest five years earlier.

[4] Carlos Castilho Cabral, *Tempos de Jânio e Outros Tempos*, p. 170.
[5] *Ibid.*
[6] Victor, *Cinco Anos que Abalaram o Brasil*, p. 61.
[7] *Ibid.*, p. 57.

The presidential race had also become a three-cornered one. Millionaire Ademar de Barros, who enjoyed campaigning as much as he disliked Quadros, again was nominated by the PSP. Using a word he had coined, *gerencialismo,* he asserted that what Brazil needed was a good general manager (*gerente*), namely himself.

3. Achieving the Presidency

As EXPECTED, Luís Carlos Prestes declared that the Communists favored Lott and Goulart. Quadros, while abroad in 1959, had remarked "I'm not interested in the position of Luís Carlos Prestes, whom I consider defunct." But Quadros, supported by conservative anti-Getulistas (such as the publisher of *O Estado de S. Paulo*), needed votes of leftists, and these he attracted in a number of ways. First he accepted, as Lott did not, an invitation from Fidel Castro to visit Cuba.

With Quadros on the jaunt to Havana receptions went Senator Afonso Arinos de Melo Franco, whom the candidate was eyeing as a good choice to be his Foreign Minister. The group of travelers included two others who hoped to become Quadros' Foreign Minister: Castilho Cabral (of the Movimento Popular Jânio Quadros) and João Ribeiro Dantas, the director of the Rio daily, *Diário de Notícias,* who had previously accompanied Quadros on calls on Tito and Khrushchev. Also visiting Cuba with Quadros were Deputado Paulo de Tarso, of the Christian Democratic Party's left wing, and Francisco Julião Arruda de Paula, a politician who sometimes called himself a Communist and frequently a Marxist. Julião was becoming known as the mystical leader of the peasant leagues in the Brazilian Northeast.[1]

For his Brazilian guests, Fidel Castro listed Cuba's principal export products (Raúl Castro adding, "and revolution").[2] Fidel had recently

---

[1] Although much wooed by Quadros, Julião in 1960 finally followed the line of the Communist Party of Brazil and supported Lott.

[2] Carlos Castilho Cabral, *Tempos de Jânio e Outros Tempos,* p. 189.

disappeared mysteriously and then returned, "reclaimed by the people," apparently more popular than ever. Quadros, fascinated by this episode, kept asking Cubans for explanations.[3]

The Brazilians returned home via Caracas, where Venezuela's Rómulo Betancourt, in a playful mood, told Jânio: "See here, Quadros, one should pay attention to Fidel. He is a practicing revolutionary, not a demagogue—like us, like you and me." Then Betancourt laughed, but Jânio maintained an uneasy silence.[4]

Back in Brazil Quadros praised the Castro revolution and came out in favor of diplomatic relations with the Soviet Union.

Lott's case was different. Like his running mate Goulart, Lott had, throughout the campaign, the full support of the Communist press and the crowd-producing apparatus of the Communist Party of Brazil. Lott stressed that he was an anti-Communist who opposed Castro, the legalization of the PCB and the re-establishment of relations with the Soviet Union. Prestes unworriedly dismissed these statements with the explanation that Lott did not yet have "a well-formed mentality about political doctrines."[5]

Quadros' theatrics contrasted sharply with the performance of Lott, the stodgy military man who had never campaigned before. Lott's foes revealed that "the hero of the Getulistas" had been one of the twenty-seven generals who had signed the manifesto of August 1954, calling on Vargas to resign. The manifesto, the Janistas declared, had driven Vargas to suicide. Getúlio's son, Lutero, accused the opposition of producing a "new Brandi letter."[6] But there was nothing Lutero or Lott could say when Janistas came out with reproductions on television and in the press. Lott's signature was there, together with those of other anti-Vargas generals like Fiuza de Castro, Canrobert Pereira da Costa, Juarez Távora, and Alcides Etchegoyen.[7]

In the last week of campaigning Lott suffered another setback. A

---

[3] Prudente de Morais Neto, interview, Rio de Janeiro, August 31, 1963.

[4] Afonso Arinos de Melo Franco, *A Escalada: Memórias*, p. 464.

[5] *O Estado de S. Paulo*, July 12, 1960.

[6] Castilho Cabral, *Tempos de Jânio*, p. 206.

[7] Bento Munhoz da Rocha Neto, interview, Curitiba, November 28, 1965. Bento Munhoz da Rocha, *Radiografia de Novembro*, Appendix 16, pp. 118–119.

platform collapsed under him, injuring a leg so badly that he had to abandon further appearances. It was Goulart, then, who concluded the PSD-PTB effort in the grand manner, presiding over a huge rally in São Paulo. As in the case of the final São Paulo rally of the PSD-PTB in 1955, Communist Party workers made their presence vividly evident. Some were on the platform with Goulart.

The so-called Prestes-Goulart Alliance, mentioned with abhorrence by conservatives during the 1958 election, seemed to be in full swing during 1960. Early in August Prestes declared that Goulart had the "obligation to be a leading fighter for the legality of the Brazilian Communist Party."[8] Prestes went on to reiterate that his party would work for the formation of an over-all national labor union organization (*central sindical*) at the forthcoming Third Congress of Brazilian Trade Unions. When this congress took place, later in August, the anti-Communists disappointed Goulart by opposing a *central sindical* and by getting into a row with the Communists and their allies (men who had sought to put the labor movement behind Kubitschek and Goulart in 1955). The result was a break between Goulart and the anti-Communist leaders of organized labor that left Goulart closer to the Communists and their allies.

In September 1960 the PTB was represented at the closing session of the Communist Fifth Party Congress. After the delegates applauded "small and heroic Cuba," Prestes declared that the day would soon come when Goulart would be able to appear in a public square to sign a pact of action with the Communists.

Goulart's campaign for the vice-presidency was given a boost when some of Jânio's supporters urged voters to split the ticket and push for a Jânio-Jango victory. This "Jan-Jan" campaign was effectively organized in São Paulo by Dante Pelacani, the dynamic graphic workers' leader who was close to Quadros and Goulart and who had left the PCB two years earlier. Jânio's failure to condemn this campaign led observers to speculate that he wanted an outcome that would appear to be more a personal victory than a party victory.

Quadros stated that he was still a PTB congressman, and he described

8 *Correio da Manhã*, August 6, 1960.

Vargas as a "great patriot."[9] Although his broom implied much, Quadros disappointed the UDN by refraining from attacking the administration of Kubitschek, who maintained a neutral attitude throughout the campaign.

Quadros flew over 155,000 miles. He delivered over one thousand speeches, and these generally revealed him to be a nationalist and a friend of labor. At the end of the campaign he said that he had reached "the extreme of my resistence." As one observer remarked, he could have won "with any party, without any party, or against any party."[10] The "Fenômeno Jânio Quadros" swept Brazil more powerfully than it had swept São Paulo before. Quadros received almost six million votes, nearly equal to the combined total cast for Lott and Ademar de Barros.

Once again Goulart edged past Milton Campos. But the UDN, nevertheless, found much to be happy about. Magalhães Pinto captured the governorship of Minas Gerais; and Lacerda became the first governor elected to head Guanabara, the tiny state that replaced the old Federal District when the national capital was moved from Rio to Brasília.

Businessmen shrugged off as politics Quadros' campaign appeal to "the Left," and looked forward to an administration that would do for Brazil what he had done for São Paulo. They were impressed on October 19, when the President-elect, about to take a steamer for Europe, made a sober, nonpartisan call for unity over a television-radio network. Quadros put "economic-financial" conditions at the head of the list of matters needing attention.

In London Quadros underwent an eye operation. He kept himself secluded from favor-seekers but remained in constant touch with his efficient São Paulo team, which was suggesting administrative appointments. From Rio Lacerda was able to advise him that Kubitschek's War Minister, Odílio Denys (organizer of the 1955 coup against Luz), would guarantee his inauguration.

Brazilian Embassy personnel in Portugal were surprised on New

[9] A careful analysis of the campaigning in 1960 is given in Vladimir Reisky de Dubnic, *Political Trends in Brazil*, pp. 102–124.

[10] Prudente de Morais Neto, interview, August 31, 1963.

Year's day, 1961, when Quadros and his family unexpectedly arrived in Lisbon by airplane. Quadros was cold to the ambassador, Kubitschek's friend, Francisco Negrão de Lima. But well into a bottle of Scotch in a night club, Brazil's President-elect revealed some of his thoughts to one of the embassy's top men. Charming the couples who came to his table to greet him, Quadros confided: "If I wished, I could be elected head of Portugal." He went on to observe that the President of Brazil was the most powerful head of any democratic nation. "Like an emperor," said Quadros. Then he added that during his first week as President he would have to make 473 appointments and therefore wanted time in Lisbon to relax and study matters.

On January 20, 1961, eleven days before the inauguration, a steamer brought Quadros to Brazil, the scene of acrimonious debates about the merits and defects of the outgoing regime. The new cabinet list was issued on the eve of the inauguration. Pedroso d'Horta and Quintanilha Ribeiro, of the Quadros São Paulo team, became, respectively, Justice Minister and head of the presidential Casa Civil. Some high posts went to men who had long struggled for the UDN: Afonso Arinos de Melo Franco was named Foreign Minister, Bahia banker Clemente Mariani became Finance Minister, and Congressman João Agripino took over the newly created Ministry of Mines and Energy. The new Labor Minister belonged to a current in the PTB which opposed Goulart.

War Minister Denys stayed on under Quadros. He continued to regard his 1955 movement as the step that prevented Zenóbio da Costa and "leftist" Movimento Militar Constitucionalista (MMC) officers from assuming Army control under Kubitschek.

The anti-Kubitschek feeling in the Navy and Air Force was given dramatic recognition with the appointments of Sílvio Heck and Gabriel Grün Moss to head these ministries. Grün Moss immediately made longtime-colonel Adil de Oliveira a *brigadeiro* and put him in charge of the important Second Air Zone, with headquarters in Recife.[11]

Burnier, Veloso, and others who had been in exile since the Aragarças rebellion returned to Brazil during the first part of 1961. They were arrested but put at liberty after arguing that they had revolted to

[11] Gabriel Grün Moss, interview, Rio de Janeiro, December 12, 1965; João Adil de Oliveira, interview, Rio de Janeiro, December 20, 1965.

prevent the success of a "leftist" rebellion. Testifying on behalf of the Aragarças rebels, Brigadeiro Adil de Oliveira referred to Kubitschek as "Colonel Juscelino of the Minas Military Police." [12]

On inauguration day, January 31, 1961, rain made a muddy place of Brasília, where it was difficult to grow grass. Quadros, toying with his horn-rimmed spectacles at Planalto Palace (the presidential offices), gave the outgoing President credit for having "consolidated the principles of a democratic regime."

The rain became a torrent by the time Kubitschek and his party reached the airport to board an airplane for France. After a speech by Israel Pinheiro, Kubitschek's right-hand man in building Brasília, Juraci Magalhães praised the former President and wished him a good trip.

Kubitschek, flying to France, heard with surprise and bitterness a radio broadcast of Quadros' first presidential message to the Brazilian people: "The economic and financial situation is no more serious than the moral, administrative, and political-social crisis in which we have been submerged. . . . I see scandals of every sort. . . . My government will act on the cry of revolt of six million voters who decided to end the cycle of insanities." [13]

While Quadros prepared to name investigating commissions to look into what he called the wrongdoings of the Kubitschek regime, many congressmen and a part of the press observed that Quadros' message had been "unnecessarily indelicate."

[12] *Jornal do Brasil*, June 28, 1961.
[13] *O Estado de S. Paulo*, February 1, 1961.

4. Quadros, a Novel Chief Executive

QUADROS PROVIDED an air of efficiency and left no doubt that he was running Brazil. His relations with the members of his administration were formal and correct. Yet incidents led commentators to describe these people as often "shivering and trembling" before him.

His *bilhetinhos*, published daily in the press, usually set some deadline, before which government officials were ordered to accomplish this or that. "This whole method of confirming instructions in writing," a Brazilian general points out, "is similar to the way such matters are handled in military circles." However, a spokesman of the PTB told Justice Minister Pedroso d'Horta that Quadros' personal style, "divulging immediately all his administrative acts by means of his famous memoranda," threatened to provoke "an institutional crisis."[1]

Bilhetinhos ordered an end to "bikini" beauty contests and upset the Jockey Clubs by ruling that horse racing should take place only on Sundays and holidays. Fifty per cent of the music at night clubs was to be Brazilian music.

The President changed the customary working hours of public servants, making it difficult for them to hold, simultaneously, additional jobs. To this new *horário duplo*, which specified hours in the morning and afternoon with some time off for lunch, he decreed a strict observance. A similar experiment in Rio Grande do Sul had been unsuccessful, but Quadros believed that the arrangement would, in six months, get rid of thousands of "bad public servants." As Quadros expected, it was met with some sabotage and much criticism. "Where are the women public servants going to leave their children?" asked a sentence scrawled on the obelisk in downtown Rio. A reply soon appeared underneath: "Where the commercial employees leave their children." When one Communist sympathizer complained to Quadros about the specific number of hours of work demanded, Quadros told him that "in a nation which you admire, they work fifteen hours a day and do not object."

Quadros dispensed with the services of all bureaucrats who since September 1, 1960, had been added by the past regime to the public payroll. When Congress voted that over 5,500 NOVACAP workers, who had constructed Brasília, become permanent government employees, Quadros vetoed the bill (only to have his veto overruled).

A retired general, one of Kubitschek's heads of Petrobrás, contradicted Quadros' criticism of his past management of the petroleum

---

[1] *O Estado de S. Paulo*, February 11, 1961, p. 3.

monopoly and was, therefore, arrested by order of the President. Another former Army man, who had also once headed Petrobrás, was ordered arrested for giving a press interview opposing the transfer of Petrobrás' headquarters from Rio to Salvador, Bahia. Neither act was outside the tradition, established in 1956 by Lott, of disciplining retired military officers for statements that might be considered political. But in the press and in Congress there were expressions of uneasiness, especially after Quadros ordered Rádio Jornal do Brasil to be silent for three days as punishment for issuing a bulletin described as untrue and dangerous.

Presidential instructions pushed forward projects for regulating radio broadcasting and the profession of journalism and for dealing with economic monopolies. Only the title of the administration's proposed legislation for "restricting profit remittances abroad" seemed likely to please ultranationalists; the proposed bill had little to do with the subject and seemed unlikely to restrict the remittances of foreign firms. The UDN's conservative Milton Campos was selected to head a group to study agrarian reform.

The President felt the outlook for fulfilling the administration's program was not bright. Congressmen were notably slow to act and were not famous for spending a great deal of time in the new capital. To make matters worse for the President, Congress was a carry-over from the previous regime, and supporters of the administration were in a minority.

These supporters were disappointed when the President, showing his independence of the UDN, sometimes courted the PTB. The UDN expressed displeasure when Quadros chose a PTB favorite, General Amauri Kruel, to be ambassador to Bolivia. Kruel, Kubitschek's police chief, was close to Goulart and had gotten into a scrap with former Police Chief Menezes Côrtes, whose ties were with the UDN.

Quadros was known to believe that his 1960 victory superseded the victories of congressmen, all achieved in 1958. Some of the lawmakers had the impression that Quadros "detested" Congress. At any rate, the new President was not a man who sought legislative votes by jovially slapping congressmen on the back. When they sought to see him they usually received word from Planalto Palace that they should see Pedroso d'Horta. The disappointment of being denied Quadros' time was sometimes aggravated when they found the busy Justice Minister a bit brusque.

Congressmen resented the President's tendency to appeal directly to the people. They heard rumors about how the planners in Planalto Palace, feeling a need of reforming the legislature, were studying the arrangements that De Gaulle had set up in France.

Quadros made sure that plenty of publicity would be given to the words he expressed at the cabinet meeting of July 6. On the next day newspaper readers learned that the President, at the meeting, had been "at times almost tearful, and at times vehement" as he insisted that he had the confidence of the people, and as he demanded the enactment of "the great reforms."[2]

What were the "great reforms" to which the President referred so dramatically? Although the public had no clear idea of their nature, Quadros had gone on to tell his cabinet that the nation was demanding their enactment and that they constituted the only commitment he had assumed during the election campaign.

Kubitschek, back from Europe and elected senator from Goiás, joined Ernâni do Amaral Peixoto and other friends in a discussion of Quadros' theatrical behavior. Quadros, the former President predicted, would either push for the election of a docile Congress in 1962 or else seek to act against the democratic regime.[3]

Quadros, so that he and his cabinet could familiarize themselves with local problems, initiated a system whereby for one week each month he and the cabinet would govern Brazil from a different state capital. At such times the authorities of the region would flock to meetings with programs and requests for federal funds, most of which the Quadros administration would promise to furnish.

High officials of the southern states of Paraná, Rio Grande do Sul, and Santa Catarina attended such a session held in the capital of Santa Catarina. There Paraná's state secretary of agriculture praised the possibilities of Saracen wheat. In front of the federal and state cabinet

[2] *Ibid.*, July 7, 1961, dateline Brasília, July 6, 1961.
[3] *Ibid.*, July 8, 1961, dateline Rio de Janeiro, July 7, 1961.

ministers, state governors, and other dignitaries, Quadros broke a piece of bread made from this wheat. He solemnly tasted it, nodded, and then had all those present follow his example of tasting.[4]

[4] Mário Braga Ramos, interview, Brasília, October 19, 1965.

5. Reactions to the "Independent" Foreign Policy

IN MARCH 1961, at the start of his administration, Quadros boldly did away with multiple currency exchange rates. They had been instituted by Finance Minister Aranha in 1953 and had been retained by the Café Filho administration in spite of Whitaker's desire to abolish them. When Kubitschek's first cabinet was evenly divided on what to do about the matter, Kubitschek had decided to back Finance Minister Alkmin, who opposed exchange reform.

During the Kubitschek years the multiple exchange rates, used to subsidize imports of petroleum, wheat, and newsprint, had allowed the public to buy these items at approximately half their true cost. Quadros' step, establishing realistic sales prices, was part of his financial program and was hailed by international bankers. It was helpful to Walter Moreira Sales and Roberto Campos, the well-chosen negotiators whom Quadros sent abroad to obtain new foreign financial commitments and the postponement of due dates of past loans that could not be repaid. But the step was abhorrent to the IMF-hating Left and brought back memories of Gudin's austere term as Café Filho's Finance Minister.

Quadros, in a dramatic television-radio speech, stressed that his cancellation of the subsidies was required by fiscal, financial, and moral considerations. As for the price of paper, he held up for his viewers a copy of a Sunday newspaper and described it as unnecessarily bulky. After appealing to all Brazilians, especially the "powerful" ones, to help the collectivity, he emotionally vowed that he would do what was right, regardless of the effects on his popularity.

While the Left criticized the financial program, it became more and more delighted with the new administration's course in international affairs.

Adolf Berle, a man Vargas had liked to blame for his 1945 downfall, learned something from Quadros about Brazil's foreign policy when he made a short trip to Brazil late in February 1961. At the time of the arrival of this special representative of President Kennedy, the Brazilian press published Khrushchev's wire thanking Quadros for a message about a Russian achievement in space. The Brazilian people, Khrushchev said, "can count, like others in Latin America, on the backing of the U.S.S.R. in their aspirations to liberate themselves from foreign dependency."[1]

When Berle and Ambassador John Moors Cabot called on Quadros at Planalto Palace on March 2, Cabot noted two new decorations in the presidential office: an unsigned photograph of Tito and an ebony statue sent by Cuba's Che Guevara.

Berle reiterated the willingness of the United States to loan Brazil 100 million dollars. But Quadros did not feel that such an amount would solve Brazil's problems. He said that his financial program was going to be drastic and in six months would make him the most unpopular man in Brazil.[2] Therefore, he said, he would need the fullest United States backing for it.

Berle, speaking of Cuba and his apprehension of an explosion in the Caribbean, urged that Brazil join the United States and other OAS nations in an inter-American action. Quadros made it clear that he would not support this idea. Berle concluded that the Brazilian President planned to use foreign policy to achieve the good will of the Brazilian Left.

It had been a frank but cordial discussion. However, as soon as Berle returned to Washington the Brazilian press pictured it as anything but friendly. News items mentioned that Quadros had refused to shake Berle's hand when he saw him out of his Planalto office, and that the Foreign Office had failed to extend the usual formal farewell courtesies

[1] *O Estado de S. Paulo*, February 28, 1961.
[2] Adolf A. Berle, interview, Austin, Texas, March 8, 1963.

to the foreign dignitary. While such misleading reports were delighting leftists, it was confirmed that Quadros had invited Tito to visit Brazil before the end of the year.[3]

Quadros, addressing Congress on March 15, said that Brazil "could not ignore the vitality and dynamism of the Socialist States. Therefore steps have been taken for the establishment of diplomatic relations with Hungary, Rumania, and Bulgaria, and studies are being made to normalize our relations with all countries." The Brazilian delegation to the United Nations, he said, would vote for the full acceptance of the credentials of the representatives of the People's Republic of Hungary and for considering the representation of the People's Republic of China.[4]

As the unsuccessful Bay of Pigs invasion of Cuba got under way, Quadros cited principles of self-determination and expressed his profound apprehension about the threat to Castro. Lacerda, on the other hand, welcomed the Cuban invasion "as the beginning of the liberty of a people betrayed by a revolutionary transformed into a tyrant."[5]

In May 1961 the Red Chinese sent a commercial mission to Brazil. Late in July Quadros, dressed in a white jacket and white slacks, received a good will mission from the Soviet Union. A few days later the press published Quadros' *bilhetinho* instructing Foreign Minister Afonso Arinos to take steps to re-establish diplomatic relations with the U.S.S.R.

The new "independent" foreign policy of Quadros was to reverse "the subsidiary and innocuous diplomacy of a nation aligned with worthy though alien interests."[6] It was to provide Brazil a position of leadership among "uncommitted nations" (those which were not pro-West, pro-East, or even in the "neutralist" bloc). Particular emphasis

[3] *O Estado de S. Paulo*, editorial, March 5, 1961. Regarding the invitation to Tito, this editorial says: "This is the first act of the new government for establishing a new direction for foreign policy. This newspaper opposes this direction."

[4] Jânio Quadros, *Mensagem ao Congresso Nacional Remitida pelo Presidente da República na Abertura da Sessão Legislativa de 1961*, p. 94.

[5] Mário Victor, *Cinco Anos que Abalaram o Brasil: de Jânio Quadros ao Marechal Castelo Branco*, p. 239.

[6] Jânio Quadros, "Brazil's New Foreign Policy," *Foreign Affairs*, 40, no. 1 (October 1961), p. 19.

was to be given to the emerging nations of Africa where some new Brazilian embassies were established. To please the U.S.S.R., diplomatic relations with non-Communist diplomats who claimed to represent Lithuania, Latvia, and Estonia were to be broken.[7]

Even before announcement of the renewal of diplomatic ties with the U.S.S.R., Quadros' foreign policy evoked heated debate. *O Estado de S. Paulo, O Globo,* and *Tribuna da Imprensa,* dailies that had supported Quadros' effort to reach the presidency, expressed grave concern.

Admiral Pena Bôto and his Cruzada Brasileira Anticomunista attacked the new foreign policy so bitterly that Quadros had the admiral put under house arrest. The order was carried out by Pena Bôto's former *Tamandaré* companion, Navy Minister Heck.

Luís Carlos Prestes praised Quadros in May 1961 for his steps "to strengthen the national economy and free it from foreign influences." Late in July 1961, when Cardinal Jaime de Barros Câmara was condemning the renewal of relations with the Soviet Union, Prestes wrote Quadros of "the applause of the Brazilian Communists." "Obeying the clamor of our people and attending the interests of the nation, Your Excellency established relations with Bulgaria, Rumania, and Albania, and you have now decided to do the same with the U.S.S.R., a great socialist nation."[8]

The National Union of Students and a part of organized labor acclaimed the President's foreign policy. It helped increase the warmth between the President and some PTB leaders—a warmth that showed signs of weakening the traditional bond between the PTB and the PSD. Francisco San Tiago Dantas, the clever lawyer and former Green Shirt who had recently become a prominent PTB congressman, accepted Quadros' invitation to head the Brazilian delegation to the United Nations.

Afonso Arinos was kept busy making explanations to congressmen. Although Minas Governor Magalhães Pinto expressed enthusiasm for Quadros' foreign policy, Afonso Arinos noted that most of his old associates in the UDN did not care for it.[9] One of these was Deputado

---

[7] Vasco Leitão da Cunha, interview, Washington, June 24, 1966.

[8] Luís Carlos Prestes' letter to Quadros is given in full in *A Gazeta,* August 4, 1961.

[9] Afonso Arinos de Melo Franco, interview, Brasília, October 16, 1965.

Raimundo Padilha, who, after making a particularly bitter attack on it, was called in to see the President.

Padilha found the President nervous and not much interested in discussing foreign policy. "Some day," Quadros sorrowfully told him, "you may become President of the Republic, in which case you should be a very sad man. The job should only be accepted if all the people get on their knees, pleading that you take it."[10]

[10] Raimundo Delmiriano Padilha, interview, Brasília, October 13, 1965.

6. The João Dantas Mission (May–June 1961)

IN MAY, before announcing that diplomatic ties should be renewed with the U.S.S.R., Quadros sent newspaper publisher João Ribeiro Dantas to Eastern European countries. Dantas, who had visited the Soviet Union with Quadros in 1959, was to prepare the way for closer diplomatic ties with these countries and push for another favorite objective of Quadros: the opening of nontraditional markets in order to increase trade wherever possible.

Many observers felt that, practically speaking, opportunities for increased trade with the Socialist nations were small. Nevertheless, wide publicity was given to the commercial agreements that the Dantas mission signed with Albania, Bulgaria, Czechoslovakia, Hungary, Poland, Rumania, and Yugoslavia; an agreement was also made with East Germany, to the discomfiture of the West Germans. At the time the West Germans, important to Brazilian trade, were preparing to receive Roberto Campos for discussions concerning standby credits for Brazil.

Headlines about the protocol with East Germany revealed that it had been signed by João Dantas as traveling ambassador and that it included references to understandings reached "between two countries." The West Germans did not have to remind Quadros of the Hallstein Doctrine, wherein they had proclaimed that any nation which diplomatically recognized East Germany thereby automatically ceased having diplomatic relations with West Germany. Foreign Minister Afonso Arinos had explained the matter to Quadros; he had also persuaded Quadros to issue a telex message to the Foreign Ministry confirming that Dantas' trip to East Germany was to be simply a personal "unofficial" visit.

After Dantas signed the protocol, Roberto Campos found the West Germans unwilling to discuss credits. Therefore, Campos telephoned Vasco Leitão da Cunha, the career diplomat who was general secretary of the Brazilian Foreign Office. In Rio on May 31 Leitão da Cunha issued a press release declaring that Dantas had no credentials to East Germany. The release was a timely help to Campos; but, in making it, Leitão da Cunha surprised Afonso Arinos and infuriated Quadros.

Quadros told his Foreign Minister to fire Leitão da Cunha for an act of indiscipline. After Afonso Arinos replied that he wanted first to hear what Leitão da Cunha had to say, the President paced the floor. Then, putting one hand on the Foreign Minister's head and the other on the Foreign Minister's heart, Quadros declared that a politician must never put his heart ahead of his mind. He went on to tell Afonso Arinos that he understood from him that he wished to leave his post. Afonso Arinos protested, saying that he only wanted an end to a situation in which he found himself a subminister (not fully running his office himself).

"Who said that I should be President of Brazil?" Quadros asked. Before the question was answered, Quadros explained that in spite of personal wishes he was not thinking of resigning. Then he spoke emotionally of Brazil and its people and added that sometimes it is more difficult to stay in office than to leave office.[1]

Leitão da Cunha, informed of Quadros' reaction to his press release, quickly left his lofty Itamarati post—a step that allowed Afonso Arinos to continue in office. Generals congratulated Leitão da Cunha. Osvaldo Cordeiro de Farias, Chief of Staff of the Armed Forces, stressed the need of "rigorous respect for agreements solemnly made with all nations, especially in the Americas."

---

[1] Afonso Arinos de Melo Franco, interview, Rio de Janeiro, December 15, 1967.

7. A Decoration for Che Guevara (August 19, 1961)

E CONOMIST CELSO FURTADO reported that, during his discussions in Washington, about the Brazilian Northeast, United States officials always asked whether he was submitting large enough figures.[1] More than once, "limitless resources" had been mentioned by men of the Kennedy administration.[2] The same spirit apparently infected Treasury Secretary Douglas Dillon, head of the forty-two man United States delegation to the launching of the Alliance for Progress at Punta del Este, Uruguay. Dillon and his associates, on their way to Uruguay in August 1961, were received amicably by Quadros in Brasília. Quadros learned of United States interest in seeing Brazil's ambitious Emergency Plan put into operation.[3]

After the delegations gathered at Punta del Este, it was reported that the Alliance for Progress would furnish Latin America twenty billion dollars over a ten-year period.

The chief discordant note was provided by the exchanges between Douglas Dillon and the bearded Che Guevara, the only uniformed member of the forty-five man Cuban delegation. The United States, in order not to betray "thousands of patriotic Cubans," refused to recognize the Castro regime. Dillon said that, as the Cuban government was

---

[1] *O Estado de S. Paulo*, August 5, 1961.

[2] *Ibid.*

[3] The Emergency Plan for development, described as a forerunner of a "Five Year Plan," was signed by Quadros on July 21, 1961, after the National Economic Development Bank and various planning groups had examined eight hundred projects submitted by local governments and sectors of the federal government. As explained by presidential adviser Cândido Antônio Mendes de Almeida, the Emergency Plan was designed to allow an orderly presentation of foreign assistance requests at the forthcoming Punta del Este conference. It called for the expenditure of "over 95 billion cruzeiros (or 487 million dollars)" for undertakings listed under the following headings: regional plans (Northeast and South), colonization, agriculture and fishing, housing, education, health, energy, transportation, and basic industries. (See *O Estado de S. Paulo*, July 22, 1961.)

controlled by the Soviet Union, the United States would offer no financial assistance to Cuba. [4]

A dramatic walkout by the Brazilian delegation would have been
unthinkable (except, perhaps, in the mind of Governor Leonel Brizola,
"special adviser" to the Brazilian delegation). Nevertheless, Quadros
wanted to re-emphasize the independence of Brazil's international
position. He spoke to representatives of the Soviet press about "the enthusiasm with which the Brazilian people follow the gigantic efforts of
the Soviet people to reach prosperous levels." He appointed Vice-President Goulart to head a sixteen-man mission to make an official visit to
Red China, stopping first to spend several days in Moscow.

Che Guevara, Cuban Minister of Industry and Commerce, sought to
bolster Cuban prestige by conferring with heads of state. Argentina's
President Frondizi received him, an act that helped stir up the Argentine military against Frondizi.[5]

Guevara's request for an audience with Quadros was passed on to
Brasília by telephone from Uruguay by Finance Minister Mariani on
August 18. The Brazilian President replied that he would be happy to
see Guevara early the next morning. Quadros, thinking he might get
for Brazil some Cuban commerce that no longer interested the United
States, had sent a high-caliber trade mission to Cuba. Quadros also
wanted to straighten out the unpleasant situation resulting from the
crowding of over 160 refugees in the Brazilian Embassy in Havana.
Espionage was common in the embassy building; one spy, pretending
to be a refugee, had been killed.

Most important, Quadros wanted somehow to become the father of
the readmittance of Cuba into the American family.[6] João Dantas,
whom he would send to Havana to obtain safe-conducts for the refugees, would discuss with Castro the admission of Cuba into the Latin
American Free Trade Association. Dantas would then see some of the

---

[4] de Lesseps S. Morrison, *Latin American Mission*, pp. 91–92. See also *O Estado
de S. Paulo*, August 18, 1961

[5] Morrison, *Latin American Mission*, p. 103.

[6] João Ribeiro Dantas, interview, Rio de Janeiro, December 20, 1965.

United Nations people in New York and later, Dantas believed, be sent to Moscow as Brazil's new ambassador to the Soviet Union.

Guevara was received by Quadros at the President's Planalto office at 7:00 A.M. on August 19. For half an hour the revolutionary listened as Quadros appealed on behalf of the refugees in Havana and the Cuban Catholics. Then Guevara was escorted by the Brazilian President to be the leading figure at a small ceremony in the Green Room of the palace. Newsmen and photographers were present, but Quadros was the only important Brazilian official there. Even the chief of the Casa Militar, usually on hand for such occasions, was absent.

In awarding Che Guevara the highest order of the Brazilian decoration for foreigners, the Cruzeiro do Sul, Quadros said that the recipient had frequently demonstrated his desire for stronger economic and cultural relations between the governments of Cuba and Brazil. This, said Quadros, was an objective he shared. He decorated Guevara "to show our appreciation to the people and the government of Cuba."

Guevara, after accepting the decoration on behalf of all the people of the Cuban revolution, held a news conference. In an almost inaudible voice, he explained that the Alliance for Progress is basically "imperialistic" and that Dillon's final speech at the conference had been full of lies.[7]

The wily Quadros ordered his press chief to release the story about the decoration without first clearing it with Quintanilha Ribeiro, head of the Casa Civil.[8] When Quintanilha Ribeiro and Casa Militar Chief Pedro Geraldo de Almeida spoke to Quadros about the decoration, Quadros pointed out that in Brazil all foreign cabinet ministers are decorated. The military ministers were displeased and noted that the decoration "to an undesirable visitor" had been given without the usual prior approval of the appropriate council. However, they refrained from protesting publicly in order to avoid creating "a crisis of unfathomable depth."[9]

[7] *O Estado de S. Paulo*, dateline Brasília, August 19, 1961.

[8] Pedro Geraldo de Almeida, interview, Rio de Janeiro, November 4, 1965.

[9] Gabriel Grün Moss, declaration in *Jornal do Brasil*, November 7, 1967.

8. Lacerda's Night in Brasília (August 18–19, 1961)

LACERDA, whose strenuous attacks on the administration's foreign policy had become constant, reached Brasília the evening before Guevara was decorated. In Rio he had spoken to Quadros' wife Eloá, explaining that he wished to see Jânio, whom he considered in the role of a father, because he had to discuss a "tremendously serious" personal problem.[1] Immediately a federal government airplane had been put at his disposal.

By the time Lacerda reached Alvorada Palace, the modernistic presidential residence, Quadros had dined and was watching a film with a few friends in the cinema in the basement. After a long day, Quadros liked to relax in the evenings, drinking Scotch and watching American westerns or films such as "Butterfield 8" (starring Elizabeth Taylor). Advised that Lacerda was being served dinner and would be down later, Quadros said "Good, I'll talk with him."

The two master politicians spoke while Lacerda ate. Lacerda's tremendously serious personal matter concerned financial losses being incurred by the *Tribuna da Imprensa,* managed by one of Lacerda's sons. Perhaps he should resign the governorship and give more attention to the newspaper. Lacerda said that the commercial indebtedness of the *Tribuna* was twenty million cruzeiros (about $80,000) and kept growing.[2]

But other matters were on Lacerda's mind, although they did not fit the father-son relationship. It soon became clear to Quadros that Lacerda was considering a dramatic resignation to be accompanied by

[1] Eloá Quadros' statement, August 26, 1961, as reported in *O Estado de S. Paulo.*
[2] Pedro Geraldo de Almeida, interview, Rio de Janeiro, November 4, 1965. Lacerda's visit to Brasília on the evening of August 18, 1961, was mentioned in Lacerda's radio-television speech on the night of August 24, 1961, and Pedroso d'Horta's radio-television speech on the night of August 25, 1961. Lacerda describes it in "Rosas e Pedras do Meu Caminho," *Manchete,* ch. XI, June 24, 1967. Oscar Pedroso d'Horta discusses it in "As Rosas e as Pedras do Caminho de Lacerda," *Manchete,* August 12, 1967. It is also described by John Dos Passos in *Brazil On the Move,* pp. 162–167.

a declaration that the President was holding up promised financial assistance to Guanabara because the governor attacked the administration's foreign policy. Mentioning that policy, Lacerda told Quadros that he wanted to retire from public life in order not to play a part in a "farce" or be the "victim of some drama."

Not for thirty or forty days, said the President, would he be in a position to discuss some of the matters brought up by the governor. What preoccupied Quadros was a Congress he considered uncooperative. Earlier, at a regional meeting of governors in Rio, Quadros had mentioned this concern to Lacerda; he had asked Lacerda whether he or the governors of Minas or Bahia could accomplish anything in the face of problems created by state legislatures.

The Alvorada Palace meal over, the President escorted Lacerda downstairs to the movie projection room. Thus the President, whose schedule for the next morning included the Guevara meeting and a trip to the port of Vitória, cut short Lacerda's opportunity for discussion. However, Quadros interrupted his film viewing long enough to telephone Justice Minister Pedroso d'Horta and explain that Lacerda evidently had much that he wanted to get off his chest. At the President's suggestion, a somewhat displeased Lacerda accepted the Justice Minister's invitation to come to his apartment.

There Pedroso d'Horta interrupted his conversation with San Tiago Dantas and presidential secretary José Aparecido de Oliveira and took Lacerda to a separate room where he heard what he calls "a heart-rending story." Lacerda surprised the Justice Minister with the news that he was resigning the Guanabara governorship. He gave four reasons: The *Tribuna* deficits, the Quadros foreign policy, difficulties with the state assembly, and an inability to get Quadros to hear him out in heart-to-heart sessions. He had just been unsuccessful in Alvorada Palace; and the President, the only man in the world he trusted implicitly, was leaving for Vitória in the morning without having asked him to accompany him.[3]

Pedroso d'Horta tried to reassure his visitor on all four points. The problem of the twenty million cruzeiros, he said, "is not a problem

[3] Pedroso d'Horta, "As Rosas e as Pedras do Caminho de Lacerda."

for you or me."[4] He pledged the support of São Paulo friends and asked Lacerda to send him the manager of the *Tribuna*. Foreign policy, Pedroso d'Horta admitted, was a controversial matter; but he added that Lacerda's divergences with the administration's policy did not worry the administration, and he asked why they so upset the governor. The Justice Minister explained that the President could not very well have Lacerda at his side when he disembarked at Vitória to be greeted by Espírito Santo's PSD governor. However, the President was going on from Vitória to Rio, and there, Pedroso d'Horta promised, Lacerda could have a long chat with him.

Lacerda's reference to problems with his state legislature provided more exciting information; for both Quadros and Pedroso d'Horta, worrying about a similar problem on the federal level, had concluded that Brazil needed a reform in its juridical-political structure to give the President more authority.[5] Speaking now with Lacerda, Pedroso d'Horta said that the troubles that the Guanabara governor was having with his state legislature were no greater than those which Quadros was having with the federal Congress. Pedroso d'Horta went on to ask Lacerda for copies of newspaper articles he had written in 1955 urging a constitutional reform. Lacerda, who felt that conditions had changed since 1955, was interested in the opinions of the military ministers. Pedroso d'Horta pictured the War and Navy Ministers as probably inclined to favor a strong executive. Navy Minister Heck, he reported, had really beamed for the first time when Quadros had ordered troops to put down student demonstrations in the Northeast.[6] As for Air Force Minister Grün Moss, it would be well, the Justice Minister said, if Lacerda, who had good connections in the Air Force, would sound him out.

Just before Lacerda left Pedroso d'Horta's apartment, he said that his suitcase was at Alvorada Palace. To save Lacerda the long walk between the palace and its gate, Pedroso d'Horta, after his visitor departed, telephoned the palace and arranged to have the suitcase waiting for him at the gate.

[4] Pedro Geraldo de Almeida, interview, November 4, 1965.
[5] Jânio Quadros and Afonso Arinos de Mello Franco, "O Porquê da Reúncia," *Realidade*, II, no. 20 (November 1967).
[6] Carlos Lacerda, interview, Rio de Janeiro, October 11, 1967.

By the time Lacerda found his suitcase in the hands of a guard there, Quadros was asleep. Not much later Pedroso d'Horta answered a call from the Hotel Nacional and heard the irate governor announce his resignation. "I was thrown out of the palace. They put my suitcase at the garden entrance gate and this is an insult to me personally and to the governor of Guanabara. They cover me with ridicule."

Pedroso d'Horta rushed to the hotel. Until the first signs of daybreak he tried to persuade the pyjama-clad governor not to resign. He explained the misunderstanding about the bag and pointed out that no arrangements had been made in the first place for Lacerda to spend the night at Alvorada Palace. Lacerda, however, spoke of using television to reveal the antidemocratic intentions of the President and the Justice Minister.

After a fair amount of whiskey had been consumed, Lacerda thanked Pedroso d'Horta for his efforts at reconciliation. He added: "I hope that this political crisis will not harm our personal relations." Expressing the same hope, Pedroso d'Horta promised to keep quiet about the affair of the governor's black suitcase.[7]

Lacerda, about to return to Rio, advised some UDN *deputados* that he was resigning and that Pedroso d'Horta knew the reasons. He also gave Casa Militar Chief Pedro Geraldo de Almeida a message for Quadros. "I'm going to do what I said I was going to do."[8] Thus Quadros, just before he received Che Guevara, learned of Lacerda's decision to resign.

[7] Pedroso d'Horta, "As Rosas e as Pedras do Caminho de Lacerda."
[8] Pedro Geraldo de Almeida, interview, November 4, 1965.

9. Lacerda Breaks with Quadros

AFTER GUEVARA had been decorated, Quadros and his party flew to Vitória. Early in the afternoon they reached Rio. Lacerda, already there, was replying to Quadros' act of decorating the Communist. A key to the city of Rio, the highest honor the city could offer, was presented publicly to the leader of a group of anti-Castro Cubans. The recipient praised Lacerda and reminded his listeners that all nations run the risk of falling into Communist hands.[1]

In Brasília Pedroso d'Horta, who had reported to Quadros about his sessions with Lacerda, soon had to deal with telephone calls from Rio. Lacerda said that he would not go to Rio's Laranjeiras Palace to call on Quadros unless asked by the President. The President telephoned to say that it would be improper for him to invite the governor; but he acceded to Pedroso d'Horta's urging and had Afonso Arinos bring Lacerda to Laranjeiras Palace.

That evening the Quadros-Lacerda rift apparently ended. Mrs. Quadros and Mrs. Lacerda, having visited Petrópolis together, were at Laranjeiras Palace while their husbands had a friendly talk. It was decided that the Lacerdas would accompany the Quadroses to São Paulo the next morning. Quadros gave assurances that Guanabara would receive federal assistance. Lacerda agreed not to resign.[2]

The President and his wife, preparing to leave Rio with the Lacerdas on August 20, were surprised to receive a note from the governor. "Who is Sebastião?" Quadros asked, as he read that the Lacerdas had decided to remain in Rio to greet Sebastião (a son arriving from abroad).

Lacerda did more than greet his son. That evening, in a widely broadcast speech, he said that he was officially representing the people of his state for the last time. He cried that Quadros' "suicidal" foreign policy, "a capitulation to Communist tyrannies," was dashing the hopes of the Brazilian people.

In Rio Lacerda surprised Air Minister Grün Moss by telling him to be ready to be asked to participate in a coup. The incredulous *brigadeiro* asked about the other military ministers. Lacerda, in indicating that perhaps the War and Navy Ministers did not really favor a coup, was giving an accurate description.

Lacerda went on to São Paulo to give impetus to National Unity

---

[1] *O Estado de S. Paulo*, August 20, 1965.
[2] Pedro Geraldo de Almeida, interview, Rio de Janeiro, November 4, 1965.

Week by delivering a speech on the twenty-third which *O Estado de S. Paulo* hailed as one of the most important in recent times. Youthful hecklers, chanting "Jânio yes, Lacerda no! Guevara yes, Yankees no!," interrupted Lacerda as he made his main point: the Vargas government in 1935 had encouraged Communism in order to have an excuse for imposing dictatorship in 1937.

While in São Paulo, Lacerda called on Governor Carvalho Pinto and urged him to invite Quadros to reveal his "great reform program" at a meeting of governors. The governors, Lacerda explained, could back the reforms and thus work against any presidential pretext for closing Congress.[3] But Cavalho Pinto declined the suggestion, saying that neither Jânio nor Pedroso d'Horta had spoken to him about the matter. These men, Lacerda then observed, had not consulted Carvalho Pinto because "they think you will mull over the matter for six months, and they are in a hurry."

Late at night on August 24, seventh anniversary of Vargas' suicide, Lacerda spoke from Rio's Guanabara Palace. Addressing a vast radio-television audience, he accused Pedroso d'Horta of having canceled the President's invitation that he spend the night at Alvorada Palace.

This time Lacerda's sensational message was that Pedroso d'Horta had spoken of the need of carrying out an institutional change that would send Congress on vacation and allow the administration to enact reforms. The Justice Minister, Lacerda solemnly declared, had said that two of the military ministers had already been sounded out and that Lacerda should sound out the third. Lacerda went on to explain that he had recently discovered that the military ministers knew nothing about the matter. The Justice Minister, he added, had given him false information.

The Governor told his listeners that the presidential advisers were "malevolent, incompetent and perverse." He revealed that he had toyed with the idea of resigning his Guanabara post. For one thing, the federal administration was not complying with promises of financial assistance to his state. But, Lacerda went on, he had now found the right answer: he would stay at his post so that he could alert the

---

[3] Carlos Lacerda, interview, Rio de Janeiro, October 11, 1967.

nation to the need of defending democracy; also he would remain to save the President from himself.

Lacerda's accusation brought after-midnight life to the Chamber of Deputies. Word from Kubitschek encouraged those who wanted to convert the Chamber into an investigating commission. In the end, over two hundred *deputados* approved a resolution that Pedroso d'Horta appear before the Chamber as quickly as possible.

10. Quadros Resigns

QUADROS had once publicly declared that only if dead or forcibly ejected would he leave the presidency.[1] A little later, furious at Congress for overriding his veto of tenure for workers who had built Brasília, he had confided to one of the governors: "Imagine what this country would be like if I should leave it."[2]

At Alvorada Palace late on August 24, Quadros decided to resign. The purpose of the resignation was to force the military ministers to carry out the very plan Lacerda was denouncing. Dead set against turning Brazil over to Vice-President Goulart, they would have to intervene. Quadros, according to his own account of his thinking, expected the armed forces to establish a new, more authoritarian regime, with himself or someone else at its head.[3] That this could only be himself he could not doubt. "Brazil," he said, "needs three things. Authority, capacity for work, and courage and rapidity in making decisions. Outside of myself there is no one, no one, who combines

---

[1] *Correio da Manhã*, editorial, August 26, 1961.

[2] Radio-television speech of Pernambuco Governor Cid Sampaio, Recife, September 6, 1961, as reported in *O Estado de S. Paulo*, September 7, 1961.

[3] Jânio Quadros and Afonso Arinos de Mello Franco, "O Porquê da Renúncia," *Realidade*, II, no. 20 (November 1967).

these three requisites."[4] On his side also would be "spontaneous clamor" of the people, making his return, as he put it, "inevitable."

Quadros, considering the effect of a "courageous" sacrifice and an appropriate farewell message, could take comfort from the popular reaction to the steps that Vargas, under attack by Lacerda, had taken seven years earlier. He could also reflect that, with a weekend coming up, there would presumably be few congressmen in Brasília to receive the resignation.

August 25 is the annual "Day of the Soldier." Shortly before 7:00 A.M. that morning General Pedro Geraldo de Almeida, with military ceremonies in mind, met the President at Planalto Palace. He was the first to learn of Quadros' decision. "Seeing that I cannot carry out what I promised the people, I shall not remain one minute in the presidency." "I was not born President," Quadros added.[5] Pedro Geraldo, trying to dissuade him, told him that he had the support not merely of the six million votes received in 1960, but of sixty million Brazilians. Quadros admitted to having "the mentality of a school teacher"; he could permit no breach of discipline. Authority had been undermined by remarks made against the honor and family of the Head of State. Besides, he said, he could not govern in the face of constant attacks upon his policies and his administration.[6] Pedro Geraldo then called in Quintanilha Ribeiro, head of the Casa Civil.

Quadros telephoned his wife, asking her to pack. From 8:00 A.M. to 9:00 A.M. on grounds not far from the palace he presided over ceremonies honoring Brazilian soldiers. After the presidential party returned to Planalto Palace, Pedro Geraldo called in Pedroso d'Horta and presidential secretary José Aparecido de Oliveira. The military ministers, busy exchanging the traditional "Soldiers' Day" handshakes in the War Ministry, were summoned.

To the seven men in his office Quadros explained that under existing circumstances he did not know how to carry on the work of the

---

[4] These words and those quoted in the next sentence were spoken on the day following the resignation (see Carlos Castello Branco, "O Dia Seguinte," *Realidade*, II, no. 20 [November 1967]).

[5] Pedro Geraldo de Almeida, interview, Rio de Janeiro, November 4, 1965.

[6] *O Estado de S. Paulo*, August 26, 1961.

presidency. "Since failure does not have the courage to resign, it is important that success have this courage. I shall not exercise the presidency with its authority undermined before the eyes of the world, nor shall I remain in office arguing about confidence, respect, and dignity, which are indispensable for the Head of State. This is not an accusation against any particular person. It has to do, rather, with the act of denouncing anyone who, like me, has the solemn and serious duties of a majority mandate. I was not born President. But I was born with my conscience. And that is what I must heed and respect. It tells me that the best way I can now serve the people and the nation is by resigning."[7]

Quadros wrote out a short note to Congress: "On this day and by means of this instrument, leaving with the Justice Minister the reasons for my act, I resign the mandate of President of the Republic." He also produced a longer message for the Brazilian people, and it was typed by the same girl who had typed his letter resigning as a candidate in 1959. When Quadros turned it over to Pedroso d'Horta, the military ministers and others sought to have him reconsider. Refusing to do so, Quadros pointed out that his action was unilateral and that his resignation did not ask for approval. To the military ministers he explained that he could not govern "with this Congress." "Organize a military junta and run the country," he added.[8]

At Alvorada Palace he was joined by his wife and mother. Among the luggage, he did not forget to include the presidential sash. Before boarding the presidential Viscount and heading for São Paulo, he told Pedro Geraldo and José Aparecido that he was leaving with a clear conscience. "God is witness," he said, "to the efforts I have devoted to governing well, without hates or malice." Vargas-like he added: "At this moment I am thinking of the poor and humble. It is very difficult to help them."[9]

Quadros had insisted that his resignation was not to become known until 3:00 P.M. However, at 1:00 P.M. Pedroso d'Horta telephoned

[7] Ibid.

[8] Genival Rabelo, "O Inquérito," PN (Política & Negócios) Magazine, Rio de Janeiro, October 7, 1961, p. 20. See also Mário Victor, Cinco Anos que Abalaram o Brasil, p. 309.

[9] O Estado de S. Paulo, August 26, 1961.

São Paulo to advise Carvalho Pinto, who was considered to have persuaded Quadros to withdraw his resignation in 1959.

Interrupting his lunch with the federal Labor Minister and the governors of Minas, Paraná, and Goiás, Carvalho Pinto sped to Cumbica Air Base.[10] There Quadros explained why he could not continue. The governor asked whether the military had limited his authority. Quadros stressed that, on the contrary, the acts of the armed forces had been exemplary.

Later, when Carvalho Pinto brought the Labor Minister and the three other governors to the air base, they had to go through a cordon of soldiers. Quadros, installed with his wife in the office of the commander of the base, again refused to reconsider. He described the nation as "ungovernable."[11]

Castilho Cabral, seeking guidance for the Movimento Popular Jânio Quadros, could not get through the cordon of soldiers. But he managed to get a message from Jânio. This told him that Jânio had confidence in his "prudence" and that he should "act in accordance with his conscience."[12]

Labor Minister Castro Neves asked Quadros for instructions for unions, which were considering going on strike. "I do not want to assume the responsibility for setting the nation on fire," Quadros said.[13]

[10] José Bonifácio Coutinho Nogueira, interview, São Paulo, November 22, 1965.
[11] Nei Braga, interview, Rio de Janeiro, December 21, 1965.
[12] Carlos Castilho Cabral, *Tempos de Jânio e Outros Tempos*, p. 230.
[13] Carlos Castello Branco, "O Dia Seguinte," *Realidade*, II, no. 20 (November 1967).

11. Mazzilli Becomes Acting President
(August 25, 1961)

As it was Friday, only thirty-four *deputados* assembled in Brasília for the 2:00 P.M. session of the Chamber of Deputies. The speeches were critical of Lacerda.

At 3:00 P.M. Senate Vice-President Auro de Moura Andrade interrupted a discussion about the appointment of San Tiago Dantas to the United Nations to advise that Quadros had resigned. Moura Andrade, who had been at odds with Quadros, went on to say that he would meet with congressional leaders to determine what steps to take. He and José Maria Alkmim sent taxis and buses to the airport to gather up legislators who were about to leave for the weekend.

The lawmakers heard both of Quadros' messages. In the longer one, released by the presidential office at 3:00 P.M., Quadros followed the pattern given in Vargas' farewell letter. Quadros wrote:

I was beaten by the reaction, and therefore I leave the government. In these seven months I fulfilled my duty. I have fulfilled it day and night, working indefatigably without prejudice and without animosity. But I have been frustrated in my efforts to take the nation on the road of its true political and economic freedom, the only one which can bring about the effective progress and the social justice to which her generous people have a right.

I wanted a Brazil for the Brazilians, but in the case of this dream I faced corruption, lies and cowardice which subordinated the general interests to the appetites and the ambitions of individual groups, including foreign ones.

Therefore I find myself crushed. Terrible forces arose against me and plotted against me or maligned me, even on the pretext of collaborating. If I remain, it will not be possible to maintain confidence and tranquility, already broken but indispensable for exercising my authority.

I also believe that public peace itself cannot be maintained. Therefore, with my thought turned to our people, to the students and to the workers, to the large family of the Nation, I close this page of my life and of the national life. As for me, I do not lack the courage for resigning.

I leave with thanks and with an appeal. The thanks go to companions who struggled with me and sustained me in and out of government, and in a special form they go to the Armed Forces, whose exemplary conduct, in all moments, I take this opportunity to proclaim.

The appeal is on behalf of order, harmony, respect, and esteem by each of my fellow countrymen for all; and by all for each.

Only in this way will we be worthy of our heritage and our Christian predestination. I return now to my work of lawyer and teacher.

Let us work, all of us. There are many ways of serving our Nation.[1]

[1] *O Globo*, August 25, 1961.

Moura Andrade, presiding over a special joint session, reread Quadros' shorter message. Then he declared: "As you congressmen know, the act of resignation is a voluntary act, of which the National Congress should be apprised." In accordance with the constitution he declared that, as Goulart was abroad, Ranieri Mazzilli, president of the Chamber of Deputies, was Acting President of Brazil. Then about one hundred legislators proceeded to the Green Room of Planalto Palace to witness Mazzilli's assumption of his new post.

At the Cumbica Air Base, Quadros was shocked to learn that the military ministers had permitted the government to be turned over to Mazzilli. They were, Quadros knew, determined not to allow Goulart to reach the presidency. But, while Goulart's presence in Red China may have been a reminder of old complaints against him, his very absence from Brazil made it unnecessary for the military ministers to act quickly against the constitution, as Quadros apparently had expected them to do.

Lacerda proclaimed Quadros' resignation "lamentable" and desired by no one. When Leopoldina Railroad workers went on strike on behalf of Quadros, Lacerda called the strike illegal. It did not last long and there were few other organized demonstrations in support of the former President. The stunned nation was discussing Goulart and his rights.

Quadros' military ministers stayed on, whereas the resignations of the civilian ministers were accepted by Mazzilli. Afonso Arinos, leaving the Foreign Ministry to return to the Senate, warned Congress that if it did not reject Quadros' resignation the nation would become involved in a civil war. João Agripino, back in Congress after serving as Minister of Mines and Energy, eloquently defended Quadros. "An unusual man," he said of him, "an entirely unusual man." Quadros, Agripino revealed, had told him: "We shall carry out all the reforms and we shall carry them out all together and as quickly as possible." He had also said: "João, either they will throw us out within six months, or else we shall give this nation a great administration."[2]

Members of Quadros' staff, cleaning up the President's office, re-

[2] *O Estado de S. Paulo*, August 26, 1961.

moved the four portraits that had decorated it: pictures of Lincoln, Tito, Nasser, and Sukarno.

Quadros, after spending the night at the Cumbica Air Base, spoke to intimates about the inevitability of a spontaneous clamor returning him to the presidency. His return, he now conceded, might take more time than had been calculated: three months, one year, even two years. Then he added philosophically: "If it does not happen, the resignation is complete in itself. At least I shall leave a gesture. In a nation where no one resigns, I resigned four and a half years of the presidency."[3]

Quintanilha Ribeiro observed that it might begin to appear that Quadros was a prisoner at the base.[4] Therefore, later on the twenty-sixth, Quadros drove himself to the home of an industrialist at Guarujá Beach, near Santos. Newsmen caught the motoring former President at a ferryboat toll station.

"I was elected," said Quadros, "with the most solemn and public commitments which anyone has ever contracted with the people and, above all, with those humble comrades who suffer the most. I gave assurances that I would provide a good government, and God knows I tried. Nevertheless, the circumstances which developed—and I alluded to them in my letter of resignation—were making it impossible for me to take care of the anxieties of the Brazilians. I had no doubts. I preferred to leave rather than to disappoint those who believe in and struggle for a strong, rich, just, and free nation. Now I plan to travel for a while because my presence here might be prejudicial. My successor will need tranquility to face the terrible problems of our country and I do not intend in any way to disturb that tranquility nor to serve as a reason that it be disturbed. When I return I'll reorganize my office and devote myself to law and to teaching."[5]

Two days later he sailed for Europe from Santos. His wife, mother, daughter, son-in-law, and his new granddaughter, were already aboard the *Uruguay Star* when Quadros boarded by climbing a ladder on the

---

[3] Carlos Castello Branco, "O Dia Seguinte," *Realidade*, II, no. 20 (November 1967).

[4] Pedro Geraldo de Almeida, interview, Rio de Janeiro, November 4, 1965.

[5] *O Estado de S. Paulo*, August 27, 1961.

sea side of the ship. Before leaving Brazilian soil he used a local radio station to broadcast some last tearful words: "President Getúlio spoke well when he said: 'They send me away now, but I shall return.' Take note: the defeats have only been partial ones."[6]

[6] *Ibid.*, August 29, 1961.

BOOK V: *Goulart and the Parliamentary Regime*

"In the presidency, in a regime which gives full authority and personal power to the head of the government, João Goulart without any doubt would constitute the clearest stimulus to all who want to see the nation immersed in chaos, in anarchy, in civil strife. The armed forces themselves, infiltrated and controlled, would become transformed, as has happened in other countries, into simple Communist militias."

Manifesto of military ministers
August 30, 1961

1. The Military Ministers Veto Goulart's Return to Brazil

THE STRUGGLE over the fate of Goulart was so intense that Quadros' postresignation declarations were given little attention.

Quadros, invoking themes Vargas had used successfully, was alluding to "terrible forces" that had prevented him from defending the poor and the humble. But many dismissed him as a spoiled and unpredictable eccentric who drank too much and would not play ball unless he always had his own way. The *Tribuna da Imprensa* wrote that "It is licit to conclude that Jânio Quadros, with his resignation, sought to extend what he had done as a candidate: impose his personal will on the nation by threatening a catastrophe."[1]

[1] *Tribuna da Imprensa,* September 6, 1961. Immediately after Quadros' resignation *PN (Política & Negócios)* magazine polled around 2,200 people in Guanabara state (largely workers in commerce and industry and students). Asked to choose from among the following explanations of the resignation, those questioned were reported to have replied as shown (*PN,* October 7, 1961):

An effort to return as dictator	30.9%	Imposed by the armed forces	15.5%
Pressure of foreign forces	18.2%	A display of craziness	10.0%
Cowardice in the face of pressures	16.4%	The result of illness	7.1%

Some replies gave "other reasons" or "reason unknown."

The Left found itself with a new battle and a less austere hero, Jango Goulart. It also found itself on the side of legality and made the most of this popular issue.

Marshal Lott spoke out for *legalidade*. Calling in representatives of the press in Rio on August 25, he declared that any acts of the military against the inauguration of Goulart would constitute a calamity and should be resisted by all. In such a situation, he said, he would not hesitate to play a part in defending the constitution.[2]

But the military ministers—Denys, Heck, and Grün Moss—advised Mazzilli of their veto against Goulart and hoped that Congress would act against the Vice-President as it had against Carlos Luz and Café Filho. Lott telephoned Brasília in an unsuccessful attempt to get Denys to change his mind[3] and then issued a manifesto calling on all the active forces in Brazil, including his military comrades, to protect the constitution and defend Brazilian democracy.

For this Lott was imprisoned in the rocky island fortress of Lage. For sharing his view other military officers were also jailed. Among them were over thirty Air Force officers who, like Brigadeiro Francisco Teixeira, had been active when Correia de Melo was Kubitschek's last Air Minister but had been allowed no posts under Grün Moss. A prison ship served for those with the rank of colonel or lower.

Among the dailies, *O Estado de S. Paulo* and the *Tribuna da Imprensa* were almost alone in backing the military ministers. Over the weekend the National Union of Students called a strike in defense of Goulart and "legality." To do their part on behalf of Goulart, an informal Labor Strike Command (Comando de Greve dos Trabalhadores) was set up by those who, a year earlier at the Third Trade Union Congress, had upset anti-Communists by fighting for an overall labor organization. Directors of the new CGT included non-Communists who were working with Communists against the anti-Communist leadership of most of the labor confederations. Despite its impressive title, this CGT was not very successful in organizing pro-Goulart strikes.

---

[2] *O Estado de S. Paulo*, August 26, 1961.
[3] Nelson Werneck Sodré, *História Militar do Brasil*, p. 376.

Goulart's loudest supporter was his brother-in-law, Leonel Brizola, governor of Rio Grande do Sul. "I can accept," Brizola said "no coup d'état. There was a scheme under way and its objectives were against the aims not only of Jânio Quadros but also of João Goulart." In explosive radio broadcasts, which he called "The Voice of Legality," Brizola blasted the military ministers.

On Monday, August 28, Congress made it clear that it would not declare Goulart *impedido*. It sent a warm message to Lott, who had been transferred, still a prisoner, to Fort Santa Cruz.

The UDN affirmed the principles it had proclaimed in Congress in November 1955. Aliomar Baleeiro declared: "I do not think Goulart will be a good President. But it is the duty of all Brazilians to guarantee him the right to assume the position."[4] Adauto Lúcio Cardoso, another prominent UDN congressman, asserted that Mazzilli and the military ministers were criminals, guilty of violating the constitution. The PTB's leftist congressional leader, Almino Afonso, described as "inexplicable" any reasons some military sectors might have had for opposing the constitution. The only reason that appeared in the press by the twenty-eighth was Denys' statement that "the situation obliges us to choose between democracy and Communism, and the armed forces have already decided: they will carry on to the end in the defense of our democratic traditions."[5]

On August 28 Congress received Mazzilli's formal message advising that the military ministers, "responsible for internal order," found it "absolutely inconvenient, for reasons of national security, that Vice-President João Belchior Marques Goulart return to the country."[6] Moura Andrade, opposed to the position taken by the military ministers, named a commission of six senators and six congressmen to report on Mazzilli's message.

Deputado Rui Ramos, heading a column of a dozen frenzied Gaúcho congressmen, advanced into the Chamber with his arm extended, and

---

[4] Statement, Rio de Janeiro, August 25, 1961, in *O Estado de S. Paulo*, August 26, 1961.

[5] *O Estado de S. Paulo*, August 28, 1961.

[6] *Ibid.*, August 29, 1961.

roared "Viva a Constituição! Viva a Legalidade! Viva a Democracia!"[7]
He cried out that Denys had just sought to "massacre the governor of
Rio Grande do Sul, ordering the Commander of the Third Army to assault the Government Palace and assassinate Governor Leonel Brizola."[8]

Ramos also made the startling announcement that Third Army
Commander José Machado Lopes had adhered to Brizola and "legality." Then the *deputado* asserted that if Mazzilli failed to jail Denys
within forty-eight hours, he and other legislators would either capture
Denys or die in the attempt.

On the next day, August 29, the Third Army chief of staff came
from Pôrto Alegre to Rio to announce that "the news that the military
garrison of Rio Grande do Sul adheres to Governor Brizola is completely unfounded." Nevertheless, it was clear that Brizola was putting
his state on a war footing. Besides calling for a general strike by
Pôrto Alegre dock workers, he was taking steps to prevent the Navy
from reaching the state. An admiral reported that the governor was
removing all nautical markings from Lagoa dos Patos, the large lagoon
that gives access to Pôrto Alegre.

Congressmen were presented with numerous suggestions for modifying the constitution and thus breaking the deadlock created by the
disagreement between the military ministers and the congressional majority. All these formulae, their sponsors pointed out, would be perfectly "legal" if voted by two-thirds of the members of the Chamber
of Deputies and two-thirds of the senators. *O Estado de S. Paulo* proposed an amendment that would have prevented Goulart from reaching the presidency.

The most favored amendment would have allowed Goulart to become President but would have reduced his powers under a parliamen-

---

[7] *Ibid.*

[8] In 1961 (unlike 1955) Brazil was divided by the Army into areas of four "Ar-
mies." The First (formerly the Eastern Military Zone) had its headquarters in Rio de
Janeiro, the Second (formerly the Central Military Zone) in São Paulo, the Third in
Pôrto Alegre, and the Fourth in Recife. Each of the first three Armies included two
"Military Regions," and the Fourth included three "Military Regions." The Third and
First Armies had more men than the others.

tary system of the European type. For years the adoption of a parliamentary form of government had been seriously considered by Brazilian congressmen. Parliamentarianism was well regarded by a growing bloc in the powerful PSD,[9] and the father of the idea, the PL's aging Raul Pilla, had seen the possibility of having his dream come true by an absolute majority vote two years in a row.[10]

Afonso Arinos de Melo Franco, past secretary of a congressional commission that had studied the matter, had originally opposed the parliamentary system; later, considering political events in Brazil in the 1950's, he had become an advocate of the change.[11] As he relaxed at Petrópolis on August 26, 1961, after seven strenuous months in the Foreign Ministry, he decided that the national crisis could be overcome by adopting the system. Many felt the same way. Nor had Quadros done anything to prevent congressmen from believing that they should play a larger role in the affairs of the Executive. Some blamed the presidential system for the crisis and observed that a parliamentary system would prevent the nation from being "at the mercy of the personalities of its leaders."

Armed Forces Chief of Staff Cordeiro de Farias, full of formulae, was rushing between Brasília and Rio. At Rio's Santos Dumont Airport on August 27, he heard Afonso Arinos' thought concerning parliamentary reform, agreed with it, and sent him posthaste in a military airplane to work on it in Brasília.[12]

At this point Goulart, traveling from Hong Kong, reached Paris. In press conferences Goulart stressed his "democratic ideals" and the importance of Brazil's "maintaining itself within legal order." It would be his duty, he said, to govern in accordance with the constitution, with

---

[9] Ernâni do Amaral Peixoto, interview, Brasília, October 15, 1965.

[10] Raul Pilla, interview, Brasília, October 13, 1965. The 1946 constitution, according to its Article 217, could be amended provided that the amendment be approved either (1) by two-thirds of the congressmen and by two-thirds of the senators; or (2) by an absolute majority of congressmen, and an absolute majority of senators, in two consecutive ordinary legislative sessions.

[11] Afonso Arinos de Melo Franco and Raul Pilla, *Presidencialismo ou Parlamentarismo*, pp. ix–xxiv.

[12] Afonso Arinos de Melo Franco, interview, Brasília, October 14, 1965.

the help of all political parties, and "above any personal sentiments."[13]

Goulart spent much of August 28 and 29 on the telephone in his Paris hotel room, receiving the conflicting opinions of Brazilian political leaders. Although he revealed his inclination to listen to many views before acting, he also showed himself to be a man who knows what he wants. San Tiago Dantas, the PTB's influential intellectual who was planning to run for the Minas governorship, was full of advice. He urged Goulart to resign to avoid the military's installing a "tyranny." To save Congress, he even expressed the belief that the PTB *deputados* should vote against Goulart's becoming President. Upon receiving this advice, Goulart, the color drained from his face, replied that he was "going to Brazil to take over as President. The *deputados* must vote as their consciences dictate. Their votes will be on record for the nation."[14]

PTB leaders Almino Afonso and Wilson Fadul disagreed with San Tiago Dantas. Fadul asserted that the Army barracks in his state of Mato Grosso favored Goulart's becoming President, and he suggested that Goulart make no decision for forty-eight hours.[15] On the other hand, Samuel Wainer, who was running the pro-Goulart *Última Hora,* suggested that Goulart refrain from seeking the presidency.

Afonso Arinos de Melo Franco and San Tiago Dantas heard Goulart say that, to end the crisis, he would accept a solution provided it would not cause him any loss of status.[16] Although this was not an acceptance of the parliamentary system, its advocates interpreted Goulart's words as being useful for their purpose.

The calls reaching Goulart's hotel room on the twenty-ninth were agitated. Brizola described "the generals" as threatening to bombard himself and his family in the Pôrto Alegre governor's palace, from

[13] This announcement was made by Senator Camillo Nogueira da Gama (PTB—Minas) when asked by reporters about the telephone conversations between Brasília and Paris (*O Estado de S. Paulo,* August 29, 1961).

[14] João Etcheverry, interview, Rio de Janeiro, October 3, 1968.

[15] Wilson Fadul, interview, Rio de Janeiro, November 1, 1967.

[16] Goulart said that the solution should not cause him any *diminuição moral* (Afonso Arinos de Melo Franco, interview Brasília, October 14, 1965).

which he was speaking, unless he agreed that Goulart not become President. But, said Brizola, "I shall not yield. The Brazilian people will rise up, and the military will reconsider." Kubitschek, telephoning from Rio, said: "Jango, for the love of God do not return to Brazil. This would be the most terrible of civil wars. . . . You must resign." Coldly Goulart thanked Juscelino for his call. "Tell your friends," he said, "that I shall not abdicate."[17]

In Brasília on the twenty-ninth, the congressional committee, appointed to study the position of the military ministers, rejected the veto. Although the military ministers repeated that they would not accept Goulart's return under any circumstances, the congressional committee on August 30 approved the suggestion of its secretary that a parliamentary form of government be adopted.[18] That evening the Senate unanimously, and the Chamber of Deputies by a vote of 299 to 14, resolved that on August 31 they would consider amending the constitution.

The military ministers then released a manifesto to acquaint the public with "some of their many reasons" for the veto. Mention was made of Goulart's term as Vargas' Labor Minister, when "active and well-known agents of international Communism" had infiltrated the ministry and the unions. As Labor Minister, and later as Vice-President, Goulart (the manifesto said) had, for obvious political reasons, promoted continual turmoil in union circles which was harmful to the true interests of the working classes. Recently in the Soviet Union and Communist China he had made clear his unrestrained admiration for the regimes of those nations. The military ministers stressed the dangers to Brazil at a time of international tension, when international Communism was intervening in the life of democratic nations, particularly the weak ones. In the presidency, "in a regime which gives full authority and personal power to the Head of the Government," the armed forces themselves, as had happened in other countries, would

---

[17] From article by Paul Grégor in *France Soir*, September 2, 1961, reproduced (in Portuguese) in *Novos Rumos*, Rio de Janeiro, September 15–21, 1961.

[18] Antônio Ferreira de Oliveira Brito, interview, Brasília, October 20, 1965.

become so infiltrated that they would become "simple Communist militias."[19]

[19] Manifesto of the military ministers, August 30, 1961, in José Stacchini, *Março 64: Mobilização da Audácia*, pp. 132–134.

2. The Crisis is Resolved (September 1961)

A GENERAL, secretary of the National Security Council, asked Lacerda's state government to impose press censorship.[1] But the great white gaps, which Carioca readers soon found in their newspapers, did nothing to diminish the talk about impending civil war.

One item, which Rio newspapers were allowed to print, reported that the aircraft carrier, *Minas Gerais,* was steaming to the south, where Brizola's inflaming *Voz da Legalidade* cried for Rio Grande do Sul's defense against invasion. In official circles it was admitted that Brizola was disturbing the peace. Failure of the armed forces to silence Brizola was attributed to a desire to avoid bloodshed.[2]

That the Third Army's General Machado Lopes was, in fact, adhering to Brizola's position became clear on August 30 when Marshal Denys told Mazzilli that he was firing the general and ordering Cordeiro de Farias to arrest him and take his place. In the city of Rio de Janeiro, a safe distance from Pôrto Alegre, nervous Cordeiro de Farias took command of the Third Army. Thereupon Machado Lopes imprisoned five Third Army officers and wired the War Minister that Cordeiro de Farias would be imprisoned if he set foot in Pôrto Alegre.

The commander of the Fifth Air Zone, also in the south, was dismissed by Air Minister Grün Moss, but this officer kept on with his

[1] On September 2, 1961, Guanabara Police Chief Hélio Tornaghi declared that neither he nor Lacerda had been responsible for the press censorship or prison sentences.

[2] Statement of Casa Militar Chief Ernesto Geisel, Brasília, August 28, 1961 (see *O Estado de S. Paulo*, August 30, 1961).

work, helping the Third Army prepare the Pôrto Alegre airport against the arrival of Cordeiro. Machine gun nests were installed. Army troops from throughout the state were brought into Pôrto Alegre.

Brizola called on the entire Gaúcho population to defend Rio Grande do Sul and legality. Banks, including the Bank of Brazil, moved funds out of the state, whereupon the state government issued two billion cruzeiros in small denominational notes, which were used as money and known as *brizoletas*.

Brizola and his military allies in Rio Grande do Sul were encouraged by a number of declarations made elsewhere. Although the First Army, with well-armed units in Guanabara, was reported firm in supporting Denys, some Army men between Rio de Janeiro and the far south showed reluctance to march against Brizola. The Second Army, with headquarters in São Paulo, issued a note favorable to legality and to reaching peacefully a compromise formula (as advocated by Governor Carvalho Pinto). A pronouncement by the Fifth Military Region, embracing Paraná and Santa Catarina, expressed "loyalty and obedience" to the Third Army, which has jurisdiction over all three southern states.

On the following days Gaúcho soldiers were so active "defending" their state that some of them marched into Santa Catarina and took a small town from the control of the Marines. Navy men, retreating to Florianópolis, the capital of Santa Catarina, dynamited three bridges. After the Marines requested an order to allow them to attack the invaders, Navy Minister Heck declared that the armed forces had decided that "clashes should be avoided and attacks should be resisted." Cordeiro de Farias, signing bulletins in Rio as "Commander of the Third Army," announced that the "legalist" troops in the disputed area "have orders to defend themselves at the positions they occupy. Should there be armed clashes, General Machado Lopes will be responsible before the armed forces as the initiator of the fratricidal struggle."[3]

While the military ministers worried about defections in the south, most civilians opposed their position.[4] Many who had not voted for

---

[3] *O Estado de S. Paulo*, September 5, 1961.

[4] Thomas E. Skidmore, *Politics in Brazil, 1930–1964: An Experiment in Democracy*, p. 213.

Goulart believed that the case for violating the constitution was not convincing.

Goulart continued his return trip. Before leaving Paris for New York on August 30, he opened his shirt to show a medallion of the Virgin Mary. "Have you ever seen any real Communist wearing things like this?" he asked his interviewer.[5] His flight to Buenos Aires was carried out from the west of the United States so that he would not be over Brazilian soil and subject to the charge of leaving Brazil without congressional approval—something Brazilian Presidents cannot do.[6] From Buenos Aires a special airplane took him to Montevideo late on August 31.

In Brasília that afternoon, Rui Ramos, the Gaúcho PTB *deputado* who had first advised Congress of the position of General Machado Lopes, made another dramatic speech. The military ministers, he said, had met early that morning and decided to accept the decision of Congress for solving the crisis. Ramos went on to describe how, on August 30, Amauri Kruel and some other generals in Rio had delegated General João Segadas Viana, at the top of the hierarchy, to tell Denys that they had decided to support whatever solution Congress might choose and that they did not agree with what they had read in the press about the military ministers' suspicions of Goulart. These generals, Ramos reported, included Osvino Ferreira Alves, Amauri Kruel, Nelson de Melo, and Idalio Sardenberg. Ramos said that the resulting resolution of the military ministers to accept the decision of Congress was being made known to Mazzilli.

Another *deputado* went to the rostrum to say: "Were we not in a regime of complete abnormality, anarchy, and disorder, it would be incomprehensible that the Chamber receive so important a communication from a *deputado*. Where are the cabinet ministers? Where is the President?"[7]

Denys did not deny Ramos' story. Instead, he and Heck and Grün Moss met at the War Ministry in Rio late on the thirty-first with a

[5] João Goulart, quoted in issue of *Candide* magazine, which went into circulation August 30, 1961.

[6] João Etcheverry, interview, Rio de Janeiro, October 3, 1968.

[7] *O Estado de S. Paulo*, September 1, 1961.

group of state governors. The military ministers sought to avoid direct contacts with Congress, lest pressure be alleged, and they felt that the governors might mediate, if necessary, between them and Congress. The governors, concerned about who the future Prime Minister might be, suggested Juraci Magalhães, Magalhães Pinto, and Carvalho Pinto.[8] These names, associated with the UDN, were not likely to command great strength in Congress. Juraci Magalhães, an early supporter of Goulart's right to the presidency, said that popular feeling in his state of Bahia backed Goulart. Lacerda, a UDN governor who felt differently, opposed both Goulart and the parliamentary form of government.

Kubitschek, hoping to be elected President in 1965, disliked the parliamentary system. When a military dictatorship or civil war seemed possible he did some quiet work on behalf of the compromise, but later he was reported to be expressing his opposition to it in talks with Mazzilli, Catholic Church leaders, and others. His party, the PSD, having the largest bloc in Congress, saw the parliamentary system as a method of recovering control of the Executive. A large majority of congressmen simply considered the proposed amendment an easy way to settle the crisis.

This majority included San Tiago Dantas, but he was supported by only a small group in his own party. Most of the PTB's sixty-six congressmen agreed with leader Almino Afonso, who maintained that installation of a new form of government represented a *golpe*, or coup by traditional antireform conservative forces.[9] Whenever Almino Afonso tried to telephone Goulart in Montevideo, the connection was cut.

For a while Almino Afonso and his group doubted the reported strength of the military movement in Rio Grande do Sul. They sent Deputado Luís Fernando Bocaiuva Cunha to check. After talking with such pro-Goulart generals as Machado Lopes and Peri Constant Bevilaqua, Bocaiuva Cunha returned to Brasília convinced that Goulart could successfully resist the implantation of a parliamentary form of

[8] Tancredo Neves, interview, Rio de Janeiro, October 7, 1965.
[9] Almino Afonso, interviews, Santiago, Chile, June 26 and 28, 1967.

government.[10] Bocaiuva Cunha, Almino Afonso, and other members of the PTB's leftist Grupo Compacto (Compact Group) correctly judged that only Congress could prevent Goulart from heading Brazil under a presidential system. The military ministers themselves realized that they lacked backing not only in large ranks of the Army but also among intellectuals, the clergy, and the press.[11] Much of organized labor could also be expected to back Goulart.

PSD president Amaral Peixoto did not have Almino Afonso's difficulty in telephoning Goulart in Montevideo. He explained to Goulart that Congress was not going to impeach him but that a compromise was necessary and that the best one would be a parliamentary form of government. Goulart, who might have led an effective march from the south, decided to avoid possible bloodshed. He asked Amaral Peixoto to try to convince Brizola of the usefulness of the compromise.[12]

Because Amaral Peixoto was too busy to accept Mazzilli's invitation to go to Montevideo to see Goulart, the PSD's Tancredo Neves was sent as the government's envoy. Neves had served with Goulart in the last Vargas cabinet and in 1960 had been beaten for the Minas governorship by Magalhães Pinto.

Almino Afonso felt that the airplane taking Tancredo Neves should carry a spokesman of the PTB's ideas. He asked, therefore, that Wilson Fadul accompany Neves and carry a letter advising Goulart not to accept implantation of the parliamentary system. But the airplane left without Almino Afonso or Fadul being advised, and they continued unable to telephone Goulart.

Tancredo Neves, commissioned to get Goulart's acceptance of the compromise, explained to Goulart in Montevideo on September 1 that the system about to be enacted by the Brazilian Congress would not deprive him of much of the traditional presidential power.[13] Neves considered the proposed structure a "hybrid" one. But Goulart said

[10] Luís Fernando Bocaiuva Cunha, interview, Rio de Janeiro, December 5, 1968.
[11] Gabriel Grün Moss, interview, Rio de Janeiro, December 4, 1968.
[12] Ernâni do Amaral Peixoto, interview, Brasília, October 15, 1965.
[13] Neves, interview, October 7, 1965.

that he would never stop fighting for his rights as conferred by the presidential system.

PSD and UDN leaders in Brasília knew that Brizola opposed "capitulating" to the compromise. They let it be known, therefore, that a stopover by Goulart in turbulent Rio Grande do Sul would give his return an "inconvenient revolutionary savor." He was, they said, to remain in Montevideo for forty-eight hours, while the situation "cleared," and then to come directly to Brasília. But Goulart told Tancredo Neves and former Labor Minister Hugo Farias, who also visited him in Montevideo, that he could not agree. Brizola had telephoned him to say that his presence in Rio Grande do Sul would contribute to an immediate solution. Already, Goulart told Neves and Farias, thousands of Gaúchos had come to Montevideo to accompany him on a triumphant trip to Pôrto Alegre.

PTB leaders in Brasília sought to include in the constitutional amendment a clause to provide that a plebiscite be held in 1963 to let the people determine whether to continue with the new form of government. After this suggestion was voted down, most of the PTB supported Almino Afonso in trying to block the amendment. However, nineteen PTB *deputados* "defected": they followed San Tiago Dantas and helped provide the two-thirds of the Câmara membership of 326 which was necessary for amending the constitution. The vote on September 2 was 236 for and 55 against giving Brazil a parliamentary form of government. The Senate agreed to institute the new system by a margin of 48 to 6 (Kubitschek voting against). According to this amendment, the fourth to the 1946 constitution, Congress might decide to hold a plebiscite, in which case it should take place nine months before the end of Goulart's term.[14]

Fernando Ferrari, who had opposed Goulart in the 1960 election, delivered a prophecy when he explained his vote against the parliamentary form of government. Disagreeing with jurists who said that the new system would end the unrest in Brazil, he called it an artificial remedy that would increase tension. He pointed out that it was unfair

[14] Article 25 of Amendment No. 4 to the 1946 constitution.

to Goulart and that, when he (Ferrari) and others had tried to enact a parliamentary regime in the 1950's, all had agreed that such a change should be introduced only upon the conclusion of the term of office of whoever had been popularly elected under the presidential system.[15]

[15] *O Estado de S. Paulo*, September 3, 1961.

3. Tancredo Neves Becomes Prime Minister (September 1961)

On the evening of September 1, Goulart, Brizola, and General Machado Lopes appeared on a balcony of the Governor's Palace in Pôrto Alegre. Brizola and Machado Lopes raised a Brazilian flag to the top of the palace mast, while a military band struck up the national anthem. A great mob in the square below acclaimed Goulart President of Brazil.

Twenty-four hours later, Goulart, still in Pôrto Alegre, was advised that the constitutional amendment had been enacted. He issued a statement saying that he would study it and adding that he had not contributed to bringing on the crisis. For support given him, he expressed his gratitude to the press and the people, "especially my companions of Rio Grande do Sul, resolute under the leadership of Brizola and José Machado Lopes and his commanders of the Third Army."[1]

Although Goulart announced that he expected to go to Brasília within a few hours, he had to wait several days. A commission of congressmen, preparing to leave Brasília on Sunday, September 3, to join Goulart and escort him to the capital, found it could not make the trip. Grün Moss had closed the Brasília airport, advising Mazzilli that the Air Force was in no position to guarantee any flight between Brasília and Pôrto Alegre in view of the outbreak of a "subversive movement" among Air Force officers. Some of the most rebellious of these had developed a plan, known as Operação Mosquito, to cap-

[1] *O Estado de S. Paulo*, September 2, 1961.

ture Goulart by forcing a landing of the airplane that was to bring him to Brasília.[2]

Among the precautionary measures taken by the Air Ministry was the suspension of all VARIG domestic flights. Finally, early on September 5, the military ministers felt able to guarantee Goulart's trip and investiture.

When Goulart reached Brasília that evening he found that the crowd, which had come to greet him at the airport, had been turned away. Surrounded by soldiers, he was met by Mazzilli and other dignitaries and was driven to Granja do Torto, one of the government-owned model farms used as residences of top officials. Goulart had lived there when he was Vice-President, and he planned to continue to use it, preferring its rustic atmosphere to Alvorada Palace.

The inauguration was scheduled for Independence Day, September 7. Goulart, conferring with politicians and labor leaders at Granja do Torto and at his Senate office, was described by his foes as affected by the "climate of Pôrto Alegre" and as behaving with disregard for the parliamentary system. Antônio Balbino, reportedly Goulart's choice to head the presidential Casa Civil, was at work on the sixth, dealing with legislators in the name of Goulart. Some objected that Balbino, a former Vargas cabinet minister, was invading areas that should have been reserved for the future Council of Ministers and Prime Minister. At the same time Goulart was making decisions about the cabinet.

Since the Prime Minister would have to be a member of the largest party, Goulart presented three PSD names for the legislators of that party to choose from. Auro de Moura Andrade, who had opposed the military veto and done much to help Goulart, believed that Goulart had a commitment to him. Although Goulart neither wanted him nor felt he had any commitment, he presented his name, thus including a Paulista. The other two names were Mineiros: Gustavo Capanema and Tancredo Neves.

Capanema, the only *deputado* among the three, had long served Vargas and was well-liked in the PSD. Approached by Tancredo

[2] Tancredo Neves, interview, Rio de Janeiro, October 7, 1965. Dr. Neves described Operação Mosquito as "more than a rumor."

Neves, Balbino, and San Tiago Dantas, he agreed to serve as Prime Minister and drew up a cabinet that included Neves and San Tiago Dantas.[3]

But Kubitschek preferred Neves. Goulart, reflecting on his Montevideo conversations and his past relations with Neves, agreed with Kubitschek. Neves, who had once headed the PSD-PTB assemblymen in the Minas state legislature, was acceptable to Goulart's PTB. Vargas, before committing suicide, had given Goulart a copy of his farewell message, and he had given Neves, his loyal Justice Minister, the gold pen with which he had signed it. Goulart, about to be inaugurated President, spoke to friends about his own lack of *intimidade* (intimacy) with Capanema.

On the afternoon of September 7, Goulart appeared before a joint session of Congress and promised to defend and carry out the constitution. In what was considered an appeal for a plebiscite, he stressed that "we must now get a mandate from the people, faithful to the basic precept that all power emanates from them."[4]

The PSD legislators then met on the twenty-fifth floor of the congressional office building. When Moura Andrade came out in third place on the first ballot, his name was dropped. On the second ballot the PSD chose Tancredo Neves ahead of Capanema.

The political commentator of *O Estado de S. Paulo* wrote that "the choice of Tancredo Neves was the first fruit of the conspiracy hatched by João Goulart and Juscelino Kubitschek against the parliamentary system. The candidate of the PSD directorship was Gustavo Capanema. . . . The selection of the Mineiro who used to be minister of Vargas, and who is a man identified with the worst groups of the PTB, stamps the new government with a stigma of a state of affairs which was surmounted and beaten in the ballot boxes—a state of affairs to which there belonged, besides João Goulart himself, men like Antônio Balbino and General Amauri Kruel."[5]

Some members of the UDN disliked collaborating with the new administration, but a majority felt otherwise and the opposition party

[3] Gustavo Capanema, interview, Brasília, October 23, 1965.
[4] João Goulart, *Desenvolvimento e Independência: Discursos, 1961*, p. 10.
[5] *O Estado de S. Paulo,* September 8, 1961.

received two cabinet posts. One of these went to Gabriel Passos, a Mineiro who had long attacked Tancredo Neves and Kubitschek. His appointment as Minister of Mines and Energy pleased Governor Magalhães Pinto and the Frente Parlamentar Nacionalista (Nationalist Parliamentary Front). San Tiago Dantas, the PTB Mineiro who improved his standing with Goulart by helping persuade Magalhães Pinto to accept Tancredo Neves as Prime Minister, became Foreign Minister. His former post, head of the Brazilian delegation to the United Nations, went to Afonso Arinos de Melo Franco.

Military ministers Denys, Heck, and Grün Moss were not encouraged to stay on. Goulart's close friend, Amauri Kruel, became chief of the Casa Militar. Segadas Viana, who had also opposed the veto against Goulart, became War Minister.

4. Experimenting with the New System

GOULART, a person of charm, was forty-three when he became President of Brazil. His leg injury, causing a limp, seemed to add to the affection in which many held him. In dealing with men he was inclined to be gentle and friendly, and the nation could assume that he would neither push for austerity nor wield the anticorruption broom. Despite the attainment of wealth and high position, Goulart remained a person who put the common man at ease. He was happy when he could watch his cattle fatten.

Blessed with an alert mind, he was also known to be a good listener —so good that some had reported him to be a timid conversationalist. But he could speak fluently about matters that interested him. These for long had included labor politics, and it was said that in his work he had come to know the head of every *sindicato* (union) in Brazil.

His desire to hear many opinions before acting was described as a sign of prudence and caution. Many, on giving advice to the good listener, received the impression that he was agreeing with them. Later they would be likely to say that Goulart was not one to take advice.

He was determined to play a very positive role. Upon assuming the presidency one of his primary purposes was to bring an end to the parliamentary system, which he did not consider useful. This purpose should be remembered when interpreting much that occurred during the first phase of Goulart's presidency. Goulart was little influenced by Raul Pilla, who told him that he would be rendering Brazil a great service if he would seek to make the new system work. Pilla saw some problems, particularly since President Goulart had not been chosen by Congress but by a popular election for the vice-presidency.[1]

The new amendment supported by Pilla declared that Presidents were to be elected to five-year terms by Congress. The office of Vice-President was abolished. The amendment provided that "every act" of the President had to be approved by the Prime Minister and the particular minister who was concerned with the matter. The Prime Minister and each member of the cabinet (Council of Ministers) were to retain their posts only as long as Congress approved. The cabinet, which was to reach decisions by majority vote, was responsible to Congress and was to carry on only as long as it had the confidence of Congress. With the fall of a Prime Minister, the President was to suggest a new name to Congress. Should this nomination be rejected and be followed by two more unacceptable presidential suggestions, the Senate was to make the nominations.[2] Should three consecutive Councils of Ministers fall, due to congressional votes of no confidence, the President could dissolve Congress and call for a new congressional election. The undersecretaries were to run the ministries during intervals when no Council of Ministers existed.

In practice Goulart found that he could name the president of the Bank of Brazil, could exert influence in labor unions, and could switch generals around. In these respects the new system did not seem to be the "strait jacket" some of Goulart's foes had hoped it would be. But it seemed an obstacle to the fuller powers expressed in the words "presidential President." Goulart deeply resented its implementation at the moment he took office. Nor was he pleased with newspaper cartoons showing him in the dress of the Queen of England.

[1] Raul Pilla, interview, Brasília, October 13, 1965.
[2] José Loureiro Júnior, *Parlamentarismo e Presidencialismo,* p. 56.

Quadros, in his farewell message, had referred to factors he said had been preventing him from realizing great achievements. Goulart could blame failure on the parliamentary system, and he could do so quite convincingly. Although Tancredo Neves worked conscientiously, the new arrangements made it more difficult than ever for the Brazilian Executive to provide leadership. Decisions, it was found, depended on the approval of various people who generally had different ideas and were sometimes antagonists. Making decisions became such a slow process that on the domestic front nothing of importance was settled during the Tancredo Neves ministry. In the meantime the rate of inflation increased, due in part to self-generating qualities.

A leading engineer asserted that the Ministry of Mines was becoming a Communist entity. The UDN Mines Minister, who continued antagonistic to the Prime Minister, was not a favorite with the Brazilian Communist Party (PCB).[3] He was simply more interested in promoting "nationalism" than in distinguishing between Communists and non-Communist "far leftists." It was not an easy distinction to make.

[3] In August 1961 the Prestes-led Moscow-line Partido Comunista do Brasil (Communist Party of Brazil) changed its name to Partido Comunista Brasileiro (Brazilian Communist Party). Then some Brazilian Communists, critical of Prestes and Moscow and sympathetic to the more violent ideas of Red China, organized a group that called itself the Partido Comunista do Brasil (PC do B) and claimed to be carrying on the former party (see Appendix, section 3). The initials PCB are used to denote the Moscow-line Party both before and after August 1961.

5. Establishing the CGT (General Labor Command)

GOULART AND Marxist Francisco Julião, disorganized leader of many peasant leagues, were the principal speakers at the Peasant Congress held in Belo Horizonte in November 1961 and sponsored by the Brazilian Communist Party, which was no longer friendly to large landowners. Authentic peasants and their bickering would-be leaders, with a few "progressive" priests, adopted the slogan: "We Want

Land by Law or by Force." They hailed the President when he called for a constitutional reform to allow a radical redistribution of land.

At the same time Goulart was playing a role in the most significant occurrence of the Tancredo Neves ministry—the December 1961 biennial election of officers of the Confederação Nacional dos Trabalhadores na Indústria (CNTI). The CNTI, representing between two and three million workers (less than half of them union members), was the largest of Brazil's five labor confederations. It was considerably larger than the Confederação Nacional dos Trabalhadores no Comércio (CNTC), which in turn was larger than any of the three more recently formed confederations.[1]

The outcome of the CNTI election was also considered important in labor circles outside of Brazil. Such anti-Communist international organizations as the ICFTU (International Confederation of Free Trade Unions) and its hemispheric affiliate, ORIT (Inter-American Regional Organization of Workers), followed the clash with concern. Each of Brazil's fifty-odd industrial labor federations had one vote, regardless of size. The contest was heated, with the usual charges about job offers and about the use of money.

While Goulart had presided over organized labor as Kubitschek's Vice-President, a policy of coexistence between Communists and non-Communists had generally been in effect. Leadership of the three most important confederations (CNTI, CNTC, and CNTTT) had remained in anti-Communist hands; at the same time most of the informal (non-legal) horizontal organizations, such as Guanabara's CPOS (Comissão Permanente de Organizações Sindicais), had been Communist inspired and controlled. This peaceful coexistence had come to an abrupt end at

---

[1] The five labor confederations are designated as follows: *Founded*

CNTI	National Confederation of Workers in Industry	October 1946
CNTC	National Confederation of Workers in Commerce	November 1946
CNTTT	National Confederation of Workers in Land Transport	February 1953
CONTEC	National Confederation of Workers in Credit Establishments	August 1959
CNTTMFA	National Confederation of Workers in Maritime, River, and Air Transport	June 1960

the Third Trade Union Congress of August 1960, when anti-Communist confederation heads had dramatically walked out, complaining that aggressive Communists were using unfair tactics and false credentials. Goulart had been unable to persuade the anti-Communists to make concessions on behalf of labor unity, and the congress had closed in a disunified atmosphere satisfactory to such Communist labor leaders as Roberto Morena (longtime advocate of an over-all labor organization), Osvaldo Pacheco, Rafael Martineli, and Luís Tenório de Lima. The battle had then been started to dislodge anti-Communist Deocleciano de Holanda Cavalcanti from the CNTI presidency, a post he had held for fourteen years.

Deocleciano believed that even if he were re-elected in December 1961, the Goulart administration would not allow him to take office. He declined, therefore, to head the anti-Communist ("democratic") slate again.[2] The opposing slate, favored by Goulart and actively supported by presidential labor affairs adviser Gilberto Crockatt de Sá, was led by Clodsmidt Riani, non-Communist friend of Goulart from Minas. This slate, which believed in coexistence with Communists, has been described by graphic worker Dante Pelacani as determined to give the CNTI a "renovating" leadership.[3] Pelacani was on the slate headed by Riani.

The trouble with Riani, said Deocleciano's friends, was that he had been playing the game exactly as the Communists wanted. Particularly memorable was Riani's role in 1960 at the Third Trade Union Congress. After congress President Deocleciano had tearfully walked out with other confederation heads, Riani had stepped forward to preside over the majority of delegates who decided to remain at the congress. "Nationalistic" resolutions, poorly regarded by ORIT and the American Embassy, had then been adopted; also approved was the motion calling for the formation of a single trade union center (*central sindical*).

In the election of December 1961 the Riani-Pelacani wing won control of the huge industrial workers' confederation by a vote of twenty-

---

[2] Deocleciano de Holanda Cavalcanti, interview, Rio de Janeiro, December 18, 1968.

[3] Dante Pelacani, interview, São Paulo, November 24, 1968.

nine to twenty-three federations. The losers stated that the outcome was the result of threats and job offers made by Goulart's agents to eleven "uncommitted" federation heads.[4] They also complained that they could not provide last-minute "democratic" persuasion to these key electors because Riani's men had prudently kept them closeted the night before the election.[5]

Again, this time at ceremonies installing the new CNTI officers, Brazil's President and Prime Minister shared the spotlight with Francisco Julião. "Cuba, Cuba, Cuba" was the frenzied response to the President's satisfying speech on Brazil's "independent" foreign policy.

The CNTI election result made it possible for the proponents of a *central sindical* to put together an "over-all" horizontal labor organization which, while not supported by all segments of labor leadership, could describe itself as speaking for a large force. The CNTI's new officers had the cooperation of pro-Communist leadership in the National Confederation of Workers in Credit Establishments (CONTEC) and in a large part of the National Confederation of Workers in Maritime, River, and Air Transport (CNTTMFA).

Strong federations sometimes acted against the wishes of confederations of which they were a part; similarly, large *sindicatos* (unions) sometimes behaved independently of the federations to which they belonged (and in which their voting strength was no greater than that of the smallest *sindicatos*). Thus, although the officers of the National Confederation of Workers in Land Transport (CNTTT) remained adamantly anti-Communist, the Communists and their allies could rely on one of the five federations that made up the CNTTT—the National Federation of Railroad Workers, headed by Rafael Martineli.[6] The sentiments in the directorship of the São Paulo State Federation of Metalworkers hardly represented the Communist orientation of the

---

[4] *Tribuna Esportiva*, February 7, 1963.

[5] Antônio Navas Martins, interview, São Paulo, November 22, 1968.

[6] In 1968 Rafael Martineli was expelled from the PCB for participating in "fractionizing activities" (see *Voz Operária*, no. 37 [March 1968]).

leaders of the *sindicato* of the São Paulo City Metalworkers, Brazil's largest *sindicato*.[7]

Toward the end of the first half of 1962 the new officers of the CNTI met with fellow "renovators" who headed other confederations and national federations to create an over-all labor organization that was much more substantial than the group they had quickly formed to help Goulart late in August 1961. Between June and September 1962 the new organization was known as the Comando Geral de Greve (CGG—General Strike Command) since its immediate purpose was to call general strikes. Thereafter, it was called the Comando Geral dos Trabalhadores (CGT—General Command of Workers). According to Pelacani, this command came to include himself, Riani, Martineli and Osvaldo Pacheco (of the stevedores), as well as representatives of financial workers, maritime workers, and airline personnel.[8] Deocleciano de Holanda Cavalcanti, former head of the CNTI, would add Roberto Morena (of the carpenters) and Hércules Correia dos Reis[9] (of the Guanabara textile workers) to the group because he considers these two, with Pacheco and Pelacani, the "big four" of the CGT.[10]

---

[7] The full name of Brazil's largest *sindicato* is Sindicato dos Trabalhadores nas Indústrias Metalúrgicas, Mecânicas e de Material Elétrico de São Paulo (Union of Workers in the Metallurgical, Mechanical, and Electrical Material Industries of São Paulo).

[8] Pelacani, interview, November 24, 1968.

[9] The participation of Hércules Correia in political planning meetings of PCB leaders is mentioned in the notebooks of Luís Carlos Prestes, which were seized by the authorities in 1964, and is discussed in São Paulo State, Secretaria da Segurança Pública, Departamento de Ordem Política e Social, *Relatório: Inquérito Instaurado contra Luiz Carlos Prestes e Outros por Ocasião da Revolução de Março de 1964*, pp. 253–255.

[10] Holanda Cavalcanti, interview, December 18, 1968. Clodsmidt Riani (interview, Juiz de Fora, November 2, 1968) advises that he was CGT President, Pacheco was secretary-general, and Martineli was treasurer. Riani's CGT list includes leaders of the CNTI, CONTEC, CNTTMFA (and, later, CONTAG, the Confederation of Workers in Agriculture, formed in December 1963); also included are leaders of national federations of graphic workers, railway workers, stevedores, and airline personnel (Commander Paulo de Melo Bastos). Morena did not head a confederation or national federation. Thus in a list issued in 1965 by a military investigating commission, Morena's name and that of Benedito Cerqueira (head of the Guanabara metalworkers *sindicato*) follow those of Riani, Pelacani, Humberto Menezes Pinheiro (of

The CGT was unofficial and had no place in the setup established by the Vargas Labor Law Consolidation. Stating that other countries had official over-all labor organizations and that Brazil's workers wanted one, CGT leaders made plans to hold a Fourth Trade Union Congress at which representatives of vast sectors of organized labor would urge the federal legislature to give the CGT legal status. In the meantime CGT leaders met in a room they reserved for themselves at the Rio headquarters of the CNTI, issued political pronouncements, and threatened general strikes.

With assistance from the federal government the CGT became powerful. Loans were often granted by the Bank of Brazil and the government's Caixa Econômica through intervention by the CGT,[11] which also was instrumental in deciding who occupied important union posts. Besides controlling positions in the Labor Ministry and in the pension institutes, the CGT became influential enough to control some posts in ministries not directly connected with labor matters.

Legislators began to note that Brasília's hotels were filled with labor union officials, and they suspected that the President spent more time seeing them than seeing congressmen. Many of them feared that the President wanted to be in a position to bring on a general strike by "pressing a button."[12]

As Kubitschek's Vice-President, Goulart had built up a reputation among labor leaders as a good mediator, not as the great strike proponent described by some of the press. One leader has stated that "Goulart would show us where we were in error, and tell us that we should keep our feet on the ground."[13] During his presidency Goulart found it necessary now and then to beg that leaders he had helped to power desist from calling strikes. Sometimes, however, even his most

CONTEC), Pacheco, Melo Bastos, Severino Schnaipper (of the maritime workers), Martineli, and Hércules Correia dos Reis. Morena (like Pacheco) was on the Central Committee of the PCB; in labor affairs he worked actively, although frequently he remained in the background.

[11] Arnaldo Sussekind, interview, Rio de Janeiro, October 26, 1965.

[12] Alberto Honsi, interview, Brasília, October 19, 1965.

[13] Hélcio Maghenzani, interview, São Paulo, November 14, 1968.

dramatic pleas regarding strikes and positions on national issues went unheeded, and he would be placed in a difficult situation.

When a friend asked Goulart why he assisted the faction of labor which included known Communists, he made clear his own lack of interest in the Communist cause. He added that the group he was assisting was one on which he could rely to get results. Anti-Communists compared the game he was playing to riding a tiger; but admirers of the President pointed out that he well knew Brazilian Communism and its weaknesses and that, if he found himself on any tiger, he would know when and how to get off, if necessary.

The Moscow-line Brazilian Communist Party (PCB), hoping to be declared legal and seeking to act as an important segment of a broad nonviolent "anti-imperialist front," was not mentioning Marxist principles in its statutes. Using hard-working militants and effective nationalist slogans, it concentrated much of its fire on the United States and on United States investments in Brazil and supported measures that were popular with the Left: agrarian reform, limitation on the remission of profits abroad, the nationalization of banks, less rigid strike regulations, and votes for illiterates. It was ever seeing Petrobrás threatened by the "machinations of the imperialists."

Luís Carlos Prestes explained to Crockatt de Sá that the PCB was peacefully inclined and that Brazil was in no condition to have a violent revolution. But the presidential adviser on labor union matters had been impressed by what he had seen in Red China when he had accompanied Goulart there in 1961. He felt that Red China would become influential in Latin America, and he feared that the peaceful PCB would eventually find it hard to compete with a new extremism advocated by Red Chinese leaders. Some of Brazil's Communist labor leaders, not wanting to be described as conservative, would, he felt, become attracted to, or carried along by, the violent line.[14]

Although in Brazil the PCB preached peaceful coexistence, a different possibility was not ruled out during a discussion that Luís Carlos

[14] Gilberto Crockatt de Sá, interviews, Rio de Janeiro, October 9 and 11, 1967; December 12 and 17, 1968.

Prestes and another PCB official held with Khrushchev and Suslov in Moscow in November 1961. Prestes perhaps had exaggerated the role of the PCB in the events that brought Goulart to Brazil despite the veto of the military ministers.

Suslov: The situation in Brazil has changed seriously. . . . In giving consideration to military work, we must not diminish the work with the masses. . . . Without political preparation of the masses the insurrection will be difficult. . . . As for the peasant movement . . . the essential thing is to increase the demands of the great peasant masses. . . . You orient yourselves in the correct sense of developing the action of the masses, leading them thus to insurrection. The two things are intimately connected. It is clear that with the passage of time the importance of military preparation will increase. However, this should in no way mean abandoning the action of the masses. . . . In Brazil the revolutionary potential is very large. If this bonfire gets started no one will be able to put it out. . . .

Khrushchev: . . . It is important to know how to arouse with forcefulness the demands of the peasants, who struggle against the large landowners. You speak of agrarian reform. This is right when the situation is not revolutionary. In a revolutionary situation we must know how to fight for the agrarian revolution. Then any constitutional reform will be unnecessary. . . . As for the workers, it is indispensable to reinforce the trade union movement. When we speak of armed struggle, we speak of the struggle of the great masses and not of sectarian actions of some Communists. For that would be a hazardous enterprise. Armed struggle by Communists alone is always a hazardous enterprise. Carrying out the work of the masses is the best form of preparing for the insurrection. . . .

Suslov: . . . In Brazil, contradictions are becoming seriously worse . . . [with] no problems solved, with the apparatus of the State weakened, with the masses in movement. . . . Improve [the Party's] connections with the masses. Improve also its connections with the other political parties. . . . It would be erroneous to think that one could only initiate the armed movement when one had 51% of the working class. In 1917, Lenin said that he had only 30% of the Army on the side of the revolution, but that one must take into consideration the rapid evolution of the masses with the outbreak of the insurrection. . . . He knew how to choose exactly the right moment for the insurrection.[15]

[15] From notes found in Luís Carlos Prestes' home in São Paulo in April 1964. In part these notes were reproduced in São Paulo State Departamento de Ordem Política e Social, *Relatório*, pp. 23–25.

6. "Areas of Friction" with the United States

THE MOST PUBLICIZED DECISION of the Tancredo Neves ministry concerned foreign policy. Foreign Minister San Tiago Dantas resolved to work for Brazil's "independence" and went ahead with steps already taken to renew diplomatic relations with the Soviet Union. At Punta del Este in January 1962 he criticized Dean Rusk's anti-Castro position; the Brazilian Foreign Minister found juridical reasons to explain why Brazil could agree neither with the imposition of economic and diplomatic sanctions against Cuba, nor with the expulsion of Cuba from the Organization of American States. In defending this position at home, San Tiago Dantas stated that Brazil's stand represented a victory for the Brazilian people, who were "showing their will."[1] The Brazilian Congress, after much debate, rejected a motion to censure the Foreign Minister, whose stand was bringing him the applause of nationalists, Communists, and organized students and workers.

Not to be outdone by San Tiago Dantas, Governor Brizola late in 1961 helped establish a National Liberation Front (FLN), which was supposed to bring all the Brazilian "anti-imperialists" together. Then in January 1962 the forces applauding the gallant Foreign Minister hailed Brizola for his newest "patriotic expropriation," the victim of which was the Rio Grande do Sul subsidiary of the International Telephone and Telegraph Corporation. Brizola's state government deposited an indemnization check of twenty million cruzeiros ($54,000) and then claimed that money was owed it by the expropriated foreign utility.[2]

In a public statement critical of Dean Rusk, this act was defended by General Peri Constant Bevilaqua, commander of the Third Military

---

[1] Vladimir Reisky de Dubnic, "Trends in Brazil's Foreign Policy," in *New Perspectives of Brazil*, ed. by Eric N. Baklanoff, p. 93.

[2] Testimony of Roberto Campos before Congressional Commission Investigating Situation of Foreign-Owned Utilities, June 20 and 26, 1963, reproduced in Instituto Brasileiro de Relações Internacionais, "A Compra das Concessionárias de Energia Elétrica," *Revista Brasileira de Política Internacional*, VIII, nos. 31, 32 (September, December 1965), 532.

Region; but it was embarrassing to Goulart, who was preparing for an official visit to Washington. Before Goulart left on his trip, arrangements were made "to reduce the area of friction" between the two countries by having the Bank of Brazil loan (pending court decisions) 1,300 million cruzeiros to the American owners of the expropriated property.[3]

At the White House on April 4, 1962, President Goulart suggested to President Kennedy that foreign public utilities in Brazil be "nationalized peacefully" by means of "just payments prescribed in the Brazilian Constitution." The sellers—the large American and Foreign Power Company was much in mind—would follow the example set in Mexico; they would reinvest 75 per cent of the payments received for the sales in Brazilian undertakings considered useful by the Brazilian government. Kennedy expressed his interest and urged that the operations be carried out in a manner that would not give the appearance of confiscation. Such an appearance, he said, would reduce the flow of foreign private capital to Brazil and would also make it difficult for the United States Congress to vote AID programs for Latin America.

[3] *Ibid.*, pp. 563–564.

7. Exerting Popular Pressure on Congress

THE JUDICIARY ruled that members of the Council of Ministers who wanted to run for Congress in the October 1962 elections would have to leave their posts three months earlier. In June 1962 Congress could have voted Senator Mem de Sá's project to make this requirement unnecessary but turned it down in order to show dissatisfaction with the poor record of the too heterogeneous Council of Ministers.[1] Tancredo Neves and his cabinet resigned on June 26, 1962.

[1] Tancredo Neves, interview, Rio de Janeiro, October 7, 1965.

The cabinet had run into difficulties caused by the UDN's dislike of its predominantly PSD complexion and by Goulart, who saw in the fall of the ministry an opportunity to demoralize the parliamentary system.

Many supported Goulart in his fight against parliamentarianism. The governors opposed the system because, as it had been enacted, it was scheduled to be installed in their states. Governor Magalhães Pinto, inclined to welcome opportunities to support the head of the federal government, warmly agreed with Goulart that the system was ineffective. All leaders who, like Magalhães Pinto, hoped to be elected President in 1965, disliked parliamentarianism. The parliamentary system was also opposed by the Far Left, which considered the restrictions placed on Goulart to be part of the same "plot" that had caused Vargas' suicide and Quadros' resignation. Many in Congress reflected that they had accepted the system in 1961 only as a convenient way to end a crisis.

After the fall of the Tancredo Neves ministry, Goulart proposed to Congress that San Tiago Dantas become Prime Minister. San Tiago Dantas had just explained to three thousand cheering workers in Rio that "policy is independent only if it finds backing in the popular interests." The "independent" foreign policy, he had said, should be accompanied by a corresponding domestic policy: one that would control prices and foreign capital and promote agrarian reform.[2]

The PSD was not disposed to confirm the nomination of a member of the PTB. Moreover, quite a few congressmen, particularly PSD leaders, had reservations about the Left, of which San Tiago Dantas was now a hero. In domestic affairs the term "Left" was becoming associated with "popular reforms," especially with radical agrarian reform calling for a constitutional amendment allowing bonds to be paid for expropriated tracts of land.

The leftists felt that Congress had long failed to reflect popular demand for reforms. They blamed this not only on the ineligibility of illiterates to vote, but also on congressional election procedures. They felt that conservative party bosses, connected with industrialists and

[2] *Novos Rumos*, June 8–14, 1962.

property owners, often failed to nominate congressional candidates who had "true popular ties"; furthermore, in the interior the *coroneis de barranca* (barranca colonels) continued able to deliver congressional election votes because of voter connections unrelated to national issues.

Leftists, considering transactions made with these "colonels" and reviewing the financial requirements of campaigning and the sources of the funds, felt Congress represented "the establishment" and was favorable to the status quo. They saw the press as influenced by large advertisers and United States advertising agencies. Impatient reformers and would-be populist heroes believed the situation required a "crisis climate" and great popular demonstrations for impressing congressmen and other politicians.

The leftists thought United States economic groups were taking more out of the Brazilian economy than they were contributing to it. They saw these groups—considered to be vastly influential in Brazil and backed by the United States State Department—as collaborators with Brazilian forces that opposed worthwhile reforms.

Advocates of a "crisis climate" made full use of ISEB, the Education Ministry's Institute of Superior Studies. After Roland Corbisier's successful venture into politics in 1960, philosopher Álvaro Vieira Pinto had become director of the institute. ISEB gave more and more attention to "educating" and stirring up labor leaders, workers, and sergeants. Night courses were given to extol the virtues of a bitterly anti-United States ultranationalism. At such courses speakers were likely to include Stalin Peace Prize winner Josué de Castro and Marxist historian Nelson Werneck Sodré; also Deputado Sérgio Magalhães of the Frente Parlamentar Nacionalista (Nationalist Parliamentary Front) and Rio Alderman Roland Corbisier. Francisco Julião came to explain radical agrarian reform. Men connected with ISEB helped organize a Frente Militar Nacionalista (Nationalist Military Front).

Brazil's business community included some who were willing to finance an institute that published studies whose findings contrasted markedly with those of ISEB. The Instituto de Pesquisas e Estudos Sociais (IPÊS) was established—one of its founders later said—"to create democratic public feeling strong enough to force Goulart to rid himself of the leftists surrounding and using him."[3] In its definition of the "Left," IPÊS maximized the Communist issue. In mid-1962 it was giving courses on "democracy" to women who had decided to organize actively after coming to feel that children were falling under the control of Communist student leaders.

While these women were preparing anti-Communist petitions to send to Brasília, the recently formed General Strike Command (CGG) tested its ability to exert pressure on Congress. On behalf of the nomination of San Tiago Dantas it sent busloads of workers to Brasília and prepared to call a general strike. But Congress reacted unfavorably, the PSD maintained its claim on the prime-ministership, and many *deputados* criticized San Tiago Dantas' foreign policy. On June 28, before the general strike was called, San Tiago Dantas' nomination was rejected, 174 to 110.

In an irritated mood Goulart then spoke with PSD leader Auro de Moura Andrade. After securing from him an undated resignation from the prime-ministership, Goulart submitted Moura Andrade's name for this post. Congress approved the nomination (222–51) and Moura Andrade, a strong personality, showed that he planned to run the government. He also reported to Goulart that Congress was not disposed to reamend the constitution to allow an early plebiscite regarding the parliamentary system. While he argued with Goulart about this matter and about cabinet names, the CGG demonstrated against him. Within forty-eight hours it was announced that he had rejected his new post.

The country, therefore, continued in a state of confusion and without any Council of Ministers. The War Ministry, in the absence of a minister, was being run by General Machado Lopes, who had backed Brizola during the August 1961 crisis. Anti-Goulart military men saw their fears being realized. Strikes were called, and the resulting transportation tie-ups contributed to food shortages in industrial centers. Luís Carlos Prestes, in Brasília, discussed the national situation with politicians and labor leaders. He also delivered 53,367 signatures on petitions calling for legalization of the PCB.

---

[3] Paulo Ayres Filho, "The Brazilian Revolution," in *Latin America, Politics, Economics, and Hemispheric Security*, ed. by Norman A. Bailey, p. 250.

After Moura Andrade's rejection of the prime-ministership, the President made a stunning nomination. He picked Francisco Brochado da Rocha, a PSD man who would be all that the Far Left might desire. He was little known except that, as Brizola's legal adviser, he had played a part in the expropriation of the International Telephone and Telegraph Corporation in Rio Grande do Sul.

While this nomination was pending, Goulart's supporters insisted that the country was about to collapse because the President was not getting his way. Evidence of collapse included rioting in a Rio suburb that was suffering from food shortages. A few were killed and many were injured after people had been incited to loot food stores. Critics of Goulart accused his supporters of being responsible for the shortages and the rioting.

Agents of the CGG paraded around Congress, demanding a "truly nationalistic" government. Congressmen, eager to return to their states to campaign for the October 7 election, could see that if they rejected Brochado da Rocha they might be held responsible for deliberately prolonging the crisis. The matter was resolved on July 10, 1962, when most of the congressmen agreed to accept him but not necessarily to support him.

8. The Ministry of Brochado da Rocha
(July–September 1962)

BROCHADO DA ROCHA, it turned out, was a socialist and a temperamental law professor, who favored having the electorate decide the fate of the parliamentary system by an immediate plebiscite. He arrived in Brasília with a list of the nation's twelve "most important political leaders" and confessed to Amaral Peixoto that Amaral Peixoto was the only one on the list whom he knew. Goulart named the cabinet. General Nelson de Melo, an opponent of the parliamentary system, took over the War Ministry. Admiral Pedro Paulo de Araújo Suzano, who had been arrested for his pro-Goulart position at the end of August 1961, became Navy Minister.

The new Labor Minister was Hermes Lima, an intelligent lawyer and well-known socialist professor; many recalled that after the 1935 Communist rebellion he had been jailed when the anti-Communists had overzealously accused people of supporting that uprising. The Ministry of Mines and Energy went to João Mangabeira, socialist brother of the late Otávio Mangabeira and an "intransigent" backer of the presidential system.[1] Afonso Arinos de Melo Franco, after receiving telephone calls in Paris from San Tiago Dantas and Goulart, returned to his former post of Foreign Minister to carry on with Brazil's "independent" foreign policy; his party, the UDN, neither liked that policy nor had voted in favor of accepting Brochado da Rocha as Prime Minister.

The various Far Left forces were happy with Brochado da Rocha. He promised a program that would upset what he called "an international capitalism linked with reactionary domestic groups." His administration and Governor Brizola cooperated well with the National Union of Students (UNE) and made it possible for the students to meet at the enormous, pompous Quintandinha Hotel near Petrópolis to choose once more a directorship agreed upon by Catholic leftists and Communists. Organized students, in the company of representatives from Prague and Budapest, resolved to fight against the Alliance for Progress and in favor of a socialist regime for Brazil. Students who protested this line found that those who were in control were being "protected" by stevedores.

Brochado da Rocha, attacked by Lacerda, met with cabinet ministers in Laranjeiras Palace to plead that a legal way be found to have the federal government throw Lacerda out and take over his state government. But the ministers, including General Nelson de Melo, opposed "intervention" in Guanabara. After making their views known they had a difficult time preventing the excitable Prime Minister from resigning.[2]

[1] Afonso Arinos de Melo Franco, *Planalto*, p. 231.
[2] *Ibid.*, pp. 235–236.

On August 10, 1962, Brochado da Rocha delivered his most important message to Congress. He pointed out that, as the legislators wanted to campaign, Congress should empower the Council of Ministers to legislate the reforms the nation urgently needed. The powers requested by Brochado da Rocha in his twenty-two–point program were enormous. Among other things, they would have allowed the ministers to carry out agrarian reform, nationalize the electric power and mining industries, create a federal police force, revise regulations governing strikes, control the foreign exchange market, issue a telecommunication code, and decree antitrust legislation.[3]

Again, masses of laborers surrounded Congress. The CGG warned that it would call a general strike unless the "plundering of the nation by foreign trusts" was ended and unless "the wishes and aspirations of the people" were "fully satisfied."

These "aspirations" included approval of the Prime Minister's twenty-two–point program; they also called for a plebiscite, which would be held at the time of the October 7, 1962, elections, to let the people decide between the presidential and parliamentary forms of government. The atmosphere, Afonso Arinos de Melo Franco writes, was such that he could not give the necessary attention to his own ministerial duties.[4] Nor was there anything to indicate that the parliamentary system, which he had worked to install, was going to survive. Brochado da Rocha, becoming known as "the philosopher of the early plebiscite," was arguing that the form of government was "legal," but could not be considered "legitimate" unless supported by a favorable plebiscite.[5] Important Army commanders, such as Osvino Ferreira Alves in Rio, Peri Constant Bevilaqua in São Paulo, and Jair Dantas Ribeiro in Pôrto Alegre, opposed the parliamentary system.[6]

With the nation anticipating another crisis—or an intensification

---

[3] For Brochado da Rocha's message and requested powers, see Francisco Brochado da Rocha, *Mensagem ao Congresso Nacional Remetida pelo Presidente do Conselho de Ministros, Solicitando Delegação de Poderes para Legislar*, August 10, 1962.

[4] Melo Franco, *Planalto*, p. 236.

[5] Gustavo Capanema, interview, Brasília, October 23, 1965.

[6] Melo Franco, *Planalto*, pp. 236–237.

of an existing one—War Minister Nelson de Melo stated that the plebiscite should be held on October 7. The Navy and Air Ministers then agreed.

Congressional committees were appointed to study Brochado da Rocha's twenty-two–point program, but they were reluctant to cede great legislative powers to Goulart and "his" Prime Minister. They maintained that reforms were already under study in Congress. To show that Congress was reform-minded and able to act, there was passed, and forwarded to the President in September, the more severe of the two principal versions of the long-discussed bill to limit profit remittances abroad.

The PSD, backed by landowners, wanted to be careful about agrarian reform. Furthermore, some serious reformers felt that administration politicians and socialist theoreticians, calling chiefly for "confiscation of the land," were not giving serious attention to the agrarian reform problems that most needed to be solved.[7]

The Brochado da Rocha program helped pave the way for a compromise involving the matter that most interested Goulart. To end the crisis and let the congressmen—harassed by the CGG—proceed with electioneering, PSD President Amaral Peixoto finally agreed with Kubitschek and Nelson de Melo. On the occasion of the next congressional "concentrated effort" (when the *deputados* and senators were to make an effort to concentrate in Brasília in sufficient numbers for a quorum), the PSD, Amaral Peixoto said, would set a date for a plebiscite. Goulart arranged to have the Air Force mobilize fifty airplanes to stand by to fly the campaigning *deputados* to the capital from all over Brazil.

As Brochado da Rocha prepared for a showdown, a military voice from the far south issued a warning in support of Goulart's goal. General Jair Dantas Ribeiro, commander of the Third Army, dispatched a message to the President, the Prime Minister, and the War Minister. He said that in view of the intransigence of Congress and the resulting demonstrations in the territory occupied by the Third Army, he was

[7] Hermes Lima, interview, Brasília, October 17, 1965.

not in a position to assure the maintenance of order unless Congress agreed that a plebiscite be held on October 7 at the latest.[8]

Nelson de Melo, who thought Jair Dantas Ribeiro was going too far, replied that a possible plebiscite was being discussed in Brasília in order to settle the crisis. He also advised Jair that his message was conducive to indiscipline and should not have been sent. It was up to the War Minister, Nelson de Melo said, to decide whether order could be maintained in the south; he added that he believed that Jair could maintain it.[9]

In an emotional speech in Congress, Brochado da Rocha almost collapsed while forecasting that he would either die leading the people against the reactionaries or be killed by the foes of the people. To exert pressure while Brochado da Rocha sought a vote favorable to his twenty-two–point program, the CGG called its general strike. The strike did not spread far beyond government-controlled bodies, such as port facilities, but it brought disturbances to Rio. Lacerda, maintaining that the strike was political and therefore illegal, had the Guanabara state police arrest some of the strike leaders. Soldiers of First Army Commander Osvino Ferreira Alves, accompanied by federal Undersecretary of Labor João Pinheiro Neto, freed the leaders and arrested a few of Lacerda's detectives. First Army soldiers also foiled Lacerda men who wanted to close Rio's Rádio Mayrink Veiga on the ground that it was being used by Brizola to incite Cariocas to "open rebellion."

On September 13 Congress denied Brochado da Rocha the special powers he had requested. On the next day the cabinet resigned on the ground that it was in no condition to resolve the political crisis.[10] The Foreign Minister left with the explanation that the Prime Minister was wrong to take the view that a congressional vote against an early plebiscite would be a vote of no confidence in the Council of Ministers. Brochado da Rocha retired from politics and died soon after. The country again was without a cabinet. Many questioned whether, during the

[8] Mário Victor, *Cinco Anos Que Abalaram o Brasil: de Jânio Quadros ao Marechal Castelo Branco*, p. 442.

[9] *Ibid.*, p. 443.

[10] Melo Franco, *Planalto*, p. 237.

various crises that had followed Tancredo Neves' withdrawal in June, it had had a government.

Capanema, back from studying parliamentary ways in Europe, had presented a project to prevent gaps and crises by allowing a provisional Prime Minister, appointed by the President, to govern until dismissed by a congressional vote of no confidence.[11] When the Capanema project went to the Senate, Benedito Valadares introduced a modification stating that the parliamentary system should only continue in force if supported by a "popular referendum" to be held on January 6, 1963.[12] Even Senator Afonso Arinos de Melo Franco, staunch believer in the parliamentary system, voted for the Valadares modification; he wanted to avoid civil war.[13]

On September 16 Valadares' article was accepted by the Chamber of Deputies, 169 to 83. The use of the words "popular referendum" instead of "plebiscite" hardly reversed the fact that what was really needed was a new constitutional amendment and not the ordinary law that was adopted. Thus illegally[14] Congress gave Goulart what he wanted. By this time it was what most Brazilians wanted.

[11] Capanema, interview, October 23, 1965.

[12] Jânio Quadros and Afonso Arinos de Melo Franco, *História do Povo Brasileiro*, VI, 259.

[13] Melo Franco, *Planalto*, p. 239.

[14] Olímpio Mourão Filho, interview, Rio de Janeiro, October 9, 1965; Ernâni Sátiro, interview, Brasília, October 22, 1965; Capanema, interview, October 23, 1965.

9. An Election and a Plebiscite

GOULART APPOINTED a "provisional cabinet," said to be shaped in the molds of "true nationalism." Professor Hermes Lima became both Prime Minister and Foreign Minister. João Mangabeira was moved from Mines and Energy to the Justice Ministry.

Thirty-four–year-old João Pinheiro Neto, who was discovering that cooperation with the "renovating" labor leaders offered a path to prominence, became Labor Minister. Pinheiro Neto was full of enthusiasm for the Left and dislike for the International Monetary Fund, and soon after taking office he made use of a television program to blame the country's afflictions on two members of the administration: Roberto Campos, ambassador to Washington, and Otávio Bulhões, head of SUMOC (the Superintendency of Money and Credit). After the Prime Minister dismissed Pinheiro Neto for this performance, workers gathered in front of the Labor Ministry building to show their admiration for the former Labor Minister. This demonstration was organized by the CGT (General Labor Command), new name of the CGG. Pinheiro Neto called his dismissal a "sordid move" by the government to please the IMF, but Goulart made a statement critical of the IMF and looked for another important post to give Pinheiro Neto.

That War Minister Nelson de Melo had pronounced in favor of an early plebiscite was important. But this support ended the general's usefulness to Goulart. Before joining the cabinet he had, as head of the Second Army, spent his time in São Paulo breaking up what he says were "prefabricated" strikes, organized by agitators who were financed by government funds. (Laborers, he adds, had thanked him for giving them the opportunity to work.) During his term in the War Ministry Nelson de Melo concluded that Goulart was definitely bent on turning Brazil into a syndicalized state, and he broke with the President.[1] His stern reprimand to Jair Dantas Ribeiro annoyed the CGT and made his position clear. For the Hermes Lima cabinet Goulart found a new War Minister, fellow Gaúcho Amauri Kruel.

While the elections of October 7, 1962, came and went, the government devoted some of the people's money to propaganda calling for votes against the parliamentary system in the January 1963 plebiscite.

The October elections excited much interest. Neither the Far Left nor the opposition to it were particularly well united; but polarization of viewpoints had been going forward rapidly, and the election was seen by many as more of a struggle between two camps than a struggle between political parties. The IPÊS-educated anti-Communist women's group of Rio filled the city with posters: "Dad, vote for a democrat so that tomorrow I may continue to be free." Far leftists were also

[1] Nelson de Melo, interview, Rio de Janeiro, October 28, 1965.

opposed by the Instituto Brasileiro de Ação Democrática (IBAD), which had been organized in 1959 to save for Brazil the brand of democracy now extolled by the women's groups; in 1962 IBAD assiduously solicited campaign funds to be used to defeat candidates it considered socialistic. But neither its intense work in Pernambuco nor the women's posters in Guanabara met with success.

The election was held, in part, to determine the make-up of the group of men who would play major roles on a political stage that promised to be agitated. The electorate brought Miguel Arrais to prominence in Pernambuco and Ademar de Barros to new prominence in São Paulo. Cariocas much influenced Brazil's future when they gave congressional candidate Brizola a victory of unprecedented magnitude.

Ademar's narrow victory was at the expense of Jânio Quadros, who was seeking to regain the São Paulo governorship. Quadros, who had apparently changed his mind about retiring to the practice of law and teaching, returned from Europe and tried to explain his resignation in a speech that described his helplessness in the presidency in the face of attacks unleashed by Congress, Lacerda, "a few dangerous Communists," political parties, "powerful newspapers and eminent figures in all sectors of economic, political and social power."[2]

In this long-awaited explanation, Quadros declared himself a dedicated democrat, but there was nothing in his description of how "popular reforms" had been suppressed by a powerful minority to allow listeners to feel that anything useful for the masses could be accomplished by the system established under the 1946 constitution. The speech was one of many in which Brazilians would hear the governmental structure included among the scapegoats and which implied that somehow everything would be all right if the constitution were radically altered. Again the listener was given no specific ideas about what reforms were necessary. Quadros simply stated that they would reconstruct the national life, "legitimizing popular representation" and eliminating demagogues, liars, the corrupt, and all who exploited the people on behalf of bad Brazilians and foreign greed.

Foreign scapegoats, mentioned in Quadros' speech, were Adolf

[2] Quadros' speech is given in Carlos Castilho Cabral, *Tempos de Jânio e Outros Tempos*, pp. 297–309.

Berle, Ambassador John Moors Cabot, Treasury Secretary Douglas Dillon, and the West German Ambassador. But during Quadros' campaign to recapture the São Paulo governorship his opponents began to say that the "terrible foreign forces" that had confronted him in the presidency had been Haig & Haig and other brands of Scotch.

Quadros appealed to the Far Left for support.[3] With no effective party endorsement, he faced two opponents who were backed by experienced party machines: one was Ademar de Barros and the other was a young protégé of Carvalho Pinto who had annoyed landowners by pushing an agrarian tax-reform program. From the start of the campaign Ademar identified himself solidly as an anti-Communist and a friend of the United States. Favoring typically conservative idealisms, he made the most of a growing concern in São Paulo rural areas about "Communist advances."[4] Some of the extreme leftists were trying to persuade peasants to take the matter of land distribution into their own hands.

Ademar benefited from a last-minute PSD drive—in which Kubitschek was interested—to knock out Quadros. This gave Ademar votes that were diverted from the failing candidacy of Governor Carvalho Pinto's young man. Considering the organized resistance to Quadros, his very narrow miss—the first electoral miss in his life—seemed more likely to spell temporary eclipse than doom.

The gubernatorial race in the troubled, populous Northeastern state of Pernambuco was equally close and brought national stature to winner Miguel Arrais. Arrais, who had been serving as mayor of Recife, let it be known that he was a "democrat and a nationalist," not a Communist.[5] But he was in the habit of working closely with Brazilian Communists of the peaceful Moscow line, and he believed that the principles advocated by them would benefit Brazil. Supported by a wealthy industrialist as well as by the Communist Party, Arrais had the good fortune of having two opponents whose ideology differed from his.

[3] Hélio Jaguaribe, "As Eleições de 62," *Tempo Brasileiro,* I, no. 2 (December 1962), 33.

[4] José Bonifácio Coutinho Nogueira, interview, São Paulo, November 22, 1965.

[5] Adirson de Barros, *Ascensão e Queda de Miguel Arraes,* p. 86.

Among those on the Far Left who won federal congressional seats from Pernambuco was Francisco Julião Arruda de Paula. He, too, spoke of democracy, but he defined democracy for the peasants as an uprising that would end the miserable conditions in which they existed. Julião belonged to a family of large landowners and had become a lawyer whose practice included the defense of peasants against large landowners. Beginning in 1955 he urged peasants to strengthen their interests by forming peasant leagues. Uncombed and bright-eyed, he made effective, bitter speeches. These had already gained him a seat in the Pernambuco state legislature when he was discovered, late in the Kubitschek administration, by the United States and Socialist press and was pictured as the great and mystical leader of Brazilian peasantry.

Seeking financial assistance for his peasant leagues, Julião visited Red China in 1960 and made a number of trips in 1960 and 1961 to Cuba (where he put his four children in school). He was full of praise for Mao Tse-tung and Fidel Castro. He repeatedly declared himself a Marxist and an admirer of Christ the "rebel," and Christ the "radical"; but he expressed contempt for modern Christianity, which, he said, had come to be used for the defense of dominant economic interests. During his successful campaign for federal congressman in 1962 the vicar at his birthplace threatened excommunication for Catholics who voted for him.[6]

Julião once declared that if the Brazilian people could express their view, they would invite Castro to run the affairs of Brazil. He was, at the time, receiving money from Castro to promote revolutionary change by violent means. Although Julião soon made Cubans and Chinese Reds wonder whether he really wanted a violent uprising,[7] he did use emotional phrases, which separated him from the peaceful line of

[6] Lêda Barreto, *Julião—Nordeste—Revolução*, p. 58. For Julião's views see also Francisco Julião, *Que São as Ligas Camponesas?*, and *Até Quarta, Isabela!*

[7] Diary of Wang-chin, revealed by Colonel Gustavo Borges in Rio de Janeiro on May 9, 1964; see *O Estado de S. Paulo*, May 10, 1964. Wang-chin wrote: "Julião likes fame and bragging. . . . He speaks and shrieks, but he does not want an armed movement." For a useful chapter on Julião, see Anthony Leeds, "Brazil and the Myth of Francisco Julião," in *Politics of Change in Latin America*, ed. by Joseph Maier and R. W. Weatherhead. Leeds wrote of Julião, landowner, lawyer, and successful politician: "To stir [the landless and impoverished] to true revolution would be to destroy himself; to use them is in his best interest."

Arrais and the Brazilian Communist Party. A further cause of this separation was rivalry for leadership.[8]

Leonel Brizola was serious when he advocated violence if "the establishment" would not yield peacefully, and he doubted that it would. The defeat of his candidate for the Rio Grande do Sul governorship in October 1962 constituted a setback for him, but that contest was close. It showed once again that political leaders have not been notably successful at garnering votes for protégés.

Brizola's expropriation of the International Telephone and Telegraph property and his aggressive call for land redistribution and other radical reforms appealed to Guanabara workers. He won his federal congressional seat with far more votes than any congressional candidate had ever received in the past. The setback for Lacerda was not limited to Brizola's victory. The Guanabara governor's candidate for the federal Senate, Juraci Magalhães, was beaten. So was Lacerda's candidate for the vice-governorship of the state. The new vice-governor–elect of Guanabara, Elói Dutra, no friend of "the establishment" or of Lacerda, directed his fire against IBAD's definition of democracy, IBAD's "neofascism," and what he said was IBAD's use of funds from foreign firms to attack the people's candidates.[9]

In the federal Congress the PSD apparently preserved its leadership. But Goulart's PTB, which replaced the UDN as the second strongest party, was almost in a position to take first place by means of postelection switches of the allegiance of *deputados*.[10] Luís Carlos Prestes announced that of the 409 candidates elected to the enlarged Chamber of Deputies, 17 were Communists who had run on other party tickets.

[8] Lêda Barreto, *Julião—Nordeste—Revolução*, p. 79. The PCB was unable to control Julião and did not want mass leadership in his hands.

[9] See Eloy Dutra, *IBAD: Sigla da Corrupção*. Helping to put IBAD in a bad light, Castilho Cabral, former head of the Movimento Popular Jânio Quadros, lied sensationally (see Castilho Cabral in Edmar Morel, *O Golpe Começou em Washington*, p. 52).

[10] The case of Cláudio Braga presents an example of such switching in the Pernambuco state legislature. He ran for the legislature as candidate of the small Partido Social Trabalhista (PST) because local leaders of the PTB would not nominate him. He received more votes than any other man elected to the legislature. Once elected, he rejoined the PTB (Cláudio Braga, interview, Montevideo, November 16, 1967).

The Cuban missile crisis followed the election. The official Brazilian view was shrouded in mystery after rumors were spread that the Brazilian ambassador to the Organization of American States was being recalled because his vote had favored the United States.[11]

In Brazil Ademar de Barros and Juscelino Kubitschek supported the United States position, whereas PTB congressional leader Almino Afonso spoke against it. Brizola, busy shouting against the "imperialistic" nation to the north, turned some of his fire on Kubitschek. Then, as the missile crisis unfolded, he attacked both the Soviet Union and the United States. So did the National Liberation Front, which Brizola had formed a year earlier; its offensive against the U.S.S.R. embarrassed the Brazilian Communist Party, which had been picturing itself as a potent part of the Front. General Albino Silva, chief of the President's Casa Militar, returned from a "peace-seeking mission" to Cuba and stated that Brazil had taken on the role of mediator to "save Cuba from American internal pressure designed to adopt radical measures against Castro's regime."[12]

Living costs, which had increased about 40 per cent in 1961, went up over 50 per cent in 1962. Congress approved a bill giving all urban workers an extra month's salary at the end of 1962, and the Goulart administration boosted minimum wages about 75 per cent effective January 1963. However, there was talk about this being the last such increase for three years. As the date for the plebiscite drew near, Goulart spoke of a Three Year Plan to bring financial sanity, as well as much development, to Brazil. A National Planning Commission was to be set up. These evidences of interest in planning came at a time when the United States was suggesting that Brazil should do more to help itself if it were to receive sizable assistance under the Alliance for Progress program.

Of Brazil's total electorate of around 18.5 million, only about 11.5

[11] For more about the Brazilian official view, see de Lesseps S. Morrison, *Latin American Mission*, pp. 250 and 258. Morrison states: "I attribute to [Roberto] Campos main credit for freeing Brazil's difficult vote on October 23, 1962, during the missile crisis. He finally took it upon himself to assume responsibility. After he acted, a minister in President Goulart's cabinet demanded his removal. But Campos survived."

[12] Report from Anthony Vereker, Rio de Janeiro, November 7, 1962.

million voted in the plebiscite of January 6, 1963. Of these, almost
9.5 million expressed preference for the presidential system.[13] Newspapers exaggerated a little and spoke of a six to one victory for presidentialism. Goulart, pleased with what he considered a personal victory, was proclaimed "presidential President" on January 23. Many
hoped that a return to presidentialism would result in serious attention
being given to the problems that afflicted the nation.

Some felt that in 1962 the numerous political crises and strikes had
contributed to the serious decline in the rate of growth of Brazil's domestic production.[14] There were others, however, who felt that a continuation of the "crisis atmosphere" would be necessary for Brazil's
long-run development. As they saw it, this development depended on
structural reforms that would integrate the great masses into the economy and "emancipate" Brazil from United States "economic domination." Among these reforms was a projected banking reform that would
give direction to the economy and would not restrict credit to the
"elite."

The "crisis atmosphere" had so far produced few of the reforms
mentioned by Brochado da Rocha; but it had shown that it might.
Herbert Levy, who headed the UDN in 1962, says that during that
year he watched "a determined minority take over the floor" of Congress and with the help of "the controlled unions" and the government's Executive Branch, "press the majority." The majority, Levy
states, became so "frightened" that it sometimes found itself voting
"against its own way of thinking." As an example of this, Levy cites the
profit remittance law, which, as voted, he declares to have been "a
police law and a disaster for Brazil."[15]

[13] Complete tabulation by states is given in Institute for the Comparative Study of
Political Systems, *Brazil: Election Factbook*, p. 81.

[14] This rate of growth, reported as 7.7 per cent in 1961, was reported as 3.7 per
cent in 1962. This rate amounted to little on a per capita basis, for the population growth rate was reported as 3.1 per cent.

[15] Herbert V. Levy, interview, São Paulo, November 15, 1965.

10. The Red Scare

In the Council of Ministers in 1962 the Finance Ministers had been men who could talk with international bankers and who were, therefore, loathed by the Far Left. Despite this conservatism and Goulart's trip to the United States, a good deal of evidence was presented to the public to suggest that Goulart was "taking Brazil to Communism."

The generally antiadministration press pictured Goulart—accompanied by Presidential Press Secretary Raul Riff, a former Communist —spending public funds to assure that "'Communists" or "pro-Communists" dominated labor and student groups—and as many other groups as possible. Communist infiltrators, knowing that they could count on backing from men around the President, were described as having a field day.

Civilians who abhorred the idea of socialist legislation were able to attract great numbers to their cause by pointing out that far leftism involved more than the enactment of "popular reforms." In January 1963 it became public knowledge that, in the Brazilian interior during 1962, some so-called peasant leagues led by Francisco Julião had become Cuban-financed centers for arming peasants and training them in guerrilla warfare. Not inaccurately the authorities were pictured as less than energetic in dealing with young Tarzan de Castro and other far leftist leaders of these guerrilla training camps. Because of governmental apathy, associations of rural landowners held secret meetings at night to organize a defense against those who would use force to seize their properties.

Although some advocates of "popular reforms" belonged to Catholic Action (Ação Católica) and the Christian Democratic Party, foes of far leftism were beginning to associate its goals with a grim and violent conspiracy, which felt contempt for religion and family ties. He who advocated "popular reforms" in order to "foil subversion" ran the risk of being labeled a tool of "Communist conspirators" or a "Communist conspirator" himself. Those who made this charge could point out that not infrequently Catholic leftists worked very closely with Communists.

The components of the Brazilian Far Left were agreed on a program, but they vied with each other for leadership and disagreed about method. Among those who called themselves Communists were the Trotskyite group, with only a few hundred followers, and a new Peking-line Communist Party of Brazil (PC do B), with about one thousand members. Both of these preached a violent uprising while attacking each other and the Moscow-line PCB. Peking-liners took training courses in barracks in Red China.

Prestes' PCB, preaching the peaceful line, had an estimated 35,000 members. They were well-placed. For example, they controlled the huge São Paulo City Union of Workers in the Metallurgical, Mechanical, and Electrical Material Industries (with 25,000 union members) and used the union's share of the *impôsto sindical* (union tax), corresponding to the city's 200,000 workers in those fields, to strengthen the PCB in the state.

Early in 1962 Prestes reported to Moscow that he favored setting up more peasant leagues in Brazil. Accordingly, the União dos Lavradores e Trabalhadores na Agricultura (ULTAB), which the PCB had established for this purpose in 1954, stepped up its activities, becoming a rival of Julião, whose main strength was in Pernambuco. Julião soon noted that in the neighboring state of Paraíba, the federation of peasant leagues was in the hands of the PCB.[1] During 1962 Julião's rather disorganized peasant leagues also ran into competition from Catholics, both of the Left and of the Right.

The "Red scare" brought contributions from business and professional men pouring into the São Paulo and Rio offices of IPÊS (Instituto de Pesquisas e Estudos Sociais). To create intellectual barriers against the spreading of Marxist ideas, IPÊS issued more and more "democratically oriented" studies about economic and social problems. It furnished articles to the press. It even reached the masses by issuing pamphlets that had the well-known earmarks of cheap paper and poor typography.

Silently IPÊS assisted numerous organizations that were working in

[1] Lêda Barreto, *Julião—Nordeste—Revolução*, p. 83.

other ways on the anti-Communist front. Some were training rural and urban anti-Communist labor leaders. By the beginning of 1963 IPÊS had in Rio an efficient intelligence service, run by General Golberi do Couto e Silva, who had headed the intelligence work of the National Security Council under President Quadros.

On a smaller scale, the Fundo de Ação Social, established in São Paulo in March 1962, also received contributions from firms. The Fundo, believing that "Brazil was one of the choicest battlefields of the cold war and that business could not stand idle and see itself destroyed by demagoguery and ignorance," sought "a closer cooperation of the foreign business community with its Brazilian counterpart."[2]

The anti-Communist women's groups, organized in São Paulo and Rio in mid-1962, bustled with activity. The São Paulo group (União Cívica Feminina—UCF) stormed into television stations to make their views known in a manner not typical of the Brazilian housewife. These women sent busloads of anti-Communist students to participate in student union elections.

Rio's Campanha da Mulher pela Democracia (CAMDE—Women's Campaign for Democracy), after campaigning for "democrats" in the October 1962 election, turned its attention to the Cuban crisis. Learning that missiles had been discovered in Cuba, CAMDE, within one hour, mobilized four hundred women to call on the Foreign Minister. They clashed with pro-Communists who also invaded the Foreign Office in Rio, and the police had to be called.[3]

The idea of having one nation-wide women's organization was rejected. Separate groups were established in different locations, it being felt that if an incident prompted the government to close down one group, the others would be able to carry on. In Minas Gerais the Liga da Mulher pela Democracia (LIMDE) was formed. The women's group in Recife was called the Cruzada Democrática das Mulheres do Recife (Women's Democratic Crusade of Recife). Ação Democrática Feminina was established in Pôrto Alegre.

Under resolute leadership and often working closely with IPÊS,

---

[2] Fundo de Ação Social, circular letter, São Paulo, October 18, 1965; Fernando Lee, interview, São Paulo, November 22, 1965.

[3] CAMDE, mimeographed report, 1964, p. 3.

the women attended conferences on democracy and current events. They obtained thousands of signatures on their petitions and prodded their husbands in what became a spirited campaign against "Communist penetration."

11. Concern in Military Circles

THAT SOME NAVAL OFFICERS were discontented was not surprising. In the opinion of a group of unhappy admirals, appointments to high office had come to depend on supporting the Far Left and bore no relation to ability. In July 1962, when Admiral Pedro Paulo de Araújo Suzano was named Navy Minister, six admirals asked to be discharged from their posts, a request that was accepted.[1] In December 1962, when the Naval Medal of Merit was bestowed on Brizola, these six, and some retired officers, turned in their medals. Navy Minister Suzano unsuccessfully tried to court-martial active naval officers who took this step, and he went on to award the Medal of Merit to some CGT leaders.[2]

Denys, Heck, Grün Moss, and Cordeiro de Farias, top military men in the Quadros administration, were joined in conspiracy by General Nelson de Melo, who had tried to cooperate with Goulart and who now brought worrisome first-hand reports about what he felt were the President's ultimate objectives.

Goulart made certain that his antagonists who were in active military service were without troops. Particular attention was given to seeing that top commands over the Army's formidable array of weap-

---

[1] These six were Admirals Augusto Rademaker Grünewald, Levi Aarão Reis, Ernesto de Melo Batista, Waldeck Vampré, Mário Cavalcanti, and Armando Zenha de Figueiredo. They were warmly praised by retired Commander Mário dos Reis Pereira, classmate of the four last-mentioned. The retired commander's subsequent work was such that he came to be considered one of the "group."

[2] Ernesto de Melo Batista, interview, Rio de Janeiro, December 4, 1967.

ons in Guanabara—strengthened by the United States military co-operation program—were in the hands of pro-Goulart officers.

Thus General Emílio Maurel Filho ran into trouble. Having pleased Goulart by cooperating with Denys in 1955 and by finding the Brandi letter a forgery, he headed the First Military Region, located in Guana-bara. But shortly before his friend Nelson de Melo left the War Min-istry, Maurel irritated Osvino Ferreira Alves, who headed the First Army, which had jurisdiction over Maurel's First Region. Osvino, as-sociated with Brizola and praised by admirers of Francisco Julião, assisted Carioca leaders of the September 1962 "general strike" and was frequently called "the Marxist general." During a discussion with Osvino, Maurel had suggested that Congress ought not to be closed down if it resisted Goulart and the CGT.[3]

Pressures against Maurel, one of the founders of the Escola Supe-rior de Guerra, were successful after Kruel replaced Nelson de Melo as War Minister. A presidential order transferred Maurel to a place on the Army staff. Reluctantly accepting the post, which was without troops, Maurel delivered a speech, known as the *discurso bomba*, denouncing what he said were plans for closing Congress and for having a Com-munist-dominated government.[4] Maurel was not arrested, but a pro-motion was denied him.

Admiral Sílvio Heck labeled the dismissal of Maurel Filho an open attempt against Brazil's security. He spoke of "Communist infiltra-tion" in the armed forces—a charge that had some validity in the case of sailors and Air Force sergeants—and he called for reinstatement in the security services of men who, he said, had been replaced by pro-Communists. For these "subversive statements" Heck's prison record was increased by thirty days.

An extremely discontented general who still commanded troops was Olímpio Mourão Filho. He headed the large Third Infantry Division with headquarters in Santa Maria, the railroad center of Rio Grande do Sul. A determined and impetuous little dynamo who had been an Integralista (Green Shirt) in the 1930's, he chewed on his pipe and

[3] Emílio Maurel Filho, interview, Rio de Janeiro, October 11, 1965.
[4] *Ibid.*

decided what to do after hearing a "diatribe" by Brizola on January 6, 1962. Convinced that a plot existed to make Goulart the dictator of a República Sindicalista,[5] Mourão hastened to Rio and São Paulo to suggest to War Minister Segadas Viana and Nelson de Melo that anti-Communists in the Army should act at once to overthrow the President. At that time he aroused little interest, and a few of his listeners considered him a bit of an idiot.

Back in Rio Grande do Sul he made some converts among Army officers. This limited success was a tribute to his doggedness, because overwhelmingly the Army troop commanders were devoted to "legalism" and discipline. He explains that he was assisted in Rio Grande do Sul by "Brizola's frequent radio calls for an uprising by the Radical Left, and Brizola's fondness for inciting sergeants to plan to revolt against their superiors."[6]

Mourão was among those who felt that Goulart wanted to close Congress if it failed to agree to an early plebiscite. At the time that his chief, Third Army Commander Jair Dantas Ribeiro, advised Brasília that an early plebiscite was necessary for the maintenance of order, Mourão Filho prepared to place himself on the side of *legalidade* and to lead a march north in case Congress was closed. After this crisis passed, he continued to make plans for an armed overthrow of the government. Mourão, inclined to do things in a novel manner, did not hide his purpose, but what he did to achieve it was clothed in secrecy. Government people did not take him seriously. Some felt that if he did anything it would be unsuccessful; a few reflected that such a development might justify extraordinary powers for the Executive.

[5] Olímpio Mourão Filho, interview, Rio de Janeiro, October 9, 1965.
[6] *Ibid.*

12. Robert Kennedy Visits Goulart
(December 17, 1962)

DURING THE CORDIAL DISCUSSIONS between Presidents Goulart and Kennedy in Washington in April 1962, John F. Kennedy accepted Goulart's invitation to visit Brazil. Kennedy and his advisers, enthusiastic about the proposed visit, agreed that it should be made around July 20, 1962.

Early in July, when an advance party from Washington was in Rio making detailed plans for the visit, Brazil was suddenly beset with the agitation that followed Moura Andrade's "rejection" of the prime ministership. The country had no government, the CGG was demonstrating and threatening a general strike, and rioting was occurring close to Rio. President Kennedy agreed with advisers who felt that his visit should be postponed, but he wanted a new date to be set and he wanted the postponement to create no misunderstanding. Goulart conceded that the moment was inappropriate for a visit; he asked that the reason to be given for its deferment not be linked to political difficulties in Brazil.

News of the postponement was made public amidst evidences of Washington's friendship for Goulart. Pierre Salinger, President Kennedy's Press Secretary, made a special trip to Brazil. American Ambassador Lincoln Gordon acted as interpreter during a telephone call from Kennedy to Goulart. It was explained to the public that, as Kennedy had urgent matters pending in the United States Congress, he would have to defer his Brazilian visit until November 1962. This would be soon after the Brazilian gubernatorial and congressional elections.

Following this postponement, Ambassador Gordon found reasons for increased concern about the trend of Brazilian developments. He had known Brochado da Rocha in connection with the expropriation of the International Telephone and Telegraph Corporation's property in Rio Grande do Sul and was not well impressed by his nomination to be Prime Minister. Gordon also noted strong Communist infiltration in Petrobrás and in the Postal and Telegraph Department, and he worried about some of the appointments made to the inner circle of the presidential office. He wondered whether Goulart's design was to attract support for a plebiscite that would bring back the presidential system, or whether it was of a more sinister nature. At any rate, although advance planners were once more in Brazil, Kennedy's proposed November visit was again postponed in October. Kennedy needed to stay close to his desk following the Cuban missile crisis. Goulart was agreeable, preferring to receive Kennedy after the expected death of the parliamentary system in January 1963.

During staff sessions held in Gordon's office following this second postponement, there emerged the idea of having Attorney General Robert Kennedy deliver a message, which it was hoped would be taken seriously by Goulart. The message would acknowledge that constitutional matters had made 1962 a difficult year for Brazil, and it would emphasize United States interest in Brazilian democracy and development. It would also reveal official worry in the United States. "We see two possible roads ahead," Robert Kennedy would tell Goulart. One road, that of the Alliance for Progress, would stress reforms, development, and United States-Brazilian cooperation. The other road, that of "extreme leftism," would be characterized by chaos, inflation, and the activities of Communists and their supporters.[1]

Gordon went to Washington where this idea was considered in the cabinet room by President Kennedy, Secretary Rusk, Attorney General Kennedy, the director of the CIA, and high State Department officials. Robert Kennedy, asked by the President whether he was willing to undertake the mission, replied in the affirmative.

In Brazil Gordon explained to Goulart that President Kennedy, unfortunately tied up in Washington preparing his State of the Union address, had some points he wanted to present to Goulart. Robert Kennedy, Goulart was told, would soon be in the Panama Canal Zone, half-way to Brazil, and would be pleased to exchange impressions with Goulart. The Brazilian President, irritated by a recent statement in which the United States President had demonstrated concern about Brazilian economic and financial problems,[2] was delighted at the pros-

[1] Lincoln Gordon, interview, Washington, January 17, 1969.
[2] *Jornal do Brasil*, December 19, 1962.

pect of a frank, informal conversation with Robert Kennedy. He asked Gordon to be present at the meeting, which he suggested be held in Brasília.

Besides Goulart, Kennedy, and Gordon, only an interpreter of the American State Department attended the meeting on December 17. Robert Kennedy did not follow in detail the scenario given him by Embassy officials the evening before, but he did speak of the two paths that seemed open to Brazil and expressed concern about Communist infiltration. Goulart then spoke for forty minutes, bringing up numerous matters, such as declining prices for Brazilian exports in contrast to increasing prices of equipment imported from the United States.[3] In essence the reply to Robert Kennedy's message was that descriptions of chaotic Brazilian conditions should not be taken seriously, that the parliamentary system was no good, and that specific information should be given about the Communist infiltration that had been mentioned. Gordon then referred to the situation in Petrobrás and in the Postal and Telegraph Department. Goulart did not deny Communist infiltration there, but he did not see it as a problem, and he told his visitors that they would be pleased with occurrences in Brazil after the presidency got back the powers it had held before September 1961.[4]

On the next day Goulart advised the *Jornal do Brasil* that Attorney General Robert Kennedy had "lost all the negative impressions he had formed about Brazil."[5] However, the *New York Times* said that "it can be reliably reported that Mr. Kennedy returned to Washington with continued concern over Brazil's economic and financial situation."[6] Ambassador Gordon was disappointed in the conference; but then, he had never been very confident that much could be accomplished by it.

[3] *Ibid.*
[4] Gordon, interview, January 17, 1969.
[5] *Jornal do Brasil*, December 19, 1962.
[6] *New York Times*, December 19, 1962.

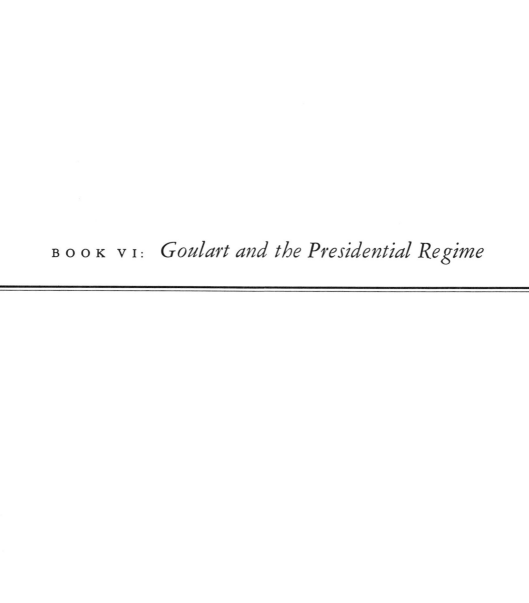

BOOK VI: *Goulart and the Presidential Regime*

"It is not by chance that all official documents of the Church condemn capitalism."

Herbert José de Souza, general
coordinator of Ação Popular

". . . taking the pulse of national reality, we feel the social Christian revolution, fully on the march. Bishops, priests, and Christian movements in the vanguard of authentic and profound reforms. Why hesitate to use the appropriate term: of the true social revolution."

Frei Carlos Josaphat
São Paulo, May 1963

1. Launching the Three Year Plan

WITH THE DEATH of the so-called parliamentary system in January 1963, Goulart announced a new cabinet. The military ministers remained, and so did the socialist Justice Minister, João Mangabeira. PTB congressional leader Almino Afonso—young, idealistic, intelligent, and honest—became Labor Minister. Antônio Balbino, whose advice Goulart had found useful, was named Minister of Industry and Commerce. Socialist Hermes Lima, as Foreign Minister, was expected to continue advancing Brazil's "independent" foreign policy.

Domestically the emphasis was to be on economic planning. Thus the Goulart regime entered a second phase, during which a few people gave some attention to combatting inflation. This would promptly and inevitably yield to a third phase, in which the talk about reforms—prominent in the first two phases—was to become a loud shout.

The second phase opened when the administration revealed its Three Year Plan, a statistics-laden document calling for the unpleasant steps deemed necessary to reduce the annual inflation rate from 52 per cent to less than 10 per cent. Blessed by the United States and approved by the International Monetary Fund (IMF), the plan hardly

seemed likely to attract those pro-Goulart forces that had demonstrated around Congress in 1962. To offset its obvious political weaknesses, the plan was, however, bathed in unrealistic glamor and was
given sponsors who were expected to be effective: Celso Furtado and
San Tiago Dantas were persuasive men who had enjoyed the support
of the Left but who had much prestige in other circles.

Furtado, a Paris-educated economist from the Northeast, was renowned for his vigorous work as head of the Superintendência do
Desenvolvimento do Nordeste (SUDENE), charged with bringing
change and development to the Northeast. He had ably attracted political support for SUDENE.[1] As Minister of Economic Planning
(without portfolio) in the last "parliamentary" cabinet, he supervised
the preparation of the Three Year Plan. Continuing as minister without portfolio in Goulart's first presidential cabinet, he made the plan
public in January 1963. Implementation of its financial clauses became the job of San Tiago Dantas, Finance Minister in Goulart's first
presidential cabinet.

Critical economists averred that the lengthy plan was largely a projection of trends handled in a way to give an optimistic forecast.[2] It
was a forecast that bore little resemblance to what might have been
possible under the best of circumstances. But it made good reading. It
spoke of reducing the inflation rate from 52 per cent in 1962 to 25 per
cent in 1963, and of containing it within 10 per cent by 1965. While
this was being accomplished, the annual rate of national production
growth was to be 7 per cent (3.9 per cent per capita).

The plan showed that this growth rate depended on Brazil's receiving (in three years) 1.5 billion dollars in foreign government assistance and 300 million dollars in foreign private investments: much of
this was to take care of servicing past foreign debts. The plan also

[1] Albert O. Hirschman, *Journeys Toward Progress*, pp. 78–86.

[2] *Análise e Perspectiva Econômica* (APEC) in its June 27, 1963, issue stated that
the Three Year Plan "in reality was no real plan but merely a package of statistics
tacked together with a thread of good intentions colored pink. However, despite its
purely publicity value, the merit of the Triennial Plan was simply to justify a series
of political-economic-financial measures which were being adopted . . . in an endeavor
to drag Brazil out of its inflationary quagmire and to re-establish its credit in the eyes
of civilized people."

made it clear that the reduction in inflation required cutting government expenditures, ending wheat and petroleum subsidies, increasing taxes and public service rates, and limiting credit.

Lucidly San Tiago Dantas appealed to the intelligence. He also acted vigorously. He conferred with visiting representatives of the IMF and trimmed the federal budget. He eliminated the wheat and petroleum subsidies and looked for more subsidies to attack. Then, early in March 1963, he sped to Washington while reports from Brasília suggested that the Brazilian government was considering modifying the profit remittance bill, which had not yet been promulgated.

Washington was impressed with San Tiago Dantas' intentions and with what he had done. But there was reason to doubt that Goulart or Brazil would long support an unpopular program that bore some resemblance to the short-lived anti-inflationary program discarded by the Kubitschek regime in 1959. Therefore, AID Administrator David Bell rather disappointed the Finance Minister. He made 84 million dollars available at once and offered an additional 315 million dollars in steps depending on Brazil's future performance.

In Brazil the Three Year Plan was assaulted almost as soon as it was made public. Men who did not admire Furtado accused him of being a Marxist with "Caesar-like aspirations" and untruthfully referred to him as "the Tsar of the Brazilian economy."

The CGT delivered a threatening memorandum to Goulart: "None of the suggestions for a truce in the fight for higher wages will be accepted." The Three Year Plan, Luís Carlos Prestes said, was "a plan against the public." Propaganda machines of the PCB and of the entire "Radical Left" worked overtime to condemn the activities of the Finance Minister. Associates of the UNE (National Union of Students) wrote that "The Three Year Plan is an attempt to conciliate imperialism and large landowners as a part of an over-all policy which the national bourgeoisie is carrying out through the government of João Goulart."[3] The Nationalist Parliamentary Front joined in the attack.

Kubitschek condemned the IMF. Miguel Arrais, featured in a pub-

[3] Quotation given in Thomas E. Skidmore, *Politics in Brazil, 1930–1964: An Experiment in Democracy*, p. 405.

lication of the Catholic Far Left, wrote that the Three Year Plan augmented the maldistribution of Brazilian resources.[4] The Dantas Mission, he said in a São Paulo speech, had obtained a "small parcel" of money, which would largely be used to benefit foreign companies in Brazil.[5] Brizola, using a chain of radio stations, lashed out against San Tiago Dantas and everything the government did in the realm of economics and finance.

Grumbling members of the producing classes, their lines of credit sharply reduced, laid off workers and cut back production to such an extent that it became doubtful whether Brazil would realize any per capita national production growth in 1963. The cost of living continued to rise as it had before San Tiago Dantas took office. It was affected by the huge money supply of 1962 (including the "thirteenth month" wage payments of December 1962), the wage increase decreed in January 1963, the elimination of subsidies, and the decline in production.

San Tiago Dantas described himself as a "leftist liberal" and his program as that of the "Positive Left." Brizola's screaming attacks on behalf of the "Radical Left" prompted the Finance Minister in mid-April 1963 to refer to the Three Year Plan's Far Left opponents as members of the "Negative Left."

[4] *Brasil, Urgente*, I, no. 11 (May 26–June 2, 1963).
[5] Adirson de Barros, *Ascensão e Queda de Miguel Arraes*, p. 113.

2. Brizola's Attacks on the Administration

BRIZOLA, his political stature enhanced by his impressive congressional election victory, would give no peace to Goulart. "We must get rid of the antireformist tripod, San Tiago Dantas, Amauri Kruel, and Antônio Balbino," he demanded. Like San Tiago Dantas, War Minister Kruel and Commerce Minister Balbino were working for the execution of an agreement reached in April 1963 for Brazil's purchase of the American and Foreign Power Company (AMFORP) properties.

For this Brizola described the three ministers on television and radio as "traitors to the national interests."[1]

Brizola's charge that the power company deal was equivalent to a gift to a "foreign imperialistic trust" resulted in the formation of a congressional investigating commission to scrutinize the government's agreement wth AMFORP. Governor Lacerda echoed Brizola's charge. The Goulart administration, he declared, was offering too high a price for "scrap iron."

War Minister Kruel, an outspoken anti-Communist, was on the blacklist of the Radical Left. He was soon having troubles with First Army Commander Osvino Ferreira Alves, darling of the CGT and the National Union of Students. In March 1963 Osvino offered Army protection for a "monster meeting" to be held by organized laborers and students to protest Lacerda's decision not to allow a pro-Cuba congress in Guanabara. Kruel reprimanded the "people's general" and made him withdraw his offer. He accused him of scheming to overthrow Lacerda. Then in April Osvino accused Kruel and the chief of the Casa Militar of having the same intention: they were, he publicly charged, planning a pro-Goulart rally in Rio in order to incite the masses to attack the Governor's Palace; the disorders would give an excuse for military intervention and the simultaneous deposal of rightist Lacerda and leftist Miguel Arrais.

Kruel submitted a memorandum warning the President of the direction in which Brizola and labor union officials were taking Brazil. The nation, he wrote, seemed headed for four stages: agitation by the unions, indiscipline by sergeants, disparagement (*desmoralização*) of military leaders, and, finally, "the assault on the power." The general expressed doubt that the President would survive the fourth stage.[2]

According to this memorandum, Brazil had already reached the second stage. There was evidence for this in May 1963 after Brizola made accusations against the commander of the Army garrison in

---

[1] David Nasser, *João sem Mêdo*, p. 82. Relations between Goulart and Brizola are discussed in Abelardo Jurema, *Sexta-Feira, 13: Os Últimos Dias do Govêrno João Goulart*, Chapter VIII ("Jango x Brizola"), pp. 67–79.

[2] Amauri Kruel, interviews, São Paulo, November 15, 1965; Guanabara, October 21, 1967.

Natal and was supported, in the ensuing furore, by a group of sergeants. Then about one thousand Army sergeants met in the Brazilian Press Association auditorium in Rio. At this affair, directed by CGT leaders and some "nationalist" congressmen, General Osvino was honored. Sergeant Gelsi Rodrigues Correia proclaimed: "We swear to defend order in this country, but not that which presently exists, for it benefits only a few privileged people."

Late in May Kruel transferred Sergeant Correia to Mato Grosso and gave him a thirty-day prison sentence.[3] At this time another sergeant, Antônio Garcia Filho, was fighting "for the good of all sergeants." Garcia had been elected a federal congressman and had reportedly joined the Nationalist Parliamentary Front; but he had a problem taking his seat because the constitution forbade sergeants from holding legislative positions. Brizola supported Garcia's cause.

Brizola, struggling to seize national control of the PTB from Goulart, assembled "peasants" outside of the halls of Congress and told them to arm themselves to fight for their rights. On another occasion he told a large crowd that "the people have the right to exert force on Congress, and, if necessary, to take up arms." Magalhães Pinto offered Congress refuge in Minas Gerais.

Using a radio network of forty stations, Brizola would sometimes speak for two to four hours at a time. In Deputado João Calmon, he found an adversary as stubborn as himself. Calmon, director of the Chateaubriand chain of newspapers and broadcasting stations, told a large radio audience that Brizola advocated following the Cuban example and should not be underestimated. "If Brazil falls into the hands of the group led by Leonel Brizola, the democratic cause, in the entire world, will be irreparably lost."[4]

In a much-publicized debate on the night of June 2, 1963, Brizola struck at the United States, the Chateaubriand chain, Kruel, and the American and Foreign Power deal. Calmon observed that the deal had been made by Goulart; Brizola admitted to having differences with his brother-in-law. Brizola exclaimed that Calmon should take a look at the wonderful agrarian reform program going forward on what

[3] Amauri Kruel, interview, Guanabara, October 21, 1967.
[4] Nasser, *João sem Mêdo*, p. 87.

was once a part of one of Brizola's properties in Rio Grande do Sul. Later in June Calmon did just that. He returned from the south to report to his radio-television audience that the so-called agrarian reform was a shield to hide a misuse of public funds which had benefited Brizola.[5]

Public debates such as this were attracting much attention. In May 1963 the one between two prominent federal congressmen from São Paulo, Herbert Levy and Paulo de Tarso, so aroused the six hundred listeners who were present that the speakers could not carry on. Paulo de Tarso, leader of the left wing of the Christian Democratic Party, called for agrarian and constitutional reforms. After his defense of popular pressures on Congress was labeled demagogic by Levy, Paulo de Tarso revealed that his words on this matter came from a speech, supporting the Marcha da Produção, made by Levy in 1958.

[5] After the fall of Goulart and Brizola, a military investigation sustained João Calmon's charge (see Nasser, *João sem Mêdo*, pp. 190–193).

3. The Fall of the First Presidential Cabinet (June 1963)

During the first five months of the presidential regime Goulart took steps that appeared to be designed to preserve his personal power.

One of these measures was the launching of a campaign to weaken the CGT. Goulart acted after an interview in which a group of São Paulo industrialists told the President that unless he broke with Communist labor leaders he would be opposed by all of São Paulo industry.[1] The campaign seemed also to answer expressions of concern about Communism which were made by War Minister Kruel and United States government officials. Goulart well appreciated that his power to bargain in organized labor would be enhanced by the build-up of a strong new force—a competitor of the CGT.

[1] Arnaldo Sussekind, interview, Rio de Janeiro, December 19, 1967.

Goulart did not turn to the violently anti-Communist Movimento Sindical Democrático (MSD). This pet of Ademar de Barros, Herbert Levy, and São Paulo industrialists had not gained much support since its organization in São Paulo in 1961. (Lacerda had helped try to install a branch of the MSD in Rio.) Instead, Goulart called on his labor affairs adviser, Gilberto Crockatt de Sá, to organize what was sometimes called a "third force" in labor, independent of the Communists and the MSD. This group, the União Sindical dos Trabalhadores (UST), was described as friendly to Goulart and "well to the left," but "neutral rather than pro-Communist." Disclaiming any government interest in its sudden appearance and growth, Crockatt de Sá said that the UST was "an absolutely spontaneous movement" whose many adherents were "all totally voluntary."[2] He tried to induce São Paulo graphic worker leader Dante Pelacani to join the UST;[3] but Pelacani decided to stick with the CGT.

The UST attracted some who had broken with Goulart and Communists during the Third Trade Union Congress. It included a number of former Janistas, former PCB member José Maria Crispim, and a leader of workers on the Santos-Jundiaí Railway. Its progress in São Paulo state disturbed the Communist directors of the local horizontal labor organizations, such as the Forum Sindical de Debates of Santos and the Pacto de Unidade e Ação (run by able stevedore leader Osvaldo Pacheco).

Crockatt de Sá, who proposed to dislodge the Communists at the year-end CNTI election, called the CGT leaders "imbeciles." Arriving in São Paulo with the title of presidential adviser on trade union affairs, he declared that: "If the CGT were a responsible organ, its dictators—the dictators of labor unionism—would lose control." Asked to name the dictators, he replied: "the Communists."[4] The presidential adviser went on to condemn the CGT for wanting to oust Kruel from the War Ministry. The "imbeciles," Crockatt de Sá added, had

[2] O Estado de S. Paulo, June 13, 1963.

[3] Gilberto Crockatt de Sá, interview, Rio de Janeiro, December 12, 1968. Pelacani reports that Crockatt de Sá offered him the presidency of the CNTI (interview, São Paulo, November 24, 1968).

[4] Brasil, Urgente, I, no. 11, (May 26–June 2, 1963).

been unwilling even to listen to Celso Furtado or San Tiago Dantas explain the Three Year Plan.

For a short while Antônio Pereira Magaldi, who headed the MSD and the National Confederation of Workers in Commerce, worked with the UST. But Magaldi and his backers soon decided that they did not like some of the people in the UST. They apparently did not like cooperating with Goulart either—even if against the Communists. To the press Magaldi described Crockatt de Sá's São Paulo visit as designed to strengthen the President.[5] As one anti-Communist labor leader has put it, a good many anti-Communists were unwilling to join Goulart in what was being described as his effort to "free himself" from the CGT.[6]

Labor Minister Almino Afonso, insisting that his ministry be run in a highly proper manner, argued with CGT leader Dante Pelacani, director of the ministry's Department of Social Welfare. Pelacani was not inclined to take instructions from the Minister. But the CGT could find little to criticize about the ideology of Almino Afonso. Furthermore, the Minister favored legality for the CGT. The matter was one for Congress to resolve, but the Labor Minister helped where he could: he withdrew old directives that had specifically prohibited the existence of "central labor groups" like the CGT.

Almino Afonso, one of the strong personalities of Goulart's first presidential cabinet, belonged to the leftist Grupo Compacto of the PTB. Under Luís Fernando Bocaiuva Cunha, Almino Afonso's successor as PTB congressional leader, the Grupo Compacto drew up a "program of action" for guiding all PTB *deputados*. By this time post-election switches had brought the PTB congressional group almost even with the PSD group. One commentary dismissed these "betrayals" as unimportant due to the decline in the influence of parties and the division of Congress into "two moving forces: the Frente Nacionalista and Ação Democrática."[7]

The Bocaiuva Cunha program of action was a bit too radical for

[5] *O Estado de S. Paulo*, May 21, 1963.
[6] Hélcio Maghenzani, interview, São Paulo, November 14, 1968.
[7] *Análise e Perspectiva Econômica* (APEC), February 27, 1963.

some of the PTB congressmen. It stressed the need of "democratizing" the government: popular referendums, or plebiscites, were to be established on a permanent basis in order to "know fundamental decisions in the country's life." Industries, insurance companies, and financial institutions were to be nationalized. The law limiting profit remittances was to be rigorously enforced. Workers were to participate in the management of enterprises that were fully or partially owned by the government. The illiterates were to be enfranchized. Government bonds, not cash, were to be used to pay for expropriated properties.

This PTB program saw agrarian reform as ending feudalism and eliminating large estates "with the redistribution of land property in a manner which will assure access thereto to farmers not possessing any land." Agricultural credits and minimum prices were to be established. Rural *sindicatos* (labor unions) were to be fostered.[8]

In developing this "Plan of Action," congressional leader Bocaiuva Cunha sought to give the PTB a firm position at a time when he felt that Goulart's main task was to lead all Brazilians—not simply the PTB. But Goulart, determined to run his party and not be run by it, was displeased with what Bocaiuva Cunha was doing.[9]

The President had created a cabinet that had much to recommend it. American Ambassador Lincoln Gordon, asked by Goulart to comment on it, called the cabinet a good one. Bocaiuva Cunha, describing it as the greatest Brazilian cabinet of the century, was particularly eloquent about the abilities of PTB members San Tiago Dantas and Almino Afonso. Among the ministers with international prestige were Celso Furtado, Mines Minister Elieser Batista, and Transport Minister Hélio de Almeida. Some said that the cabinet, and not the President, was running the country. But Goulart seemed unlikely to let that happen. One congressman, distressed to find the President about to dissolve his cabinet, asked him why he was dismissing Kruel. Goulart, he says,

[8] The "Plan of Action" was discussed with Luís Fernando Bocaiuva Cunha during interview, Rio de Janeiro, December 18, 1968.

[9] Luís Fernando Bocaiuva Cunha, interview, Rio de Janeiro, December 5, 1968.

President Juscelino Kubitschek and Vice-President João Goulart (right), 1955. Picture of Getúlio Vargas in background. (*O Estado de S. Paulo*)

Leonel Brizola, as mayor of Pôrto Alegre, Rio Grande do Sul, calls on President Kubitschek (right), October 8, 1958. (*O Estado de S. Paulo*)

João Café Filho and Carlos Pena Bôto (right). (*Manchete*)

Juarez Távora (left) and Eduardo Gomes. (*O Globo*)

1955 election rally for Kubitschek and Goulart. Communist banners demand legality for PCB and commercial relations with the Soviet Union. (*O Estado de S. Paulo*)

Troops at Catete Palace, Rio de Janeiro, November 21, 1955. (*O Estado de S. Paulo*)

The *Tamandaré*. (*O Estado de S. Paulo*)

Aboard the *Tamandaré*, November 13, 1955. Front row, left to right: Bento Munhoz da Rocha Neto, Carlos Luz, Carlos Pena Bôto, and Otávio Marcondes Ferraz. José Eduardo do Prado Kelly stands behind Luz and Pena Bôto. (*O Globo*)

Milton Campos and José Eduardo do Prado Kelly. (*Jornal do Brasil*)

President João Café Filho (left) with Casa Militar Chief Juarez Távora. (*Manchete*)

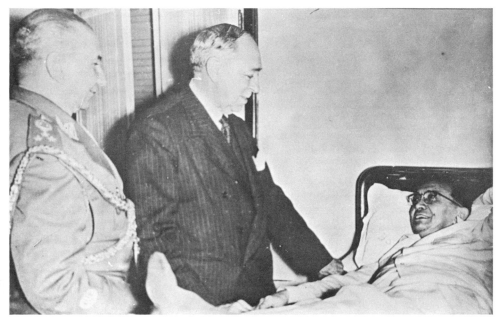

General Floriano Lima Brayner (left) and Nereu Ramos call on João Café Filho at the Government Hospital for Public Servants. (*O Estado de S. Paulo*)

João Café Filho (lower right) at clinic. Counterclockwise from top: Gabriel Passos, Bento Munhoz da Rocha Neto, Aliomar Baleeiro, Alim Pedro, Brigadeiro Antônio Guedes Muniz. Rio de Janeiro, November 21, 1955. (*Manchete*)

Jacareacanga rebellion, 1956: Major Haroldo Veloso and Captain José Chaves Lameirão (right) at Santarém Airport. (*O Estado de S. Paulo*)

War Minister Henrique Batista Lott, late November 1955. (*O Estado de S. Paulo*)

Geraldo Menezes Côrtes (left) and Sílvio Heck. (*O Globo*)

First Army Commander Osvino Alves (right) calls on Marshal Henrique Lott, August 1962. (*O Estado de S. Paulo*)

Oscar Pedroso d'Horta. (*Jornal do Brasil*)

Gabriel Grün Moss, September 22, 1962. (*Jornal do Brasil*)

First Army Commander Odílio Denys, September 7, 1958. (*Agencia Nacional*)

Governor José de Magalhães Pinto of Minas Gerais (left) and Governor Carlos Alberto Carvalho Pinto of São Paulo, 1961. (*O Estado de S. Paulo*)

UDN leaders from Minas Gerais, late 1959. Left to right: José de Magalhães Pinto, Afonso Arinos de Melo Franco, and Gabriel Passos. (*O Estado de S. Paulo*)

Jânio Quadros (left) and João Goulart. (*Manchete*)

Juscelino Kubitschek (left) and Jânio Quadros.
(*O Estado de S. Paulo*)

Inauguration at Brasília, January 31, 1961: Left to right: João Goulart, Jânio Quadros, out-going President Juscelino Kubitschek, and General Nelson de Melo. (*Manchete*)

President Jânio Quadros speaking, early August 1961. Seated at far left: São Paulo Governor Carvalho Pinto. Seated at far right: Guanabara Governor Carlos Lacerda. (*O Estado de S. Paulo*)

General Pedro Geraldo de Almeida (left) and
President Jânio Quadros. (*Jornal do Brasil*)

Cumbica Air Base, August 25, 1961. Arrival of
Jânio Quadros after he resigned the presidency.
(*Manchete*)

"I am no longer President," says Quadros during drive to the coast, August 26, 1961. In rear
of car are his wife and mother (with glasses).
(*O Estado de S. Paulo*)

Quadros making an emotional appeal. (*PN*)

Left to right: Prime Minister Tancredo Neves, São Paulo Governor Carvalho Pinto and São Paulo Cardinal Carlos Carmelo de Vasconcelos Mota, January 1962. (*O Estado de S. Paulo*)

Troops near the São Paulo-Paraná border, early September 1961. (*O Estado de S. Paulo*)

Granja do Torto, Brasília, September 6, 1961. Left to right: Governor José de Magalhães Pinto, PSD President Amaral Peixoto, UDN President Herbert Levy, João Goulart, and Senator Gilberto Marinho. (*O Estado de S. Paulo*)

João Goulart.
(*Última Hora*)

Left to right:
President Goulart, Senate leader Auro de Moura Andrade, and Deputado Sérgio Magalhães. (*Última Hora*)

Professor Hermes Lima.
(*Correio da Manhã*)

Education Minister Paulo de Tarso.
(*Manchete*)

Labor Minister Almino Afonso, 1963.
(*Jornal do Brasil*)

Darci Ribeiro.
(*Correio da Manhã*)

Raul Riff, presidential press secretary 1961–1964.
(*Correio da Manhã*)

João Pinheiro Neto.
(*Última Hora*)

Brasília, September 7, 1961. In foreground, left to right: Casa Militar Chief Amauri Kruel, President Goulart, Acting President Mazzilli, and Former Casa Militar Chief Ernesto Geisel. (*Manchete*)

Leonel Brizola (left) embracing João Goulart. (*Correio da Manhã*)

Justice Minister Abelardo Jurema (left) and President João Goulart. (*Jornal do Brasil*)

President Goulart with Labor Minister Amauri Silva (seated at left). (*Jornal do Brasil*)

President Goulart (left), General Osvino Ferreira Alves, and General Amauri Kruel, 1962. (*Jornal do Brasil*)

Labor leaders Roberto Morena (left) and Dante Pelacani. (*Última Hora*)

Antônio Balbino. (*Correio da Manhã*)

Ademar de Barros. (*Correio da Manhã*)

Luís Carlos Prestes.
(*Correio da Manhã*)

Francisco San Tiago Dantas.
(*Jornal do Brasil*)

Prime Minister Francisco Brochado da Rocha speaking to Navy Minister Pedro Paulo de Araújo Suzano (right) and other Navy officers. (*Jornal do Brasil*)

Left to right: Rui Ramos, Juscelino Kubitschek, José Maria Alkmim, Raul Pilla. (*Manchete*)

Demonstration by peasants. (*Jornal do Brasil*)

Guanabara Governor Carlos Lacerda with students, February 1964. (*O Estado de S. Paulo*)

Rally of March 13, 1964, Rio de Janeiro. Signs call for agrarian reform and a banner shows Vargas and words from his farewell message: "This people whose slave I was will no longer be slave of anyone." (*Manchete*)

Rally of March 13, 1964. (*Manchete*)

Rally of March 13, 1964. Goulart flanked by
Mrs. Goulart and Osvaldo Pacheco. (*O Globo*)

Rally of March 13, 1964. Brizola speaking;
Pelacani at right. (*O Globo*)

Miguel Arrais (left) and Admiral Cândido Aragão at Rally of March 13, 1964, Rio de Janeiro.

Dante Pelacani (CGT and CNTI) addressing mutinying sailors, Guanabara Metalworkers Union Building, March 26, 1964.

Cabo José Anselmo (far right) and Congressman Max da Costa Santos (second from left). (*O Globo*)

Guanabara Metalworkers Union Building, Rio de Janeiro, March 1964. Mutinying sailors in windows, Army police in foreground. (*Manchete*)

Admiral Pedro Paulo Suzano with rejoicing sailors, Rio de Janeiro, March 27, 1964. (*O Globo*)

Celebration of mutinous sailors, Rio de Janeiro, March 27, 1964. (*Manchete*)

Admiral Cândido Aragão with rejoicing sailors, March 27, 1964. (*O Globo*)

President Goulart with sergeants at the Automobile Club, Rio de Janeiro, March 30, 1964. (*Manchete*)

Victory celebration, Rio Branco Avenue, Rio de Janeiro, April 2, 1964. (*O Globo*)

Francisco Julião, 1961. (*Correio da Manhã*)

Francisco Julião in prison. (*Manchete*)

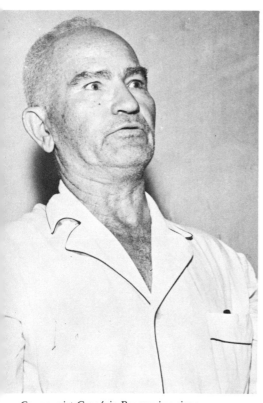

Communist Gregório Bezerra in prison.
(*Manchete*)

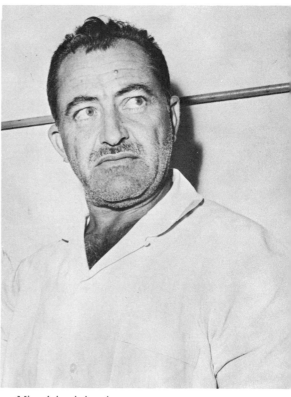

Miguel Arrais in prison.
(*Manchete*)

Former President Eurico Gaspar Dutra.

General Osvaldo Cordeiro de Farias, December 1960. (*O Estado de S. Paulo*)

Brigadeiro Francisco de Assis Correia de Melo, April 1964. (*O Estado de S. Paulo*)

Marshal João Batista Mascarenhas de Morias. Behind (at right): Juarez Távora. (*O Estado de S. Paulo*)

Marshal Odílio Denys (using telephone) and General Olímpio Mourão Filho (right). (*O Globo*)

Governor Carlos Lacerda at Guanabara Palace, April 1, 1964. (*O Estado de S. Paulo*)

Left to right: War Minister Artur da Costa e Silva, President Humberto Castelo Branco, and General Mário Poppe de Figueiredo, Pôrto Alegre, May 1964. (*O Estado de S. Paulo*)

Anti-Goulart conspirators of Minas Gerais and São Paulo. Front row, left to right: General José Lopes Bragança; São Paulo Guarda Civil Commander Reynaldo Saldanha da Gama; Carlos Luís Guedes, Olímpio Mourão Filho, Father Caio de Castro Alvim; Colonel José Canavó Filho; General Dalísio Mena Barreto. (Kindness of Eldino Brancante)

Meeting of cabinet of President Castelo Branco (at head of table), May 1964. Far side of table, left to right: Casa Civil Chief Luís Viana Filho, Navy Minister Ernesto de Melo Batista, Foreign Minister Vasco Leitão da Cunha (partly hidden), Transportation Minister Juarez Távora, and Education Minister Suplici Lacerda. Near side of table: Justice Minister Milton Campos (right) and Casa Militar Chief Ernesto Geisel. (*O Estado de S. Paulo*)

replied that "if I don't replace Kruel, all the people will tell me that I have no power."[10]

In dismissing the entire cabinet after it had served only five months, Goulart showed that Brazil could continue to expect a rapid turnover of administrative personnel. Whenever "crises" developed they were to be solved by dismissals and new appointments.

Goulart could argue that a cabinet change was required because of widespread attacks against it, because it lacked harmony, and because it appeared unable to muster enough congressional strength to assure the passage of reform laws. The congressional Ação Democrática and the conservatives it represented were suspicious of the President and of the reforms he favored. Members of the Nationalist Parliamentary Front and of the CGT increasingly condemned him for supporting men whom they labeled as antireformists and who were identified with the "AMFORP deal" and the politically disastrous Three Year Plan.

The self-declared "positive leftists," who hardly appeared leftist and who were few in number, suffered from more than the vicious attacks of the Radical Left. They suffered also from the mild economic depression. The experience of four or five months disproved the featured figures of the Three Year Plan's forecast and seemed to confirm the doom predicted by the plan's detractors. The cost of living in Guanabara rose 25 per cent between December 1962 and May 1963, indicating that 1963 would be more inflationary than 1962. The decline in sales and production of automobiles, television sets, and refrigerators brought further worker layoffs.

Celso Furtado, critical of the financial policy of the ailing but determined San Tiago Dantas, found himself unable to do anything to implement his Three Year Plan. He fretted at his inability to develop an area of colonization near the Maranhão-Amazonas border. It seemed to Furtado's admirers that Goulart had no interest in Furtado's ideas and did not mind clipping his wings.[11] The Three Year Plan,

---

[10] Maurício Goulart, interview, São José do Rio Prêto, November 12, 1968.
[11] Leonides Alves da Silva Filho, interview, Recife, October 14, 1968.

Furtado concluded, "served merely to give João Goulart victory in the plebiscite."[12]

In Washington San Tiago Dantas had spoken of limiting Brazilian wage increases in 1963 to 40 per cent. Labor Minister Almino Afonso could not accept this, and he denounced the Three Year Plan as "too rigid." When Osvaldo Pacheco and other labor leaders presented the CGT's unfavorable analysis of the plan to Goulart, the President acknowledged that he found himself in a difficult position. He vowed that he would never betray his past at the side of labor and said that he preferred leaving the presidency to repressing the workers.[13] The labor leaders told him to remain in office and to rely on the workers and the people for the backing he needed for his reform program.

The anti-inflationary steps originally advocated by the Finance Minister could not have been expected to show desirable results without exhausting the patience of labor and capitalists. In the face of clamor from all who would be squeezed by a tight wage policy—and this group included the military—the cabinet showed preference for the "less rigid" ideas of Almino Afonso. It was agreed in May that the forthcoming wage increases for government workers (which set the pattern elsewhere) should reflect living cost increases rather than ideas expressed by San Tiago Dantas in Washington.

Goulart, tired of squabbles and attacks, was eager to head dramatically a popular campaign for reforms. This goal appeared easier to attain with the removal of ministers who were becoming centers of controversy. By dismissing every member of the cabinet the President was able to avoid a show of partiality.[14]

To succeed Kruel as War Minister, Goulart chose Jair Dantas Ribeiro, who had been rebuked in 1962 by Nelson de Melo for insisting

[12] Alessandro Porro, "Porque Êle É um Cassado," *Realidade,* August 1967.

[13] Luís Tenório de Lima, interview, São Paulo, November 21, 1968.

[14] After the dismissal of the cabinet in June 1963, the following were appointed to serve: Justice: Abelardo Jurema; Finance: Carlos Alberto Carvalho Pinto; Labor: Amauri Silva; Foreign Affairs: Evandro Lins e Silva; Education: Paulo de Tarso; Industry and Commerce: Egídio Michaelsen; Mines and Energy: Antônio Ferreira de Oliveira Brito; Health: Wilson Fadul; Agriculture: Osvaldo Lima Filho; Transportation: Expedito Machado; War: General Jair Dantas Ribeiro; Navy: Admiral Sílvio Mota; Air: Brigadeiro Anísio Botelho.

that an immediate plebiscite was necessary for the preservation of order in the south. Kruel had earlier offered to step aside, but the President had dismissed the thought and added that if a change were necessary Kruel would be the first to be told. As things worked out, Kruel was among the last to learn.

Congressman Maurício Goulart—long an observer of, and participant in, Brazilian political affairs—considered the first strong presidential cabinet to be a guarantee against a coup by the President. With the cabinet's dismissal he believed that Goulart hoped to perpetuate himself in office. The congressman was not alone in his worry. Lincoln Gordon saw much to indicate that President Goulart proposed to follow the path against which Robert Kennedy had warned him in December 1962. The American ambassador came to feel that Goulart wished to engineer a coup that would make him dictator, and that Left Wing radicals—Communists and their allies, all of whom were interested in autocratic power—supported this. A visit by President Kennedy to Brazil was no longer discussed.

4. Troubles with Washington

THE FALL OF THE CABINET, a confirmation of the Three Year Plan's death, was considered a victory for Brizola. Luís Carlos Prestes, in a speech praising Pernambuco Governor Miguel Arrais, expressed satisfaction with the dismissal of Kruel and the defeat of the Three Year Plan. The Communist leader cited these as examples of the victories resulting from the PCB's "alliance" with the PTB and Goulart. The PCB's alliance with the "progressive forces," he added, could yet bring to Brazil "a nationalist and democratic" government "along the same path we are going, without bloodshed, without the need for a civil war."[1]

[1] *Análise e Perspective Econômica* (APEC), August 27, 1963; *O Estado de S. Paulo,* August 17, 1963.

The "victories" hailed by Prestes were, however, of no help to the negotiations regarding the American and Foreign Power Company (AMFORP) properties. These negotiations were viewed with much interest in international circles, especially after August 1962, when the United States Congress voted the Hickenlooper Amendment, cutting off aid to countries that expropriated without fair compensation. Studies, following the impetus of the Kennedy-Goulart talk in April 1962, had for a while gone ahead in routine fashion. In May 1962 Prime Minister Tancredo Neves had created a commission, headed by a general, to work out purchase terms with foreign utility companies.

The commission was concluding its work with AMFORP early in 1963 when Finance Minister San Tiago Dantas, at Goulart's suggestion, invited Marshal Lott, Professor Carvalho Pinto, and General Jair Dantas Ribeiro to constitute a task force to review the work. After they declined, a group of cabinet ministers was formed to act as such a task force and to bring the negotiations to a close. In April 1963 San Tiago Dantas, on behalf of this group, authorized Ambassador Roberto Campos to sign a "memorandum of understanding" with AMFORP in Washington.

This memorandum declared that the Brazilian government and AMFORP would enter into a contract calling for the former to pay 135 million dollars for AMFORP's Brazilian assets. The down payment of 10 million dollars was to be made no later than July 1, 1963. The remainder was to be covered by interest-bearing notes, which were to be paid off in installments over twenty-two years.

In June 1963, after Brizola denounced the deal, a congressional investigation commission (which included Brizola) questioned men like Amauri Kruel, San Tiago Dantas, and Roberto Campos.[2] San Tiago Dantas addressed a plenary session of the Chamber of Deputies to defend the "letter of understanding" and to argue that the arrangements with AMFORP had not, as charged, been handled in a secret

[2] See Instituto Brasileiro de Relações Internacionais, "A Compra das Concessionárias de Energia Elétrica," Part II, *Revista Brasileira de Política Internacional,* VIII, nos. 31, 32 (September, December 1965).

manner.[3] It was only a few days later that all the cabinet ministers, including San Tiago Dantas, lost their jobs.

In the resulting government reorganization, Darci Ribeiro, the brilliant, dynamic anthropologist who had been first head of the University of Brasília, resigned as Education Minister and became chief of the Casa Civil. Ribeiro, no friend of foreign businessmen, provoked Lacerda into suing him. Lacerda's lawyer, famed old Heráclito Sobral Pinto, declared that the activities of the new Casa Civil chief were part of a government plan for spreading Communism. Luís Carlos Prestes, when asked about Darci Ribeiro during a television interview, declared that Ribeiro had been a Communist "but he is no longer because he heads the Casa Civil."[4]

The new cabinet included the man whom Brizola had unsuccessfully supported for the Rio Grande do Sul governorship in 1962. Brizola himself was reported to have wanted the Finance Ministry, a devilish thought for the financial community. But this post went to Carvalho Pinto, whose persistent presidential aspirations had been hurt by the election of Ademar de Barros as governor of São Paulo. Cautious Carvalho Pinto appeared to be a progressive who opposed extremes.

On July 1, 1963, the last day for Brazil to make its down payment to AMFORP, Presidents Goulart and Kennedy were in Rome for the funeral services of Pope John XXIII. Goulart, managing to spend a few moments with Kennedy, requested some financial assistance for Brazil and mentioned difficulties brought on by the AMFORP "letter of understanding." Goulart received the impression that Kennedy could not help as fully as he might have liked because he found his hands somewhat tied in the United States.[5]

In a letter of July 10 to Goulart, Kennedy referred to the latter's request for a sixty- or ninety-day postponement of the AMFORP

[3] See *ibid.*, Part I, *Revista Brasileira de Política Internacional*, VIII, no. 30 (June 1965), 260–274.

[4] L. C. Prestes on television (Tupi) program, reported in *O Estado de S. Paulo*, January 4, 1964. Darci Ribeiro (interview, Montevideo, November 13, 1967) has asserted that he was a technocrat, "not involved with the PCB or any political party."

[5] Darci Ribeiro, interview, Montevideo, November 13, 1967.

"understanding" and stated that any amendment about the date should be negotiated directly with the company and should confirm the purchase terms.

Goulart wrote back, saying that his words in Rome had not been well understood by Kennedy. The Brazilian President mentioned the importance of public opinion and explained that he was seeking to avoid the situation in which purchase arrangements with foreign public utilities designed to reduce the "areas of friction" between the countries actually increased these frictions. Such arrangements, Goulart wrote, should not be worked out in an isolated manner but as part of a large-scale over-all collaboration between Brazil and the United States.[6] Brazil did not make the down payment to AMFORP.

In Washington AID Administrator Bell had become aware that the Brazilian performance, mentioned in his March talks as necessary for the additional 315 million dollars in AID funds, was not being carried out. Therefore, as had happened in the case of the Kubitschek administration, large "additional funds," which had been promised conditionally to the federal government, were held up. Washington was not, however, adverse to continuing with assistance for a number of specific programs when it found "islands of administrative sanity." Some of the states, among them Guanabara and Rio Grande do Norte, benefited in this way.

[6] See Instituto Brasileiro de Relações Internacionais, "A Compra das Concessionárias de Energia Elétrica," Part I, *Revista Brasileira de Política Internacional*, VIII, no. 30 (June 1965), 275–280.

5. Paulo de Tarso in the Education Ministry

IN THE CABINET REVISION of June 1963, Paulo de Tarso, Herbert Levy's opponent in the recent debate, became Education Minister. He was devoted to Ação Católica (Catholic Action), which, he explained, favored radical reforms in order "to transcend Communism and liberal capitalism."[1]

At the moment "liberal capitalism" seemed to be the big culprit, because Paulo de Tarso and Catholic far leftists assisted known Communists and were supported by them. Speaking late in 1961 on behalf of the legalization of the PCB, Paulo de Tarso had said: "The rulers of the industry of anti-Communism do not hesitate to sell the national sovereignty itself to the United States."[2]

In the early 1950's Ação Católica had established a number of Catholic Youth organizations. Among them were Juventude Operária Católica (JOC) for the working youth, Juventude Estudantil Católica (JEC) for secondary school students, and Juventude Universitária Católica (JUC) for university students.[3] Around 1961 these youth organizations resolved to play an active role in bringing about a radical change in Brazil, because its social and economic structure appeared to them to leave much to be desired. Members of JUC believed that if Brazil were socialist it would be more Christian.

Although at lower levels the PCB was frequently at odds with JEC and JUC, agreements were reached at upper levels. Thus, for some important secondary-school union elections JEC and the PCB formed a united front. Elections to the directing board of the National Union of Students (UNE), official voice of Brazil's 100,000 university students, further confirmed agreements reached between the PCB and JUC.

In 1962, when Catholic bishops objected to JUC's activities, Ação Popular (Popular Action) was born in Minas Gerais to carry on with JUC's recent political work. Guided by some advanced Catholic priests, it found warm friends among such politicians as Paulo de Tarso and Almino Afonso. The UNE directorship, its majority divided about evenly between members of Ação Popular and the PCB, retained

[1] Paulo de Tarso, "Explicação Inicial," (May 1963), an introduction to the publication of two of his speeches in Congress.

[2] *Novos Rumos,* October 27–November 2, 1961.

[3] Thomas G. Sanders, "Brazil's Catholic Left," *America* (November 18, 1967); Emanuel de Kadt, "Religion, the Church, and Social Change in Brazil," *The Politics of Conformity in Latin America,* edited by Claudio Veliz.

strong ties with the Communist International Union of Students with headquarters in Prague.

Herbert Levy, contemplating the role of the Catholic Far Left, described Paulo de Tarso as a "new Christian type of Communist." Paulo de Tarso, no Communist, called on the Attorney General to ask Congress to allow Levy to be prosecuted for making this remark.

Among student leaders Paulo de Tarso was popular, but he felt that his lack of backing elsewhere limited his independence. He was especially handicapped by bad press relations, due in part to a decree he issued affecting comic strips (most of which originated in the United States): within four years, he announced, 60 per cent of the comic strips appearing in Brazil should deal with Brazilian themes.[4]

To the Education Ministry Paulo de Tarso brought Professor Paulo Freire, who, with some help from the United States AID program, had advanced the fight against illiteracy in the Northeastern state of Rio Grande do Norte.[5] Freire's innovations had included the introduction into teaching materials of pictures and expressions appropriate to the environment. But as Freire worked to put his literacy campaign on a national basis, anti-Communists scrutinized the expressions and decided that they aimed at teaching "subversion" as well as literacy.

The Education Ministry gave financial support to the Movimento de Educação de Base (MEB). This organization had been established, by an agreement between Quadros' Education Ministry and the National Conference of Brazilian Bishops, to make use of the radio in

---

[4] Paulo de Tarso, interview, Santiago, Chile, June 27, 1967.

[5] Neale J. Pearson, (*Small Farmer and Worker Pressure Groups in Brazil*, pp. 152–153) quotes from Antônio Callado (*Tempo de Arraes*, p. 28) to explain the teaching methods devised by Recife University Professor Paulo Freire. Pearson's translation reads in part: "The Paulo Freire method has as an objective to suddenly reveal the world to man. Instead of starting with [letters] as a basic unit toward a vocabulary, the illiterate absorbs entire words. . . . With drawings and with entire words, the illiterate . . . learns to divide the world into that of nature and that of culture. A leftist existentialist Catholic, of the Gabriel Marcel group, Paulo Freire not only teaches the peasant to read. As everyone in Pernambuco is indoctrinating the backwoods ruffian (*cabra*), he uses the fastest possible means, explosive words of great socio-political connotation. With the folder of illustrations (*letrume*) . . . he seeks to locate the illiterate in the social struggle that the illiterate does not know about, that what ought to be given to the man that learns the idea of learning to read is learning to struggle to improve life."

advancing basic education. By 1962 MEB had become involved in politics and issued voting instructions. With Paulo de Tarso in the Education Ministry, MEB prepared to apply Paulo Freire's procedure on a wide scale. Members of Ação Popular, using funds from the Ministry, were to distribute MEB's reading primer, which spoke of God, calling him "Justice and Love." The primer went on to tell the adult, who was beginning to read, that "The Brazilian peasants continue to be expelled from the land," "A complete change in Brazil is necessary," and "The people have a duty to fight for justice." Other phrases for the peasant to practice were: "The Brazilian people are an exploited people; Exploited not only by Brazilians; There are many foreigners exploiting the people; How can one free Brazil from this situation?"[6]

Student leaders, always busy, were particularly active in July 1963. The International Union of Students (of Prague) held a conference in Salvador, Bahia, during the week ending July 13. This was followed by the annual meeting of Brazil's UNE at Santo André, a suburb of São Paulo.

The meeting in Salvador, called "the International Week of Students of Underdeveloped Nations," attracted delegates from Cuba, Red China, and the Iron Curtain countries as well as representatives of the UNE. Members of the Brazilian Democratic Youth Front—opposed to the UNE directorship—criticized the Brazilian Education Ministry, the Foreign Ministry, the mayor's office of Salvador, and Petrobrás for providing money to sponsor what they said was not a meeting of students but, rather, a group of "professional agitators trained in Prague and Moscow."

Some of the "Democrats," following a practice they had used a year earlier at the UNE Quintandinha meeting, surreptitiously added ingredients to the food, making participants in the seminar mildly ill. Bahian anti-Communists amused themselves by arranging to have students receive anti-Peking literature in envelopes whose stamps indicated that it was posted in the U.S.S.R.; likewise, anti-Soviet literature was distributed in a way to indicate Red Chinese origin.

Foreign Communists went on to be present at the UNE Santo André

---

[6] Movimento de Educação de Base, *Viver É Lutar: 2⁰ Livro de Leitura Para Adultos.*

meeting, and there they heard speeches by Brizola, Paulo de Tarso, and Almino Afonso. Luís Carlos Prestes was present when Ação Popular and the Communists divided up UNE directorship posts for the year ahead. A few posts were allotted to members of Política Operária (POLOP), a hard-hitting independent Marxist revolutionary organization established in 1960 by a group that included a former Trotskyite.

The new UNE president, José Serra, described himself as a Catholic "but not of the Western type." As head of the São Paulo State Student Union, he had already allied himself with São Paulo Communist labor leaders to fight for the program of the Radical Left.

One of Congressman Herbert Levy's sons, an active opponent of the winning slate, was labeled "the whelp of a gorilla" by the São Paulo edition of the pro-Goulart, Petrobrás-assisted *Última Hora.* Later Levy and other Paulistas founded *Notícias Populares* to take some circulation away from *Última Hora* of São Paulo.

Following the Santo André meeting, Paulo de Tarso went to Bogotá, Colombia, for the Third Inter-American Conference of Education Ministers. There he pictured the Alliance for Progress as representing "the interests of conservative and privileged groups." While he felt that Brazil wanted a peaceful solution to its problems, he warned that the privileged classes, favoring the status quo, might "precipitate matters."

6. The Great Race for the Hearts of Rural Workers

RECIFE, CAPITAL OF TROUBLED PERNAMBUCO, was sometimes described as the "reddest" of Brazilian cities even though PCB membership in Pernambuco was less than in Guanabara and far less than in São Paulo. Miguel Arrais, governor of Pernambuco, condemned the Alliance for Progress, the United States wheat shipments to Brazil, and the Three Year Plan. Vargas' suicide and Quadros' resignation he blamed on "financing by imperialists." "Large landownings," he said, "are allied with North American imperialism and must be liquidated." Arrais lacked Brizola's oratorical sensationalism, but his apparent sincerity was effective.

In spite of his leftism and his important post, Arrais had no representation in the federal cabinet. He loomed as a rival of both Goulart and Brizola, and he wondered whether either wanted a peaceful presidential election in 1965. Goulart told General Joaquim Justino Alves Bastos, head of the Fourth Army, with headquarters in Recife: "Watch out for Arrais. He is very dangerous."[1]

Like Kubitschek, Lacerda, Magalhães Pinto, and Ademar de Barros, Arrais and Brizola hoped to succeed Goulart. For Brizola, legally ineligible for election in 1965 because his wife was Goulart's sister, the most immediate opportunity lay in constitutional change or violence. Arrais, however, supported peaceful, legal solutions, and so did the PCB members and their sympathizers who occupied posts in his state government.

At this time Francisco Julião, preacher of peasant violence, was suffering a series of reverses. Arrais, squabbling with him, jailed one of his right-hand men in Pernambuco.[2] More disasterously, Julião's guerrilla training camps, financed in 1962 by Cuban money, were becoming recognized as great fiascos; the few peasants who had seemed seriously interested in training for violence were bewildered by the utter lack of organization.[3]

As Julião looked around, particularly in the northeastern states of Rio Grande do Norte, Alagoas, and Sergipe, he could see great peasant-organizing activity, sponsored by the rising progressive wing of the

[1] Adirson de Barros, *Ascensão e Queda de Miguel Arraes*, p. 97.

[2] Artur de Lima Cavalcanti, interview, Recife, October 26, 1967.

[3] Report of a Castro agent, whose baggage was found after the crash (near Lima, Peru, on November 27, 1962) of the airplane in which he had left Brazil (document reproduced in *O Estado de S. Paulo,* January 29, 1963). See also "Report from Cuban Agent Coincides with the Facts Gleaned by the Brazilian Military" (translated from *Correio da Manhã,* February 1, 1963), given in U.S., Congress, Senate, Testimony of Jules Dubois in Hearing before the Subcommittee to Investigate the Administration of the Internal Security Act and Other Internal Security Laws of the Committee on the Judiciary, United States Senate, 88th Cong., 1st sess., October 2, 1963, *Documentation of Communist Penetration in Latin America,* pp. 99–101. Lieutenant-Colonel Nicolau José de Seixas' report is given in Appendix II (pp. 389–391) of the same hearing.

Catholic Church and inspired by Pope John XXIII's encyclical *Mater et Magistra*.[4] In Rio Grande do Norte Bishop Eugênio Sales had started to organize legal *sindicatos* of peasants in 1961, and soon similar work was begun in Julião's own state of Pernambuco, where Fathers Paulo Crespo and Antônio Melo set up the Serviço de Orientação Rural de Pernambuco (SORPE) for that purpose.

The 1963 Statute of the Rural Worker, which had spent eleven years making its way through Congress, was largely the work of Fernando Ferrari. It was supposed to do for rural labor what Vargas' legislation had done for urban labor. With the statute's promulgation by the Goulart administration on March 2, 1963, Governor Arrais set to work to enforce the clauses that benefited peasants.

The issuance of the statute coincided with the federal government's great show of interest in the organization of rural *sindicatos*. In January 1963 there were about 200 rural *sindicatos* in Brazil, many of which were the work of Catholics. To bring the number quickly to 1,800 became the aim of a new National Commission for Rural Syndicalization and its two creators: the Labor Ministry and the Superintendência de Política Agrária (SUPRA), which had been established late in 1962 to hasten agrarian reform. João Pinheiro Neto, the young professor from Minas who had lost his job as Labor Minister for publicly attacking Roberto Campos and Otávio Bulhões, was now in charge of SUPRA. To speed the formation of rural *sindicatos*, the new commission organized a staff of five thousand all over Brazil and made use of a fleet of vehicles. It paid rentals on behalf of the new *sindicatos*, and it furnished them with lawyers and accountants who were to assure the peasants of their rights, including the right to a minimum wage. The commission listened to the arguments of the four groups that were competing with each other to form rural *sindicatos*: the Communist União dos Lavradores e Trabalhadores Agrícolas do Brasil (ULTAB), Ação Popular (AP), non-AP progressive Catholics, and conservative Catholics.

Luís Carlos Prestes, finding more and more evidence that Communist principles could be established in Brazil without insurrection, decided early in 1963 that the PCB's past emphasis on peasant leagues was

---

[4] Márcio Moreira Alves, interview, Rio de Janeiro, November 11, 1967.

in need of change. Accordingly ULTAB, once the fashioner of Communist peasant leagues, joined the government's mad dash and began
to register rural *sindicatos* with the Labor Ministry. As the then-director
of the National Commission for Rural Syndicalization has explained
it, the ULTAB people were present, more than those of any other
group, at the Labor Ministry's day-to-day work for organizing rural
sindicatos. If the commission needed someone to go to a distant district,
the ULTAB people were willing to send someone. "I felt," he has
said, "that they worked more efficiently than other groups."[5] Particularly in the Northeast and far south, ULTAB was a great help to those
dreaming of suddenly giving Brazil 1,800 rural *sindicatos*. ULTAB
hoped to dominate the confederation of agricultural workers which was
scheduled to be organized.

Another important force, with friends in high circles, was Ação
Popular; it had government funds for distributing MEB primers to
illiterates and was particularly strong in its natal state, Minas Gerais.

Neither the progressive Catholics, such as those administering
SORPE in Pernambuco, nor the more conservative Catholics, such as
the Confederação Brasileira dos Trabalhadores Cristãos (CBTC), felt
that they received any assistance from the government. The CBTC had
long been setting up Christian "circles" of workers. Now seeking to
organize peasant *sindicatos*, it joined forces with São Paulo's José Rotta,
who had some experience in this work. This CBTC-Rotta alliance received financial assistance from IPÊS, the businessmen's organization
that hoped to save Brazil from Communism.

Men from SUPRA, ULTAB, and Ação Popular traveled around
Brazil in jeeps, getting signatures on *sindicato* registration forms, or
sometimes just writing in the names of people who did not know that
their names were being used. In this way over one thousand new rural
sindicatos were created in 1963. In each district, the Ministry gave preference to the group that submitted its application first. Upon finding
a district where the peasants said they had no *sindicato*, opponents of
ULTAB and Ação Popular would establish one but often discover later
from the authorities that their competitors had registered a *sindicato*
already. SORPE complained of persecution by the Labor Ministry and

---

[5] Sérgio Luiz Rocha Vellozo, interview, Rio de Janeiro, October 8, 1968.

by SUPRA.[6] Rotta, who found himself unable to get *sindicato* registration forms, has stated that late in 1963 Labor Minister Amauri Silva (Almino Afonso's successor) let the "leftist" *federações* participate in the creation of the *confederação* of rural workers even if they had not had time to register with the Labor Ministry.[7]

During the interval in which *sindicatos* formed state *federações*, rival groups submitted applications that would allow them to have as many as three federations in one state, because the ministry was recognizing *federações* of wage earners, small property owners, and those working leased areas on their own. The question of what to do about the rival applications was far from settled when the representatives of twenty-seven so-called *federações* met in Rio in December to establish the Confederation of Workers in Agriculture (CONTAG).[8]

Ação Popular had nine *federações*; the Communists (ULTAB), with the most *sindicatos,* also had nine; and the non-AP Christians had nine. Although AP and the Communists had shown keen rivalry in forming *sindicatos,* they reached an agreement at the summit, as they had done in the case of the UNE directorship. This agreement gave CONTAG's top posts to Communists.[9]

[6] Padre Paulo Crespo, interview, Recife, October 16, 1968.

[7] José Rotta, interview, São Paulo, November 30, 1965.

[8] After Goulart's fall, the Castelo Branco government declared that all but eleven of these *federações* were *fantasmas* (ghosts).

[9] Padre Paulo Crespo, interview, Recife, October 16, 1968. See Leonard D. Therry, "Dominant Power Components in the Brazilian University Student Movement Prior to April 1964," *Journal of Inter-American Studies,* VII, no. 1 (January 1965), 27–48.

7. Mourão Filho in São Paulo
(February–August 1963)

IN FEBRUARY 1963 General Olímpio Mourão Filho, who had been conspiring against Goulart in Rio Grande do Sul, was transferred to São Paulo to serve under Second Army Commander Peri Constant Bevilaqua. Bevilaqua had defended the inauguration of Goulart in

August 1961 and had criticized Dean Rusk for remarks made after Brizola expropriated the International Telephone and Telegraph Corporation subsidiary.

Mourão, as commander of São Paulo's Second Military Region, believed that he could count on many heads of Army barracks to follow him in overthrowing Goulart before it was "too late." He asked Colonel José Canavó, former commander of the Fôrça Pública, to determine the sentiment in this state militia in the interior of São Paulo. The colonel submitted a pessimistic report that mentioned poor armaments, infiltration, and much apathy.[1]

Despite this report, Mourão felt that São Paulo, becoming infected with the rebellious spirit of 1932, was full of possibilities. Governor Ademar de Barros, he learned, was disgusted to find Goulart continuing to work closely with the CGT. The governor planned to increase the fifteen-thousand-man Fôrça and the ten-thousand-man Guarda Civil (city police) and furnish them with newer weapons. Mourão further noted that a group of Air Force officers was conspiring with Colonel João Paulo Moreira Burnier, who had headed the Aragarças rebellion. These officers were in touch with some of the more aggressive associates of the São Paulo branch of IPÊS and with Júlio de Mesquita Filho, director of O Estado de S. Paulo.

Mourão did not underestimate the work being done by Paulista civilians—much of it in the field of publicity and education. Some of this work was defensive; people were organizing to fight in case Janguistas, Brizolistas, and their "Communist friends," and perhaps "infiltrated groups of sergeants," turned to violence. To protect themselves and their properties against a peasant uprising, members of the Sociedade Rural Brasileira were arming themselves and loyal farm workers.

Mourão, not inclined to wait for a Communist revolution to break out, organized a civilian staff headed by retired General Dalísio Mena Barreto. It included groups that supervised use of mass psychology, sabotage and countersabotage, intelligence, and transportation. Pam-

[1] Eldino Brancante, interview, São Paulo, November 23, 1965. Regarding armaments, see "Depoimento que o Col. José Canavó Filho Prestou a José Stacchini," O Estado de S. Paulo, June 27, 1965.

phlets were issued to remind citizens of what had happened in Czechoslovakia and to counteract "Red propaganda." This term was used to
refer to more than the Communist periodicals printed in Brazil and
the mass of Communist literature that came to Brazil from abroad;
publications of the non-Communist Radical Left, including the Catholic Far Left, were considered equally dangerous.

To spread alarm quickly, Mourão's civilian staff conversed with
business executives, local political party leaders, and the presidents of
clubs. Most helpful to Mena Barreto were the sporting clubs, some of
which supplied target ranges as well as men.

Late in May 1963 Mourão wanted to know how many civilian
disciples had been attracted. He told Mena Barreto to pass the word
along that all of them were to gather in front of Pacaembu Stadium
at 10:00 A.M. Sunday morning, June 2, and sit in automobiles, reading newspapers for half an hour. At the appointed time Mourão drove
to a spot where he could look down on the gathering. He saw about
one hundred cars parked, and in them about two hundred newspaper
readers.[2]

Organizers of this *concentração* expressed their disappointment at
the small turnout when they met with Mourão and Mena Barreto the
next day. But Mourão and Mena Barreto seemed pleased and remarked that those who had shown up were leaders. They had seen
several bank presidents and relatives of the UDN's Herbert Levy.[3]

Most of the São Paulo groups that favored organizing against the
Far Left sponsored a rally at a gymnasium on June 22. Among the
four thousand who attended were some from other states and men who
had been at odds in the past. Ademar de Barros, Carlos Lacerda, and
Júlio de Mesquita Filho were present. The ebullient Ademar, in an
almost endless speech, expressed his opposition to socialism and his
disappointment at not having been consulted by Goulart about the
new federal cabinet. Lacerda, in his vehement style, blamed the Pres-

[2] See Maria Helena Brancante, "Coube-me a Honrosa Delegação de Saudar o
General-de-Divisão Sebastião Dalyzio Menna Barreto," paper presented at meeting of
the Instituto Histórico e Geográfico de São Paulo, June 5, 1964. (Typewritten.)
[3] Eldino Brancante, interview, November 23, 1965.

ident's office for labor unrest. He accused Goulart of plotting his removal from the Guanabara governorship but added that Communist
infiltration in the Army had not gone so far as to let him get away with
it.

While the press commented on the "Lacerda-Ademar alliance,"
Mourão continued with his plot. After careful study, he recommended
that a factory turn out a lot of cheap, short, .22-caliber rifles, which
were light because much plastic was used. These appeared fairly in-
offensive and were acceptable for registration with the police. The
necessary munitions were easy to obtain and could be carried in good
supply.[4] Thanks to effective financial backing, a few thousand of these
weapons were produced and distributed to civilians in São Paulo, Rio
Grande do Sul, and the south of Minas Gerais. In Guanabara, Mourão
continued to find little interest.

In August 1963 Mourão was transferred to the command of the
Fourth Military Region, whose headquarters were in Juiz de Fora,
Minas Gerais. His São Paulo followers were depressed, but Mourão
told them that this shift, his "punishment," was providential. He said
that a revolution starting in São Paulo might not be properly interpreted, considering what had happened in 1932 and considering that São
Paulo is not well understood elsewhere. Furthermore, the proximity of
southern Minas to the city of Rio would best permit surprise.[5]

With Mourão's departure from São Paulo, Mena Barreto lost prestige. He could see that the anti-Goulart work among civilians was
being carried on more and more by groups that ignored him. He sometimes felt that these groups, critical of his advocation of the use of
Molotov cocktails, placed too much emphasis on long-term propaganda.

However, long-term propaganda was not the sole interest of these
groups. Many were getting ready to shoot it out with "Red guerrilla
fighters" and with those who were being encouraged to arise in arms if
Congress proved balky. Large numbers of anti-Communist labor leaders were being trained and sent to infiltrate Red unions. The sons of
those who had participated in the three-month anti-Vargas Constitu-

[4] Olímpio Mourão Filho, interview, Rio de Janeiro, October 9, 1965.
[5] Eldino Brancante, interview, November 23, 1965.

cionalista rebellion of 1932 prepared for a tough fight. Among them were the sons of Júlio de Mesquita Filho and Herbert Levy.

With São Paulo's numerous anti-far leftist civilian groups going their own ways, Mena Barreto turned his attention to advancing Mourão's ideas among young Army officers. An emissary of Mourão arrived to tell him of the anti-Communist work that had been done in Minas before Mourão's transfer. Men active there included General Carlos Luís Guedes (commander of the Tenth, Eleventh, and Twelfth Infantry Regiments), retired General José Lopes Bragança (whose work with civilians resembled the work Mena had done under Mourão in São Paulo), and Father Caio de Castro Alvim.

8. Congress Blocks the Administration's Agrarian Reform Program

V ARGAS WAS SAID to have integrated the urban workers into the political life of Brazil. Darci Ribeiro, who was head of Goulart's Casa Civil, has stated that if Goulart, by a radical agrarian reform, could have done the same thing for the rural workers, he would have "broken the PSD and the UDN, dependent on votes controlled by landowners."[1] According to Darci Ribeiro, Brazil had forty million peasants under the control of thirty-two thousand large landowners.

In 1960 Darci Ribeiro, then a professor, had studied agrarian reform at President Kubitschek's request. Although Kubitschek had refused to sponsor the ideas that Ribeiro had then developed, these found a warm advocate later in President Goulart, and they became the principal features of the Goulart administration's agrarian reform program. Goulart, Ribeiro has pointed out, wanted Brazil to have ten million rural property owners instead of two million. To make this change, the Goulart administration favored the expropriation of properties rather than the use of high taxes on unused properties. Never, in

[1] Darci Ribeiro, interview, Montevideo, November 13, 1967.

the opinion of Darci Ribeiro, has agrarian reform been accomplished anywhere in the world by means of property tax measures.[2]

Considerable publicity was given to the key point of the Goulart program, that of using bonds to pay for expropriated properties— a matter requiring a constitutional amendment. But Darci Ribeiro's ideas, which were adopted by Goulart, included other features. A certain percentage of agricultural land in each region would have to be devoted to raising food. Landowners who did not comply would have to lease to those who would. The new lessees and the three million farm workers who were already leasing were to be highly favored. Their expulsion by property owners would be made very difficult. Rentals were never to exceed 10 per cent of the value of production, a percentage so much lower than what was usual that the value of rural properties would decline precipitously ("reducing speculation in land").[3]

After Goulart opened the new congressional session on March 15, 1963, with a plea for agrarian reform, the PTB presented the administration's controversial proposal, which would force landowners to rent their properties if they were considered to be holding them in an antieconomic or antisocial manner. The proposal also contained a provision for a constitutional amendment authorizing the government to pay for land expropriations with 6 per cent bonds whose face value adjustments (due to currency depreciation) would have been limited to annual increases of no more than 10 per cent. Study of the proposal was begun by a congressional commission late in April, by which time much opposition had developed against it. Even the PTB was torn, with many of its members reluctant to support the radical reform ideas of the party's Grupo Compacto.

The PSD, representative of many landowners, came out against the compulsory rental of land and insisted that the face value of the proposed bonds should be fully adjustable to cover currency depreciation. Unlike most of his colleagues, Abelardo Jurema, PSD congressional leader from the Northeast, was more friendly to the President's ideas

[2] *Ibid.*
[3] *Ibid.*

and went so far as to say that the question should be decided by a plebiscite.

Lacerda was able to persuade a UDN convention to vote its disapproval of any reform of the constitution. His success demonstrated the support he had acquired in the party whose nomination for the presidency he expected to receive; it also indicated the prevailing UDN sentiment. However, Lacerda's antireform position antagonized a number of "progressive" UDN party leaders, including Governor Magalhães Pinto, who sought leftist support for his own presidential ambitions and who was becoming very friendly with Miguel Arrais. Goulart, advised that Magalhães Pinto wanted to help push the agrarian reform program through Congress, sent PTB leader Bocaiuva Cunha and other reform-minded congressmen to make speeches in Minas. Their mission, Magalhães Pinto told them, was very important.[4]

Herbert Levy, freer to act after completing his term as chairman of the UDN, met in the Library of Congress with twenty-one other *deputados*. They decided to distribute subjects for speeches, part of a "counteroffensive" to recapture from the Left the initiative on the floor of Congress.[5] Levy visited 230 towns to mobilize public opinion against the program of the President and the PTB.

Late in May the congressional committee, which had been studying the administration's bill for agrarian reform, came out against it. Representatives of the PSD, UDN, and PSP opposed the bill; representatives of the PTB and PDC (Christian Democratic Party) favored it. Then some Christian Democrats unsuccessfully espoused a compromise whereby the size of the adjustments on the bonds would depend on whether they were in payment of lands expropriated from small, medium-sized, or large holdings.

In July, after months of further negotiating, the Chamber of Deputies defeated (164–69) a proposal known since the Quadros administration as the Milton Campos bill.[6] It did not appeal to the PSD because it would have forced landowners to rent unused or "under-used" acreage. The administration considered it inadequate, for it included

[4] Luís Fernando Bocaiuva Cunha, interview, Rio de Janeiro, December 5, 1968.

[5] Herbert V. Levy, interviews, São Paulo, August 9, 1963; November 15, 1965.

[6] George W. Bemis, *From Crisis to Revolution: Monthly Case Studies*, p. 122.

no constitutional amendment. However, the enactment of an amendment, requiring a two-thirds majority, appeared extremely unlikely; the administration could not secure even a simple majority.

PSD leaders then presented Goulart with a program that would have protected from expropriation all properties being used productively and all properties of less than ten thousand hectares (24,700 acres). It would have allowed bonds, issued in payment of expropriations, to have a maximum annual value adjustment (for currency depreciation) of 50 per cent. The PSD also insisted that the government draw up "a coherent plan" and appoint a commission of "competent people."[7] When Goulart rejected these proposals as not radical enough, PSD leaders concluded that his interest in agrarian reform was "purely political."

Addressing a crowd of thirty thousand in one of Recife's main squares late in July 1963, Goulart declared that "those who combat agrarian reform do not know the risks they are running." He also called for a tax reform that would strike at the wealthy. In his numerous public appearances he made vigorous appeals to support the reforms and was effectively backed by the organizing apparatuses of the CGT, PCB, and UNE.

In August Goulart asked labor adviser Crockatt de Sá to stop working for the anti-Communist "third force" in labor. He explained that he needed labor's backing and that, if labor were divided, his enemies would say that he was weak.[8]

Labor unions, in bulletins issued for their members, pointed out that unless the constitution were modified, the government would have to issue "the fabulous sum of THREE TRILLION cruzeiros, or ten times the money in circulation, for expropriating large landholdings." The bank workers learned that a banking reform would force banks to funnel their credits to the development of agriculture and industry, thus providing all the goods needed by the working class and producing such prosperity that the threat of unemployment would disappear. To force the enactment of such reforms and to exert pressure on the

[7] Filinto Müller, interview, Brasília, October 15, 1965; Ernâni do Amaral Peixoto, interview, Brasília, October 15, 1965.

[8] Gilberto Crockatt de Sá, interviews, Rio de Janeiro, October 9 and 11, 1967.

President, Brizola and other "radical leftists" had already set up what they called the Frente de Mobilização Popular (Popular Mobilization Front). This *frente* established local chapters, made up of state labor leaders, state student leaders, and local "nationalist" politicians.

The vote on the PTB agrarian reform project taken in Congress early in October indicated that an impasse on "leftist reforms" had been reached. The project was beaten 176 to 121. Goulart felt convinced that this outcome did not represent the popular will, and some of his advisers considered another plebiscite.

Reminding Goulart that time was running out, Kubitschek and Lacerda began their campaigns for the October 1965 election. (In July 1963, Ademar de Barros, also preparing to run, said that this was the first time electioneering for the presidency had started "thirty months ahead of time.") Kubitschek, who wanted PSD and PTB support, faced a problem on agrarian reform but let it be known that he was studying the matter. In the Northeast he praised Miguel Arrais and promised to fight against the "vultures which try to take everything from the Brazilians for their own benefit." Lacerda, also traveling about making speeches, ran into CGT-organized opposition in Rio Grande do Sul. Supporters of his presidential hopes described him as being "what Quadros had been believed to be."

9. The Sergeants' Rebellion (September 12, 1963)

GOULART FELT that sergeants should be allowed to hold legislative posts.[1] However, as the constitution explicitly forbade this, the Supreme Court was expected to rule unfavorably on the seating in Congress of Sergeant Antônio Garcia Filho, member of the Nationalist Parliamentary Front. Adepts of violence, including a few agents of the Chinese

[1] Abelardo Jurema, *Sexta-Feira, 13: Os Últimos Dias do Govêrno João Goulart,* p. 109.

Communists,[2] organized the sergeants for a rebellion throughout Brazil in case of an adverse decision.

War Minister Jair Dantas Ribeiro asked Justice Minister Abelardo Jurema to try to get the Supreme Court to postpone acting.[3] But on Wednesday, September 11, the court voted seven to one against the sergeants. The lone vote in their favor was cast by Hermes Lima, who had recently been appointed to the high tribunal by Goulart.

As in the days before the 1935 Communist uprising, anti-Communists had infiltrated groups of potential rebels. They learned, therefore, that a revolt was to break out on Saturday night, September 14, when the authorities would be away from Brasília for the weekend.[4] Speaking to a large group of irate Marine and Air Force sergeants in Brasília on the night of the eleventh, an anti-Communist infiltrator urged that the rebellion begin at once. He argued that the government secret service had learned of the Saturday plan. The outbreak, therefore, took place in Brasília before dawn on September 12 without any coordination with similar groups that were ready to act elsewhere in Brazil on the fourteenth. The sergeants in Brasília, also at the suggestion of anti-Communist infiltrators, started out by cutting off Brasília's communications and thereby contributed to making the movement in Brasília an isolated one.

The six hundred sergeants, corporals, and enlisted men who rebelled in Brasília roved around in bunches before daybreak, claiming to be in control of the airport and the Justice and Navy buildings. They "arrested" a few dignitaries, including a Supreme Court Minister. But the rebels were disorganized and poorly led. Later in the morning they were subdued by Army contingents, some of which Jair

<hr />

[2] One Red agent from China, writing from Switzerland on March 20, 1963, to his successor for "work in Brazil," stated that "In the principal work of joint struggle, Sergeant Garcia Filho and Sergeant Paulo Prestes and [Congressman] Max da Costa Santos are new relations in the Brazilian Government for us." Documents found with nine Chinese captured after Goulart's fall, reproduced in *O Estado de S. Paulo*, May 10, 1964.

[3] Jurema, *Sexta-Feira, 13*, p. 108.

[4] The source of information in this and the succeeding paragraph prefers to remain anonymous.

Dantas Ribeiro had posted in Brasília soon after he became War Minister. The only person killed was an innocent passer-by.

About one thousand rebels, subversives, and suspects were made prisoners. Of the more than one hundred sergeants who had rebelled, only two or three were Army sergeants. Army officers attributed this to the existence of a closer relationship between commissioned and noncommissioned officers in the Army than in the Navy or Air Force.

That night Goulart reached Brasília by airplane from Rio Grande do Sul and issued a statement that was kindlier to the rebels than were those issued by the Justice and Military Ministers.[5] Almost all the men who were captured were found to have simply followed the orders of about one hundred sergeants and were rapidly set at liberty.

The uprising was not a complete failure. It persuaded Goulart and Darci Ribeiro that the regime should have better relations with, and do something on behalf of, the military men in the lower ranks.[6]

The War Minister's vigorous action raised his prestige. Unkindly commentators described the Navy and Air Force Ministers as having been unprepared because they were giving all of their attention to the wrangle about which branch of the service should control the airplanes on the aircraft carrier *Minas Gerais*.

Following the end of the short revolt in Brasília, a group of São Paulo sergeants called for "continuation of the struggle until victory." The CGT praised the "vigorous protest" of the Brasília sergeants and declared a planned series of strikes to be the "sole alternative to succumbing to employers' impositions, stemming from a juridical and economic setup which no longer meets the needs of Brazil." Army officers in São Paulo arrested two labor union leaders.

Six days after the sergeants' rebellion, Second Army Commander Peri Constant Bevilaqua issued a thunderous directive in São Paulo. He condemned the Brasília rebels for having taken up arms against the constitution they had sworn to defend. In words that were certain to arouse a storm, the General warned of the need of being on guard against accepting support from "syndical evildoers": the CGT, the

[5] Jurema, *Sexta-Feira, 13*, p. 120.
[6] Darci Ribeiro, interview, Montevideo, November 13, 1967.

Forum Sindical de Debates of Santos, and the Pacto de Unidade e Ação (PUA). He described these "subversive traitors" to democracy as attempting to set up a superpower. To accept their support, he said, was to "smear the honor and dignity of the Brazilian soldier."[7]

The General was violently attacked by Arrais and by organized labor. He was congratulated by the heads of the Third and Fourth Armies and by the usually silent former President Dutra. São Paulo anti-Communists prepared to present him with a sword of gold. Cordeiro de Farias and other conspirators, hoping that Bevilaqua would agree to lead troops in rebellion, flocked to the Second Army headquarters.[8]

But Bevilaqua, who did not favor armed revolt, disappointed these people. The War Minister called him to Rio and gave him a reprimand for his pronouncement. The statement from the War Ministry spoke of Bevilaqua's "improper conduct" and the resulting "distortion" of the general's words by political factions opposed to the administration. This statement did not close the incident, because the War Minister continued to be seriously worried about Bevilaqua[9] and sought an opportunity to deprive him of his command of troops.

[7] George W. Bemis, *From Crisis to Revolution: Monthly Case Studies*, p. 138; Mário Victor, *Cinco Anos que Abalaram o Brasil: de Jânio Quadros ao Marechal Castelo Branco*, p. 452; Araken Távora, *Brasil, 1º de Abril*, p. 45.

[8] José Stacchini, *Março 64: Mobilização da Audácia*, p. 62.

[9] Jurema, *Sexta-Feira, 13*, p. 129.

10. Kidnap Attempts (early October 1963)

SENATE PRESIDENT MOURA ANDRADE, speaking late in September 1963, summed up the situation as he saw it: "Illegal organizations and agitators create public disorder without being punished, keeping the country in a state of political turmoil, and sapping the nation's economic strength. It cannot be denied that the gravest kind of subversion is now under way in Brazil."[1]

[1] Araken Távora, *Brasil, 1º de Abril*, p. 44.

At about the same time—during a period of widespread strikes—
Lacerda spoke to the Rio correspondent of the *Los Angeles Times*. In
a taped interview, which first appeared in the *Los Angeles Times* and
then found its way to the Brazilian press, Lacerda described the Brazilian government as being in the hands of Communists and others who
were determined to "stop the country," to stop transportation, to make
work difficult and to "degenerate the whole public economy and the
whole public spirit. And the whole damned thing is done from the
top down."

Lacerda pictured the "masses" as "nauseated, fed up with the artificial revolution, with this cabinet agitation and subversions." Speaking of the price-wage spiral, he said that "the Communists know they
will be answered 'yes' the day before they ask for an increase." Lacerda
viewed agrarian reform as "untimely." "Social and political reform
must come first, along with education of the peasants. It has been discovered that Brazilian farm labor is not even prepared—I would not
say to run the land—but even to use it properly."

The Governor advised that the United States should withhold further aid to Brazil. Under the circumstances it would accomplish nothing. It would be "like trying to sell roses in an opium den, or tran-
quilizers to people already gone amok." "Nonintervention is one thing
but another thing is to ignore what is going on." The United States
Department of State, Lacerda said, must learn "after all these years"
that it makes a difference to know who is running Brazil.

Lacerda described the military as debating whether "it is better to
tutor him [Goulart], to patronize him, to put him under control to
the end of his mandate, or to choke him off right now." His words
were interpreted as forecasting that Goulart would soon be toppled,
because he said: "I don't think this thing will go to the end of the
year."[2]

The three military ministers considered Lacerda's remarks unpatriotic and perhaps even an invitation to the United States government to

---

[2] Excerpts from Lacerda interview with Julian Hartt based on AP cable from Los
Angeles, given in *Brazil Herald*, October 1, 1963.

intervene in Brazilian affairs.[3] In a joint manifesto they praised Goulart's discernment and farsightedness and condemned extremist minorities of the Left and of the Right. In particular they condemned Lacerda, the "bad citizen" who was using techniques "learned when he was a leader of the Communist Youth." He was accused of presenting "our country like a subcolonial little republic" just when Finance Minister Carvalho Pinto was about to leave for important discussions with financial authorities in the United States.

The military ministers also condemned Governor Ademar de Barros, who had recently said that "some people want to establish a socialist regime in Brazil" and that he did "not quite believe" that elections would occur in 1965.[4] Ademar has since explained that on several occasions Goulart invited him to join in a move to depose Lacerda, long an adversary of Ademar. Apparently Ademar always declined, telling Goulart that after the removal of Lacerda "then you will put me out."

By September 31, 1963, when the military ministers rebuked the governors of Guanabara and São Paulo, Ademar had broken with the President. The break occurred when Goulart, at the São Paulo University, made an address Ademar interpreted as an accusation against "free enterprise people, described by Jango as sharks responsible for misery and poverty."[5] That night Goulart, still in São Paulo, telephoned Ademar. The Governor said: "What do you want after that stupid speech?" Goulart wanted to explain it, and so Ademar and General Bevilaqua joined the President at a private residence. They found him surrounded by "over forty Communists," who booed the Governor and the General when they arrived. "Jango" explained that he could not abandon his friends, the labor union leaders. Ademar considered all these leaders Communists and blamed them and their Forum Sindical de Debates (the "local strike command" in Ademar's words) for practically continuous strikes, which were ruining São Paulo's economy. Strikes on the railroads and at the port of Santos ("the Brazilian Moscow") created an economic blockade.

[3] Abelardo Jurema, *Sexta-Feira, 13: Os Últimos Dias do Govêrno João Goulart,* p. 123.

[4] *Brazil Herald,* October 1, 1963.

[5] Ademar de Barros, interview, São Paulo, December 1, 1965.

After the military ministers pronounced against Lacerda and Ademar, Ademar expressed surprise that their statement had not come from the Justice Minister, "the voice of the government." He added that his own state government opposed "fabricated strikes, which are responsible for new currency issuances, and each new currency issuance is a step toward complete collapse." Lacerda said that the military ministers were "pathetically" trying to find third parties to blame "for the impoverishment and demoralization to which the innocent people are being condemned."

Even before this "jeer" at the military ministers, the government had been carefully examining the National Security Law of 1953 (against subversion) to find a justification for using the First Army to punish Lacerda, throw him out of office, and institute federal *intervenção* in Guanabara.[6] Reformers in the President's office felt that the removal of Lacerda and Ademar, to be followed by a state of siege, might strengthen the Executive and produce emergency conditions, perhaps the only ones in which reforms could be implanted. Although Goulart opposed illegal removal of the two governors, a few of his military supporters went ahead with plans to "arrest," or kidnap, Lacerda. The first of two "plots" was limited to words, but the second resulted in action.

While Goulart's supporters plotted Lacerda's downfall, three anti-Goulart civilians developed plans—unknown to Lacerda—for capturing the President at his "weekend farm property," "Capim Melado," at Jacarepaguá in Guanabara state.[7] These civilian sleuths (one of them was brother of the head of a Guanabara special police department) had been spying on Goulart when he went there. Noting that occasionally he met with PCB leaders (including Prestes), they hoped to capture him in the company of Communists. They made friends with a Portuguese who owned property nearby, and there they built up a cache of arms belonging to Guanabara state. After Francisco Julião arrived at "Capim Melado" in an Air Force helicopter, they felt that

[6] The federal government would "intervene" and take over the powers of the state government (Jurema, *Sexta-Feira, 13*, p. 126). See also Araken Távora, *Brasil, 1º de Abril*, pp. 47–48.

[7] Charles Borer, interviews, Rio de Janeiro, October 5, 1966 and October 6, 1967.

their moment had come. But before they and their men acted, a neighbor, putting out an unexpected brush fire, discovered the arms cache and reported it to Vila Militar.[8] Army officers arrived and the plotters went into hiding for a few days.

During the ensuing investigation, which made headlines throughout much of October, Lacerda and state Security Secretary Gustavo Borges claimed that the arms were needed to protect rural properties from land invasions by Communist guerrillas. Justice Minister Jurema pointed out that there had been no guerrilla operations in the area. He called attention to the secret manner in which the arms cache, so close to Goulart's property, had been built up; and he proclaimed it significant that, after its discovery, those immediately responsible had gone into hiding.

Like Goulart, Lacerda, too, escaped a poorly executed kidnap attempt—this one promoted by Paratroop General Alfredo Pinheiro. Following discovery of the state arms cache near "Capim Melado," a group of paratroopers from Vila Militar set out to grab the Governor near Miguel Couto Hospital while he was making a morning tour to inspect construction work. But the group was small because some of the General's subordinates, including two lieutenant-colonels, refused to obey his orders.[9] One young man sent a warning to state cabinet member Sandra Cavalcanti, and she alerted two Air Force officers, a Naval officer, and state Security Secretary Borges. A vehicle, used by the would-be kidnappers, broke down due to sabotage by three junior officers.[10]

[8] *Ibid.*
[9] Olavo Bilac Pinto, *Guerra Revolucionária*, p. 50.
[10] Sandra Cavalcanti, interview, Rio de Janeiro, October 21, 1966.

11. The Request for a State of Siege (October 1963)

CHARGES ABOUT "kidnap attempts" had not yet been publicly made when the military ministers, meeting with the President, discussed Ademar de Barros' declaration in response to their manifesto attacking the governors of Guanabara and São Paulo. As the ministers worriedly paced back and forth on a veranda of Rio's Laranjeiras Palace, they concluded that Lacerda and Ademar had joined forces and were planning to use arms to overthrow the federal regime.[1] At the suggestion of the War Minister, they decided to ask Congress to declare the nation in a state of siege (martial law). Other "solutions" (drastic measures against governors) strayed from *legalidade* and thus held little appeal for a large body of the military.

With this decision reached at an all-night session in Rio, Goulart and his advisers sped to Brasília before dawn on October 4. Early that afternoon Congress received the administration's request for the thirty-day state of siege. This was the maximum time allowed under the constitution, but it could later be renewed by Congress. It would suspend numerous constitutional guarantees, such as free expression of opinion, the right to hold meetings, and the granting of habeas corpus.

Reasons for the request were given in messages from Justice Minister Jurema and the military ministers. "Strikes keep reoccurring and serve as a pretext for political conspiracy," the military men said. "Dissatisfied groups preach violence and subversion as the solution of the problems which afflict the laboring classes. State governors forget the responsibilities of the posts to which the people elected them, and they rebel against democratic legality."[2]

Goulart called in Dante Pelacani and Rafael Martineli to advise them that a state of siege had been requested, and that it was necessary for the nation's good. He asked them to convince their labor com-

---

[1] Abelardo Jurema, *Sexta-Feira, 13: Os Últimos Dias do Govêrno João Goulart,* p. 127.

[2] Mário Victor, *Cinco Anos Que Abalaram o Brasil: de Jânio Quadros ao Marechal Castelo Branco,* p. 438.

panions of this decision.[3] But although in August Goulart had told Crockatt de Sá to desist in his anti-CGT work so that he might have the fullest possible backing by labor leaders, the CGT, scared of a state of siege, was unwilling to cooperate with Goulart. When Pelacani and Martineli met other CGT leaders in Rio, they resolved to call a general strike should the state of siege be enacted. Then each CGT leader went to his own state to work against the administration's request.

While the request was studied by the congressional Justice Commission, some reform-minded legislators, who had prematurely celebrated the forthcoming strong government at Laranjeiras Palace on the evening of October 3, had second thoughts; they worried lest the state of siege be used against them.[4] They also were affected by the loud public outcry against the government's request. Understandably the press, as well as radio and television stations, shuddered at the news of Goulart's plans to appoint censors. Jurists, such as former Ministers João Mangabeira and San Tiago Dantas, defended constitutional guarantees. Almino Afonso, who had once done legal work for a São Paulo labor federation, hastened to São Paulo to stir up the workers there against a state of siege.

Labor groups were easily convinced that exceptional presidential powers might be used against them, particularly as the press had been blaming wage increases for the inflation. The CGT issued a manifesto reminding the President that "the maintenance and amplification of democratic liberties are irreplaceable and necessary for the struggle against enemies of the people. What the people demand, and the workers defend, are concrete steps against imperialism and large land ownership and the agents of these things in Brazil."[5]

With the CGT taking this position, Brizola let the President down. He had agreed with Goulart that a state of siege was necessary, but now he found it more convenient to oppose the President's plan.[6] Thus he adopted the position taken by Miguel Arrais from the outset. The Pernambuco Governor, fearing that extraordinary powers for the federal

[3] Dante Pelacani, interview, São Paulo, November 24, 1968.
[4] Gilberto Crockatt de Sá, interview, Rio de Janeiro, December 12, 1968.
[5] Victor, *Cinco Anos Que Abalaram o Brasil*, p. 460.
[6] Luís Tenório de Lima, interview, São Paulo, November 21, 1968.

executive would be used against him after they had been used against
Lacerda and Ademar de Barros,[7] criticized the President severely.
Rumors described Goulart as planning to move simultaneously against
Lacerda and Arrais, thus giving his "bid for emergency powers a po-
litically 'neutral' character."[8]

PTB congressional leader Bocaiuva Cunha felt that the rumors
about a move against Arrais were invented by leftists to strengthen
the campaign against the state of siege. Bocaiuva Cunha had learned
from the Ministers of Health and Agriculture that the administration's
request was to be quickly followed by a movement of troops and tanks
in Guanabara, and perhaps also in São Paulo, showing great Army
support for a federal government with exceptional powers.[9] Backers
of this point of view felt that the Army would help depose Lacerda
and that the resulting strong government would decree reforms being
"demanded" by the people. For forty-eight hours Bocaiuva Cunha
worked in Congress for the state of siege.[10] But he noted that in the
meantime the military did not take the steps he had been led to believe it would take. On Sunday, October 6, he declared his opposition
to the administration's request. He described it as "reactionary," "in-
opportune," and "antilabor."[11]

By then it seemed that every group in Brazil, from the Far Left
to the Far Right, was assailing the idea of exceptional powers for
Goulart. A majority of the congressmen "remembered 1937," when
following a state of martial law Vargas had closed down all legislative chambers with the help of the military. The congressional Justice
Commission declared that the request of the Goulart administration,
as it was worded, was unconstitutional.

Congress was preparing to reject the request when suddenly it received, on October 7, new messages from the President, the Justice
Minister, and the military ministers. These messages withdrew the

[7] Jurema, *Sexta-Feira, 13,* p. 130.

[8] Thomas E. Skidmore, *Politics in Brazil, 1930–1964: An Experiment in Democracy,* p. 263.

[9] Luís Fernando Bocaiuva Cunha, interview, Rio de Janeiro, December 5, 1968.

[10] The *Brazil Herald* reported on October 6 that a correspondent in Brasília on
the fifth found 190 legislators against, and 160 for, approval of the state of siege.

[11] George W. Bemis, *From Crisis to Revolution: Monthly Case Studies,* p. 150.

request, although nothing had occurred to change the situation described two days earlier as requiring the state of siege. This time the President mentioned his "natural aversion" to emergency measures. The military ministers admitted that the request had run into trouble.

Goulart announced that "making a withdrawal, in order to side with the people, is not a withdrawal." But nothing could hide the humiliation his regime had suffered. He felt depressed by the problems his high office had brought him.[12] At the same time he felt bitter that men he had supported had turned against him.

The Frente de Mobilização Popular, which had disappointed Goulart, lost no time in telling him how he could "reconquer the good will" he had lost with the state of siege request. This front, in which Brizola, Almino Afonso, the UNE, the CGT, and the Nationalist Parliamentary Front were said to be participating, denounced what it called the President's vacillation and failure to adopt a "popular" program. Now it demanded agrarian reform, voting rights for illiterates, political rights for soldiers and noncommissioned officers, the suspension of payments on foreign debts and the prohibition of the remission of profits abroad, government monopolies covering all exports and foreign exchange, the expropriation of the Capuava (private) oil refinery, and the expulsion of the Hanna Mining Company from Brazil.

The Frente de Mobilização Popular existed more in press reports than in actual fact. Neither it nor the Nationalist Parliamentary Front had the unity that the newspapers implied.[13] The Brazilian Communist Party (PCB) liked the idea of participating in "Fronts" and therefore Communist members of the CGT considered the CGT a part of the Frente de Mobilização Popular even though the PCB felt uneasy about some of Brizola's violent ideas and found him difficult to get along with. Non-Communist CGT leaders declared that the CGT did not belong to the Frente. They stated that when Communist labor leaders attended meetings—which were described as meetings of the Frente—they merely did so as CGT "observers" (as in the case of Hércules Correia) or as representatives of labor organizations of their

---

[12] Jurema, *Sexta-Feira, 13*, pp. 131–135.
[13] Bocaiuva Cunha, interview, December 5, 1968.

own (as in the case of Roberto Morena, head of the Movimento Sindical da Guanabara).[14]

[14] Clodsmidt Riani, interview, Juiz de Fora, November 2, 1968.

12. The São Paulo General Strike (late October 1963)

THE "GENERAL STRIKE," which broke out in São Paulo late in October 1963, revealed the CGT to be weaker than it claimed. The strike also advanced the antigovernment conspiracy in the São Paulo barracks, ended General Bevilaqua's career as a troop commander, and reflected the new tendency of Labor Tribunal judges to declare strikes illegal. (Most of these judges held lifetime appointments, made before the CGT had come to power.)

Leaders associated with the CGT worked hard in advance to assure that the strike would halt all activity in the state unless their demands were met. They called for industry-wide contract revisions to provide 100 per cent pay increases, with living cost adjustments every three months. Goulart described these demands as "justified." State government officials denounced the impending strike as a scheme for creating chaotic conditions, which would allow the federal government to intervene in São Paulo.

The strike was most formidable on its first day. But, even then, less than half of the 700,000 workers associated with the eighty-odd striking *sindicatos* heeded the strike call. Of these, the Communist-leaning metalworkers and textile workers were in the vanguard. The city of Santos was paralyzed. On the other hand, power and transportation in the city of São Paulo continued to function; anti-CGT labor leaders have taken some credit for preventing a more wide-spread breakdown.[1]

The State Police and troops of the Second Army were active in arresting strike leaders and protecting workers who stayed on their jobs.

[1] Olavo Previati, interview, Rio de Janeiro, December 18, 1968.

Delegates arriving in São Paulo for an Inter-American Economic and Social Council meeting found the city police busy trying to protect those taxi drivers who ignored strike orders.

Second Army Commander Bevilaqua sent a battalion to Santos to help troops there maintain order. The battalion's deputy commander, Major Ner Augusto Pereira, had been unsuccessfully trying to follow Mena Barreto's instructions to get young Army officers to plan a revolt against Goulart. At the Santos docks the strikers laughed at the troops, which were supposed to guarantee that nonstrikers could work. When the commander in Santos ordered soldiers to load and unload ships if workers would not do so, Major Ner declared his action unconstitutional. He further told the commander that if he wanted the dock work done he should arrest the Labor Minister,[2] who appeared to be a puppet of the CGT.

Ner, imprisoned for thirty days, suddenly found himself a hero to young officers. His work for rebellion went better. So did similar efforts of Major Rubens Resstel, who had been plotting rebellion for over a year. With the advance of the conspiracy in the São Paulo barracks, the Friday night meetings of young anti-Goulart officers were better attended. Partly as a result of the general strike, sixty or seventy officers would gather where once there had been five or six. Army Colonel Cid Camargo Osório joined the conspirators and took the lead in carrying out the work, which included the development of a system of coded radio communications with conspirators in other states.[3] Paulista civilians, under the direction of Herman de Morais Barros, Paulo Quartim Barbosa, and Paulo Egydio Martins, were inspired by the general strike to prepare with greater urgency to have a movement to overthrow Goulart.

The strike lasted for four days, during which employers insisted that varying industry conditions made an over-all settlement impractical. Crockatt de Sá, Goulart's anti-CGT adviser, noted that more workers returned to their jobs each day. He telephoned the São Paulo Regional

[2] Eldino Brancante, interview, São Paulo, November 24, 1965.
[3] Luís Werneck, Flávio Galvão, Roberto Brandini, Luís Maciel Filho, and Heber Perillo Fleury, interview, São Paulo, November 24, 1965.

Labor Tribunal, urging that it not succumb to a strike that was about to collapse.

The tribunal backed the employers' thesis in a four to three decision; although the tribunal disappointed the taxi drivers, in most cases it ruled an 80 per cent pay increase with assurances that another increase would be considered in six months. At the same time it declared the strike illegal. The decision meant that employers were not to pay for time lost and spelled the end of a "general" strike that had demonstrated little of the intensity of São Paulo's famed general strike of 1917, led by Anarchists in the days when governments persecuted strike leaders.

In declaring the strike illegal, the São Paulo Labor Tribunal adopted a concept recently developed by the Guanabara Labor Tribunal: since lengthy strikes, particularly in transportation, seemed to be "leading to chaos," and since the Labor Ministry, which had customarily ruled on the legality of strikes, now showed no inclination to declare strikes illegal, labor tribunals should decide whether strikes were legal or not.[4]

During the São Paulo strike the state Fôrça Pública arrested over six hundred workers. The arrest of labor leaders by Army Commander Bevilaqua deeply disturbed Goulart,[5] who saw the General falling under the influence of Ademar de Barros, Cordeiro de Farias, and Nelson de Melo.

Bevilaqua was, therefore, named Chief of Staff of the Armed Forces, a post that had become largely decorative. To the disappointment of conspirators, who pleaded that he resist the Goulart regime and remain in charge of troops, he accepted the appointment.[6] Amauri Kruel became the new commander of the Second Army.

Other command changes were made to strengthen the *dispositivo militar* (military backing) of the President. Having a hand in these arrangements was the new Casa Militar chief, Argemiro Assis Brasil, Gaúcho friend of Goulart and of retired "Red Marshal" Osvino

[4] Gustavo Simões Barbosa, interview, Rio de Janeiro, December 16, 1967.

[5] Abelardo Jurema, *Sexta-Feira, 13, Os Últimos Dias do Govêrno João Goulart*, p. 137.

[6] Eldino Brancante, interviews, November 23; December 3, 1965.

Ferreira Alves. Assis Brasil was the brother of an outstanding Brazilian Communist who had died in Europe.

After Lieutenant-Colonel Francisco Cavalcanti Boaventura lost his post of chief of the paratroopers in Rio, he publicly charged that the War Minister had dismissed him because he had refused to participate in the early October plot against Lacerda. His place was taken by an officer who was said to have agreed to act against Lacerda.[7]

Poorly educated Cândido Aragão was promoted to admiral and put in charge of the Marines. Shocked naval officers, who saw Aragão as a man who would agree with anyone who advanced him beyond his merits, issued a vehement manifesto. In it they pointed out that Aragão was a "disgraceful" element who had once been expelled from the Navy for swindling. Sílvio Heck, the first to sign the manifesto, spent Christmas in prison.[8]

[7] Araken Távora, *Brasil, 1º de Abril*, p. 56.
[8] Sílvio Heck, interview, December 13, 1965; Távora, *Brasil, 1º de Abril*, p. 58.

13. Efforts to Reform without the CGT

IN OCTOBER BOCAIUVA CUNHA, who had turned against the state of siege request, lost his job as PTB congressional leader. In November the President, disappointed also in the CGT leaders' response to that request, authorized Crockatt de Sá to resume his mission of defeating Communists and their allies in the forthcoming election of officers of the Industrial Workers' Confederation (CNTI).

Working indefatigably for reforms, Goulart held a discussion with thirteen governors (Lacerda and Ademar declined to be present) and received some vague expressions of support. He gathered with PSD leaders who were interested in PTB backing for Kubitschek, and some of them spoke about restudying agrarian reform. Following the PSD's expression of concern about inflation (approaching 100 per cent on an annual basis), Goulart upset Finance Minister Carvalho Pinto by expressing similar concern in a magazine article. "I am much attacked, but I do not attack," Goulart told the governors. Speaking to PSD leaders, Goulart pointed out that he was being rudely assailed by the Brazilian Communist Party. He could have added that leaders of the Frente de Mobilização Popular, in the habit of handing him ultimatums, were also giving him trouble.

Brizola, the Frente's crisis-climate–provoking coordinator, continued to work to weaken Goulart's control of the PTB.[1] The Guanabara congressman, head of the PTB in Rio Grande do Sul, was cheered by the margin with which his candidate won the mayorship of Pôrto Alegre in November. Late that month, with the help of nationwide broadcasts, Brizola issued a call to the people to organize into Groups of Eleven Companions (Grupos de Onze Companheiros). In his widely circulated eleven-page brochure, "nationalist leader" Brizola explained that an upheaval was in the offing and that the people must organize to avoid being oppressed. The Groups of Eleven were to help bring about agrarian reform and "free Brazil from international spoliation."[2] Rio's Rádio Mayrink Veiga, which Brizola used, received several thousand forms, filled in by Groups of Eleven. Many of the groups were made up of misfits,[3] but news of them put fear into Brizola's foes, who were generally unaware of their worthlessness.[4] CGT leaders felt that Brizola's new move was designed to "weaken the syndical movement."[5]

Crockatt de Sá presented a greater threat to the CGT. In December Dante Pelacani was dropped from his influential Labor Ministry post, that of Director-General of Social Welfare. Pelacani had not only rejected Crockatt de Sá's offer to lead the UST against the CGT; he had turned up at a UST congress and told an unfriendly audience that there

---

[1] João Cândido Maia Neto, interview, Montevideo, November 16, 1967

[2] Leonel Brizola, *Organização dos "Grupos de Onze Companheiros" ou "Comandos Nacionalistas,"* Rio de Janeiro, November 29, 1963. (11-page brochure.)

[3] Osneli Martinelli, interview, Rio de Janeiro, October 12, 1966.

[4] João Cândido Maia Neto, who was a director of Rio's Rádio Mayrink Veiga (then owned by São Paulo Senator Miguel Leuzzi), opposed the idea of the Groups of Eleven. The groups, he says, were formed for Brizola's political purposes (interview, Montevideo, November 16, 1967). Brizola explains that he organized the Groups of Eleven "in view of the great weaknesses, errors, and failures of the government of Goulart" (interview, Atlántida, Uruguay, November 14, 1967).

[5] Dante Pelacani, interview, São Paulo, November 24, 1968.

was no need to have a UST. Pelacani, whose relations with the Red Chinese were good, had been participating in discussions concerning the creation of CUTAL (Central Única de Trabajadores de América Latina), a Communist-line Latin American labor organization. The post, which Pelacani lost in December, was filled in accordance with the votes of two representatives each of labor, management, and the government. When the representatives of management and the government, at Crockatt de Sá's suggestion, joined forces to replace Pelacani with a government man, the CGT claimed that the government had united with the company owners against the workers.[6]

Pelacani then disclosed to the press that Crockatt de Sá had threatened such a step should he (Pelacani) refuse to "betray his companions"[7] in the forthcoming CNTI election, now scheduled for early January 1964. He added that Goulart had broken "with the syndical movement." CNTI President Clodsmidt Riani, long a Goulart man, asserted that the government had abandoned the workers, who had always backed it. Hércules Correia dos Reis proclaimed that the break between the government and "the entire syndical front" was "total."[8] The newspapers also carried the protests of Osvaldo Pacheco (of the stevedores), Commander Melo Bastos (of the airline personnel), Luís Tenório de Lima (of workers in food industries), and Benedito Cerqueira (of the Guanabara metalworkers). Cerqueira was a federal congressman; Riani and Correia were state assemblymen.

Tenório de Lima spoke for Pacto de Ação Conjunta (PAC—Pact of United Action). Correia was presiding over the Permanent Commission of Union Organizations (CPOS) and held high posts in many of them, including the PUA. Pacheco, the serious-minded and hard-working head of the PUA, had been voted the "best Brazilian syndical leader" in a poll of São Paulo City *sindicato* heads conducted by the anti-Communist Instituto Cultural do Trabalho.[9]

[6] Clodsmidt Riani, interview, Juiz de Fora, November 2, 1968.

[7] *Jornal do Commercio*, December 24, 1963.

[8] *O Estado de S. Paulo*, December 27, 1963.

[9] Dante Pelacani and Antônio Pereira Magaldi tied for second place in the poll and were followed by Roberto Morena. Altogether the thirty-three who voted distributed their votes among seventeen labor leaders (see J. V. Freitas Marcondes, *Radiografia da Liderança Sindical Paulista*, p. 51).

In reply to this barrage from the Communists and their allies, Crockatt de Sá asserted that he had exerted no pressure against Pelacani. "What Dante Pelacani, Clodsmidt Riani, and others are feeling is their coming defeat in the election for the directorship of the CNTI," he said.[10]

Already in October Education Minister Paulo de Tarso had resigned with the assertion that his leftist opinions did not allow him to collaborate further with the government. Former Labor Minister Almino Afonso expressed his disenchantment with the regime late in the year when Finance Minister Carvalho Pinto, having had administrative difficulties with Goulart, was succeeded by Nei Galvão. Galvão's appointment, Almino Afonso said, was "either a joke or a lack of respect for popular forces."

Bocaiuva Cunha's dismissal from the PTB congressional leadership was for a moment felt to be helpful to the extinct "PSD-PTB coalition." But Darci Ribeiro minimized the break between Goulart and Bocaiuva Cunha, and PSD congressional leaders continued wary of the President. They took the lead in arranging for a watchdog session during the regular congressional recess (December 15 to March 15). Congressmen feared that otherwise Goulart might take it upon himself to declare a state of siege. Auro de Moura Andrade was instrumental in getting signatures on behalf of the watchdog session, and Goulart, therefore, sponsored an effort to remove him from the presidency of the Senate. Goulart failed.

The single-minded President[11] saw two ways to achieve reforms, and he prepared to use them both. The first method permitted the Executive to act on his own in certain cases. The second method involved bringing popular pressure to bear on Congress.

To begin the "executive phase," Goulart ruled in December 1963 that private oil refineries had to use either petroleum that the government would import or petroleum produced in Brazil by Petrobrás. In

---

[10] *O Estado de S. Paulo,* December 27, 1963.

[11] Some men close to President Goulart had liked to think of the reform efforts of the "three Johns": Pope John XXIII, John Kennedy, and João Goulart. With the assassination of John Kennedy on November 22, 1963, following the death earlier in the year of Pope John XXIII, Goulart was pictured as being left alone, to carry on without the other two Johns.

January 1964, he signed the regulations implementing the rigorous bill, voted by Congress in September 1962, to restrict profit remittances abroad. The matter had been left pending during unsuccessful efforts to renegotiate debts with the United States. The bill provided that the 10 per cent ceiling on annual remittances was to be calculated only on the money and equipment originally brought into Brazil and not on the so-called national capital made up largely of reinvestments. (This national capital, Darci Ribeiro estimates, was between 70 and 80 per cent of the total Brazilian investments of foreigners.)

The bill, a blow to foreign investment, was not considered radical by the Far Left, which had come to favor the outright nationalization of all foreign capital.[12] By the time the bill became effective, the political and economic climate was such that foreigners were not investing in Brazil anyway, and Brazilians were building up huge assets in foreign banks.[13] Brazil's national production growth had fallen in 1963 to about 2 per cent, a decline on a per capita basis.

The most controversial "reform by executive decree" was derived from an interpretation of a constitutional provision which allowed the government to expropriate lands along the margins of public improvements "in the social interest." A decree was drawn up authorizing SUPRA (under João Pinheiro Neto) to expropriate landholdings within ten kilometers of federal highways, railways, or water projects. In January 1964 Goulart presided over a meeting of SUPRA officials and the military ministers. It was agreed that the armed forces would assist SUPRA by providing aerial surveys and mapping.

The proposed SUPRA decree did not deal with the big issue of changing the constitution to allow bonds to be used for the payment of expropriated properties, but it did evoke much excitement when Goulart submitted it to the consideration of some political leaders. Reform-minded Magalhães Pinto (who was becoming vexed at the federal government's failure to advance fifteen billion cruzeiros to his state) suggested regional planning rather than uniform application. Kubi-

[12] Darci Ribeiro, interview, Montevideo, November 13, 1967.

[13] Speaking at the Rotary Club of São Paulo in July 1962, San Tiago Dantas said that the total of Brazilian capital in the United States, Switzerland, and other foreign countries was 150 per cent of the maximum that the Brazilian government could hope to obtain from the entire Alliance for Progress program.

tschek spoke of collaborating with Goulart to insure democratic elections in 1965; but for the most part the PSD assailed the proposed SUPRA decree. Auro de Moura Andrade declared that it would lead to the "Cubanization" and "Communization" of Brazil. The UDN's José Bonifácio de Andrada called it unconstitutional.

SUPRA's João Pinheiro Neto advised that properties of less than two hundred hectares (494 acres) would not be expropriated. In a reference to a remark of Lacerda to the *Los Angeles Times*, Pinheiro announced that peasants should get land whether or not they had been trained to use it.

14. A Victory for the Communists and their Allies

EARLY IN 1964 UDN President Bilac Pinto accused Goulart of collaborating with "his brother-in-law, his political ally," in steps that would bring about a "revolutionary war" for the implantation of a Communist dictatorship.[1] But Goulart, speaking of his brother-in-law at this time, said to his Justice Minister: "Brizola, instead of hurling himself against our common enemies, against the opposition and our principal adversaries, uses his time, his ink, paper, and adjectives against me. Against me!"[2] Nor did the Brazilian Communist Party agree with Bilac Pinto. It declared that "with respect to the present government, the position of the Communists is one of opposition, of struggle against its policy of conciliation with imperialism and large landholdings."[3]

In the Union of Secondary School Students (UBES) the PCB had taken full control after a hassle with the Catholic Student Youth (JEC). Thus the PCB seemed to be moving ahead in the "peaceful"

[1] Olavo Bilac Pinto, *Guerra Revolucionária*, pp. 77, 104–105.

[2] Abelardo Jurema, *Sexta-Feira, 13: Os Últimos Dias do Govêrno João Goulart*, pp. 77–78. Goulart was referring to articles in Brizola's weekly, *O Panfleto*.

[3] Partido Comunista Brasileiro, "Teses Para Discussão" (in preparation for Sixth Party Congress), special supplement of *Novos Rumos*, March 27–April 2, 1964.

manner that Luís Carlos Prestes felt would result in legality for the party. Internally, however, the PCB was torn by the common problem of the times: whether to join those who saw an uprising on behalf of "popular demands" as inevitable, or to be left behind with a conservative image.

In its official program for agrarian matters the PCB tended to favor violence. It is true that the PCB helped persuade Goulart to amend the SUPRA decree so that it would not touch properties under five hundred hectares; the PCB therefore appeared more conservative than Pinheiro Neto, who had been prepared to protect only properties under two hundred hectares.[4] But, at the same time, the PCB encouraged armed bands to invade properties that exceeded five hundred hectares. Such invasions, it said, were legitimate and healthy.[5]

The PCB's greatest strength was in the top ranks of organized labor. In part this was due to effective work by Communists and in part it was due to a government policy of "peaceful co-existence" with Communism in labor. The future of that policy, to be revealed at the CNTI election of officers early in January 1964, was perhaps Goulart's most important decision. When the election was less than a week away, twenty-two CNTI federations were reported definitely opposed to the CGT's pro-Communist incumbents, and an equal number were reported in their favor. Among the remaining ten "uncommitted" federations, Crockatt de Sá saw that he had enough strength to win the day from the Communists.

Casa Civil Chief Darci Ribeiro and Casa Militar Chief Assis Brasil, like the Labor and Justice Ministers, insisted that Goulart would hurt himself by a clash with the Communists. On the other hand, Crockatt de Sá argued that Goulart would be making a fatal mistake if he did not "free himself and Brazilian labor" from the Communist "idiots" who wanted to take the nation "to anarchy." Speaking with Goulart in Petrópolis, Crockatt de Sá argued that the

[4] João Pinheiro Neto, interview, Rio de Janeiro, October 8, 1968. (The PCB did this in the hope of attracting owners of medium-sized properties to the "anti-imperialist front.")

[5] "Teses Para Discussão," special supplement of *Novos Rumos,* March 27–April 2, 1964.

unsuccessful general strike in São Paulo revealed the CGT to be without support among the working masses. The presidential adviser had also been encouraged by a pro-Goulart demonstration held at Volta Redonda by the UST without any Communist assistance.

At the last minute Goulart decided against Crockatt de Sá. Thus Riani retained the CNTI presidency. Vice-President Pelacani became secretary-general. Luís Tenório de Lima, São Paulo Communist leader, was made secretary in charge of organization, and Deputado Benedito Cerqueira, of the Guanabara metallurgical workers, became secretary for social security matters.[6] The Communists hailed Cerqueira's appointment as presidential adviser to replace Crockatt de Sá, whom they accused of having offered money and public posts to defeat them. After their re-election some of them went to call on anti-Communist Second Army Commander Kruel to invite him to help celebrate their victory. But they could not find the General.

The outcome of the CNTI election strengthened the position of Communists in other labor organizations (just as a Communist defeat would have had the opposite result). The National Confederation of Workers in Commerce (CNTC), Brazil's second largest confederation, had been run by Antônio Pereira Magaldi, who was labeled "an extreme rightist" by *Última Hora* because of his work with the anti-Communist Movimento Sindical Democrático (MSD). "Independents" in the CNTC, impressed by the victory of Riani, Pelacani, and Tenório de Lima in the CNTI, joined with CNTC pro-Communists to tie the CNTC election at ten federations for each side. Twice more the electors gathered, only to provide the same result. The federal government then took temporary control of the CNTC, and Magaldi traveled to Argentina on international labor matters.

For a while longer Goulart continued independent of the Frente de Mobilização Popular, whose composition contained some elements thoroughly disliked by a majority of congressmen. While Communist labor leaders celebrated their CNTI victory, he turned to Deputado

[6] Benedito Cerqueira was, and has continued to be, a director of the Communists' World Federation of Trade Unions. Luís Tenório de Lima belonged to the Central Committee of the PCB.

San Tiago Dantas to unite the entire Left behind a new Front Supporting Basic Reforms (Frente de Apoio às Reformas de Base).

Goulart began seeing more of Miguel Arrais. He called him to Rio late in January and got his endorsement of the San Tiago Dantas Front. Arrais, as he told the press after seeing Goulart, planned to reach understandings with "all sectors of the popular forces, without excepting a single one." He added that: "João Goulart and I" know of the "corruption by economic power," and know that "external pressure on Congress makes reforms difficult."[7]

Arrais helped to get the minimum wage in Pernambuco set at a figure above those of neighboring states.[8] The new rate frequently was not paid, employers often claiming that they could not do so; but Arrais did his best to enforce laws that favored the underprivileged. Late in February 1964, plant owners in Pernambuco were so disturbed by the state government and by constant strikes, "threats," and "acts of subversion" that they themselves went on strike; sugar mills and shops closed. Public messages backing Arrais were issued by the Frente de Mobilização Popular and the UNE; Riani, as head of the CGT and CNTI, Pacheco, as head of the PUA, and Hércules Correia and Roberto Morena, Communist labor leaders in Guanabara, also announced their support.

By television and radio Arrais appealed to workers to start cutting sugar cane. They did as he asked and mill owners, not wanting the cane to spoil, started up their plants again.[9]

[7] *Última Hora,* São Paulo, January 22, 1964.

[8] Nilo de Souza Coelho, interview, Brasília, October 15, 1965; Antônio de Oliveira Brito, interview, Brasília, October 20, 1965.

[9] Artur de Lima Cavalcanti, interview, Recife, October 24, 1967.

15. Seeking Popular Support for Reforms

In February 1964 San Tiago Dantas (suffering from cancer) delivered his new front's bulky program to newsmen. He explained that he and Miguel Arrais were the principal "consultants" of the new movement, which was to ensure parliamentary and popular support for reforms.

The so-called San Tiago Dantas Plan included the following: votes for illiterates, legalization of the Communist Party, the eligibility of noncommissioned officers and enlisted men to participate in politics, the use of adjustable-value bonds to pay for expropriated properties, tax reforms, periodic wage adjustments, state monopolies covering coffee and ore exports, and the revision of all mining concessions. It also called for the immediate promulgation of the SUPRA decree-law, which would start expropriating all but small properties along highways, railways, and water projects.[1]

San Tiago Dantas, looking for support for his Front Supporting Basic Reforms, heard federal Congressman Marco Antônio Coelho—spokesman for Luís Carlos Prestes' PCB—say that its program was acceptable. Some PSD leaders agreed to discuss the program provided that the "Radical Left"—Brizola, the CGT, and the UNE—not be included in his front.

The "Radical Left" was not of one mind. On the whole the CGT thought well of San Tiago Dantas' program; but memories of the AMFORP "deal" and the Three Year Plan were fresh. Brizola had no intention of going along with the man who a year earlier had called him a "negative leftist." He and his representative, Max da Costa Santos, heaped abuse on San Tiago Dantas when they met with the CGT to discuss the position of the Frente de Mobilização Popular. Brizola used his recently founded weekly, *O Panfleto,* to accuse San Tiago Dantas of having put Brazilian money at the disposal of the United States; for this he was sued by the former Finance Minister.

---

[1] *Brazil Herald,* February 15, 1964.

On January 18, 1964, when the press was carrying the first reports of San Tiago Dantas' new "mission," Brizola met with the Frente de Mobilização Popular to urge that the President act. This meeting included representatives of the CGT, UNE, UBES, Ação Popular, and the Liga Feminina Nacionalista. A note was released stating that "the Frente de Mobilização Popular—after hearing Governor Miguel Arrais and Deputado Leonel Brizola, who told of their conversations with President João Goulart—manifests its willingness to discuss the national crisis with his Excellency."[2] This note listed numerous matters that, it said, the President had full authority to handle himself. These included issuance of the SUPRA decree and the expropriation of the country's largest privately owned oil refinery so that it would come under the management of Petrobrás.

Headlines during the first two months of 1964 did little to recommend such an arrangement. Two Petrobrás directors, recently appointed to please some labor leaders, accused the organization's president, General Albino Silva, of graft. The accusation was described as part of a plan of one Far Left faction to gain from another the control of "annual commissions of five million dollars" derived from contracts. Silva was replaced by Marshal Osvino Ferreira Alves. Arrais wired "the peoples' marshal" to make "as few changes as possible in Petrobrás."

Silva declared that Petrobrás was a "rats' nest," crooked and in Communist hands, and he charged that the Communists were using the oil monopoly to take over the country. Armed Forces Chief of Staff Bevilaqua made a similar charge. Glycon de Paiva, an eminent engineer, then let it be known that of the organization's twenty-nine key posts, twenty-one were in the hands of "militants of the Russian line" with one in the hands of a follower of the Chinese line. He called Petrobrás "the most important Communist bastion in America, after Cuba." It was also, he said, a bank for financing subversion and a very practical "school of corruption."[3]

On behalf of his Front Supporting Basic Reforms, San Tiago Dantas met with congressmen. After he spoke with CGT leaders, it was an-

[2] *O Estado de S. Paulo,* January 19, 1964.

[3] Glycon de Paiva, "Petrobrás como Banco da Subversão Nacional e Escola Prática de Corrupção," *Jornal do Brasil,* February 16, 1964.

nounced that in Rio on March 13 the President would preside over a great mass meeting that was to give impetus to the offensive for reforms. While CGT-affiliated labor organizations prepared to furnish a crowd, CGT leaders took over the direction of the program and the speaking arrangements. Featured speakers were to be Goulart, the vice-governor of Guanabara, and a CGT representative; the themes were to be the signing of the SUPRA decree and the expropriation of the Capuava petroleum refinery.[4]

The rally's organizers had a difficult time with Brizola, whose ideas had become too radical for them and who appeared likely to scare most Brazilians. The President feared that Brizola might make remarks that would be embarrassing to him and harmful to the forthcoming discussions about rescheduling foreign debts. When the CGT asked Brizola to be present on March 13 but not to speak, Brizola declined the invitation.[5] But there was always the chance that Brizola, in an area where he had demonstrated massive vote appeal, would appear anyway and "yield to demands" that he speak.

For the meeting Goulart selected Cristiano Otoni Square, between the Pedro II Railway Station and the War Ministry. Lacerda, maintaining that the Guanabara state government had the authority to decide which public places could be used for meetings, ruled out the use of the square. His ruling ignored, Lacerda said that the Army was being called on to guarantee "an illegal act promoted by the agents of a foreign power."

While the arrangements for the "monster rally" occupied the public's attention, the presidency announced a 100 per cent increase in minimum wages. It was reported that the salaries of federal employees would likewise be increased by 100 per cent.

Meanwhile presidential candidates continued to prepare for October 1965. Ademar de Barros, with Rio newspaper director João Calmon as his running mate, came out against legalizing the PCB. Kubitschek announced that the PCB should be legalized and that Brazil should

---

[4] Dante Pelacani, interview, São Paulo, November 24, 1968.
[5] *Ibid.*

recognize Red China and support its application for United Nations membership.

Magalhães Pinto arranged financial assistance for newspapers. The grateful *Última Hora* of São Paulo valiantly defended the Minas governor against Lacerda's "gorillas" and declared that his campaign was the campaign of the cruzeiro against the dollar.[6] Magalhães Pinto warned that Lacerda's candidacy would excite passion dangerous to the democratic system, and he went to seek the support of Quadros, who was preparing to campaign for the mayorship of São Paulo.

As the UDN prepared to nominate Lacerda, Magalhães Pinto considered seeking the presidency on some other ticket. He hoped that Miguel Arrais, always cold to the United States and its officials, would be his running mate. But Arrais was a presidential candidate himself. The Governor of Pernambuco had worked hard to become more than a regional figure. Favored by much of the CGT and by Ação Popular, highly satisfactory to the PCB, and backed by the PTB's Almino Afonso,[7] Arrais agreed to be "a true radical reform candidate" for President.

Brizola was predicting that chaos would wreck the prevailing order of things long before the presidential election. What concerned Arrais was that the federal administration was doing nothing to prevent an explosion, and he spoke to Goulart of his fear.

[6] *Última Hora*, São Paulo, January 6 and 14, 1964.

[7] Pelacani, interview, November 24, 1968; Luís Tenório de Lima, interview, São Paulo, November 21, 1968; and Almino Afonso, interview, Santiago, Chile, June 28, 1967.

16. Far Leftists Find Hostile Audiences in São Paulo and Minas

PAULO DE TARSO, Brizola, Arrais, Almino Afonso, João Pinheiro Neto, and Guanabara Vice-Governor Elói Dutra frequently received stormy receptions in São Paulo. Some disorders were caused by Paulista

women, many of them members of the União Cívica Feminina. Others
were caused by Ademar de Barros' tough police, who were sometimes
disguised as students.

Eight hundred of Ademar's "students"—some of them carrying
books—were present to hoot and whistle early in October 1963 when
Education Minister Paulo de Tarso tried to give an address at the
Mackenzie University. The meeting became a brawl. To save himself
from being pulverized by blows, the speaker jumped over a high wall
and fled.[1] When the federal authorities telephoned the governor to
ask what he had done to the Education Minister, Ademar expressed
his regret at the "deplorable event."

Paulo de Tarso's leftism was also causing him difficulties in Congress and in his own Christian Democratic Party. A congressional investigating commission, looking into funds supplied by the Education Ministry to the National Union of Students, asked him to explain
the appointment of some school inspectors. The new inspectors, commission members said, were dangerous professional agitators who had
been associated with guerrilla fighters in Ecuador. Soon after, conservative leaders in the Christian Democratic Party accused Paulo de Tarso
of betraying the party with his extreme views. It was then that Paulo
de Tarso resigned his Education Ministry post.

In March 1964 Goulart was upset by the experience João Pinheiro
Neto had with Ademar's sham "students" and with state policemen
who joined them on the pretext of quieting them. The SUPRA head
told the press: "I saved myself only by a miracle." He said that he had
driven up to the São Paulo Law School to give a speech and had been
greeted by bombs and bursts of machine gun fire. (According to the
Governor, the visitor also received a punch on the nose before he decided to drive off in his car instead of delivering his address.[2]) "I
hope," Pinheiro Neto said afterwards, "to return to the Paulista capital
with Army guarantees, which I shall today request of President Goulart. The Paulista police gave me no protection, and unfortunately the
Army also failed."[3]

[1] Ademar de Barros, interview, São Paulo, December 1, 1965.   [2] *Ibid.*
[3] *Correio da Manhã,* March 18, 1964. For full details see *Última Hora,* São Paulo,
March 18, 1964.

"You can't do that!" Goulart exclaimed in a telephone call to the Governor. Ademar blamed the incident on a clash, which he said he could not prevent, between "democrats and Communists."

São Paulo anti-Communist women showed their spirit. In February 1964 thirty UCF members joined an audience of three thousand workers and teachers who were calling for legalization of the Communist Party. The featured speakers had difficulty making themselves heard because, whenever they spoke, a UCF member in the audience simultaneously delivered an address in a loud voice. In this way Deputada Conceição da Costa Neves disturbed the evening for the friends of the Communist Party and got some of them to hit her and spit on her.[4]

A few days later fifty Paulista women tried to attack Miguel Arrais, who was to be the star of a television interview. They were prevented by what they have described as a wall of "Communists" who were protecting him; they also had to contend with three busloads of Santos dockworkers, who had come to be inspired by Arrais' presence. The women's shouts against the Pernambuco governor almost started a riot. Arrais was upset because he had to enter the studio by a back door. The women, also annoyed, resolved not to ignore back doors in the future.[5]

Women of Minas Gerais, priding themselves on the state's Catholic tradition, were also effective in opposing national leftist leaders. Shocked to learn in January 1964 that Governor Magalhães Pinto had approved the holding of a convention of the Central Única de Trabajadores de América Latina (CUTAL) in Belo Horizonte, they played a significant role in the protest. This Communist-inspired Latin American labor organization saw the opportunity of making an effective showing in Brazil. Presidential hopeful Magalhães Pinto, not blind to the strength of forces that had given Brizola a large vote in Guanabara in 1962, could be expected to be more cooperative than Ademar de Barros or Lacerda. As for CUTAL's planned meeting, the Governor cited the constitutional right of free assembly and expression. Com-

---

[4] Regina Figueiredo Silveira and other officers of the União Cívica Feminina, interview, São Paulo, November 24, 1965.
[5] *Ibid.*

munist leader Roberto Morena, one of the three hundred Brazilian delegates to the CUTAL convention, praised the forthcoming gathering in Belo Horizonte as another step forward "in the creation of conditions for overcoming the present division of the syndical movement in all of the continent."[6] Among the countries sending observers were Czechoslovakia, Hungary, and Rumania.

Belo Horizonte's Archbishop made public his message to the Governor telling of the "total dismay" with which the people had learned about the holding of "a clearly Communist congress" in Belo Horizonte.[7] At the suggestion of Church leaders, Mineiros prayed that Magalhães Pinto see the light.[8]

Belo Horizonte's Mayor Jorge Carone led a huge street meeting. The mob, after visiting São José Church, moved threateningly on the Palácio da Liberdade bearing a manifesto with thousands of signatures. The Governor remained behind locked gates. Speakers discouraged an invasion by reminding the people that they would soon have opportunities to show their determination. Women had resolved to lie down on the airfield, covering it completely with their bodies to prevent airplanes from arriving with CUTAL delegates. Taxi drivers refused to serve three members of a Soviet group who had already arrived.

Finally, Magalhães Pinto issued an announcement telling of the "voluntary decision" of the workers to transfer their meeting from Belo Horizonte to Brasília.[9] The proadministration *Última Hora* remarked that Magalhães Pinto had done all he could for CUTAL but had been faced with a "furious wave of McCarthyism."[10]

Early in 1964 conservative Mineiros also combatted plans for agrarian reform. They noted that a few laborers (rural and otherwise) were organizing themselves to descend on Rio and Brasília to demand land. Brizola, claiming that his Groups of Eleven totalled 200,000 members, was urging the peasants to prepare themselves to seize the land.

A group of farmowners from the Minas city of Governador Valadares declared themselves "fully resolved to open fire on anyone who

[6] *O Estado de S. Paulo,* January 21, 1964.

[7] *Ibid.*

[8] Oscar Dias Corrêa and family, interview, Brasília, October 18, 1965.

[9] *O Estado de S. Paulo,* January 24, 1964.

[10] *Última Hora,* São Paulo, January 25, 1964.

invaded" their properties. Inspired by the Biblical tones of Father Pedro Maciel Vidigal, a PSD federal congressman from Minas, landowners forcibly prevented SUPRA from holding a meeting at Corinto, in the north of the state. Pinheiro Neto, who wanted to check the validity of rural property titles in Minas, was prevented from speaking when he tried to give a talk about SUPRA in Governador Valadares in February. "I escaped alive," he has said, "because I belong to an oligarchy."[11] (The Pinheiro name and family are highly regarded in Minas.)

Federal officials threatened to have the Army disarm the landowners. Pinheiro Neto announced that the expropriation of two foreign-owned landownings in Minas might take place "even before the SUPRA expropriation decree is signed by President Goulart." If the landowners would not negotiate with SUPRA, they would, he said threateningly, have to face "something worse."

Late in February the anti-Communists of Minas, particularly the women, made sensational headlines. A few days before Brizola was due to arrive to install a local Frente de Mobilização Popular, they held a meeting of the Mobilização Democrática Mineira. This meeting was well attended because of the efforts of Father Caio de Castro Alvim and other Catholic Church leaders who asked the women to be there to protest the Governor's allowing Brizola to come. The speakers included Sílvio Heck, Mayor Jorge Carone, Father Vidigal, and other prominent Minas federal congressmen. The Governor was asked to fire two "leftist" members of the state cabinet.

The same large auditorium had been reserved for the evening of February 25 by the Frente de Mobilização Popular. As the time for Brizola to arrive drew near, Magalhães Pinto ordered the state police to surround the building, to guarantee his right to free expression, and, if necessary, to protect him.

Hundreds of women came with their rosaries and umbrellas. Many were poor, brought from the *favelas* by priests. They seemed peaceful enough, and the police let them in. Among the seats they occupied were those at the speaker's table. When the first supporters of the Frente de Mobilização Popular tried to take their places, the women

[11] João Pinheiro Neto, interview, Rio de Janeiro, October 8, 1968.

unleashed an assault with chairs and umbrellas. Husbands and sons participated, and the meeting turned into a fight, carried by television to screens throughout the state.

This chaotic situation prevailed when Brizola arrived. His party included his wife, Neusa Goulart Brizola, and "the two musketeers of Brizola"—Congressmen Max da Costa Santos and José Guimarães Neiva Moreira. He was also accompanied by Minas state cabinet secretary José Aparecido de Oliveira. With microphone in hand, Brizola stood at the head of the stairs outside the meeting room to which the women had barred his entrance. Whenever he opened his mouth, the women prayed. Using their rosaries and reciting the Ave Maria, they drowned out his words.[12]

Brizola, followed by a hostile crowd, fled down the street. A member of his group used a pistol to oblige a passing car to stop, and Brizola and his friends got in. One of the original occupants of the car, not knowing who had entered, was shouting epithets about Brizola and was thrown out. While the crowd hurled oranges and stones at the car, the owner was forced to drive to the airport. Late at night Brizola flew to Rio.

Belo Horizonte hospitals took care of some of the wounded. Among the fifty persons reported wounded was a "leftist" congressman whose skull had been fractured. The police detained marines who had come from Rio with Brizola, and they relieved them of their tommy guns and revolvers. One of the marines remarked that in Rio things would have been different due to protection by Marine Commander Aragão.

Max da Costa Santos said that Belo Horizonte had "transformed itself into a national Dallas."[13] The attack on Brizola was condemned by Magalhães Pinto as reflecting the sort of radicalism the UDN should avoid. It was condemned by Ação Católica and Catholic Youth organizations, which rebuked "extremist political groups" for "seeking to manipulate religious sentiment."[14]

According to Brizola, the Minas government had "lost control over the reactionaries."[15] However, not much later, that government gave

[12] Dias Corrêa and family, interview, October 18, 1965.
[13] *Última Hora*, São Paulo, February 26, 1964.
[14] *Ibid.*, February 28, 1964.
[15] *Ibid.*, February 26, 1964.

effective guarantees when Miguel Arrais spoke in Juiz de Fora, the second largest city of Minas. On the instructions of Magalhães Pinto, thousands of members of the state police protected the speaker and his audience by surrounding the theater. But the police were stoned.

After this reaction, the commander of the state police, which had twenty-two thousand men in active service and eighteen thousand in the reserve, told the governor that he could no longer guarantee such meetings "against the popular will."[16] The state police had a strong anti-Communist spirit.

[16] Dias Corrêa and family, interview, October 18, 1965.

"Christianity never was a shield for privileged people. Nor can the rosaries be lifted up as arms against those who call for the distribution of private landed property, still held in the hands of a few fortunate people."

President Goulart
March 13, 1964

"In the crisis of 1961 these same hypocrites, who today show a false zeal for the constitution, wanted to tear it up and bury it in the cold grave of Fascist dictatorship. . . . Who is speaking about discipline today? Who is trying to stir up trouble for the President in the name of discipline? They are the same ones who in 1961, under the name of false discipline, arrested dozens of officers and Brazilian sergeants."

President Goulart, addressing
sergeants, March 30, 1964

1. The Rally of March 13, 1964

On MARCH 11, under an option plan devised by the federal government, two thousand members of the Guanabara traffic department followed the example of firemen and others who had transferred their services from the state to the federal government. At the same time buses and trains were bringing workers to the city of Rio from neighboring states so that on March 13 they might participate in the mammoth meeting at which the President and far leftists would spearhead the drive for "basic reforms."[1]

This rally, to be held three days before the opening of the regular session of Congress, was directed by CGT leaders. It was to be followed by other such affairs, at which Goulart would also preside. The future dates were not yet definitely fixed. For São Paulo consideration was given to May 1. For Belo Horizonte some spoke of April 21, the day on which Tiradentes, hero of Brazilian independence, is honored. Minas women again resolved to lie down all over the Belo Horizonte air field. Some of their husbands swore they would make Goulart

---

[1] The transportation cost has been estimated at 400,000 dollars (see Clarence W. Hall, "The Country That Saved Itself," *The Reader's Digest,* November 1964, p. 146).

prisoner. Noting his reliance on the CGT, they asserted that his interest in constitutional changes sprang from an interest in continuing in office—as chief of a *República Sindicalista*.

CGT leaders, in charge of all the arrangements of the Rio *comício* (rally) of March 13, wrote the speech for their own representative, the head of the new rural labor confederation; they assigned him the spot immediately preceding Goulart's closing speech. After the original list of three main speakers had been greatly expanded, those making arrangements fell into a violent dispute with Brizola.

Communist labor leader Luís Tenório de Lima has described spending the entire night before the rally arguing with Brizola because Brizola was planning a speech so radical that it threatened to make trouble for Goulart and strengthen the camp of the antireformists.[2] Brizola, Tenório de Lima has said, seemed unwilling to take instructions from, or get along with, anyone. While CGT leaders were having this all-night discussion, Goulart telephoned and was informed of Brizola's position. Then the President said that perhaps he, himself, would not show up at the rally. Finally Brizola "accepted some of the CGT's instructions."[3] He was placed on the "official list of orators" given in *Última Hora* on the thirteenth; but Pelacani had in mind physically preventing him from getting onto the speakers' platform.[4]

With the approach of the hour for the rally, Crockatt de Sá saw Goulart and an Army officer in an unsuccessful attempt to fill the area nearest the speakers' stand with anti-Communists.

In Rio the women of CAMDE engaged in a telephone campaign, asking people not to attend the March 13 meeting. They also persuaded residents along the route between Laranjeiras Palace and Cristiano Otoni Square to put lighted candles in windows, so that Goulart could reflect on these signs of mourning when he made his trip to and from the rally.[5]

[2] Luís Tenório de Lima, interview, São Paulo, November 21, 1968.
[3] *Ibid.*
[4] Dante Pelacani, interview, São Paulo, November 24, 1968.
[5] Amélia Molina Bastos and other CAMDE officers, interview, Rio de Janeiro, December 13, 1965.

Thousands of Army soldiers and marines were guarding the square at 3:00 P.M. when it began to fill up with organized workers and students. Group after group marched into the square. Petrobrás workers bore torches, some of which started a fire, causing ten minutes of confusion. But nothing could dampen the enthusiasm of the enormous crowd.

By the time that 120,000 had assembled, the square was a sea of placards and banners. Signs called for the legalization of the Brazilian Communist Party, whose rights were declared to be "sacred." Beside a huge portrait of Vargas, a placard quoted from his farewell message: "This people whose slave I was will no longer be slave to anyone." Signs glorified SUPRA and Pinheiro Neto. A great banner urged quick action: "We await your orders, Jango! Don't delay any more in freeing Brazil! We want radical reforms!" A seven-foot wooden gorilla represented the foes of "the people." Television and radio networks carried the wild shouts of "Jan-go, Jan-go, Jan-go" and "Get the fire going, Brizola!" ("*Manda Brasa, Brizola!*")

The speakers' platform, it had already been announced, was the same platform from which Vargas had spoken in the past. Fifteen speakers would precede President Goulart, among them Brizola, Arrais, SUPRA's João Pinheiro Neto, Student Union President José Serra, Guanabara Vice-Governor Elói Dutra, and the heads of the Guanabara Metalworkers Union and the new Confederation of Rural Workers. After these leaders of the Frente de Mobilização Popular had stirred the crowd, Goulart was to make a dramatic entrance and give the final address.

The oratory began at 5:00 P.M., when the head of the metalworkers' union accused Lacerda of turning Guanabara into a police state. Mention of the governor always brought boos and hoots. Deputado Sérgio Magalhães, representing the Nationalist Parliamentary Front, was about to give the third speech when a special announcement was made: at Laranjeiras Palace Goulart had just signed the decree whereby SUPRA would begin expropriating lands within ten kilometers of federal highways, railways, and water projects. News of this step brought a tremendous ovation. Then Sérgio Magalhães condemned "large landholdings and imperialism" as responsible for the exploitation of the Brazilian people for four centuries.[6] Elói Dutra emphasized that it had become impossible to defeat the organized masses.

Brizola's speech was the most audacious. He exhorted the President (whose name was always cheered) to "drop the policy of conciliation and organize a strictly populist and nationalist government." He "guaranteed" that, if a plebiscite were held, the Brazilian people would vote for "overthrowing the present Congress and installing a constitutional assembly with a view to creating a popular Congress, made up of laborers, peasants, sergeants, and nationalist officers, and authentic men of the people." He anticipated that his proposal would be considered illegal, subversive, and unconstitutional, but he said that it was "the only pacific solution for the impasse" that had been reached and the only way "to eliminate disgraceful reactions." He emphasized that "our path is peaceful, but, in the face of violence, we shall reply with violence."[7] Assailing Congress, Brizola said that it was giving the people nothing because in no way was it identified with popular aspirations. "If the branches of the government do not decide, why should we not transfer this decision to the people, the source of all power?"[8]

Shortly before the President arrived, the military ministers and Justice Minister Jurema made short appearances before the throng. Ovations greeted them all, particularly War Minister Jair Dantas Ribeiro.

Goulart, looking tired, took his place at 8:00 P.M. and received a thunderous acclaim: "Jan-go, Jan-go, Jan-go." His attractive wife was on one side. On the other side of the President was stevedore leader Osvaldo Pacheco (member of the Central Committee of the Communist Party).

Goulart spoke for over an hour. First he attacked "those so-called democrats" who would label the rally an offensive by the government against the democratic regime, "as if in Brazil it were still possible to

[6] *Correio da Manhã*, March 14, 1964.

[7] *Ibid.*

[8] Mário Victor, *Cinco Anos que Abalaram o Brasil: de Jânio Quadros ao Marechal Castelo Branco*, p. 475.

govern without the people." For these "so-called democrats," democracy, he said, "is a thing of privileges, intolerance, hate, the liquidation of Petrobrás, democracy of national and international monopolies, democracy which took Getúlio Vargas—to the extreme sacrifice." A great shout of approval greeted Vargas' name. The crowd reacted joyfully when Goulart told of having just signed the SUPRA decree, "with my thoughts turned to the tragedy of our Brazilian brother who suffers in the interior of our country."[9]

But Goulart asserted that the SUPRA decree was not agrarian reform. He said that large landowners and "odious and intolerable" speculators ought not to benefit by land value increases brought about by public expenditures for highways, railways, and water projects. "Agrarian reform, with prior payment in cash to unproductive large landowners, who are radically opposed to the interests of the Brazilian people, is not agrarian reform." "In no civilized nation does the constitution include the need of prior payment in cash." Goulart also pointed out that General Douglas MacArthur, who could not be called a Communist, promoted agrarian reform in Japan.

After stating that Brazil would have no agrarian reform without a reform of the constitution, Goulart called the constitution "antiquated. It no longer takes care of the cravings of the people or the needs for developing the nation." He would, he said, tell Congress within forty-eight hours what was needed. He would do this "in the name of the Brazilian people—in the name of the 150,000 or 200,000 who are here."

Prompted by Osvaldo Pacheco, Goulart held up a paper and thrilled the organized workers and students with the news that at the meeting itself he had just signed a decree expropriating all private oil refineries. "Brazilian workers! From today on, from this very moment on, the refineries belong to the national patrimony!"

Looking over the mass of attentive and hopeful humanity, Goulart felt that his listeners were probably less interested in basic reforms than in concrete steps to improve their living conditions.[10] He prom-

---

[9] *O Estado de S. Paulo,* March 14, 1964.
[10] Abelardo Jurema, *Sexta-Feira, 13: Os Últimos Dias do Govêrno João Goulart,* pp. 147–148.

ised that within forty-eight hours he would hand down a decree establishing rent ceilings. The government would also exert pressure on the domestic market "because there are great supplies of textiles and shoes —all on the shelves of the shops."

Before finishing, Goulart directed a remark to women's groups, such as the one that had used rosaries and Ave Marias to drown out the words of Brizola in Belo Horizonte. "Christianity never was a shield for privileged people, condemned by the Holy Fathers. Nor can the rosaries be lifted up as arms against those who call for the distribution of private landed property, still held in the hands of a few fortunate people."[11]

After the meeting was over, the thought of it exhilarated Goulart. He looked forward to signing new decrees at future rallies.

On the next day he signed the rent ceiling decree. This stipulated that advertisements of apartments were to quote rentals in cruzeiros according to a tabulation based on the number of rooms offered and the minimum wage for the region. (For example: "Living room, plus one room and kitchen or kitchenette: three-fifths of the minimum wage.") Advertisers whose announcements were vague or who quoted foreign currencies would be considered "collaborators with profiteers."

At the same time, João Pinheiro Neto announced that, at the President's suggestion, the first properties to be expropriated under the SUPRA decree would be the properties of Goulart that were affected by it.

Then Goulart sped to Brasília to call on Congress to amend the constitution. Among the purposes of the amendments, Goulart listed: votes for illiterates, the expropriation of properties without immediate cash payment, legalization of the Communist Party, and the delegation of legislative powers to the Executive. Goulart's message also suggested that a way be found for holding plebiscites, in which everyone over eighteen could express his opinion about "basic reforms."[12]

Organized labor spoke of calling a general strike unless the Presi-

[11] *Correio da Manhã,* March 14, 1964.
[12] George W. Bemis, *From Crisis to Revolution: Monthly Case Studies,* pp. 227–229.

dent's program were enacted. Labor Minister Amauri Silva proclaimed that the CGT should be made a legal entity.

Congressmen discussed impeaching Goulart. Ademar de Barros agreed that this was the step to take against a Chief Executive "who publicly preached subversion of public order." The CGT retorted that a move for the President's impeachment would touch off a general strike and probably be followed by the closing of Congress "by the people."

An atmosphere of elation filled Brasília's Planalto Palace. There Goulart decreed, retroactive to March 1, wage increases of 100 per cent for all military and civilian personnel of the government. Justice Minister Jurema, delighted with the March 13 rally, said that the opposition would not have the courage to try impeachment. He added that the President was "the nation's greatest popular leader," and that the opposition's desires had absolutely no popular support and were poorly regarded in the armed forces.[13]

The UDN's Pedro Aleixo expressed his amazement that no military minister had arrested Brizola during the March 13 rally.

The country was shaking with repercussions of the rally when the PSD convention met in Rio on March 19 to nominate Kubitschek for the presidency. It was impossible to get a majority of those at the convention to approve the customary message of solidarity with the President of the Republic, who had been elected on the PSD ticket.[14]

Kubitschek promised peace, development, and reforms. "Reforms," he said, "are in the soul and conscience of the people and I am certain that they will get prompt consideration in Congress." He added: "We want a flag of reform but not a reform of the flag."[15]

News of Kubitschek's nomination was officially conveyed to Goulart by PSD leaders Amaral Peixoto, Mazzilli, Capanema, and Filinto Müller. "Your friend Juscelino Kubitschek has been nominated," said Amaral Peixoto. Goulart replied that the people were not thinking in terms of men or elections but were interested in "basic reforms."[16]

[13] *Correio da Manhã*, March 17, 1964.

[14] Gustavo Capanema, interview, Brasília, October 23, 1965.

[15] Ernâni do Amaral Peixoto, interview, Brasília, October 15, 1965.

[16] Amaral Peixoto and Filinto Müller, interviews, Brasília, October 15, 1965.

Amaral Peixoto explained that the PSD leaders wanted an alliance such as had elected Kubitschek and Goulart in 1955 and had been responsible for Goulart's victory in 1960. The President kept talking about reforms. Müller pointed out that Kubitschek had spoken in favor of reforms. But Goulart said that words had not been enough and that, if the PSD congressmen wanted him to support Kubitschek, they should vote for the reforms.[17] The President, Amaral Peixoto said, already knew the position of the PSD on agrarian reform, and he added that the PSD could go no farther than its traditions allowed.

Brizola, learning of Kubitschek's nomination, told the press that the nation had reached such a chaotic and explosive state of affairs that he did not believe a presidential election would occur in 1965.[18]

[17] *Ibid.*
[18] *Correio da Manhã,* March 21, 1964.

2. The São Paulo March of the Family with God for Liberty

Luís Carlos Prestes, in an address at the auditorium of the Brazilian Press Association, stated that the March 13 rally had been organized as the result of his suggestion to San Tiago Dantas.

Lacerda, working for a coalition of anti-Goulart governors, called the rally "an attack on the constitution and the honor of the people. Sr. João Goulart's speech is subversive and provocative, besides being stupid." He considered suing Goulart and the organizers of the rally for holding it in a place forbidden by the state. He even made a public declaration he hoped would result in an understanding with his old foe Kubitschek—an understanding whereby these two presidential candidates would work together "to exercise control over the President."[1] But Kubitschek, preoccupied with getting Goulart's support, replied with a statement irritating to Lacerda.

[1] Carlos Lacerda, interview, Rio de Janeiro, October 11, 1967.

Ademar de Barros announced that Goulart "has more farms than I have." He told landowners that the SUPRA decree was "confiscation, in violation of the most sacred juridical constitutional traditions." Pinheiro Neto then announced that the federal government would take over the São Paulo government if Ademar used force to prevent expropriations in accordance with the SUPRA decree.

Even former President Euríco Gaspar Dutra had something to say: "Respect for the constitution is the word of order of patriots."[2] Lacerda and other Guanabara high officials rushed to his home to congratulate him.

In horrified tones anti-Goulart women accused the President of having insulted the rosary. Some of them bowed their heads in the belief that Goulart had shamed the whole nation in the eyes of the Lord. At a hospital in São Paulo on the night of March 13, Ana de Lurdes, a nun, suggested to Deputado Antônio Sílvio Cunha Bueno that a parade be organized, to be called the March to Make Amends to the Rosary.[3] Later that night, at the Cunha Bueno home, plans were discussed and a telephone campaign was started. Everyone who was telephoned was asked to call five others and to repeat this request.

When about fifty São Paulo civic leaders met on the fourteenth, the name of the march was changed in order to attract non-Catholics. The final version, the March of the Family with God for Liberty, was the suggestion of Conceição da Costa Neves,[4] who had earlier gained prominence by interrupting the speeches of friends of the Communist Party. The march was to take place on the nineteenth, the day of St. Joseph, patron of the family. Starting at 4:00 P.M. the participants would walk from the Praça da República (the Square of the Republic) to the Praça da Sé, where the cathedral stands.

The governor and his wife joined the organizers. Help came from numerous São Paulo civic organizations, their members believing that Brazil was on the road to civil war. Children met after school to work on arrangements for the march. Loudspeakers were used to advertise it.

[2] *O Estado de S. Paulo,* March 19, 1964 (dateline Rio de Janeiro, March 18).
[3] Rodrigues Matias, *Marcha da Família com Deus pela Liberdade: Um Ato de Fé numa Hora de Trevas.* (Pages not numbered.)
[4] *Ibid.*

Airplane and bus companies offered free transportation for representatives from all of São Paulo's municipalities and from other states. The third and last of the preparatory meetings was held at Rio Branco College and was attended by two thousand.

At the office of the Sociedade Rural Brasileira, general headquarters of the march, posters, banners, and flags were made. Some said: "Resignation or impeachment," "The constitution is inviolable," "Reforms yes, with Russians no," and "Down with the Red imperialists." One sign read: "Getúlio arrested the Communists; Jango rewards Communist traitors."

At 3:00 P.M. on March 19, São Paulo commerce, industry, and banks closed. By then, an hour before the march was to start, the Praça da República was crowded, and soon it became impossible to carry out plans as to what groups were to march in what order. The two public squares and the three kilometers of street between them were packed with hundreds of thousands, many of them singing *"Um, Dois, Três; Jango no Xadrez"* ("One, Two, Three; Jango in the Jail"). The band of the Guarda Civil played the national anthem and "Paris Belforte," hymn of the 1932 Constitutionalist Revolution. Women from Rio's CAMDE sang the Guanabara song, "Cidade Maravilhosa." Some shouts in favor of Goulart and Brizola were drowned out by the yells of women carrying signs reading: "Not here, João."

Auro de Moura Andrade was at the Praça da Sé with Lacerda, Nelson de Melo, and others. He addressed the throng: "For the Christian conscience of Brazil we are present at this manifestation. This is a decisive day for the existence of Brazil. We have faith in the armed forces; we have faith in democracy." A representative of São Paulo's União Cívica Feminina declared that the women of São Paulo "are united, like those of Minas, replying with their action to the enemies of liberty."[5] At the cathedral a mass was held for the "salvation" of democracy.

Disapprovingly, the left wing of the Catholic Church expressed its "profound amazement at the exploitation of the faith and sentiment of the Brazilian people and the political use of religion, creating a

[5] Mário Victor, *Cinco Anos Que Abalaram o Brasil: de Jânio Quadros ao Marechal Castelo Branco,* p. 487.

climate of division in the Church, springing from differences of ideas in the temporal field."[6] This view was shared by São Paulo's Cardinal Carlos Carmelo de Vasconcelos Mota.

São Paulo law student leaders expelled from their union all students who had marched in the parade. They also resolved to have a ceremony at which they would bury effigies of Ademar de Barros and the state secretary of safety.[7]

On the other hand, the organizers of the Marcha regarded the huge outpouring of people as "a miracle of faith."[8] Thrilled and surprised, they spoke of 500,000 or more participants.

Women of CAMDE, back in Rio after their superb experience, planned a mammoth march in Guanabara. By then Santos had been assigned March 25. CAMDE, deciding to wait until after Holy Week, selected April 2 for the Carioca parade.[9] As in the case of São Paulo's Marcha, the affair in Rio was to be sponsored by as many civilian groups as possible. So many wanted to help that organizational meetings had to be held in a movie theater.

Women of Minas were reported to be busy with plans "for Making Amends to the Rosary" in Belo Horizonte on April 21, a date that had earlier been mentioned as a possible one for Goulart's Belo Horizonte appearance.

Santos was considered such a stronghold of the CGT that the organizers of the march there were worried. Maria Paula Caetano e Silva, an unusually effective leader, went from São Paulo to the port city to do what she could in the few days before March 25.[10] After it was over, the Santos parade of an estimated thirty thousand was considered a great success. It so encouraged the advocates of Family Marches with God that plans were made to have them take place all over Brazil, two or three each week.

Brazil prepared for the battle of mass demonstrations. Women of

---

[6] *Ibid.* Also see Wilson Fiqueiredo, "A Margem Esquerda," in Alberto Dines, *et al., Os Idos de Março e a Queda en Abril,* p. 215.

[7] *Correio da Manhã,* March 20, 1964.

[8] Salvio de Almeida Prado, interview, São Paulo, November 18, 1965.

[9] Amélia Molina Bastos and other officers of CAMDE, interview, Rio de Janeiro, December 13, 1965.

[10] Wladimir Lodygensky, interview, Brasília, October 21, 1965.

the Radical Left (belonging to the Movimento Nacionalista Feminino and the Liga Feminina Nacionalista da Guanabara) decided to stage a mass meeting in Rio on April 3—the day after the Family March was to be held there. Brizola's wife (sister of Goulart) would address the crowd.

For April the CGT scheduled rallies, at which Goulart was to appear, in five states. But the greatest attention was given to the mammoth one to be held in São Paulo on May 1. For this, with the help of trainloads from distant points, the CGT hoped to produce a crowd of one million; and it hoped that Goulart would give it great significance by signing a decree expropriating all companies that were distributing gasoline in Brazil.[11]

When Second Army Commander Amauri Kruel was consulted by the CGT he agreed to speak with the War Minister but said that he personally saw no need for a rally and was not disposed to give it coverage. Goulart, he said, should be more careful. Kruel added that he himself did not favor some of the reforms being advocated, such as votes for soldiers.[12]

After getting this reply, CGT leaders considered the possibility of a "rightist coup"; but they concluded that its sponsors would be "defeated, as in 1955 and 1961."[13] They believed that Kruel would be unable to stop their preparations for May 1.

[11] Luís Tenório de Lima, interview, São Paulo, November 21, 1968.
[12] *Ibid.*
[13] *Ibid.*

3. The Sailors' Mutiny (March 25–27, 1964)

POLITICIANS ALSO DIRECTED their attention to the armed forces. In the Army they appealed to sergeants, who are career men, and largely ignored the soldiers, who are conscripts serving about ten months.[1]

[1] In Brazil's Army of about 150,000, between 80,000 and 100,000 are conscripts.

Most important in the Navy, however, were the sailors, who are volunteers, normally serving three or six years. They frequently make navy life a career with promotion to petty officer their goal.

After Goulart became President in 1961, some Communist law students enlisted in the Navy. In March 1962 they helped organize a sailors' association, the Associação dos Marinheiros e Fuzileiros Navais, which came to have the warm backing of Darci Ribeiro.

Following the Paulista demonstration of March 19, 1964, the sailors' association resolved to congratulate the workers of Petrobrás for the expropriation of the private oil refineries. Navy Minister Sílvio Mota then warned the association that political pronouncements were out of bounds.

During the following days the sailors celebrated their club's second anniversary by holding rallies and making demands. One meeting was held at the headquarters of the Communist-dominated Rio Bank Workers' Union. At another, in the auditorium of Rádio Mayrink Veiga, the sailors broadcast demands for better living conditions and for the right to hold political office. The Navy Minister let it be known that he was willing to grant some improvements in living conditions for the sailors, but that he would not condone breaches of discipline.

Although elite anti-Goulart admirals regarded Navy Minister Sílvio Mota as a man who "compromised values in order to hold his high post," they appreciated that he was a sincere anti-Communist. The Minister, like these admirals, was appalled by the sailors' show of "indiscipline." On March 24 he ordered ten days imprisonment for eleven directors of the sailors' association. "I must declare," he said in a speech that was broadcast on all the naval ships, "that the present directorship of the Associação dos Marinheiros e Fuzileiros has let itself become infected by the subversive ideas of elements foreign to its setting, and that the naval authority will under no circumstances permit these ideas to be spread to our ships and barracks."[2]

The sailors' association issued a press release calling the Navy Minister's position "infantile and unworthy of a cabinet minister." Then the association, with the blessing of the CGT, used the Guanabara Metalworkers' Union building to hold a tumultuous session, which

[2] *O Estado de S. Paulo*, March 25, 1964.

began on the evening of Wednesday, March 25. About 1,200 sailors attended. Representatives of the CGT and of Brizola's Groups of Eleven were present. To make the occasion as meaningful as possible, ninety-two–year-old João Cândido, who had led a sailors' rebellion in 1910, was carried into the union building by four sailors.

Goulart, before leaving Rio to spend the last part of Holy Week in São Borja, asked Justice Minister Jurema to represent him at the meeting. The President criticized the Navy Minister's attitude toward the sailors' association and said that the government did not want to lose the support of "more than twenty thousand sailors" who were "in rebellion against the decisions of the Minister";[3] he further observed that "fifteen thousand" were to be at the meeting at the union building. After Goulart left, Jurema investigated and decided not to attend.

At the meeting a message from the six imprisoned officers of the sailors' association was read. The association's president, José Anselmo dos Santos, was present because, like four other association officers, he had not turned himself over for imprisonment. His latest sentence made his record as a sailor (more than thirty days of prison sentences in less than one year) so bad that he was due to be expelled from the Navy.

Cabo (Corporal) Anselmo assailed Brazil's institutional arrangements, and defended "basic reforms." He demanded amnesty for those still held on account of the 1963 sergeants' rebellion ("movement of protest") in Brasília, a revision of the Navy's disciplinary regulations, official recognition of the sailors' association by the naval authorities, and no interference in its internal affairs by the admiralty.[4]

Anselmo was deliriously applauded when he replied to the Navy Minister's reference to "subversive ideas." He proclaimed that "those in this nation who try to subvert order are allied to the hidden forces which drove one President to suicide and another to resignation; they tried to prevent the inauguration of Jango, and now they try to prevent the realization of basic reforms." He accused the Navy Minister

[3] Abelardo Jurema, *Sexta-Feira, 13: Os Últimos Dias do Govêrno João Goulart*, pp. 152–155.

[4] *Correio da Manhã*, March 26, 1964.

of having tried to prohibit seamen from hearing radio broadcasts of
the March 13 rally; thus, said Anselmo, the Navy Minister had tried
to be "subversive."[5]

It was past midnight, and the CGT's representatives (Pacheco and
Humberto Melo Bastos) had left, when news reached the Metalworkers' Union building that the Navy Minister had ordered the imprisonment of the forty sailors who were said to have organized the
meeting. In response, the sailors declared themselves in a "permanent
session," which was not to end until March 30. Their statement to the
press advised that "some perverted minds, controlled by the Washington Pentagon and by interests opposed to the nation and the people,
have again unleashed a blow against the democratic sentiments of our
people."[6]

On the morning of Thursday, March 26, Navy Minister Mota announced that about six hundred sailors and marines had assumed a
frankly indisciplinary attitude, and he put the Navy on the "alert,"
ordering all the personnel to be at their posts. He sent a detachment
of forty marines to arrest rebels, who were still at the meeting. Before
this troop reached its destination, Admiral Cândido Aragão, commander of the Marines, visited the Metalworkers' Union building and
had a friendly chat with the rebels. When the forty marines reached
the building, practically all of them put their weapons on the ground
and joined the rebels inside. The rebels then sang the national anthem
and drew up a manifesto hailing "the greatest of victories": the adherence of "our companions, the brave marines."

Disgruntled admirals assembled in "permanent session" in the Navy
Ministry and fiercely told Minister Sílvio Mota "to make himself
obeyed." The Minister fired Aragão and sentenced him to ten days in
prison. Unable to reach War Minister Jair Dantas Ribeiro (who was
undergoing surgery), the Minister persuaded General Genaro Bontempo to send twelve Army tanks and five hundred soldiers to the
streets outside of the union building.

Early in the afternoon, after the soldiers and onlookers had been

[5] Mário Victor, *Cinco Anos que Abalaram o Brasil: de Jânio Quadros ao Marechal Castelo Branco*, pp. 495–496.

[6] *O Estado de S. Paulo*, March 26, 1964.

standing around the building for a while, the Navy Minister sent another marine contingent (the Riachuelo Battalion) under Admiral Luís Felipe Sinai, who had been Aragão's chief of staff. The Army men withdrew around a corner, out of sight of the building, and then, at 5:00 P.M., Sinai went into the building to try to reason with the rebels. After a twenty-minute wait, Sinai learned from the sailors that they would take no "backward step" because "the people" wanted them to "keep the torch of liberation burning." Cabo Anselmo said the sailors would "resist until death."[7]

Sinai, who had orders to use force if negotiation failed, left the building. But before giving any orders to his marines he sent an aide into the building to invite two colonels, representatives of Casa Militar Chief Assis Brasil, to join him in a sidewalk conference. Communist labor leader Hércules Correia rushed from the building to Laranjeiras Palace. The two colonels telephoned the Palace and were able to speak with Darci Ribeiro, who was conferring with labor leaders.

The CGT was endeavoring to solve the crisis, although not in a manner satisfactory to the admiralty. As a first step Dante Pelacani addressed the sailors in the CGT's name, advising them that the CGT neither opposed the mutiny nor the sailors' demands, but that it felt the mutiny should be aboard ships and not in a labor union building.[8]

Pacheco and Pelacani then spoke with cabinet ministers. At a discussion at the War Ministry, government officials and military officers, who had not left their desks for Holy Week, decided that "military intervention in a *sindicato*" would lead to serious trouble and should not be carried out.

Sinai, outside of the metalworkers' building, was joined by the two colonels of the Casa Militar and told that the President's office had determined that under no circumstances should a conflict take place. Sinai himself did some telephoning (from a nearby shop) and then advised his marines that the Armed Forces General Staff had given strict orders against an attack on the building. Brizola's "Musketeer," Congressman Max da Costa Santos, used a loud-speaker to let the crowd know that the order for the withdrawal of the marines had been

---

[7] *Ibid.*, March 27, 1964.
[8] Dante Pelacani, interview, São Paulo, November 24, 1968.

delivered by Darci Ribeiro. This brought applause, and some *vivas* for "Jango." One more sailor and one more marine adhered to the mutiny.

Navy Minister Sílvio Mota resolved to submit his resignation. All during the day there had been rumors that he would do this, but the determined admirals around him had been dissuading him. These admirals, Brizola said, were "persecuting sailors and marines." The CGT announced that "the elite of the Navy is at this moment carrying out a coup against the people, the basic reforms, and the President."

The mutineers prepared to spend their second night as the guests of the metalworkers. Cabo Anselmo laid down the conditions of the sailors' association: the rebels would leave the building only when the federal government, through a new Navy Minister, freed association members who had been arrested on Sílvio Mota's orders. The sailors, during this second night, were praised by visiting labor leaders and congressmen. They were comforted by women belonging to the Liga Feminina Nacionalista of Guanabara and entertained by a show put on by members of the National Union of Students.

At 1:00 A.M. on the morning of Good Friday Goulart and Casa Militar Chief Assis Brasil arrived from Rio Grande do Sul to deal with the crisis. There was a wave of relief, for it was felt that Goulart would find the answer. The President followed his custom of listening to various groups. These included the CGT. Leading advisers asserted that the anti-Goulart admirals had forced the sailors to behave as they had. The important thing, it was felt, was to get the sailors to leave the union building without a military invasion.

The long conference at Laranjeiras Palace produced the decision that, since the sailors refused to be arrested by Navy men,[9] Army troops would take the rebelling sailors from the Metalworkers' Union building to Army barracks and hold them until Monday, March 30, when they would be freed and an investigation begun.[10] At around 4:00 A.M. trucks brought three hundred soldiers from Vila Militar to the city, and they were stationed in front of the union building.

Near the Navy Ministry a skirmish occurred at dawn. A new group

[9] *Ibid.*
[10] Abelardo Jurema, *Sexta-Feira, 13*, p. 160.

of about one hundred sailors, having left ships that were alongside Ilha das Cobras (the Island of Snakes), decided to join their comrades in the union building. Defying orders of naval officers, they advanced along the bridge that connects the island with the mainland in front of the Navy Ministry.[11] As they made their way, officers on the Ministry's ground floor ordered sentries to intimidate them by shooting.[12] Soon both sides were exchanging shots. The sailors, four of whom were wounded, did not pass across the bridge.

Aboard the ships the atmosphere was tense. Chief petty officers, petty officers, and a majority of the senior sailors opposed the rebellion.[13] The elite admirals felt that most of the vessels continued under the control of their captains.

In the Metalworkers' Union building Pacheco, Pelacani, and Labor Minister Amauri Silva were having difficulty persuading the sailors to accept the solution reached at Laranjeiras Palace. Sailors, all offering ideas at once, made a confusing scene. The negotiators then held a separate meeting with the leaders of the mutiny and advised them that the sailors, after leaving the building under arrest, would be given amnesty.[14] Although the terms of this arrangement were more favorable for the sailors than those established at Laranjeiras, Cabo Anselmo opposed them, described the labor leaders as traitors, and refused to call an assembly of the sailors.

It was, therefore, the labor leaders who now called the sailors together. Even though Pelacani's eloquence did not persuade Anselmo and other leaders, a majority of the sailors accepted the settlement. Then, Pelacani has stated, "the sailors selected Paulo Mário to take over the Navy Ministry." Pacheco and Pelacani informed the CGT of this decision. Then the CGT took the name of Paulo Mário to Gou-

[11] Levi Aarão Reis, interviews, Rio de Janeiro, December 13 and 15, 1965; Ernesto de Melo Batista, interview, Rio de Janeiro, December 4, 1967.

[12] Shooting was ordered by Admiral Arnoldo Hasselmann Fairbairn. Twenty-six years earlier Hasselmann had seized the Navy Ministry building briefly on behalf of the Integralista uprising; this act had been one of the few examples of courage shown during that affair of May 11, 1938.

[13] Arnoldo Hasselmann Fairbairn, interview, Rio de Janeiro, December 6, 1965; Levi Aarão Reis, interviews, December 13 and 15, 1965.

[14] Pelacani, interview, November 24, 1968.

lart.[15] Paulo Mário da Cunha Rodrigues was a frail sixty-nine–year-old retired admiral who had been serving as president of the Maritime Tribunal.

Later in the morning, when Goulart, Darci Ribeiro, and Assis Brasil met with the CGT leaders, it was decided that Navy Minister Sílvio Mota's resignation should be accepted and his post filled by Paulo Mário. Labor Minister Amauri Silva and CGT leaders returned from Laranjeiras Palace to the union building.

A delay in conveying the sailors to the Army barracks at São Cristóvão was ordered by Goulart at the request of Hércules Correia dos Reis and Dante Pelacani. These labor leaders needed another conference with the President to ensure that the Army trucks would have a friendly and unarmed appearance. In spite of the delay, the applauded sailors were on their way by 1:30 P.M., when the new Navy Minister, Paulo Mário, assumed his post. "My God," he remarked, "how tough is the fight against moribund imperialism."[16]

Paulo Mário canceled the order to arrest Cândido Aragão and let him return to the command of the Marines. The new Navy Minister also freed the rebel sailors, telling them to go to their homes and report back to the Navy on April 1.

That evening the rebels celebrated Good Friday with a happy victory march. They received flowers from the Liga Feminina Nacionalista of Guanabara. After stopping at Candelaria Church to thank God for the victory, they poured down the nearby streets, singing and shouting. For a while they carried on their shoulders the two "People's" admirals, Marine Commander Cândido Aragão and former Goulart Navy Minister Pedro Paulo Suzano, who had just been named Navy chief of staff.

[15] *Ibid.*
[16] *O Estado de S. Paulo*, March 29, 1964.

4. Repercussions of the Events in the Navy

The Saturday morning newspapers carried front-page photographs of the scenes created in the streets by the jubilant sailors with Aragão and Suzano. As Justice Minister Jurema has written, "the repercussions were the worst possible."[1] Some newspapers saw similarities between the recent events and sailors' uprisings in Russia prior to the Bolshevik Revolution.

O Estado de S. Paulo editorialized: "Already we have no Air Force worthy of being called such, and what remains of the Navy truly does not deserve the description of a military corporation. Changes in high Army commands continue at an alarming rate with officers who refuse to transform themselves into a praetorian force being replaced by men who have the unlimited support of the Far Left. This is the plan announced a short while back by Sr. Luís Carlos Prestes when he affirmed that his gang was governing the nation although the Power was not yet in its hands."[2]

As this editorial implied, the situation in the Air Force did not offer hope to those who opposed the advance of the Far Left.[3] Late in 1963 Air Force Chief of Staff Correia de Melo—who had served as Kubitschek's last Air Minister—became so worried about Communist infiltration in Air Force ranks that he issued a brochure, *Como Eles Destroem* (How They Destroy).

As for the Navy, the CGT announced—after the events of Good Friday—that CGT-affiliated sailors had immobilized most of the fleet. The cruiser *Barroso,* the CGT said, could still function but was under

---

[1] Abelardo Jurema, *Sexta-Feira, 13: Os Últimos Dias do Govêrno João Goulart,* p. 162.

[2] *O Estado de S. Paulo,* March 29, 1964.

[3] Haroldo Veloso has stated that by late March 1964 the Air Force had become "much infiltrated by Communists . . . ; the sergeants, in particular, were very, very infiltrated" (interviews, Marietta, Georgia, January 6–7, 1966). During March 1964, Veloso, who had carried out the Jacareacanga revolt in 1956, was in close touch with São Paulo conspirators Júlio de Mesquita Filho and Luís Werneck.

the control of these same sailors.[4] Anti-Goulart admirals were now saying that "some ships, such as the small mine sweepers" could still be "trusted."

The São Paulo branch of the Partido Libertador telegraphed Luís Carlos Prestes, using for the address the presidential palace in Brasília. The message said that although the PL was avidly opposed to Communism, it could not refrain from congratulating His Excellency upon the complete destruction of the hierarchy of the armed forces. "At the same time we appreciate your feeling of frustration upon not having gotten Cabo José Anselmo appointed Minister of the Navy."[5]

Furious admirals who wanted to use force to depose Paulo Mário and Aragão included Augusto Hamann Rademaker Grünewald, Levi Aarão Reis, Ernesto de Melo Batista, Waldeck Vampré, Mário Cavalcanti, and Armando Zenha de Figueiredo.[6] Finding their Army acquaintances cool, they held a series of meetings at the Navy Club. They declared that the performance on the streets on Good Friday had been "a shocking exhibition."

On Saturday night, March 28, four admirals took a memorandum, signed by themselves and twenty-three colleagues, to the Navy Minister. It spoke of the newspaper photographs of Suzano and Aragão wearing their uniforms in the streets (unusual for officers) and being carried by sailors "whose uniforms were in disarray." Suzano and Aragão were declared to have participated in discipline-destroying events and to lack the qualities needed for holding their offices. All the admirals, Paulo Mário was told, would leave their posts unless Suzano and Aragão were fired.[7]

With the four admirals in his waiting room, Paulo Mário telephoned Goulart, who had concluded his Good Friday activities by flying to Brasília for some rest at Granja do Torto. After midnight (on Sunday, March 29) the Navy Minister and the President detailed three

---

[4] Wilson Figueiredo, "A Margem Esquerda," in Alberto Dines, et al. Os Idos de Março e a Queda em Abril, p. 235.

[5] O Globo, March 30, 1964.

[6] Ernesto de Melo Batista, interview, Rio de Janeiro, December 18, 1965.

[7] Ibid., December 4, 1967.

investigations. These were made known in a Navy Ministry note that implied the admirals were the violators of discipline. The investigations would cover: (1) the events leading up to the sailors' arrival at the Army barracks; (2) the parade of these sailors, and the accusations against Suzano and Aragão; and (3) the origins and implications of the decision of the memorandum-signing admirals "who were guilty of patent indiscipline . . . on account of impositions made on the Minister."[8]

Thousands of Naval officers filled the Navy Club on Sunday. They were enraged by an interview in which Paulo Mário was reported to have said that he had committed himself not to punish the mutineers. They scoffed at Assis Brasil's announcement that the CGT had had nothing to do with Paulo Mário's selection.

The first short "Warning to the Nation," drawn up by Admiral Levi Aarão Reis and signed by some of the admirals, asserted that the mutiny and its outcome threatened all Brazil's institutions. A longer manifesto, issued by the Navy Club, condemned the government for having broken its word to Sílvio Mota that the rebels would be punished. It blamed the rebellion on infiltration by "agents of subversion" and said that "the Army and Air Force cannot remain indifferent."[9]

The Military Club, supporting the Navy Club, declared that the disorderly sailors had been "insidiously indoctrinated by union leaders at the service of Moscow." The venerable Association of Noncommissioned Naval Officers issued a manifesto to express its agreement with the pronouncements made at the Navy Club.

On Saturday morning in Brasília Goulart had received a telephone call from Amauri Kruel. Kruel might have communicated earlier with the President: the general's special airplane, rushing him to São Paulo on Good Friday from his Espírito Santo country place, had stopped at the Rio airport, and there he had been told that Goulart wanted him to come to Laranjeiras Palace. Although the general had plenty to say to the President, he felt that he would be in a stronger position if he spoke from his São Paulo post.

[8] *O Estado de S. Paulo,* March 30, 1964.
[9] Full texts of the manifestos are given in *O Globo,* March 30, 1964.

When he did this on Saturday, he told Goulart that Brazil had reached the third of the four phases he had mentioned a year earlier: the period of disparaging the military leaders. He also told Goulart to fire Paulo Mário and Aragão and to come from Brasília to Rio to deal personally and effectively with the sailors who had mutinied. The President abruptly ended this conversation. But later in the day Goulart returned the call; he promised some corrective measures and said that he would fly to Rio to deal personally with the problems created by the crisis.[10] Kruel urged energetic action for the sake of public opinion and for the sake of the armed forces. By the time Goulart made the trip to Rio late Sunday afternoon, Kruel in São Paulo was receiving the applause of fellow Army officers.

Upon reaching Laranjeiras Palace, Goulart called in Assis Brasil and credited Kruel with having been loyal and correct in describing the tremendous impact of the naval affair in Army circles. But Assis Brasil dispelled the President's worries. He had, he said, just spoken with General Euriale de Jesus Zerbini, who was under Kruel's command and had charge of important units in Paraíba Valley, between Rio and São Paulo. Zerbini, a supporter of Goulart and Assis Brasil, had reported that all was calm in Army circles.

The most distraught admirals, plotting to grab the Navy Ministry building, radio station, and ammunition depot, found the anti-Goulart generals in Rio reticent to receive them.[11] These generals felt they had no reason to spend their time with elite admirals, who, as they saw it, had no control over Navy ships and had nothing to offer but manifestos. On the few occasions when admirals and generals met, the generals advised caution and patience. The admirals concluded that they could count only on Olímpio Mourão Filho, who, they knew, was eager to act in Minas.[12]

---

[10] Amauri Kruel, interviews, São Paulo, November 16, 1965, and Guanabara, October 21, 1967.

[11] Melo Batista, interview, Rio de Janeiro, December 4, 1967.

[12] Levi Aarão Reis, interviews, Rio de Janeiro, December 13 and 15, 1965.

5. Goulart Speaks at the Automobile Club
(March 30, 1964)

GOULART HAD ALREADY AGREED that he and his cabinet ministers would honor the Benevolent Association of Military Police Sergeants by attending the commemoration of the association's fortieth anniversary at Rio's Automobile Club on the evening of March 30. The President and his top staff worked energetically to assure the success of the celebration.[1] Numerous groups, such as the trainees in the Firemen's Corps, were invited because Goulart hoped to be surrounded by many thousands when he addressed the sergeants. The presidential Casa Militar guaranteed transportation for all who wanted to attend, especially for sergeants and corporals in the various services.

While the presidency was thus occupied, pro-Goulart and anti-Goulart members of the Guanabara state assembly spent their time exchanging insults. Twenty-eight Guanabara state assemblymen—about half of the membership—signed a resolution in favor of the Navy Club. Among them was Admiral Augusto Amaral Peixoto, brother of the president of the PSD. Augusto, a rebel of the 1920's and a Vargas admirer, lamented that Getúlio was not present to repudiate much that Goulart was doing.

Deputado Tancredo Neves believed that the presence of the President at the Sergeants' Association gathering would be provocative because the meeting followed so closely the amnesty given the rebel sailors. When he visited the President in his Copacabana apartment to discuss his fear, Neves found Goulart in the company of General Assis Brasil, Justice Minister Jurema, Labor Minister Silva, Press Secretary Raul Riff, speech writer Jorge Serpa, and Samuel Wainer of *Última Hora*. Assis Brasil said with firmness that there was nothing to worry about, that Goulart could count on military power such as no other President had possessed.[2] Neves' opinion irritated Goulart, who

[1] Abelardo Jurema, *Sexta-Feira, 13: Os Últimos Dias do Govêrno João Goulart,* pp. 168–169.
[2] *Ibid.,* p. 171.

was not inclined to listen to civilians with warnings about the military situation.[3] The former Prime Minister left with a final remark: "God knows I hope I am wrong, but I feel that this step by the President will provoke the inevitable and will be the final reason for an armed conflict."[4]

Raul Riff and Serpa helped prepare a speech in which the President would defend reforms but would not aggravate the tense military situation.[5] However, while it was being typed, Goulart became increasingly incensed about the aggressive tone of the pronouncements then being made at the Navy and Military Clubs. He decided to disregard the carefully worded text and reply to these "subversive" clubs with a show of strength. He hoped to make this television appearance in the company of twenty thousand admiring sergeants and corporals. The Automobile Club, which could not have accommodated twenty thousand, was well filled. But the crowd consisted mostly of civilians, many of them relatives of the two thousand sergeants and corporals who were present.

Reports about military and political troubles in Minas Gerais were hardly mentioned in conversations at the Automobile Club. The prevailing mood suggested that they were unimportant in view of the vast armed strength on which the President could count. But some guessed that they might be responsible for the absence of so many members of the armed forces, including numerous top officers friendly to the administration.

The celebration was attended by the entire cabinet, with General Genaro Bontempo appearing on behalf of hospitalized Jair Dantas Ribeiro. Marine Commander Aragão received a thunderous ovation. Other heroes of the occasion were "Sergeant-Deputado" Antônio Garcia Filho and Sailors' Association President Anselmo. It was a thrilling occasion for Cabo Anselmo. In the company of the President and the cabinet, he was the object of frenzied acclaim.

The speeches were aggressive and optimistic. They were the ex-

---

[3] Luís Fernando Bocaiuva Cunha, interview, Rio de Janeiro, December 5, 1968.

[4] Jurema, *Sexta-Feira, 13*, p. 171.

[5] Antônio Callado, "Jango ou o Suicídio Sem Sangue," in Alberto Dines *et al.*, *Os Idos de Março e a Quebra em Abril*, p. 266. *O Estado de S. Paulo*, March 31, 1964.

ultant words of men who were making it clear that their triumphant victory march could not be slowed down. In the words of one speaker, the successful struggle was against the "narrow-minded mentality of those who make of military discipline an accursed whip to enslave the Brazilian people."[6] No longer would Brazil tolerate "foreign colonial capital or foreign and national trusts." Justice Minister Jurema exclaimed that "all people who are with Jango are with the people."[7]

If the President wanted to "pay to see" his opponents cards, he could not have done better. The show at the Automobile Club was one long taunt at his foes, and it was rumored that officers of the Military and Navy Clubs would march to the Automobile Club in protest. Throughout the nation the television screens showed the President being pushed this way and that by a great sea of "anti-imperialists." Again radio listeners heard the chant of reform-minded youths: "Jango, Jan-go, Jan-go." Jostlings by sergeants sometimes made it difficult for the tired President to carry on with his improvised address. But his words were strong, those of the chief of invincible troops.[8]

He would not, he vowed, allow any disorder to be carried out in the name of order. He explained that the national crisis had been provoked by the privileged minority. This minority, made up of powerful groups that opposed unity in the armed forces and created a climate of intrigues and hates, feared to face the bright future in which millions of Brazilians would become integrated into the nation's economic, social, and political life. These minority groups, opposing the enlargement of popular conquests, were led by "the eternal enemies of democracy." "In the crisis of 1961 these same hypocrites, who today show a false zeal for the constitution, wanted to tear it up and bury it in the cold grave of Fascist dictatorship.

"Who is speaking about discipline today? Who is trying to stir up trouble for the President in the name of discipline? They are the same

---

[6] Mário Victor, *Cinco Anos que Abalaram o Brasil: de Jânio Quadros ao Marechal Castelo Branco*, p. 506.

[7] *O Jornal*, April 1, 1964.

[8] Jurema, *Sexta-Feira, 13*, p. 174.

ones who in 1961, under the name of false discipline, arrested dozens of officers and Brazilian sergeants."[9]

The next morning the anti-Goulart newspapers angrily condemned the fraternization of Goulart and his cabinet, particularly the military ministers, with men like Anselmo and Garcia Filho ("of notorious Communist affiliation").[10]

Kubitschek, fearing an explosion, rushed to see Goulart. The former President spoke of the importance of discipline and respect for hierarchy in the military. But Goulart, who appeared convinced of the loyalty of the armies, particularly the most powerful First and Third Armies, kept repeating to Kubitschek phrases he had used in addressing the sergeants.[11] He felt that at the Automobile Club he had used just the right words and had given exactly the message he wanted to give to Brazil.[12] His timetable now included plans to lead a "nationalist" rally in Santos on April 3.

Following his unsatisfactory talk with Goulart, Kubitschek issued a manifesto lamenting the "divorce which today separates Brazilians," and observing that it was not too late to preserve peace and legality by means of "re-establishing discipline and the hierarchy."[13]

The confused citizenry heard numerous appeals for peace. One such appeal came from middle-of-the-roader Carvalho Pinto, who, soon after the March 13 rally, had announced that he would run for the presidency. Now he telephoned Miguel Arrais and Nei Braga simultaneously and then, in a worried mood, asked Brazilians to reject any steps that might be illegal; such steps, he said, would please both "leftist revolutionaries" and "rightist reactionaries."[14]

Auro de Moura Andrade was more aggressive. "All who want to be free," he said, "must mobilize in defense of democracy. They must do more. They must free themselves from those who would turn the liber-

---

[9] *Correio da Manhã,* March 31, 1964.
[10] Editorial, *O Jornal,* April 1, 1964.
[11] *O Jornal,* April 1, 1964.
[12] *O Estado de S. Paulo,* April 1, 1964.
[13] *O Jornal,* April 1, 1964.
[14] *Ibid.*

ties of Brazilian democracy over to international Communism."[15] One
of the federal congressmen declared that "with dumbfoundedness, per-
plexity, and disgust, the nation has witnessed the total and complete
subversion of order and discipline."[16]

[15] Victor, *Cinco Anos que Abalaram o Brasil*, p. 510.
[16] Deputado Joaquim Mariano Dias Menezes quoted in *O Jornal*, April 1, 1964.

6. Calls for a Far Left Uprising

In the name of Brizola, "Supreme Commander of National Liberation," secret instructions were prepared for his Groups of Eleven
Companions. The Grupos were told to arm themselves. A general
strike was to be the signal for them to start their work. Special groups,
"humble, strong, and full of hatred for the powerful," were assigned
special tasks. They were to back those authorities who cooperated with
the movement that was to liberate the nation from international capitalism and its allies and create a government "of the people, by the
people, and for the people." These special groups were to seize all
other influential politicians and authorities, particularly local ones.

In these instructions Brizola's followers were told that surprise was
the principal factor for initial success, and that defeat was "improbable
but not impossible."

Today we have everything in our favor, including the goodwill of the government and the complacency of powerful civilian and military sectors,
frightened and fearful of losing their present and ignominious privileges.

The Groups of Eleven Companions will have to carry the weight of all
of the initial operation. The [China-line] Partido Comunista do Brasil will
be our principal ally at the side of powerful organizations, such as the
Comando Geral dos Trabalhadores (CGT), the Pacto de Unidade e Ação
(PUA), the Comando Inter-Sindical (CIS), and all the nationalist *sindicatos*.

It is necessary that all companions of the Groups of Eleven saturate themselves with mystical feeling.

This message from Brizola spoke poorly of Luís Carlos Prestes, advocate of the peaceful path. Prestes was blamed for turning the Moscow-line Partido Comunista Brasileiro (PCB) into quarreling factions. Praise was lavished on the much smaller China-line PC do B. "Daily it grows with the help of the ideas of Mao Tse-tung and Stalin, which are, in the last analysis, those of Marx and Engels. In this wing, today more powerful than that of Moscow, we shall go to find the source of material and military potential for the struggle of national liberation. Happily it is completely at our side, for its militants have the same fierce determination that we have."[1]

There was nothing secret about some of the calls for a violent uprising by the Far Left. In a brief manifesto that was widely distributed, "the students of São Paulo" declared that the time had come for a violent change even if this meant "bloodshed."

The struggle of Cuba is our struggle. Down with the large landowner. Down with the bourgeoisie. Down with private property. Down with the "gorillas." . . . Down with the conservative clergy. . . . Only the Revolution of the Proletariat will give us BREAD, PEACE, LAND, EQUALITY, and the Brazilian Popular Socialist Communist Republic. We shall fight against all, including our relatives, who oppose the ascension of the proletariat to Power. Long live self-determination of peoples! Long live the Progressive Clergy! Long live the CGT! Long live the UNE! Long live the sergeants! Long live the Nationalist Parliamentary Front! Long live the proletariat! United we shall win.[2]

Some of the impassioned cries gave the impression that an uprising was imminent, and that, due to its overwhelming popularity, it would be quickly victorious. It would free the downtrodden who would find themselves, suddenly, in a beautiful world, which would be the result of "basic reforms" and the elimination of injustice—a world of plenty, thanks to a banking reform.[3]

---

[1] "Brizola secret instructions," found in Niterói, and reproduced in *O Estado de S. Paulo*, July 16, 1964; also given in Inquérito Policial Militar No. 709, *O Comunismo no Brasil*, IV, 396–408.

[2] Handbill issued by "the students of São Paulo," addressed to "Railway Workers, Sergeants, Peasants, and Students" in Sorocaba, São Paulo.

[3] Undated *Boletim Informativo Sindical* for São Paulo bank workers.

But the downtrodden lacked the violent intentions some of their saber-rattling "leaders" thought they should have. Calls for a violent uprising succeeded chiefly in scaring a lot of people.

7. Goulart and the CGT

OF ALL THE GROUPS calling for radical change, the CGT deserves the most serious attention. Fronts such as the Frente de Mobilização Popular and the "San Tiago Dantas Front for Basic Reforms" needed the CGT if they were to make good showings in the battle of mass demonstrations. Just when Goulart was addressing sergeants at the Automobile Club, the colorful Dante Pelacani was in Bahia carrying out a part of the CGT's preparation to convey workers from all over Brazil to São Paulo in hopes that one million would attend the rally there on "national May Day" (*1º de Maio nacional*).

While Pelacani was at work in Bahia, CGT officers in Rio—such as Clodsmidt Riani, the president, Osvaldo Pacheco, the secretary-general, and Rafael Martineli, the treasurer—were preparing to call on Goulart to make sure that Paulo Mário da Cunha Rodrigues would be retained as Navy Minister and that amnesty would be granted to the sailors who had mutinied.[1] Whatever the President's views, seemingly he had reached a position where he could ill afford to break with the CGT.

The CGT had the funds necessary for putting on great rallies and was able to make use of official labor organizations. Only one of the six labor confederation presidents took an anti-CGT position. This was Mário Lopes de Oliveira, pipe-smoking leader of the land transport workers (CNTTT), and he lacked the support of Martineli's National Federation of Railroad Workers. Mário Lopes, a resolute anti-Communist, would lock himself in his office and keep two revolvers ready at his desk.

---

[1] Clodsmidt Riani, interview, Juiz de Fora, November 2, 1968.

It would be a mistake to overlook the considerable amount of artificiality about labor organization. Most of the *sindicatos,* federations, and confederations existed only because the government kept them alive by collecting and distributing the *impôsto sindical* (trade-union tax). Legally each *sindicato* was supposed to have a membership of at least one-third of those in the occupational category over which it had jurisdiction, but frequently this was not the case.[2]

Regardless of such factors, the CGT in March 1964 was in an excellent position to tie up the nation's economy. The CGT leaders had more than the aid provided by the somewhat artificial system they dominated. They were apt to be genuine leaders who in past years had learned how to struggle and gain followings when the government and the official labor hierarchy had opposed them.

The first two labor confederations, the CNTI and the CNTC, had been established during the strongly anti-Communist presidential regime of Marshal Dutra (1946–1951) with the help of his regime. At that time the Communists, barred from holding union posts, carried on illegally. Noting the warm relations between government officials and the heads of the legal labor bodies, the Communists derisively called the government-supported labor leaders *pelegos* (a *pelego* is a sheepskin that is placed between the saddle and the animal being ridden).

After Getúlio Vargas took over the Brazilian presidency from Dutra in 1951, his predecessor's tough restrictions against Communists in the labor movement were relaxed. The Communists, using the cream of the Party's organizers, worked hard to reconquer the prestige that, before their unsuccessful 1935 rebellion, they had enjoyed in *sindicatos* of bank workers, printers, textile workers, maritime workers, and metalworkers.[3] Good progress was made in the early 1950's by such outstanding Communists as Roberto Morena, Dante Pelacani, Osvaldo Pacheco, Hércules Correia dos Reis, Eugênio Chemp, Rafael Martineli, and Luís Tenório de Lima. Nevertheless the anti-Communists, assisted by the advantages that incumbents enjoyed, remained well entrenched at the top of the labor confederations.

[2] Ophelia Rabello, *A Rede Sindical Paulista,* p. 142.
[3] Ari Campista, interview, Rio de Janeiro, October 9, 1968.

This situation continued during the Kubitschek years (1956–1961), with the anti-Communists dominating the CNTI, CNTC, and CNTTT. With non-Communists who would cooperate with them, the Communists therefore organized "united labor fronts" that were outside the official labor organization set-up. Thus while Kubitschek was President there came into being the CPOS (Permanent Commission of Syndical Organizations), the PUA (Pact of Unity and Action), and the Forum Sindical de Debates of Santos.[4] The "renovators," as the Communists and their allies called themselves, were far more "nationalistic" than the "democrats" (anti-Communists). In fact their main appeal was to an anti-United States nationalism. They complained that Brazil's old labor chieftains, busy cooperating with the United States labor attaché and with international anti-Communist groups such as ORIT and the ICFTU,[5] had no contacts with the workers and should be replaced by new, progressive, dynamic leaders. "Democrats" complained that "renovators" had a habit of unnecessarily prolonging *sindicato* meetings so that elections would occur at unreasonable hours, by which time more "democrats" than "renovators" would usually have left.

Vice-President Goulart, handling labor affairs during Kubitschek's administration, worked at the difficult job of promoting "peaceful coexistence" between "democrats" and "renovators." Crockatt de Sá has mentioned labor congresses at which Deocleciano de Holanda Cavalcanti, the CNTI's anti-Communist founder, would preside with the assistance of Roberto Morena. He has added that such coexistence, "without struggles between the right and the left," provided good results.[6] During this era of "peaceful coexistence" (1956–1959) "renovators" came for the first time to have a little influence in the

---

[4] The CPOS, a council of industrial workers' leaders in the city of Rio de Janeiro, was organized by Ari Campista, Roberto Morena, Benedito Cerqueira, and Hércules Correia dos Reis; some time after it was clear that the Communists had full control, Campista left. The PUA, representatives of maritime and railroad workers, first came into being when these workers went on strike for better wages during Kubitschek's presidency.

[5] Organización Regional Interamericana da Trabajadores and the International Confederation of Free Trade Unions.

[6] Crockatt de Sá, interview, Rio de Janeiro, December 12, 1968.

cúpula (top of the legally organized hierarchy). A step in this direction was the formation of two new labor confederations, CONTEC and CNTTMFA, with "renovating" leaderships. At Goulart's urging, non-Communist "renovator" Riani became vice-president of the CNTI, thus serving under his "democratic" foe, Deocleciano.

In the eyes of the "democrats," the "renovators" were using "peaceful coexistence" to achieve the supreme power. Complaining of the Communists' "undemocratic and aggressive" tactics, the "democrats" broke with "peaceful coexistence"—and with Goulart—at the Third Trade Union Congress in 1960. Thus in 1961, when Goulart found himself in the presidency—a presidency that military and political leaders had just stripped of its customary powers—the least surprising occurrences were the rise of the "renovators" to the top of organized labor (at the CNTI election of December 1961), their establishment of the CGT, and their demonstrations on behalf of full presidential powers for Goulart.

After Goulart got those powers, he and the CGT had an off-again on-again affair during 1963, with neither submitting to the other. To those who would criticize the CGT leaders for being *pelegos* at the service of the "vacillating" administration, the CGT replied with demonstrations of independence from Goulart, and its leaders sometimes resorted to strikes against the President's wishes.

Goulart, by giving victory to the CGT in the January 1964 CNTI election, avoided what he felt would be a serious split in organized labor—a split that he had earlier declared would allow his enemies to say he was weak. He also avoided breaking with men who had assailed him when Pelacani had lost his Labor Ministry post and with men who had taken control of the new confederation of agricultural workers (CONTAG).

The CGT was, therefore, in a strong position to make demands on the President. Goulart, however, was resolved to serve as no one's puppet. When he addressed the sergeants at the Automobile Club on March 30, he disregarded rather cautious words that some advisers had urged upon him—words calculated not to aggravate the worst fears of suspicious military leaders. Instead, he forced a military decision at a time when he knew that some Army officers were plotting against him.

Some analysts feel that Goulart believed General Assis Brasil's assurances about loyal troops. At any rate, the President's words put those promises to the test. If Assis Brasil's assurances were unfounded, Goulart would be overthrown, defending the poor and the humble. On the other hand, if Assis Brasil was right, there could well emerge that strong government dreamed of before the state of siege request. It would be a government capable of enacting reforms, but it would also be a government such as the CGT leaders had feared when they had disappointed Goulart by playing a role in defeating the enactment of a state of siege.

BOOK VIII: *The Military Movement of 1964*

"Should the armed forces join a revolution to turn Brazil over to a group which wants to dominate it . . .? To guarantee the strength of the pseudo-syndical group, whose leadership lives on subversive agitation, daily more costly to the public coffers? To submit, perhaps, the nation to Moscow Communism? This, indeed, is what would be unpatriotic, against the nation and against the people.

"No. The armed forces cannot be traitors to Brazil. To defend the privileges of the rich classes is to follow the same anti-democratic line as to serve Fascist or syndical-Communist dictatorships."

Army Chief of Staff Humberto Castelo Branco
confidential circular, March 20, 1964

1. Conspirators in the Army

GENERAL CARLOS LUÍS GUEDES, in charge of three infantry regiments with headquarters in Belo Horizonte, had served on the staff of War Minister Denys. He trusted Goulart as little as Denys did. Long before the provocations of March 1964, he was preparing for a military operation against Goulart. These preparations were already underway in August 1963, when Olímpio Mourão Filho was transferred from São Paulo to take over the Fourth Infantry Division and the Fourth Military Region, which included Guedes' regiments.

Guedes took the newly arrived Mourão to call on Governor Magalhães Pinto. The governor, assisted by José Aparecido de Oliveira, member of his state cabinet, was preparing his campaign as a reform-minded candidate for the presidency. Finding it more and more difficult to deal with Goulart, Magalhães Pinto was beginning to fear that there might be no election in 1965. When Mourão spoke to the Governor about plans to overthrow Goulart, Magalhães Pinto stated that he would side with such a revolution.[1] Mourão then asked for a mani-

[1] Primeiro Exército, Comando da 4a Região Militar, 4a Divisão da Infantaria e Guarnição de Juiz de Fora, Ajudância Geral, *Relatório da Revolução Democrática*

festo in which the governors of Minas, Guanabara, Rio Grande do Sul, and São Paulo would declare that Goulart was acting illegally and should be deposed.[2] It was to be used to justify an outbreak in Minas, which, Mourão hoped, would be supported by the other three states and possibly by all of Brazil. Magalhães Pinto said he would see what he could do.

When Mourão learned of the sergeants' uprising in Brasília in September 1963, he went from his Juiz de Fora headquarters to Belo Horizonte to urge Magalhães Pinto to give the word. But, by the time he saw the Governor, the sergeants had surrendered. What, asked Mourão, had come of the manifesto of the four governors? Magalhães Pinto said that securing four signatures would be easy for him, and that he should get others, such as that of Miguel Arrais. "No, Governor," said Mourão, "I want to make a clean revolution."[3]

Although the right moment was slow in coming, Generals Mourão and Guedes and their staffs prepared for it. Mourão visited Rio each weekend, seeing something of Admiral Rademaker and his group, as well as Denys, Heck, Grün Moss, Nelson de Melo, and Cordeiro de Farias. These unhappy officers commanded no troops.

Mourão was often reminded of the military situation in Guanabara, where modern arms created a compact force as powerful as that in all the rest of Brazil.[4] First Army Commander Armando de Morais Ân- cora was unswervingly loyal to Goulart, as was First Region Commander Ladário Pereira Teles. Some of their subordinates might not care for Goulart, but, as good military men, the majority could be ex- pected to uphold legality and obey orders.

Mourão came to feel that no revolution would break out unless he started one; and he considered it imperative to begin before May 9, when—according to Army records—he would reach retirement age. He felt Magalhães Pinto was vacillating between pleasing Janguistas

---

Iniciada pela 4a RM e 4a DI em 31 de Março de 1964, Special Bulletin, Part I, Juiz de Fora, May 9, 1964.

[2] Carlos Luís Guedes, interview, São Paulo, November 18, 1965.

[3] José Stacchini, *Março 64: Mobilização da Audácia,* p. 33.

[4] Guedes, interview, November 18, 1965.

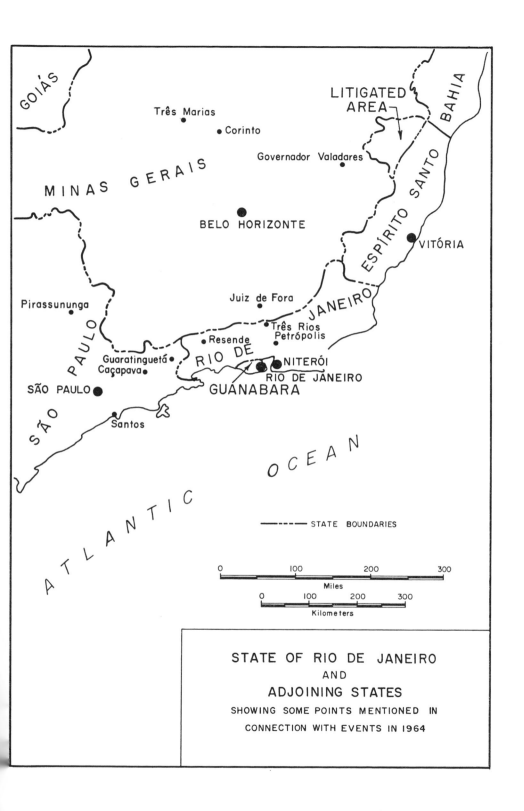

GOIÁS

MINAS GERAIS

Três Marias

• Corinto

Governador Valadares

BELO HORIZONTE

LITIGATED AREA

BAHIA

ESPÍRITO SANTO

• VITÓRIA

Pirassununga

Juiz de Fora

JANEIRO

Três Rios
Petrópolis

Resende

RIO DE

Guaratinguetá
Caçapava

NITERÓI

RIO DE JANEIRO

SÃO PAULO

GUANABARA

Santos

ATLANTIC OCEAN

------- STATE BOUNDARIES

0   100   200   300
Miles

0   100   200   300
Kilometers

STATE OF RIO DE JANEIRO
AND
ADJOINING STATES
SHOWING SOME POINTS MENTIONED IN
CONNECTION WITH EVENTS IN 1964

and anti-Janguistas.[5] After the demonstrations against CUTAL in Belo Horizonte in January, Magalhães Pinto was advised by General Guedes that a military movement could be started "for guaranteeing legality." But the Governor told Guedes that he was uninterested in backing a "rightist coup."[6] The Governor, a skillful Minas politician, was willing to support a revolution to preserve democracy in Brazil, but he wanted it to be a successful and popular movement. During January and February he did not believe the conditions were right. The federal administration, he felt, had too great a control of fuel supplies and had too much backing in the Army and among organized laborers.[7] He did what he could to build up the Polícia Militar (state police force), and late in February he pleased its officers by dropping leftist José Aparecido de Oliveira from his state cabinet.

After the Rio rally of March 13, Army Chief of Staff Humberto Castelo Branco, one of the intellectuals of the Escola Superior de Guerra's "Grupo da Sorbonne," meditated on the meaning of legality. Then this sixty-three–year-old veteran of World War II put his thoughts in a confidential circular for officers of his staff.

Acknowledging that "intranquility" had prevailed in the armed forces following the March 13 rally, Castelo Branco noted two threats: the advent of a constitutional assembly for obtaining basic reforms and increased agitation by "the illegal power of the CGT."

The armed forces, Castelo Branco wrote, should not let themselves be used to serve the privileges of the rich or to support either Fascist or Communist–labor union dictatorships. The armed forces were to uphold the constituted powers and the proper application of the law, but that was not to say that they should defend specific government programs; much less should they defend government propaganda.

Castelo Branco saw achievement of the proposed constitutional assembly as involving revolutionary violence, the closing of the existing Congress, and the institution of a dictatorship. While declaring it legi-

---

[5] Olímpio Mourão Filho, interview, Rio de Janeiro, October 9, 1965.

[6] "Gen. Guedes Relata o Começo do Movimento," *Correio da Manhã*, April 3, 1964.

[7] Carlos Castello Branco, "Da Conspiração à Revolução," in Alberto Dines *et al.*, *Os Idos de Março e a Queda em Abril*, 293.

timate for people to turn to insurrection, he expressed the feeling that the Brazilian people were not at the moment asking for a constitutional assembly or a civilian or military dictatorship.

The armed forces, he added, would be acting against the people and the nation if they were to help "the pseudo-syndical group whose leaders live on subversive agitation, which is daily becoming more costly to the public coffers" and which might "submit the nation to Moscow Communism."

In conclusion, Castelo Branco wrote that he had spoken with the War Minister and received the assurance that he would respect Congress, the elections, and the inauguration of those who won at the polls.[8]

Cordeiro de Farias persuaded Castelo Branco that these thoughts should have wider distribution than their author had intended. On March 20, therefore, mimeographed copies, turned out in Cordeiro's Rio apartment, were distributed among numerous officers who commanded troops.[9] Although Castelo Branco had signed the generals' memorandum of August 1954, calling on Vargas to leave office, he had a great reputation for being always "rigorously within the law." His confidential circular carried much weight and made it certain that he would lose his job, even though it was not a job with a command of troops.

The settlement of the sailors' mutiny was a clear reply to Castelo Branco's sober words. The terms of the settlement adhered precisely to assurances that had previously been given by CGT leaders to congressmen belonging to the Frente de Mobilização Popular.[10]

These terms gave a new urgency to planning against a coup by the Far Left. Planning in Rio was headed by top-ranking Generals Artur da Costa e Silva (chief of the Army Department of Production and Works) and Castelo Branco. They held, respectively, the second and third positions in the Army Almanac's list of eight four-star generals in

[8] Text of Castelo Branco's circular given in Araken Távora, *Brasil, 1º de Abril,* pp. 78–79.

[9] Sebastião Chaves, interviews, São Paulo, November 20 and 22, 1967.

[10] Carlos Castello Branco, "Da Conspiração à Revolução," in Dines et al., *Os Idos de Março,* p. 297.

active service.[11] (Cordeiro de Farias, first on the Almanac's list, was not really in active Army service; he had been conspiring for some time and was the only one of the eight to hold no Army post. Of the other five—all promoted by Goulart late in 1963—four were the commanders of Brazil's four armies.) The sixty-one–year-old Costa e Silva had headed the Fourth Army (with headquarters in Recife) at the start of the Goulart regime, but he had displeased Brizola and Goulart and had been transferred to desk jobs in Rio.[12]

Castelo Branco and Costa e Silva sought a compact with important troop commanders; it provided that all would remain on the alert and act together if it became necessary to prevent a coup by Goulart or those around him.[13] This idea was presented to the commanders of the Second and Fourth Armies. Castelo Branco and Costa e Silva could expect no help from the commanders of the stronger First and Third Armies, but they had the support of some troop-leading subordinates in these armies. Colonel José Costa Cavalcanti, UDN congressman from Pernambuco, visited garrisons to promote Castelo Branco's ideas.

From Rio a colonel sped to Recife and brought back a letter in which careful Fourth Army Commander Joaquim Justino Alves Bastos subscribed to Castelo Branco's position. Alves Bastos' adherence was considered significant in spite of the fact that the colonels under him had already given the Fourth Army a strongly anti-Goulart complexion. Alves Bastos—once an opponent of the Democratic Crusade—had been fence-sitting.

The Fourth Army is by far the smallest of Brazil's four armies. Therefore, if the antiadministration generals were to be in a position to present a well-backed ultimatum to Goulart and the War Minister, much more was needed than Alves Bastos' letter. Retired General Riograndino Kruel was sent to São Paulo to seek the adherence of his brother Amauri. Like Alves Bastos, Amauri Kruel headed an army that was full of anti-Goulart officers. His relations with Costa e Silva

---

[11] Rank in the list depends on the length of time spent as a four-star (Army) general.

[12] Nelson Dimas Filho, *Costa e Silva: O Homem e o Líder*, p. 35; João Adil de Oliveira, interview, Rio de Janeiro, December 20, 1965.

[13] Chaves, interviews, November 20 and 22, 1967.

were good, but his personal ties with Goulart continued to be the predominant factor. Amauri Kruel, willing to act if and when he was convinced that it was necessary to save Brazil from a coup by the Far Left, wanted to press upon the President the need to change his advisers.

2. Minas Decides to Revolt

FOLLOWING THE RALLY of March 13, Magalhães Pinto sped on airplanes to confer gravely with fellow governors and fellow presidential candidates about the need for understandings regarding the "defense of the nation's institutions." Back in Belo Horizonte on March 20 he appeared before a battery of microphones and television cameras to deliver what he called the "Manifesto of Minas." In his statement he expressed disapproval of any coup or "revolution commanded at the top." Then he went to the adjoining state of Espírito Santo and arranged with its governor that Minas might use the port of Vitória in case a civil war should make that necessary.

The "Manifesto of Minas," intended to suggest that the Governor was breaking with the President, was so carefully worded that it did not much worry Goulart. What did upset Goulart was a meeting of Magalhães Pinto and Lacerda at Belo Horizonte on March 24. The discussion at the lunch table at the Palácio da Liberdade largely concerned the UDN's forthcoming national convention, but Goulart's reaction to the meeting of the UDN rivals was that Magalhães Pinto had joined the "intolerant opposition to the federal government."[1]

On Friday morning, March 27, when Goulart was handling the sailors' mutiny, Magalhães Pinto called Mourão Filho from the colonial town of Ouro Preto, where the General and his wife had settled down to spend the end of Holy Week. At the Palácio da Liberdade,

[1] Pedro Gomes, "Minas: Do Diálogo ao 'Front'," in Alberto Dines et al., Os Idos de Março e a Queda em Abril, p. 91.

Magalhães Pinto and Carlos Luís Guedes showed Mourão newspaper stories about the mutiny, which, besides being serious, was turning the opinion of civilians and military officers against the President. All three decided to send emissaries all over Brazil to seek backing for a revolution that they hoped would begin as quickly as possible.[2] Guedes, the most impatient, wanted the uprising to break out on March 30.

Magalhães Pinto sent two members of his state cabinet—José Monteiro de Castro and Osvaldo Pieruccetti—to Rio to get the views of Marshal Dutra, Castelo Branco, and Denys. These Army men emphasized the importance of having the adherence of Amauri Kruel.[3] Dutra said that Kruel's backing was essential, for Minas could not go it alone. Castelo Branco, hopeful about Kruel, was equally emphatic.

At Denys' suggestion, Magalhães Pinto's two representatives went to São Paulo to have their second talk with Kruel. On their first visit, made to Kruel's residence shortly after midnight a few days earlier, Kruel had been surprised at Magalhães Pinto's sending men he did not know. He had simply assured them that he would not allow Brazil to become a República Sindicalista and much less would he allow it to become a Communist state; he would march on Rio if necessary to prevent chaos.[4] The second visit was held in Kruel's office early on March 28. Afterward Magalhães Pinto's representatives returned to Belo Horizonte to report that Kruel would make up his mind after discussing the situation with Goulart.

Mourão was at his Juiz de Fora headquarters, waiting in vain for Magalhães Pinto to inform him of the text of a forthcoming manifesto —a manifesto in which Mourão thought the Minas governor should make a really strong declaration of war against Goulart.[5] Instead, Mourão learned that the Governor had called for a new conference.

For this conference, held at the Juiz de Fora airport on Saturday afternoon of March 28, Denys came from Rio to urge Magalhães

[2] Olímpio Mourão Filho, interview, Rio de Janeiro, October 9, 1965; Primeiro Exército, *Relatório da Revolução Democrática Iniciada pela 4a RM e 4a DI em 31 de Março de 1964*, Special Bulletin, Part 1. "Gen. Guedes Relata o Começo do Movimento," *Correio da Manhã*, April 3, 1964.

[3] Gomes, "Minas: Do Diálogo ao 'Front'," pp. 92–93.

[4] Amauri Kruel, interview, Guanabara, October 21, 1967.

[5] Primeiro Exército, *Relatório da Revolução Democrática*, Special Bulletin, Part 1.

Pinto, Mourão, Guedes, and the state police chief that the time had come to act.[6] The optimistic picture he painted of the sentiment among Army officers dispelled ideas about waiting in the hope that fuller coordination be achieved with the adherence of Kruel.

Mourão kept demanding the much discussed manifesto. Magalhães Pinto, agreeing that time would not allow other governors to sign a joint one, offered to draw up one of his own. This, Mourão understood, would include a phrase stating that the struggle would continue until Goulart had been overthrown.[7] The wording was to be made known to Mourão, but the manifesto was not to be released until Mourão's troops were well on their way to Rio.[8]

No sooner had Magalhães Pinto left the airport than one of Mourão's men arrived from São Paulo. In reply to Mourão's appeal that "together we save the nation from Communism," Kruel had told Mourão's emissary that it would be best to await one more provocation by Goulart. "This fact will certainly appear because each day the federal government commits new illegal acts." Kruel had censured the First Army and its commander, Armando de Morais Âncora, for their failure at the time of the Navy crisis. "If I had been there, the CGT, PUA, and other organs of Communism and agitation would have been closed." Kruel's message went on to say that the São Paulo civilian authorities were "poorly informed." The General added that he had telephoned Goulart, "to whom, on account of personal friendship, I owe a certain consideration." The President had promised that on Monday, March 30, an investigation of the Navy mutiny would begin.[9]

Kruel concluded by observing that a movement in the armed forces should be a coordinated, not an isolated, one.

On Sunday, March 29, the authorities in Minas made preparations for the state to start the revolution alone. At Juiz de Fora Mourão insisted that civilian support would depend on Magalhães Pinto's manifesto. Guedes maintained that the words of Cabo Anselmo constituted

---

[6] José Stacchini, *Março 64: Mobilização da Audácia,* p. 64.
[7] Mourão Filho, interview, October 9, 1965.
[8] Primeiro Exército, *Relatório da Revolução Democrática,* Part 1.
[9] *Ibid.*

an excellent manifesto for giving their movement civilian support.[10] Mourão picked April 1 as a good "psychological date" for the outbreak. But Guedes insisted that the movement should start on March 30, and he asserted that he himself would start it then. Asked why he had chosen that date, Guedes avoided further discussion by stating that this would be the last day of the full moon.[11]

From Belo Horizonte José Maria Alkmim, with Magalhães Pinto at his side, telephoned Herbert Levy in São Paulo. Alkmim, the PSD's perfect political prognosticator, had taken a strong anti-Goulart position. Now he heard Levy report that most of the young São Paulo Army officers, many of them approached by Nelson de Melo, were ready to topple the President.[12] Kruel was said to know that only a few Second Army generals would support Goulart. The São Paulo state government, Levy said, would stand by Minas.

With this news Magalhães Pinto officially placed the Minas state police under the orders of Guedes. In manpower this force was more than twice the size of the Army in the state, but the seven thousand Army men were much better armed.

Guedes had been giving a good deal of attention to the defense of the state. The Governor and his associates were preparing for the possibility of a struggle of several months in which Minas, like São Paulo in 1932, might find itself disappointed by those who offered alliances. The state cabinet was modified to include nationally prominent Mineiros who would give it a wider political horizon. Alkmim became finance secretary. Milton Campos and Afonso Arinos de Melo Franco became secretaries without portfolio. Afonso Arinos, it was hoped, would be useful in case the revolution, in control of Minas and a part of Espírito Santo, needed to negotiate the importation of arms from abroad.[13]

In Belo Horizonte on March 30, Guedes initiated the outbreak by requisitioning all gasoline and by arresting ninety-three "pro-Com-

---

[10] Carlos Luís Guedes, interview, São Paulo, November 18, 1965.

[11] "Gen. Guedes Relata o Começo do Movimento," *Correio da Manhã*, April 3, 1964; Guedes, interview, November 18, 1965.

[12] Herbert Victor Levy, interview, Brasília, October 20, 1965.

[13] Afonso Arinos de Melo Franco, interview, Brasília, October 14, 1965.

munists," including three state legislators. "Someone has to start," he remarked.[14]

He telephoned Mourão to advise that he had met with his men and they had all declared themselves in rebellion. He also said that the Governor had released a manifesto to the press.[15] This last piece of news enraged Mourão, who had expected first to look it over and who felt that it would be dangerous to release it before his troops reached Rio.

Guedes described the manifesto over the telephone. "The first part," Guedes said, "is not of interest at the moment because it speaks only of basic reforms; however, it ends with the sentence: 'Minas will struggle with all the energy of its people for the restoration of constitutional order which in this hour has been dangerously compromised.' "[16] Commenting on the manifesto, Mourão said: "Thank God! No one will pay any attention to that." However, he instructed Guedes to depose and imprison Magalhães Pinto for "being a traitor."[17] The Governor, he felt, wanted to be a revolutionary or not, depending on the outcome.

Magalhães Pinto, neither deposed nor jailed, telephoned Mourão. The general declared that he would not change his attitude about the need for a new, more incisive manifesto. Late that evening Alkmim and Monteiro de Castro brought the Governor's manifesto to Mourão in Juiz de Fora. It was the same one Guedes had mentioned on the telephone, and had been released at noon.

Mourão explained to his visitors that he would not lead his troops against Goulart. A military uprising, he said, needed a complete civilian coverage not provided by the insufficiently revolutionary manifesto of Magalhães Pinto.[18]

Later that night Mourão heard Goulart's Automobile Club speech on the radio. He immediately decided to march against Rio "regardless

[14] Gomes, "Minas: Do Diálogo ao 'Front'," p. 104.

[15] Mourão Filho, interview, October 9, 1965.

[16] Primeiro Exército, *Relatório da Revolução Democrática,* Special Bulletin, Part 1.

[17] Mourão Filho, interview, October 9, 1965; Stacchini, *Março 64: Mobilização da Audácia,* p. 7.

[18] José Monteiro de Castro, quoted in letter from Oswaldo Pieruccetti to J.W.F.D., January 18, 1968, p. 3.

of Magalhães Pinto."[19] Before daybreak on March 31 he telephoned Guedes, asking that an infantry battalion be sent rapidly to Juiz de Fora to participate in what was to be called the Tiradentes Column. Messages were passed on to some conspirators in Rio who wanted to join the Minas troop; messages were also sent to Sílvio Heck in Rio and to Ademar de Barros and Dalísio Mena Barreto in São Paulo. Mourão prepared his own manifesto.

In Rio at 7:00 A.M. on the thirty-first, Deputado Armando Falcão received a telephone call from Mourão telling of his plans. Falcão immediately advised Lacerda and Castelo Branco, who, like Falcão, was a native of Ceará. Castelo Branco could not believe what Falcão told him, but Falcão telephoned Mourão and received confirmation.[20]

Two hours later Castelo Branco, by then convinced that Mourão was about to march, got in touch with Magalhães Pinto and Guedes. Castelo Branco felt that it was too soon to start a military outbreak because the coordinating work had not been completed and an isolated movement might be crushed with disastrous results. Speaking with Magalhães Pinto he insisted that the Governor hold the troops where they were. Mourão's troops had not left Juiz de Fora; but the Governor—who could hardly have influenced Mourão—told Castelo Branco that the Minas forces were "already approaching the Paraibuna River,"[21] one section of which separates the states of Minas Gerais and Rio de Janeiro.

Guedes advised Castelo Branco that an Army battalion was on its way to Juiz de Fora and that a state police battalion was on its way to Três Marias, another point in the state. "You are being precipitous," Castelo Branco told Guedes. Then, after advising Guedes to be careful, he added that he would inform those who were working with him. He set out to have Mourão's march supported as fully as possible in Rio.

Mourão was preparing to have about 2,500 men (with about 200 vehicles) advance on the might of Vila Militar. Meeting with his

[19] Mourão Filho, interview, October 9, 1965.
[20] Armando Falcão, interview, Rio de Janeiro, November 30, 1966.
[21] Oswaldo Pieruccetti, letter to J.W.F.D., January 18, 1968, p. 5; also see Stacchini, Março 64, p. 77, and Gomes, "Minas: Do Diálogo ao 'Front'," p. 106.

subordinate officers at Juiz de Fora, he invited them "to die" with him. All but four accepted the challenge.[22]

[22] Primeiro Exército, *Relatório da Revolução Democrática*, Special Bulletin, Part 1.

3. The Tiradentes Column Leaves Minas for Rio (March 31, 1964)

IN JUIZ DE FORA on the morning of March 31, Mourão ordered the execution of three long-planned operations: *gaiola* (cage), *silêncio* (silence), and Popeye (named after pipe-smoking Mourão).

Gaiola, which Guedes initiated in Belo Horizonte on March 30, consisted of imprisoning labor union leaders and others considered dangerous to the success of the rebellion. In Juiz de Fora the police chief and his staff made use of card indexes prepared by the rebels; the suspects were confined at the Army barracks.[1]

To carry out *silêncio*, communications from Rio to Minas were controlled to give the impression outside the state that all was normal.[2] Vehicles coming to Minas were allowed to proceed but departures were prohibited. Of those going from Rio to Belo Horizonte, only gasoline tankers were stopped; thirty of them were taken over at Juiz de Fora by Mourão's revolutionaries.[3] All telephone calls between Minas and Rio went through Juiz de Fora. People speaking from Minas had to be careful lest the line suddenly be cut. Local radio stations cooperated with Mourão's staff.

Operation Popeye, the assault on Rio, was to be undertaken by the 2,500 men of the Tiradentes Column, leaving most of the troops behind

[1] Primeiro Exército, *Relatório da Revolução Democrática Iniciada pela 4a RM e 4a DI em 31 de Março de 1964*. Special Bulletin, Juiz de Fora, May 9, 1964, Part 3 (Intelligence).

[2] *Ibid.*

[3] Olímpio Mourão Filho, interview, Rio de Janeiro, October 9, 1965.

to defend the state at its various points of entry. The column was commanded by General Antônio Carlos da Silva Murici, who, as head of the Natal garrison in 1963, had been assailed by Brizola. Mourão called him from Rio to Juiz de Fora at the last moment.

The vanguard, an Army regiment, left Juiz de Fora at 12:30 P.M. on March 31 and proceeded along the highway until, at 2:00 P.M., it reached the state of Rio by crossing the Paraibuna River. It protected the bridge and awaited the arrival of two Army regiments and one state battalion from Juiz de Fora.[4] These reached the river between 5:00 and 6:00 P.M.

In Juiz de Fora at 5:00 P.M. Mourão went on the radio and read his manifesto to the nation and the armed forces. This spoke of "spurious organizations of political syndicalism, manipulated by enemies of Brazil, confessedly Communist" and "particularly audacious" because of the "support and stimulation" provided by President Goulart. The government, Mourão asserted, allowed these organizations to name and dismiss cabinet ministers, generals, and high officials in order to destroy the democratic institutions. Mourão referred to the work of demoralizing and humiliating the Navy "in the most depraved and shameless outrage against its discipline and hierarchy."

"The people, state governors and armed forces, animated by fervent patriotic sentiment, oppose this process of degradation of the vital forces of the nation, so well conceived and capriciously carried out by the President of the Republic." Mourão expressed the certainty that the head of the government was about to annihilate Brazil's civic liberties. The armed forces, he said, could not remain silent lest they become collaborators.

Calling on all Brazilians to restore the authority of the constitution, Mourão accused Goulart of failing in his duties and turning himself into the chief of a Communist government. He should, Mourão concluded, be thrown out of the position of power he was abusing.[5]

[4] "Relatório das Atividades do Destacamento Tiradentes," signed at Juiz de Fora, April 7, 1964, by General Murici (Primeiro Exército, *Relatório da Revolução Democrática*, Special Bulletin, Appendix 11).

[5] *O Jornal*, April 1, 1964.

This ended *silêncio*. Amidst an avalanche of statements, Brazil awaited the outcome of the Minas uprising. This would depend on the attitude of important military units. First to make their reactions known were civilians. In Pernambuco, Miguel Arrais raised his voice in favor of Goulart's government. Nei Braga, governor of Paraná, sent a radio message to Mourão advising that his state was joining the "democratic movement." "Your pronouncement," he said, "has filled us with elation and was applauded in the streets."[6]

At 8:00 P.M. Magalhães Pinto made the revolt a state uprising by broadcasting another manifesto. Many times in this, and in statements to the press, the Minas Governor emphasized that he was a great believer in "reforms . . . indispensable for development and the emancipation of our people." However, he stated in this manifesto to the Brazilian people, the reforms should be carried out within the framework of the "democratic regime." "The military forces in Minas, responsible for the safety of the institutions . . . , consider it their duty to go into action. . . . Consistency and harmony oblige us to back this patriotic action. All Mineiros are at our side." He asked for the support of all Brazilians, so that legality might he restored, making Christian and democratic reforms possible.[7]

Both Magalhães Pinto and Carlos Luís Guedes affirmed that Minas was not separating itself politically from the rest of Brazil. Guedes, sending troops and trucks to Mourão in Juiz de Fora, told the press that Minas could defend itself for an indefinite length of time. It had, he said, great stocks of gasoline; moreover, mountain chains along its borders were useful for defense. Not mentioned publicly by Guedes was the state's preponderant supply of munitions for heavy artillery, due to the manufacturing plant at Juiz de Fora.

The federal government ordered an impressive armed array to march from the Rio area under General Luís Tavares da Cunha Melo to deal with the Tiradentes Column. The rebels were to be overpowered by the First Battalion of Riflemen (from Petrópolis), the Third Infantry

---

[6] *Ibid.*, April 1, 1964.
[7] *Ibid.*

Battalion, and a part of the Second Infantry Battalion; also by the celebrated First Infantry Regiment, which, known as the Sampaio Regiment, had gained fame in Italy during World War II.

War Minister Jair Dantas Ribeiro, directing operations from the government hospital, asserted that, although he was convalescing, he would not hesitate to sacrifice his health to fulfill his duty to the democratic regime. He announced that the government controlled the situaation, and that troops loyal to legality would put down the subversive movement led by Guedes and Mourão.

Raul Riff's note from the presidential office described the "subversive movement" as one that was connected with previously unsuccessful coups, "always repudiated by the democratic sentiment of the Brazilian people and by the legalistic spirit of the armed forces."

4. Kruel's Decision (March 31, 1964)

THE REBELLION IN MINAS and the short march of the Tiradentes Column forced decisions on many men.

It has been stated that if Minas had not rebelled when it did, a well-coordinated military move to overthrow Goulart—planned before Goulart addressed the sergeants—would have occurred early in April. But the history of such movements in Brazil include numerous dates that have been postponed. In this instance, the importance given to getting Kruel's adherence, and the position he took when Mourão appealed that "together we save the nation from Communism," indicate that all was not well regarding a coordinated uprising for April 2 or thereabouts.

"In the Army Staff," Castelo Branco had recently said, "a calculated risk is admissable, but an *aventura* [hazardous venture] never is. Without Kruel's adherence, all will be an *aventura*."[1] On March 30,

[1] Araújo Netto, "A Paisagem," in Alberto Dines *et al., Os Idos de Março e a Queda em Abril,* p. 46.

at a meeting of Rio conspirators, Costa e Silva is reported to have agreed with Kruel and to have said: "There is still no reason for a revolution; it is best to wait."[2] After this meeting, Cordeiro de Farias, planning another trip to São Paulo, was told by Costa e Silva that Kruel preferred that he not go.

Mourão telephoned Kruel at 9:00 A.M. on March 31 and surprised him with the news that he was about to attack Rio with his small force. When this outbreak changed the picture, all eyes—with more concern than before—turned to Kruel. On behalf of the Minas revolutionaries Kruel was visited by Antônio Balbino, who had fallen from the Goulart cabinet when Kruel had.[3] Costa e Silva telephoned Kruel from the Rio Yacht Club. Justice Minister Jurema also tried to reach him, but Kruel would not accept the call.

Jurema has written that the hopes of the entire staff of the First Army and its willingness to go out and fight "for legality" depended on the position to be taken by Kruel.[4]

Military men around the President had long felt that, in case of trouble, the outcome would be decided by the troops in Guanabara, São Paulo, and Rio Grande do Sul.[5] After the Minas outbreak—and while Kruel was deciding what to do—the government re-examined the situation in Rio Grande do Sul, where conspirators in the Army had been causing uneasiness. It was decided to send First Region Commander Ladário Pereira Teles to take over the large Third Army from Benjamim Galhardo.[6] Galhardo was appointed to replace Castelo Branco as Army chief of staff.

While the troops of the First Battalion of Riflemen marched from Petrópolis to oppose the Tiradentes Column, Goulart telephoned Kruel four or five times from Rio. Kruel always suggested that Goulart leave the people who were surrounding him lest he "sink with them."[7] But

---

[2] José Stacchini, *Março 64: Mobilização da Audácia*, p. 98.

[3] Pedro Gomes, "Minas: Do Diálogo ao 'Frente'," in Dines *et al.*, *Os Idos de Março*, p. 117.

[4] Abelardo Jurema, *Sexta-Feira, 13: Os Últimos Dias do Govêrno João Goulart*, p. 192.

[5] *Ibid.*, p. 196.

[6] *O Jornal*, April 1, 1964.

[7] Amauri Kruel, interview, São Paulo, November 16, 1965.

the President invariably replied that he could not carry on without the support of the "politicians."

In Rio Goulart tried to reassure his intimates: "Kruel is my friend; he is with us; but he's always talking about this Communism business —about infiltration in the CGT and the PUA. . . . But everything is all right."[8]

Ademar de Barros and other Paulistas were worried. Hours had passed since Guedes and Mourão had started the revolution in Minas. São Paulo, the "bastion of democracy," had taken no position. Around 6:00 P.M., while Kruel was having another, and final, telephone conversation with Goulart, General Nelson de Melo joined Ademar and his friends. Nelson de Melo was the only one in the group who seemed to have no worries. He felt sure that, with few exceptions, officers under Kruel would act in support of the movement in Minas. Moreover, many were preparing to do so. Plans had been developed to have subordinates of Kruel make him a prisoner if he did not adhere; Nelson de Melo, a former Second Army commander, was to be put in his place.[9]

Kruel, in the meantime, was asking Goulart whether he preferred the support of the politicians around him to the support of the armed forces. Goulart repeated that he could not do without his politicians. "In that case," said Kruel, "from this moment on we are separated."[10]

Kruel spent the next four hours dealing with three generals who were under his command but who strenuously balked at opposing the Goulart administration. He also took steps to have Second Army troops move toward Rio.

At 9:00 P.M., when Kruel's position was still unknown, Ademar de Barros finally made a declaration on video tape which was carried on the air about an hour later. Those who wanted to know whether São Paulo was joining Minas in military action against Goulart found this declaration indecisive. But, amidst a mass of worthy sentiments about São Paulo's readiness to defend the democratic regime, Ademar did say that the Mineiros could "count on us," and that it was necessary

[8] Jurema, *Sexta-Feira, 13*, p. 193.

[9] Prudente de Morais Neto, interview, Rio de Janeiro, October 6, 1965.

[10] Kruel, interview, November 16, 1965.

to end the regime which "threatens, which disturbs, and which paralyzes human activities."[11]

At the headquarters of the Second Army, Kruel was threatening to arrest the two Goulart-supporting generals whom he had been able to detain in his office. One headed the Second Military Region (São Paulo state); the other commanded three infantry divisions, two artillery divisions, and some mechanized squadrons. The third uncooperative general, Euriale de Jesus Zerbini, had charge of troops in Paraíba Valley, between Rio and São Paulo; a close friend of Assis Brasil, he refused to come to Kruel's office.

While Kruel was trying to work things out with these subordinates, another telephone call came from Goulart. Kruel refused to answer it. When Costa e Silva telephoned from Copacabana, Kruel advised that the last words of his manifesto were being typed. By then he had persuaded the two generals who were with him to oppose "the Communists around the President." Kruel fired Zerbini, whose subordinates had already declared their support of the Minas uprising.

It was nearly 11:00 P.M. when Kruel issued his manifesto stating that the fight of the Second Army "will be against the Communists, and its objective will be to break the circle of Communism which now compromises the authority of the government of the Republic."[12] Since the revolt had started early in the morning, no important troop commander outside of Minas had made public adherence to it. Kruel felt that he risked much in making his decision and that there was a good chance of trouble from a resisting powerful First Army in Rio. Upon releasing his manifesto, he received messages asking whether it was authentic. These came from Magalhães Pinto, the Fourth Army's Joaquim Justino Alves Bastos, and General Emílio Garrastazu Médici, commander of the military academy at Resende, in Paraíba Valley.

Ademar, following a midnight session with Kruel, returned to Campos Elísios Palace. He was full of his old confidence and fight when he addressed the nation at 1:40 A.M. on April 1. "The troops of the Second Army are marching through Paraíba Valley to join the troops of the Fourth Military Region." They would go on to Guanabara

[11] *O Estado de S. Paulo,* April 1, 1964.
[12] *O Jornal,* April 1, 1964.

"to re-establish constitutional order." Ademar also revealed that the position of São Paulo and Minas had been backed by the governors of Goiás, Mato Grosso, Paraná, Rio Grande do Sul, and Santa Catarina. He told of having placed the São Paulo Fôrça Pública under the command of "this great military figure, General Amauri Kruel." And he advised his listeners that his words were being recorded in the presence of a distinguished audience, which included Generals Nelson de Melo and Cordeiro de Farias.[13]

While Kruel was reaching his decision, the Tiradentes Column from Minas was joined by Mourão at the Paraibuna River. There it faced the battalion from Petrópolis. No one was in a hurry to start shooting. Efforts of the column's officers to negotiate with Lieutenant-Colonel Kerensky Túlio Mota, commander of the battalion, consumed much time. They made it possible for a Tiradentes Column lieutenant to have talks with officers of the battalion, many of whom decided that they wanted to become a part of the movement against Goulart.[14] After midnight most of Kerensky's battalion joined the revolutionaries from Minas, and Kerensky was reported to be returning to Petrópolis to try to find men who would fight for Goulart.

At 3:30 A.M., after Kruel's decision became known, the Tiradentes Column received a visit from Marshal Odílio Denys. The former War Minister declared that he was going to gain the adherence of the powerful Sampaio Regiment,[15] which was approaching the Paraibuna River from Rio. Denys then telephoned the regiment's commander, Colonel Raimundo Ferreira de Souza, a man who had worked under him for fourteen years, much of the time as his secretary.[16]

"We must overthrow Goulart," the Marshal told the Colonel. "Are you going to fight for the Communists?" Colonel Raimundo and his famed regiment adhered.[17] The Colonel explained that this step was

[13] *O Estado de S. Paulo*, April 1, 1964.

[14] "Relatório das Atividades do Destacamento Tiradentes," signed at Juiz de Fora, April 7, 1964, by General Murici (Primeiro Exército, *Relatório da Revolução Democrática Iniciada pela 4a RM e 4a DI em 31 de Março de 1964*, Special Bulletin, Juiz de Fora, May 9, 1964, Appendix 11).

[15] *Ibid.*

[16] Stacchini, *Março 64*, p. 45.

[17] Odílio Denys' declaration to José-Itamar de Freitas, "Denis Conta Tudo," *Fatos & Fotos*, May 2, 1964. (Also published as a separate brochure.)

not being taken out of fear. "I'm presenting myself and joining you because there are no leaders in Rio."[18]

Mourão believes that Raimundo's decision was all-important. Had the Colonel started to combat the column's vanguard, "the rest of the Army would have come to crush me."[19] The revolution, Mourão says, was victorious when it was joined by the Sampaio Regiment.[20]

The Tiradentes Column, greatly enlarged by its new adherents, left Paraibuna at about 7:00 A.M. on April 1 for Três Rios, on the way to Rio. General Cunha Melo, charged with stopping the march, saw his army disintegrate.

Like Mourão, Kruel was cheered by continued actions of support. The first came from military academy Commander Garrastazu Médici, in a position, at Resende, to have cadets try to block the road between Rio and São Paulo. On the morning of April 1 Kruel learned that a First Army column of eight jeeps and one truck was moving from Rio along this road. The adherence of this column, secured by one of Kruel's officers after a one-hour negotiation, was the signal for Kruel that the outcome would be unfavorable for "the Communists."[21]

At the Air Force school in Pirassununga, São Paulo, where Haroldo Veloso was an instructor, some of the Goulart sympathizers took to the air in order to support government Army troops. There, as elsewhere, occasional airplanes took off despite efforts of antiadministration Air Force officers to keep them on the ground; the commands at the important Air Force bases were in the hands of officers loyal to the President.[22] But proadministration planes, once in the air, found no troops to support.

When no airplanes acted against Mourão's troops, Nelson de Melo telephoned Grün Moss to congratulate him and his fellow officers for the work they had long been carrying out among Air Force pilots.

[18] Olímpio Mourão Filho, interview, Rio de Janeiro, October 9, 1965.

[19] Stacchini, *Março 64,* p. 45.

[20] Mourão Filho, interview, October 9, 1965.

[21] Kruel, interview, Guanabara, October 21, 1967.

[22] Márcio de Souza e Melo, interview, Rio de Janeiro, December 17, 1965.

5. Events in Rio

FOR A CONSIDERABLE period before the outbreak on March 31, American Ambassador Lincoln Gordon had been approached by worried Brazilians. As far back as late 1962 and early 1963, some, who had seemed a bit hotheaded, had spoken of "starting a revolution within the next thirty days." Although they had often claimed the support of most of the Brazilian military, the plotters had nevertheless wanted assurances of United States military backing and promises that United States aircraft carriers would appear suddenly if developments should go badly. The Ambassador had let them know that they should not rely on being "rescued" by the United States. He had sought to discourage those who had wanted to precipitate an uprising but who had seemed unable to carry it through. He had felt that it would be dangerous for them to start something the Goulart government could put down; an unsuccessful revolt might give an excuse for the Goulart government to act successfully against its enemies.[1]

The Ambassador had been well impressed with businessmen connected with IPÊS, and he had agreed with their evaluation of the Brazilian situation. But he had continued to maintain that the "solution" ought to be Brazilian. Talks with IPÊS officers had been "atmospheric" (in general terms). The Ambassador had always been "cautious and diplomatic." While IPÊS officers may at times have had specific ideas in mind, these ideas had not been stated even by them in conversations with Gordon. Perhaps because of preconceived ideas at which they only hinted, the IPÊS officers might sometimes have come away feeling that they had gained the Ambassador's agreement.[2]

---

[1] Lincoln Gordon, conversation, Rio de Janeiro, December 18, 1965.

[2] In "When Executives Turned Revolutionaries" (*Fortune,* September 1964), Philip Siekman writes as follows about some Paulistas conspiring against Goulart: "they sent an emissary to ask U. S. Ambassador Lincoln Gordon what the U. S. position would be if civil war broke out, who reported back that Gordon was cautious and diplomatic, but he left the impression that if the Paulistas could hold out for forty-eight hours they would get U. S. recognition and help." In this connection, Ambassa-

In Rio on the afternoon of March 31 Gordon received a visit from a well-known American resident of São Paulo who asked what the Ambassador could provide for the cause of the "revolution" against the Goulart government. The visitor seemed to be suggesting that things were not going well for the anti-Goulart group and that the United States government ought to do something to improve the chances of the movement. Gordon replied that his visitor should return to São Paulo. He added that the "revolutionaries," instead of "dreaming of some *deus ex machina*," should persuade Amauri Kruel to side with the movement against the Goulart regime.[3]

CGT leaders met in Rio on March 31 to decide on a general strike. But the National Stevedores' Federation building, where they gathered, was invaded during the afternoon by state police sent by Colonel Gustavo Borges. With the aid of tear gas, the police made a rich haul of twenty men, including Osvaldo Pacheco, Rafael Martineli (head of the railroad workers' federation), and the head of the local bank workers' union. Hércules Correia, whose legislative immunities were respected by the police, went to fetch Marine and Air Force contingents. But the police got away with their prisoners.

Protesting the arrests, workers of the local Leopoldina Railroad went on strike, and it was reported that their example would be followed by bank, textile, metallurgical, dock, and other railroad workers. Remaining CGT leaders prepared to meet, under the protection of Aragão's Marines, to make arrangements for the nationwide general strike.

Goulart, no longer able to communicate with Kruel, had San Tiago Dantas telephone Belo Horizonte and propose, in the name of the President, a discussion "to resolve the impasse between the federal administration and the Minas government."[4] San Tiago Dantas told

---

dor Gordon (conversation in Rio de Janeiro, December 18, 1965) stated that he could recall nothing about the "forty-eight hours" mentioned in the *Fortune* article and that his conversations with the people referred to in the article had been in general terms, "without anything specific; without any details and without mention of operational matters."

[3] Gordon, conversation, December 18, 1965.

[4] "Minas Hora a Hora," *O Cruzeiro-Extra,* April 10, 1964, pp. 16–17.

Afonso Arinos de Melo Franco, new member of the Minas cabinet, that the commanders of Brazil's four Armies were faithful to the federal government and that the Minas revolt would, therefore, be crushed immediately.[5] The former Finance Minister suggested that Magalhães Pinto authorize Afonso Arinos to come to Rio and work out a settlement with San Tiago Dantas in order to save Minas, of which they were both natives, from destruction, and to prevent the useless sacrifice of lives. But San Tiago Dantas was not persuasive, and, even if he had been, the men in the Palácio da Liberdade could not have controlled the Army officers who were making the march on Rio. Magalhães Pinto told Afonso Arinos that he would not change his course.[6] Afonso Arinos told San Tiago Dantas that the Minas uprising would be called off only if Goulart left the presidency.[7]

In Rio the War Minister suffered hemorrhages in the hospital. First Army Commander Morais Âncora and Vila Militar Commander Oromar Osório watched the collapse of the President's "great military *dispositivo* [layout]." Officers at Vila Militar were convinced by fellow officers that to sustain Goulart would be to advance Communism and that it was better to adhere to the position advocated by Castelo Branco and Costa e Silva. Army officers who had been effectively spreading Castelo Branco's ideas included Otacílio Terra Ururaí, Edson de Figueiredo, José Pinheiro de Ulhôa Cintra, Ademar de Queiroz, and Augusto César Moniz de Aragão.

Shortly after midnight of March 31–April 1, First Army Commander Âncora sought to have the Navy send warships to blockade Santos. But the Navy Minister said that exit from Guanabara Bay would be impossible for the fleet because most of Rio's forts opposed the President.

The commander of Fort Copacabana's 650 men made his decision early, and on the morning of April 1 he received a group of twenty anti-Goulart officers belonging to the Army Staff Command School (ECEME—Escola de Comando de Estado Maior do Exército). Civilians in the vicinity of the fort saw some action around midday when

[5] Oswaldo Pieruccetti, letter to J.W.F.D., January 18, 1968, pp. 5–6.
[6] *Ibid.*
[7] Afonso Arinos de Melo Franco, interview, Brasília, October 14, 1965.

soldiers from the fort moved against the nearby Coastal Artillery headquarters, whose commanding general supported Goulart. About twenty
shots were fired and two men were wounded before Colonel César
Montagna de Souza, of the Army Staff Command School, and other
officers gained control of the Coastal Artillery headquarters.[8]

From the hospital War Minister Jair Dantas Ribeiro submitted his
resignation and was replaced by First Army Commander Morais
Âncora. By then Goulart, who opposed bloodshed, knew that the game
was over. "Our military plan inexplicably failed," he told Justice Minister Jurema. "I can only count on the Third Army and that is not
enough."[9] Although cabinet ministers urged that he remain in Rio to
sustain the morale of progovernment forces there, he left by airplane
for Brasília at 1:00 P.M., accompanied by his secretary, Eugênio
Caillard.

Aragão's Marines, the only active progovernment military force in
Rio, dedicated their energies to nonmilitary matters. After protecting
CGT leaders, who called the general strike, they invaded the offices of
some sharply antiadministration newspapers. One report described
Aragão himself as heading the troop that took over *O Globo* and as
exclaiming: "Newspapers like this will circulate again only if Kruel
wins."[10]

Long before dawn on the first, rumors had been spreading about
Aragão's supposed intention of bringing heavy cannons to bear on
Guanabara Palace. Castelo Branco had telephoned to urge that the
Governor leave the palace since it was not "martyrs" that the cause
needed. But Lacerda had resolved to remain at his post, a decision
favored by Marshal Dutra and Brigadeiro Eduardo Gomes.[11]

Help for defending the palace came from numerous volunteers, as
well as from contingents of the Guanabara state police, under Colonel
Gustavo Borges. Retired military men, such as Eduardo Gomes and
Admirals Amorim do Vale and Pena Bôto, joined the Governor. Al-

---

[8] Glauco Carneiro, "Forte de Copacabana Não Foi Tomado" (based on interview
with César Montagna de Souza), *O Cruzeiro*, April 25, 1964, pp. 85–86.

[9] *O Estado de S. Paulo*, April 2, 1964.

[10] *Ibid.*

[11] Carlos Lacerda, interview, Rio de Janeiro, October 11, 1967.

though the palace was soon being defended by about forty machine guns and six hundred men, they would have been no match for Aragão's cannons.

The volunteers were headed by João Paulo Moreira Burnier, leader of the Aragarças rebellion. Not long after the unsuccessful kidnap attempt, Lacerda had gotten in touch with him and with Jacareacanga rebels Haroldo Veloso and Paulo Vítor.[12] As a result, Burnier had been organizing a group that frequently met at a nurses' training school near Guanabara Palace. There, on April 1, arms were passed out to civilians who wanted to defy Aragão's cannons. Burnier had been constructing *gafanhotos* (grasshoppers), jeeps bearing rockets, and these were now brought out as part of the defense. An Air Force lieutenant-colonel arranged to have heavy garbage collection trucks block the streets leading to the palace. Hand grenades were furnished to people in nearby apartments.

Protectors of Guanabara Palace, likening themselves to the defenders of the Alamo, were known as members of the Grupo Azul e Branco (Blue and White Group).

Lacerda was unable to use the Guanabara television and radio stations because the federal government had taken control of them. In the morning, when an attack on the palace was expected, Lacerda used a telephone to speak over Minas radio stations: "Brazil does not want Cain in the presidency. Cain, what are you doing to your brothers? Your brothers who are going to be killed by your Communist accomplices; your brothers who are robbed in order that you transform yourself into the largest landholder and biggest thief in Brazil. Down with João Goulart!" Then: "Guanabara Palace is being attacked, at this moment, by a band of desperados. Marines, lay down your arms, because you are being deceived by an unscrupulous officer. Aragão, coward, incestuous, leave your soldiers and come here to settle the matter with me. I want to kill you with my revolver."[13]

But no attack materialized.

---

[12] Luís Werneck, Flávio Galvão, Roberto Brandini, Luís Maciel Filho, and Heber Perillo Fleury, interview, São Paulo, November 24, 1965.

[13] Carlos Lacerda quoted in Cláudio Mello e Souza, "O Vizinho do Presidente" in Alberto Dines *et al., Os Idos de Março e a Queda em Abril,* p. 183.

With Goulart's departure for Brasília, some tanks, which had been guarding Laranjeiras Palace, were taken over by officers of the Army Staff Command School. Three of these tanks, under the command of Army Lieutenant-Colonel Leo Etchegoyen (son of General Alcides Etchegoyen), headed for Guanabara Palace. At first this move was hailed with delight by pro-Goulart onlookers. But after the Army officers had spoken with Air Force Colonel Paulo Vítor, the garbage collection trucks moved aside to let the tanks draw up to Guanabara Palace. This they did with their guns pointing away from the palace.

At about 4:00 P.M., shortly before this happened, Lacerda at last found himself able to give a radio-television talk directly to the Cariocas: "At this moment the Justice Minister is limiting his habitual slander to that which he issues from the cuspidor which has been made of Rádio Mayrink Veiga, bought with Petrobrás money for Leonel Brizola and the Communists."[14] With the arrival of the friendly tanks, Lacerda told his audience of the elation in Guanabara Palace. He said he wanted to make it clear that he had had little to do with the revolution; it was a revolution by the military. He likened Brazil's politicians to cats playing with a ball of knitting. They have time and again messed things up, he said, and the Army has had to come in to straighten the country out.[15] Finally Lacerda broke down and concluded his broadcast with the words: "God pities the people. God is good." Around the palace joyful crowds sang the national anthem and "Cidade Marvilhosa."

At Cinelandia, in downtown Rio, Goulart sympathizers had been holding a mass meeting since 2:00 P.M. Speakers called on the people to lynch the "gorillas" who were responsible for Jango's difficulties. A mob then tried to invade the Military Club. But at nearby Monroe Palace the guard of the Armed Forces General Staff (EMFA) was ready to repel the attack. In the shooting, two would-be invaders were wounded and died soon after.[16]

Later in the afternoon, anti-Communist students took over the headquarters of the National Union of Students. They threw literature,

[14] *Ibid.*, p. 185.
[15] Report of William T. Boone to J.W.F.D., Rio de Janeiro, November 1967.
[16] "Guanabara Hora a Hora," *O Cruzeiro-Extra,* April 10, 1964, pp. 36–37.

boxes, banners, and furniture out of the windows and set fire to them in the doorway. Likewise the offices of *Última Hora* were invaded and the newspaper company's furnishings were damaged. Samuel Wainer, managing director of *Última Hora,* found asylum in the Chilean Embassy.

Anti-Goulart admirals, who for days had been laying plans to take over strategic naval points including the Ministry building, at first expected a long fight. Under the leadership of Admiral Augusto Rademaker they entered the Navy Ministry at 5:00 P.M. on April 1. Meeting no resistance, they called on Navy Minister Paulo Mário and told him that Goulart was no longer President. Old Paulo Mário withdrew, and the six admirals issued a message stating that they were taking over the command of naval affairs.[17] The order of signatures reflected seniority: Rademaker, Levi Reis, Melo Batista, Waldeck Vampré, Mário Cavalcanti, and Zenha de Figueiredo.

In this way Rademaker, a vice-admiral, took charge of the Navy. Like his five erudite colleagues, he was not among those in the top section of the hierarchy in the admiralty. Ahead of him were four fleet admirals and five vice-admirals.

Principal supporters of the Goulart regime were arrested when they were found. First Army officers made a prisoner of Admiral Aragão. Justice Minister Jurema, preparing to take an airplane to join Goulart in Brasília, was picked up by officers who were taking courses at the Army Staff Command School. This school was headed by General Jurandir Mamede, whose funeral oration had precipitated a crisis in 1955. The officers attending it played a notable role; besides dominating the Coastal Artillery headquarters and taking the tanks guarding Laranjeiras Palace, they handled prisoners and watched over the personal safety of Castelo Branco.

---

[17] Levi Aarão Reis, interviews, Rio de Janeiro, December 13 and 14, 1965.

6. The Fall of Arrais (April 1, 1964)

On the morning of March 31, news of Mourão's march first reached the Northeast in coded messages sent to a few conspirators. Then colonels in Pernambuco began ordering the roundup of men considered subversive.

Fourth Army Commander Joaquim Justino Alves Bastos sent an assistant by airplane from Recife to Rio to confer with Generals Castelo Branco and Costa e Silva. While awaiting developments the commander issued an order prohibiting meetings and strikes. Then at the end of the day he learned of the authenticity of Kruel's manifesto.

When Goulart telephoned Recife from Rio at 2:00 A.M. on April 1, Justino Alves Bastos advised him that the Fourth Army was on "rigorous alert." This news apparently reassured Goulart, for he spoke of it a little later, upon receiving Governor Seixas Dória of Sergipe at Laranjeiras Palace. The President was suggesting that the governors in the Northeast make a joint appeal in favor of a "general understanding." "General Justino Alves Bastos, who is my friend and is completely in favor of maintaining the regime—as he just informed me by telephone —will be able to coordinate such a movement." Goulart concluded this talk by saying: "In any event, Seixas, I have no intention of taking the nation to civil war, whose consequences would be disastrous for the future of our children."[1]

At 3:00 A.M., Justino Alves Bastos received a radio message from the assistant he had sent to Rio. The message advised that the Fourth Army could start its work. At dawn, therefore, Justino Alves Bastos and the Third Naval District commander signed a proclamation supporting Mourão and Kruel.[2]

Governor Arrais reiterated his opposition to violent eruptions. When soldiers of Justino Alves Bastos surrounded the governor's palace (the Palácio das Princesas) they met with no resistance from the governor's guard, made up of men of the state police. Next, Army men dismissed

---

[1] Seixas Dória, *Eu, Réu Sem Crime*, pp. 47–48.
[2] Joaquim Justino Alves Bastos, *Encontro Com o Tempo*, pp. 350–359.

the guard and took its place. Arrais offered no objection. He declared that his primary interest was the preservation of order, and that he did not want to use the state police against the Army or against anyone else. But when he was told to dismiss his secretary of public safety he refused on the ground that, if he acquiesced, he would be carrying out his mandate under improper pressure.[3]

At 7:00 P.M. the colonel commanding the Fourteenth Infantry Regiment saw Arrais descending the palace stairs with about twenty companions. He arrested the Governor on the charge of supporting Goulart and opposing the armed movement. Arrais took it calmly, observing that he was not on anyone's side and only sought to carry out his constitutional obligations and support legality.

Refusing to resign, Arrais was taken from the palace at 8:00 P.M. and imprisoned at the barracks of the Fourteenth Infantry Regiment. This act provoked some popular manifestations in Recife on his behalf. In putting them down, the Army killed two and wounded many.[4] General Justino Alves Bastos then decided that it would be best to move Arrais from Pernambuco, and on the next day he was shipped to the Fernando de Noronha Island prison.

Even before Arrais was arrested, Bastos fired the Governor's public safety secretary and state police commander. On the General's instructions, an Army colonel, accompanied by two infantry groups and a mechanized squadron, invaded the Derby Barracks, headquarters of the state police. The colonel had orders to arrest the pro-Arrais commander, Major Hugo Trench, and to take his place. Trench wanted to telephone the Governor but he was told that "your governor doesn't exist any more."[5] He surrendered, and the state police, under its new commander, helped the Army round up "Communists and subversives."[6]

The state assembly, after receiving a communication from the military at 6:00 P.M., met to vote on "impeaching" Arrais. With the

[3] Miguel Arraes de Alencar, letter to lawyers Sobral Pinto and Antônio and Roque Brito Alves, in Adirson de Barros, *Ascensão e Queda de Miguel Arraes*, pp. 153–162 (see especially, p. 156).

[4] Joaquim Justino Alves Bastos, *Encontro Com o Tempo*, pp. 365–366.

[5] Report of Silvio de Melo Cahu, in *ibid.*, pp. 362–364 (see especially, p. 363).

[6] Joaquim Justino Alves Bastos, *Encontro Com o Tempo*, p. 365.

building surrounded by troops,[7] a majority of the legislators present decided to recognize a "state of fact." When the presiding officer opened the formal session, an Army colonel in uniform appeared behind him. But the colonel quickly appreciated the "indelicacy" of this and withdrew.

The debate in the assembly lasted for six hours. Finally, early on the morning of April 2, it was announced that Arrais had been "impeached" by a vote of 35 to 20.[8] Vice-Governor Paulo Guerra, having been examined by the military and pronounced "a serious man,"[9] took over the state. Following Arrais' "impeachment," the aldermen of Recife met and handled the mayor in the same way.

Governor Seixas Dória, after his nighttime chat with Goulart at Laranjeiras Palace, returned to Sergipe and issued a proclamation in favor of *legalidade*, reforms, and respect for all popular mandates. A backer of Goulart, he had spoken at the March 13 rally, recommending that public opinion be mobilized to exert pressure on Congress in favor of basic reforms. After he made his April 1 proclamation he was, like Arrais, arrested and sent to Fernando de Noronha Island.[10]

The Fourth Army rounded up hundreds of "subversives" in the countryside, including peasant league leaders. From Alagoas, south of Pernambuco, an infantry battalion moved north to the Palmares sugar-producing area. There the victorious Army men captured sixty-three-year-old Gregório Bezerra, who had been jailed for participating in the 1935 Communist uprising and ten years later had been elected federal congressman on the ticket of the Communist Party (then legal).

Before his capture in 1964 Bezerra had been trying to mobilize peasants to resist the movement that overthrew Arrais and Goulart. After his capture he was hit and beaten on the instructions of a colonel who could not forget that Bezerra, a sergeant in 1935, had been found guilty of killing a lieutenant during the rebellion of that year. Wounded

[7] Murilo Marroquim, "Ação do IV Exército Contra Arraes," *O Cruzeiro*, April 25, 1964, pp. 42–48 (see especially, p. 48).

[8] *O Jornal,* April 2, 1964. Later the vote was reported to be 45–17.

[9] Marroquim, "Ação do IV Exército Contra Arraes," pp. 42–48 (see especially, p. 48).

[10] See Dória, *Eu, Réu Sem Crime.*

and tied up, Bezerra was publicly displayed, unclothed except for a pair of red shorts. The rope around his neck was almost choking him when the performance was ended on orders from General Justino Alves Bastos.[11]

[11] Gregório Bezerra, interview, Recife, October 24, 1967; Gregório Bezerra, *Eu, Gregório Bezerra, Acuso!*, p. 17.

7. Goulart Leaves Brasília (April 1, 1964)

IN BRASÍLIA Goulart was counting on support from his old friend, local Army Commander Nicolau Fico, and assumed his force would be bolstered by the Battalion of the Presidential Guard.

On April 1 Casa Civil Chief Darci Ribeiro, using the microphone of Rádio Nacional in Brasília, cried out against "reactionaries and gorillas." Congressmen worriedly noted that airplane service out of the federal capital had been canceled.[1] They heard reports that "three thousand" laborers in Brasília, organized by "the local CGT," had been given arms,[2] and they recalled words of Brizola which had encouraged those who would attack Congress.

At 3:00 P.M. the presidential flag was hoisted at Planalto Palace. Goulart rushed in, having been flown there in a helicopter from the Brasília airport. Speaking tersely to a reporter, he revealed that he had ordered the arrest of Lacerda in Rio. He said that he had come to Brasília to demonstrate his confidence to the world and that he planned to make visits to various parts of the country. He affirmed that the rebellion would be quickly overcome and announced that 99 per cent of the people were with him.[3]

After conferring in Planalto Palace with Darci Ribeiro and military

[1] João Calmon, interview, Rio de Janeiro, November 9, 1965.
[2] *O Jornal*, April 2, 1964.
[3] "A Crise Vista de Brasília," *O Cruzeiro-Extra*, April 10, 1964, pp. 56–57; *O Estado de S. Paulo*, April 2, 1964.

men, Goulart went by helicopter to his Brasília residence, Granja do Torto, to which he had called some congressional leaders. He telephoned Casa Militar Chief Assis Brasil in Rio. Assis Brasil advised that the situation in the Navy and Air Force was extremely satisfactory. However, in Rio Grande do Sul the developments were worse than might have been expected. Although anti-Goulart Governor Ildo Meneghetti had fled to the interior and Third Army Commander Ladário Pereira Teles was taking energetic steps in Pôrto Alegre, the infantry divisions in Santa Maria and Cruz Alta had rebelled against the President. Assis Brasil then painted a gloomy picture of the situation in Rio, basing his conclusion on a talk he had just had with Oromar Osório, new commander of the First Army. Goulart's cause was lost in Rio.

From Assis Brasil Goulart learned that Kruel had gone to Resende, near the Rio-São Paulo state border, to confer with War Minister Armando de Morais Âncora. "The best thing for me," Goulart said, "is to await the outcome of that conference."[4]

Earlier in the afternoon, before leaving Rio for Resende, Âncora had declined Costa e Silva's advice that he surrender;[5] instead, he had said that he wanted to follow Goulart's suggestion that he confer with Kruel. He had sent a radio message to Kruel, advising him of Goulart's wishes, and he had accepted Kruel's stipulation to meet in a locale controlled by the Second Army.

At Resende Âncora received further evidence of his impossible military position. The cadets and officers of the military school had declared themselves for Kruel and had joined units of the Second Army in preparing to resist the approach of First Army troops.[6]

At 5:00 P.M. Âncora was awaiting Kruel, who had been delayed by a flat tire. Âncora's radio told of the rejoicing in Rio's streets "because

---

[4] "Dialogo de Goulart com Assis Brasil, 1 de Abril," *O Estado de S. Paulo,* April 2, 1964.

[5] Nelson Dimas Filho, *Costa e Silva: O Homem e o Líder,* p. 70; Ernesto de Melo Batista, interview, Rio de Janeiro, October 13, 1966.

[6] "Amaury Kruel Foi Peça Decisiva Para a Vitória," *O Cruzeiro-Extra,* April 10, 1964, p. 49.

Goulart resigned."[7] Another radio report told of celebrations in the streets of São Paulo.

When Kruel arrived at 5:40 P.M., Âncora, nervous and apparently ill, told him that originally he had wanted to negotiate an understanding with him. But, he said, he had just learned that the President had gone to Rio Grande do Sul.[8] Under those circumstances, Âncora added, his mission had no meaning and had ended.

Kruel, confident of the situation in Guanabara, prepared to send Second Army contingents south to deal with Rio Grande do Sul. He had radio messages of support from Santa Maria and Bagé, in that state, but felt that elsewhere in Rio Grande do Sul Army circles Goulart had much support.

Âncora returned at once from Resende to Rio and advised Costa e Silva that he was resigning his post. Already Costa e Silva, a suave and respected trooper, unknown outside military circles, had become top man in Brazil; he had called in the generals in the Rio area and had told them that, as he headed the hierarchy, he was assuming the post of commander-in-chief of the Operating Forces.[9] All were in agreement. Costa e Silva's circular, issued that evening, announced that Âncora, "named acting War Minister, resigned his post in a ceremony attended by all the generals. In view of the situation created by the latest developments, I advise that, being the highest ranking member of the High Command, I assumed, at the same ceremony, the Command of the National Army."[10]

As has been mentioned, the Army Almanac for 1964, in its list of eight four-star generals (*generais de exército*) who were not officially on leave, showed long-conspiring Cordeiro de Farias at the top, followed by Costa e Silva and Castelo Branco. But the fact that Cordeiro had for some time been without any Army post, and thus outside of regular Army work, eliminated him. At the moment he was in Paraná,

[7] Eurilo Duarte, "32 Mais 32, Igual a 64," in Alberto Dines *et al.*, *Os Idos de Março e a Queda em Abril*, p. 151.

[8] Amauri Kruel, interviews, São Paulo, November 30, 1965; Guanabara, October 21, 1967.

[9] Siseno Sarmento, interview, São Paulo, November 21, 1967.

[10] Dimas Filho, *Costa e Silva*, pp. 71–72.

hoping to play in the far south the role Denys had wanted him to play in 1961. Incidentally, in the course of a political career that included governing two states, he had come to be considered by Army officers a more controversial figure than Costa e Silva.

Contrary to what Âncora told Kruel, Goulart was still in Brasília. But unfriendly Army columns were marching in that direction. A contingent of the Battalion of the Presidential Guard, retreating to Brasília from the Minas-Goiás border where it had been sent, was being pursued by Minas forces.[11] Other anti-Goulart troops were moving on the national capital from faraway Mato Grosso. These included the 1,400 Army men who made up the column of Colonel Carlos de Meira Matos. To attack the President in Brasília, some requisitioned airplanes and others used diesel trucks to carry them from the Bolivian frontier.[12]

The President prepared a proclamation: "I am determined to defend my post, at the side of the people, to whom I turn over the defense of our cause. I shall react to the coup with the backing of the popular forces and the armed forces. . . . I condemn the reactionary forces, the political and economic groups, and the exploiters of religious sentiments, who oppose my government." He concluded by asserting that "I reaffirm my decision to defend, in a battle without respite, the people who are being plundered by economic power."[13]

He left Brasília by airplane for Rio Grande do Sul at about 10:00 P.M.

[11] Oscar Dias Correia, interview, Brasília, October 18, 1965; Primeiro Exército, *Relatório da Revolução Democrática Iniciada pela 4a RM e 4a DI em 31 de Março de 1964,* Special Bulletin, Juiz de Fora, May 9, 1964, Part 2 (Operations).

[12] Mário Spinelli, "A Marcha da Coluna Meira Matos." (Publication on one sheet).

[13] *O Jornal,* April 2, 1964.

8. Goulart Becomes an Exile

A SPECIAL JOINT SESSION of Congress was called to declare that Chamber of Deputies President Ranieri Mazzilli was again Acting President of Brazil. At midnight, before the session started, General Nicolau Fico assured congressional leaders that his troops would protect Congress against any popular assaults. "My commitments to President Goulart," he said, "ended at the moment he left the capital for an unknown destination."[1]

Two hours later the Chamber of Deputies resounded with angry statements as Goulart supporters, Deputado Francisco Julião among them, insisted that it would be unconstitutional to depose the President.

At 2:20 A.M. on April 2, experienced Senate President Auro de Moura Andrade called for the reading of Darci Ribeiro's statement that Goulart had left for Rio Grande do Sul. Moura Andrade then announced that the presidency of the Republic was vacant and therefore would be filled by Mazzilli, in accordance with the constitution.

Goulart supporters cried out that the President's departure for the south did not make the presidency vacant. One irritated congressman threw a microphone. Another shouted "gorillas, gorillas." But Moura Andrade's unconstitutional act was blessed by the presence of approving Chief Justice Álvaro Moutinho Ribeiro da Costa, the only Supreme Court minister who had supported Café Filho's case against Congress late in 1955.

Next, lawmakers drove to nearby Planalto Palace. Entering cautiously by a side door, they made their way to the third floor and there installed Mazzilli in the presidential office. On the fourth floor Darci Ribeiro, eager to have the men of the Casa Militar and Casa Civil put up physical resistance, had been calling General Nicolau Fico a traitor to his face and unsuccessfully trying to persuade the chief of police to help keep Mazzilli out of Planalto Palace.

Upon becoming Acting President of Brazil for the sixth time,

[1] "A Crise Vista de Brasília," *O Cruzeiro-Extra,* April 10, 1964, pp. 56–57.

Mazzilli was at once confronted by those who were worried about violations to the immunities enjoyed by legislators. On the floor of Congress Roland Corbisier (alternate for Brizola) had spoken of the reported imprisonment of several lawmakers. Francisco Julião had asserted that without doubt a Fascist regime was taking over the country.

Mazzilli, addressing those who had joined him in the ceremony at Planalto Palace, declared that he would allow nothing to interfere with congressional immunities; if his orders to this effect were not obeyed, he would, he said, leave the presidency.

But military leaders, with other ideas, were in control of Brazil. As soon as Mazzilli became Acting President, Costa e Silva contacted him by telephone.[2] The Revolutionary High Command, Costa e Silva said, was made up of himself, Admiral Rademaker, and Brigadeiro Francisco de Assis Correia de Melo. Correia de Melo was the Air Force chief of staff who had authored *Como Eles Destroem* (How They Destroy). Due to his post, his high seniority, and his point of view, he had been the man to whom anti-Communist *brigadeiros* had gone with their many worries.

While Costa e Silva was informing Mazzilli that the Revolutionary High Command would make the important decisions, Goulart approached Rio Grande do Sul. Landing at Pôrto Alegre at 4:30 A.M. on April 2, he went to confer with Third Army Commander Ladário Pereira Teles. Governor Ildo Meneghetti, he learned, had gone with his cabinet to Passo Fundo, in the north of the state, and had issued a manifesto calling on the Gaúchos to fight against Goulart "for the survival of democracy and liberty."

In Pôrto Alegre General Ladário had taken control of the press and radio and television stations. Brizola, busy attacking Kruel in radio broadcasts, had recently participated with Pôrto Alegre's mayor in a rally at which the Gaúchos were called on to resist the "gorillas."

From the states of Santa Catarina and Paraná troops of the anti-Goulart "revolution" were marching south to join the Army units that had rebelled in the interior of Rio Grande do Sul. In Curitiba, Paraná, Cordeiro de Farias was ready to assume command of the Third Army

---

[2] Ranieri Mazzilli, interview, Rio de Janeiro, December 12, 1965.

and move against General Ladário, its other commander. But Costa e Silva had different ideas. From Rio the new Commander-in-Chief of the Revolutionary Forces telephoned Cordeiro, telling him not to go to Pôrto Alegre. "Kruel," he said, "has an old personal matter he wants to settle with Brizola. He wants to deal with Rio Grande do Sul himself. So leave Rio Grande do Sul for Amauri to handle."[3]

For the time being, anti-Goulart military operations in Rio Grande do Sul were put in the hands of General Poppe de Figueiredo, who was in the state. Kruel, preparing to march south with a strong Second Army combat team, issued a proclamation for the Rio Grande do Sul barracks.

During the morning of April 2 it was clear to Goulart that the time had come for him to withdraw. At the Pôrto Alegre airport he said: "Ladário, now I am leaving. But I know that within a month I'll be back. The generals will tear themselves to pieces for the supreme power, and then . . . ."[4]

At 1:15 P.M. the Brizola Legalidade network, in one of its last acts, annouced Goulart's departure. Goulart's decision upset Brizola and the news of it was received glumly by groups in Pôrto Alegre which had been stirred up by Brizola to carry on a fight on Goulart's behalf. Pro-Goulart military resistence collapsed, and Kruel, who had gotten his combat team as far as Curitiba, did not continue south.

Goulart flew to one of his ranches on the Argentine border and inquired from there about asylum in Uruguay, where his wife and two young children had gone. The response was favorable and on April 4 Goulart flew into hospitable Uruguay.

Throughout Brazil radical leftists, who were not seized in "Operation Cleanup" (Operação Limpeza), were fleeing the country or seeking asylum in embassies. But Brizola continued at large in Rio Grande do Sul for weeks before he finally crossed over—without his mustache —into Uruguay. The elusive chief of the Groups of Eleven, while still in Rio Grande, gave an interview. "The reaction calls us Communists," he said. "This is a lie. Jango is a Catholic. So were all of his cabinet

---

[3] José Stacchini, *Março 64: Mobilização da Audácia*, p. 99.
[4] *Ibid.*, p. 129.

ministers." Brizola spoke of the mass support Goulart had enjoyed. "In Pôrto Alegre the working masses wanted arms in order to fight. And if they could not get them what could they do? How could they stop the tanks and machine guns? To resist under those conditions would have meant a real massacre of the people." He spoke of his plans. He would go from house to house to demonstrate that "faith in Brazil is inextinguishable." "We are struggling without letup against imperialism, against large foreign capital."[5]

[5] "Brizola Diz Que a Revolução Virá," *Correio da Manhã*, April 11, 1964.

9. Celebration in Rio (April 2, 1964)

Mourão's Tiradentes Column, having sent contingents to prevent pro-Goulart demonstrations by workers at the Fábrica Nacional de Motores and at the Duque de Caxias petroleum refinery, reached the city of Rio in the rain at 3:00 A.M. on the morning of April 2. A telephone call to the First Army headquarters revealed that General Otacílio Terra Ururaí had been named commander of the First Army. The column's leaders, asking who had named him, learned that Costa e Silva had become chief of the Brazilian Army. Ururaí, they were told, owed his new post to having top seniority among the three-star generals.[1] Governor Lacerda drove out to meet the column and to offer Rio's Maracanãzinho Stadium for the encampment of its men.

A secretary of the Governor suggested that, in view of the success of the revolution, Guanabara's March of the Family with God for Liberty, scheduled for April 2, be called off.[2] Castelo Branco proposed postponing it so that full attention could be given to Operação Limpeza,

[1] Primeiro Exército, *Relatório da Revolução Democrática Iniciada pela 4a RM e 4a DI em 31 de Março de 1964*, Special Bulletin, Juiz de Fora, May 9, 1964, Part 2 (Operations).
[2] Amélia Molina Bastos and other CAMDE officers, interview, Rio de Janeiro, December 13, 1965,

the business of cleaning up the country. But determined CAMDE President Amélia Molina Bastos said: "Tell Castelo Branco not to interfere with my march."[3] She also said that "the march will demonstrate to the world that this is a true *people's* revolution—it will be a marching plebiscite for real democracy!"[4]

By 3:00 P.M. delegations of marchers, trying to take their places near Candelária Church, prevented vehicles from using Rio Branco Avenue. Songs were continually interrupted by applause for newly arrived groups. Shortly after 4:00 P.M., following the singing of the national anthem, a cavalry platoon of the state Military Police led the great parade of people, flags, and signs, under an avalanche of paper thrown from the tall buildings, to Esplanada do Castelo. So many Cariocas thronged the downtown streets to join the victory celebration that observers estimated the crowd at over a million. Placards with religious sentiments, some of them expressions of thanks to God and the armed forces, mingled with others condemning Communism. "Fortunately," said one sign, "Pernambuco was not Arrais–ified." There was a stupendous acclaim for Eurico Gaspar Dutra, who refused a car although he was almost eighty. As he walked, filled with emotion, he occasionally tired and took time out to rest.[5]

At the square of Esplanada do Castelo, the multitude heard speeches by religious leaders. In the final address, Amélia Molina Bastos concluded by exclaiming: "We extol, we praise, we glorify God and the Brazilian soldier."[6]

Osvino Ferreira Alves, the "Red Marshal" who had headed Petrobrás, was a prisoner in Fort Copacabana. Former Marine Commander Aragão was being held in Fort Lage. Abelardo Jurema was allowed by Jurandir Mamede and Castelo Branco to go to his residence.[7] As a congressman, the former Justice Minister was supposed to have guarantees under the 1946 constitution. Nevertheless, he wisely decided

[3] *Ibid.*

[4] Clarence W. Hall, "The Country That Saved Itself," *The Reader's Digest,* November 1964, p. 153.

[5] *O Jornal,* April 3, 1964.

[6] *Ibid.*

[7] Abelardo Jurema, *Sexta-Feira, 13: Os Últimos Dias do Govêrno João Goulart,* pp. 217–219.

that a trip to Brasília would be unsafe. A project, which reflected the strong wave of sentiment to oust congressmen who were "known Communists" or who had "Communist ties," was being considered in Congress, and the names of about forty victims had already been suggested.

Jurema, like UNE President José Serra and five others, took refuge in the Peruvian Embassy. The embassies of Paraguay, Mexico, Argentina, and Ecuador were also used by worried Brazilians. The most popular embassy was that of Uruguay. The fifteen who reached it quickly included Elói Dutra (vice-governor of Guanabara), Deputado Demistoclides Batista (leader of the Leopoldina Railroad workers), Paulo Schilling (director of Brizola's *Panfleto* magazine), and João Cândido Maia Neto (former director of Rádio Mayrink Veiga).

The revolution against Goulart had broken out to the surprise of most of its supporters, and it had succeeded so quickly that few knew what to expect next. Ademar de Barros was reported to be about to break with the Mazzilli government because Jurema had been released and because of the names of some being considered for the cabinet. But these were matters in the control of the Revolutionary High Command, headed by Costa e Silva. Operação Limpeza, directed by military officers, was emphasizing the need for ending the widespread corruption and for punishing those who had profited from it. It now became known that the revolution had been against corruption as well as against Communism.

On April 2, Acting President Mazzilli was called from Brasília to Rio by the Revolutionary High Command to discuss cabinet appointments on the third. Four civilians were named to the Mazzilli cabinet. They and the three military ministers each assumed two cabinet posts. Costa e Silva's friend, São Paulo University head Luís Antônio da Gama e Silva, took over the Justice and Education posts. Foreign Affairs were put in the hands of Vasco Leitão da Cunha, who had broken with Quadros when João Dantas visited East Germany.

Labor Tribunal Minister Júlio Barata spent hours in Costa e Silva's office explaining that he did not wish to accept an appointment as Labor Minister. He recommended Arnaldo Sussekind, who agreed (also becoming Minister of Agriculture) and who was soon signing decrees for the government takeover of unions that had been controlled by "Red" leaders.

10. Governors Discuss the Presidency with Costa e Silva

ACCORDING TO THE CONSTITUTION, and assuming that Goulart was not President, the Senate and Chamber of Deputies were to meet within thirty days to select a new Chief Executive.

While Cariocas were participating in the great parade and hailing Dutra, the presidential succession was being considered. Businessmen who directed that Rio office of IPÊS, pleased with the cheers in the streets below and highly satisfied with the result of their anti-Far Left work, listed the qualifications they felt the next President of Brazil should have. They decided that it would be best to have someone who had no ties with any of the three governors who hoped to win the presidency in 1965: Lacerda, Magalhães Pinto, and Ademar de Barros.

Marshal Dutra, upon becoming constitutional President in 1946, had formed a coalition between his own party, the PSD, and the UDN. His administration, regarded as unspectacular but "very civilian," had dealt reverses to the Communists. After it ended, the constitution-revering Marshal, a quiet, virtuous man of simple tastes, became a perfect former President, who was held in higher esteem and affection as each year passed. His March 1964 pronouncement in support of the constitution added to his luster. Had the 1964 revolution not ended so quickly, Dutra was to have been flown by helicopter to Minas and placed in command of some revolutionary troops. This, it had been felt, would give the revolution great respectability.

With the fall of Goulart, Dutra's name came quickly to civilian minds. The first leader to go to Dutra's house and support him for the presidency was Carlos Lacerda. Magalhães Pinto told Dutra that he was the "candidate of my heart." PSD President Amaral Peixoto asked

Dutra whether, if he were elected by Congress, he would have the necessary influence in the Army to take over.[1] To this question, which revealed the PSD's awe of Brazil's new rulers, the Marshal simply replied that he would take over if elected. He was quoted as saying that he had never been to Brasília and believed that it would be difficult to govern from there.[2]

Costa e Silva, running Brazil with Castelo Branco at his side, took the position that it was too soon to discuss the presidential succession. But nothing could stop the work being done on behalf of candidates. These included Kruel, whose decision on March 31 was considered momentous. The PTB preferred him to other military candidates, and a few politicians regarded him as a vehicle whereby the PSD-PTB majority might continue its hold on the Executive. In the eyes of many military officers he was at a disadvantage because of his long Goulart association and because he was holding a post in command of troops.

The Grupo da Sorbonne, the most politically minded force in the military, worked for its star, Castelo Branco. It reminded the UDN of Dutra's allegiance to the PSD. (In 1950, before leaving the presidency, Dutra had insisted on giving his support to a member of his own party, the PSD, to be his successor.)

The UDN, recalling speeches in 1955 by Canrobert and Mamede, had a good impression of the Grupo da Sorbonne. So did IPÊS, whose General Golberi do Couto e Silva—known as the "pope of the Sorbonne"—joined Castelo Branco's staff on the eve of the revolution. IPÊS directors and women's groups that had been close to IPÊS were soon pointing out that Castelo Branco's connections with the Escola Superior de Guerra gave him a broad point of view and civilian connections, which Costa e Silva and Kruel were said not to have. Officers connected with the Escola were known to have made studies about what needed to be done in Brazil; it was felt that these would be useful at a time when the speed of the victory had left many unprepared for the immediate future.[3]

---

[1] Sigefredo Pacheco, interview, Brasília, October 16, 1965.

[2] Eurico Gaspar Dutra declaration ("Minha Vida Não Me Pertence") to Mário de Moraes in O Cruzeiro, April 25, 1964 (see p. 38).

[3] Carlos Lacerda, interview, Rio de Janeiro, October 11, 1967.

Castelo Branco, who had been unknown to the general public, was now described in a part of the press as the brains behind the revolution and a principal reason for its success. His restricted memorandum of March 20 to Army officers was given wide publicity. Much was made of his intellectual prestige among Army officers. He was a man, it was pointed out, who not only respected discipline but knew how to impose it. Past studies, in which he had praised democracy, came to light. It was said that he had never participated in a revolutionary movement before 1964, and that he was preferred in the Army to "military-politicos" such as Osvaldo Cordeiro de Farias.

Like IPÊS, Lacerda learned much about Castelo Branco and began to worry about Dutra's political connections. After calling on Dutra on April 4, Lacerda declared that the next President should be a military man able to maintain unity in the armed forces and the nation, and able to "prevent Kubitschek from becoming a Frondizi of Brazil."[4] This statement was interpreted to mean that the backing Lacerda had recently given Dutra now depended on Dutra's not supporting Kubitschek.

Lacerda had decided that the revolution had not been fought to bring to power the politicians he had seen in Dutra's home. He reflected that the Marshal's age was against him and that Eduardo Gomes strongly opposed Dutra's return to the presidency.[5]

On April 2 a few governors and the representatives of some other governors were in Rio discussing what should be done about the presidency. Magalhães Pinto's representative insisted that if it were possible to select a civilian, the choice should be the Minas governor, the first to declare his state in rebellion against Goulart.

On April 3 at Guanabara Palace Lacerda met with four of the governors: Magalhães Pinto, Ademar de Barros, Nei Braga (of Paraná), and, surprisingly, Mauro Borges (of Goiás). Mauro Borges, who (with Brizola) was cofounder of the National Liberation Front, had been called by Lacerda. The governors expressed a preference for having

<hr />

[4] *O Estado de S. Paulo,* dateline Rio de Janeiro, April 4, 1964.
[5] Carlos Lacerda, interview, October 11, 1967.

Congress choose a new President quickly rather than leave Mazzilli in the office for thirty days.

As three of the five governors were civilians actively seeking the presidency, agreement on a civilian candidate would have been impossible. In any event, it was pointed out, any civilian at the moment would find himself "practically the puppet of the Military Revolutionary Command."[6] Most of those at the meeting were persuaded to agree with Lacerda's recommendation: the 1965 election should be presided over by an Army man who would be above parties and so respected by subordinates that he could count on the Army to support his decisions.

When Ademar proposed that a civilian be chosen, he got no support from fellow governors. "Goulart left such a devil of a mess," Ademar has remarked, "that it was felt that a military man was needed."[7]

On April 4, again at Guanabara Palace, seven governors met, the original five being joined by those from Rio Grande do Sul and Mato Grosso. They decided that it would be better to offer one name to the "Military Revolutionary Command"; the presentation of several possibilities might cause dangerous discords. Lacerda said that he had a good suggestion. Urged to overcome what he described as his reluctance to mention it, he spoke of Castelo Branco. Castelo Branco's name was being advanced by most of the military men who had close connections with Lacerda.[8]

General Augusto César Moniz de Aragão, who had worked well in Rio with Castelo Branco in the recent military movement, was in Guanabara Palace. He had come from Vila Militar, deeply impressed with the great swell of Army opinion in favor of Castelo Branco. Greeted by Gustavo Borges, he was first conducted to a room full of politicians, and there he spoke in favor of the election of Castelo Branco. His manner was emotional, sometimes tearful—hardly that of a general giving civilians the orders of the military. The applause that greeted his pronouncement was prolonged and enthusiastic.

Next Moniz de Aragão was escorted to Lacerda's office. Again, this

---

[6] Mauro Borges, *O Golpe em Goiás: História de uma Grande Traição*, p. 110.
[7] Ademar de Barros, interview, São Paulo, December 1, 1965.
[8] Carlos Lacerda, interview, October 11, 1967.

time in the presence of the seven governors, he spoke in favor of Castelo Branco's being elected. The proposal was quickly and unanimously accepted.[9] Moniz de Aragão vouched for the admiration that Army officers felt for Castelo Branco. The governors decided to present Castelo Branco's name to Costa e Silva and, after getting the agreement of the Military Revolutionary Command, to speak with Castelo Branco and the political leaders.

Admiral Rademaker, learning of the governors' decision when he called at Lacerda's home, was not pleased. Naval officers wanted a civilian. Rademaker felt that if it had to be a military man, it should be retired Marshal Denys.

The seven governors, having made an appointment with Costa e Silva, called at the War Ministry late on the night of April 4. Costa e Silva, aware that the governors had decided on Castelo Branco,[10] kept them waiting while he dealt with a problem that had come up in Rio Grande do Sul.[11]

Finally after midnight, Costa e Silva took his place at the head of a conference table, around which were gathered the governors and three men Costa e Silva brought with him: General Siseno Sarmento, his chief-of-staff; also Juarez Távora and Colonel José Costa Cavalcanti, both of them federal congressmen. The military men were surprised to find Mauro Borges among the governors, for they had known about Communist influence in the Goiás state government and did not feel Borges had done anything for the revolution.

Lacerda started to explain the governors' decision in favor of an immediate election by Congress, with a military man as the sole candidate of "the revolution." Costa e Silva quickly interrupted to point out that he was not War Minister but commander-in-chief of the Revolutionary Forces.[12] The Carioca Governor was unable to elaborate because the Commander-in-Chief went on to say that the election should

---

[9] "O Seu Castigo é Decompor-se Vivo," declaration of A. C. Moniz de Aragão in *O Globo*, August 29, 1967.

[10] Sérgio Lacerda, letter, *Jornal do Brasil*, November 24, 1966; Borges, *O Golpe em Goiás*, p. 114.

[11] Carlos Lacerda quoted in Claudio Mello e Souza, "O Vizinho do Presidente," in Alberto Dines et al., *O Idos de Março e a Queda em Abril*, p. 188.

[12] Borges, *O Golpe em Goiás*, p. 112.

not be held until Mazzilli had been in office for thirty days, during which time the nation should "suffer penance" and be purged of subversion and corruption. The new "revolutionary" administration, whose Executive was to be chosen by Congress, should be spared that disagreeable work. Mazzilli was cooperating fully and doing what was requested of him.

Lacerda then interrupted to say that the revolutionary ideals did not include having a puppet in the presidency. Besides, with the passage of a little time, Mazzilli might find himself in a position to dismiss Costa e Silva. "Mazzilli and the PSD might roll you up," said Lacerda, using the verb *enrolar.* The General affirmed that no one was going to *enrolar* him.[13]

Costa e Silva seemed cordial neither to Lacerda nor to Magalhães Pinto, who, one of the governors has recorded, spoke in a "parochial tone," trying to carry on with thoughts Lacerda had originally sought to express. Costa e Silva, in the words of Mauro Borges, "referred to the separatist character of the movement started by the Minas governor and warned that he would not tolerate any whim in that sense."[14]

Lacerda guessed that Costa e Silva wanted to hold on to the supreme power. Ademar, Nei Braga, and Mauro Borges were deciding that the meeting was fruitless and were citing urgent reasons to return to their states, when Juarez Távora interrupted to ask that Lacerda be heard. After Lacerda argued for an immediate election and a military candidate, Costa e Silva repeated his position and asserted that a military candidacy might cause disunity in the Army.

Távora politely disagreed with Costa e Silva: "I do not believe that in thirty days—or in sixty or ninety—will the Military Command of the Revolution be able to exterminate the germs of subversion and corruption from Brazil or even from its governmental machinery."[15] Távora also felt that, with the passage of that period of time, the group

[13] Carlos Lacerda, interview, Rio de Janeiro, October 11, 1967.

[14] Borges, *O Golpe em Goiás*, p. 113.

[15] Juarez Távora, "Esclarecimentos Prestados pelo Marechal Juarez Távora, á Margem de Escolha do Marechal Castelo Branco para a Presidência da República em Abril de 1964," Rio de Janeiro, October 12, 1966 (typewritten memorandum for J.W.F.D.). Full text given in Leoncio Basbaum, *História Sincera de República*, IV, 135–137.

commanding the revolution would lose the unity necessary for easily arranging to have Congress elect a good President. If governors of different political parties had been able to reach agreement, he did not see why the Army generals could not do so.

Costa e Silva smiled. "We are hearing the same idealistic and unwary *tenente* of 1930," he said.

"No, Costa e Silva," Távora answered. "It is not that way. In 1930 we exercised restraint in not wanting to assume the government directly. We thought of putting the civilians in front and handling them from nearby. What an illusion, ours! Within a short time we were pushed back, . . . unable to do any of the things we had planned."[16]

The meeting broke up at about 4:00 A.M. on the morning of April 5 with nothing settled and with Lacerda noticeably upset by Costa e Silva's coolness toward him.

[16] Borges, *O Golpe em Goiás,* p. 114.

11. The Selection of Castelo Branco

ON SUNDAY MORNING, APRIL 5, General Siseno Sarmento, chief-of-staff of the Commander-in-Chief of the Revolutionary Forces, received a letter that Lacerda had addressed to Costa e Silva. In it, Lacerda stated that the governors, hoping to find in Costa e Silva the liberator, had found, instead, the usurper. The letter further said that Lacerda, in view of the attitude revealed by Costa e Silva, was resigning the governorship and definitely retiring from political life.[1] Sarmento, to avoid a major public break between civilian and military leaders, did not pass the letter on to Costa e Silva. Instead, he telephoned friends of Lacerda and suggested that they try to persuade the Governor to withdraw his statement.[2]

Soon a group in Lacerda's apartment argued that the letter had been

[1] Mauro Borges, *O Golpe em Goiás,* p. 115.
[2] Siseno Sarmento, interview, São Paulo, November 21, 1967.

a great mistake. Juraci Magalhães, who was present, had someone retrieve it from Sarmento.[3] Lacerda asked Juraci to represent him at the new meeting that the governors had scheduled with Costa e Silva.

The newspapers that morning were proclaiming that the "seven governors who commanded the revolution of April 1" had selected Castelo Branco to succeed Mazzilli. Governor Nei Braga was quoted as affirming that this agreement on one name represented a unanimity rare in Brazilian political history. During the day Castelo Branco received numerous important callers who urged that he be available for the presidency. His name was well received when groups of Rio generals and colonels gathered for discussions.[4]

Magalhães Pinto, like Lacerda, stayed away from the Sunday evening meeting at the War Ministry. He was represented by José Maria Alkmim. At this meeting a much more amiable Costa e Silva stressed to the governors that he, himself, could not be a presidential candidate because he was chief of the Army and had to keep it united. Although he repeated the points he had made at the previous meeting, he did not insist on them, and the views of the governors prevailed. The military congressmen who were present, Marshal Juarez Távora and Colonel José Costa Cavalcanti, gave assurances that if Castelo Branco's candidacy were launched, they could guarantee a peaceful election by Congress.[5] Except for Costa e Silva, all present indicated one or more names for President, and from these it was clear that Castelo Branco was the choice.[6]

Costa e Silva was asked whether he agreed with the selection. He spoke of past Brazilian military movements and said that his concern was to "avoid splits in the Revolutionary High Command." When a more direct reply was requested, he praised Castelo Branco, whom he had first known as a classmate at the Pôrto Alegre Military School in

---

[3] Juraci Magalhães, letter to *Jornal do Brasil,* November 1966.

[4] José Costa Cavalcanti, interview, Brasília, October 15, 1965.

[5] Juarez Távora, "Esclarecimentos Prestados pelo Marechal Juarez Távora, á Margem de Escolha do Marechal Castelo Branco para a Presidência da República em Abril de 1964," Rio de Janeiro, October 12, 1966 (typewritten memorandum for J.W.F.D.). Full text given in Leoncio Basbaum, *História Sincera da República,* IV, 135–137.

[6] Nei Braga, interview, Rio de Janeiro, December 21, 1965.

1915. Calling for Castelo Branco, he learned that the Chief of Staff had gone home. "You see," he said, "General Castelo Branco is such a soldier that he does not want to deal with political matters in a barracks, which the War Ministry is."[7]

It was past midnight when the governors (or their representatives) reached Castelo Branco's home on Rio's Rodrigo de Freitas Lake. As the oldest among them, Ademar de Barros was chosen to explain the mission. Castelo Branco was quick to accept the governors' support in the presidential contest.

Ademar asked him whether his candidacy had strong military support. The general replied that his own Army companions had come to his home to propose that he be a candidate. Ademar also asked Castelo Branco whether he would preside over the 1965 elections "in a climate of equality for all." The candidate referred to his past record as proof that he would do so.[8]

When Ademar asked for the annulment of the Goulart decree expropriating private oil refineries ("to show your appreciation of the business class"), Governor Mauro Borges objected to the request and praised the law that made Petrobrás a monopoly. Juraci Magalhães observed that it was an inappropriate time for a debate about the matter. Before leaving Castelo Branco, the governors picked members of their group to advise party directorships about the candidacy they were launching.

After the governors chose Castelo Branco with the "blessing" of Costa e Silva, support for Castelo Branco grew in the PSD.[9] To some this attitude seemed useful to the PSD's survival. Among the recent victors were "hard liners" who subscribed to the view of one of the generals: the PTB and PSD should be closed down, for they had "served as the incubators of Communism in Brazil."

Some PSD leaders, among them Alkmim, had already expressed a preference for a general in active service, and most of those who did so considered Castelo Branco the most blessed with civilian and intel-

---

[7] Borges, *O Golpe em Goiás,* p. 116.

[8] *O Estado de S. Paulo,* dateline Rio de Janeiro, April 6, 1964.

[9] *Correio da Manhã,* April 7, 1964, p. 14.

lectual virtues. The PSD's Francisco Negrão de Lima, friendly with both Kubitschek and Castelo Branco, sought the former President's backing for the General. So did Kubitschek's adviser Augusto Frederico Schmidt.

Kubitschek, exclusively interested in getting assurances that the people would be able to express their preference at the polls in 1965, learned from Negrão de Lima that Castelo Branco wanted that election to take place. Kubitschek himself explored the matter when he, Negrão de Lima, Amaral Peixoto, Filinto Müller, and some other PSD leaders met with Castelo Branco at the Rio home of a congressman. Kubitschek and Castelo Branco left the others to speak alone in the library, and there the General gave more assurances, which were being sought by Kubitschek, about the 1965 election.

PSD leaders, after consulting their candidate for that election, agreed to back Castelo Branco in the forthcoming election by Congress. With this decision, the PSD received the right to choose the Vice-President who would serve with Castelo Branco. Amaral Peixoto, driving home with Alkmim after the session with the General in the congressman's apartment, expressed the thought that Alkmim was the indicated choice for the number two spot. After his service in the Minas revolutionary cabinet and before the governors had met on April 4, Alkmim had urged that Castelo Branco be a candidate. Some of the PTB congressmen continued to support Kruel for President, and a part of the PSD continued to back Dutra.

Dutra had grown bitter after he learned that Lacerda had deserted him and that an early flowery remark by Magalhães Pinto and an inquiry by Amaral Peixoto had not been serious declarations of support. Maintaining that Amaral Peixoto and the governors of Guanabara and Minas had the obligation to back him to the end in view of what they had said to him, he resolved to remain a candidate. The Marshal turned down a suggestion from Kruel's supporters that if no one received a majority on the first ballot, then either Dutra or Kruel, whoever got the fewer votes, would give his votes to the other in an effort to defeat Castelo Branco.[10] But he stubbornly remained a candidate.

[10] Sigefredo Pacheco, interview, Brasília, October 16, 1965.

O Estado de S. Paulo then reminded its readers that Dutra had been responsible for the Vargas dictatorship.

Close friends of Dutra pled with him to withdraw. But the Marshal repeated that he would carry on because Lacerda had betrayed him. He also remarked that he might have acted differently had Castelo Branco, whom he had commanded in the past, advised him ahead of time that he was going to run. He let it be known that it had been he, Dutra, who had asked Castelo Branco to join the revolution.

A senator, who was a friend of Dutra but a supporter of Castelo Branco, advised Castelo Branco that Dutra was in a difficult situation. As a way out, the senator suggested that Castelo Branco explain, in a letter to Dutra, that he had been asked to be a candidate and would accept provided that Dutra was agreeable. On April 9, after receiving this letter, Dutra withdrew.

Kubitschek then made a statement in favor of Castelo Branco "in the certainty" that he would respect the will of the people, "to be expressed at the polls in October 1965." On the next day Kruel withdrew "to preserve the climate of confidence and good understanding which should reign within the military family."[11]

[11] *Correio da Manhã,* April 11, 1964.

12. The Ato Institucional

THE DECISION MADE by Costa e Silva and his advisers about Mazzilli's successor was tied to the problem of putting Brazil on a new track, following a period characterized by considerable inflation, corruption, Communist infiltration, and poor management. A part of the military, eager for a full-fledged "revolution" and feeling the need of drastic measures, wished for a while to deal roughly with Congress, the constitution, and the Supreme Court (whose appointees had largely been made by Getulista Presidents). Some civilians felt the same way.

This "hard line" point of view went counter to ideas long held in the Army. Since the enactment of the 1946 constitution, Army leaders had intervened in political affairs from time to time when they felt that democracy was being threatened, but as a rule they had retired quickly in favor of the constitution and political democracy. The "hard line" point of view also went counter to an important segment of foreign opinion. The United States government, which had been quick to recognize the new Mazzilli administration, extolled democracy in Latin America. United States congressmen were not likely to favor foreign assistance for Latin American military dictatorships.

Costa e Silva and Castelo Branco hoped that, in the year and a half which remained of the term begun by Quadros, it would be possible to enact needed reforms and clean things up with little disturbance to the constitution. Some exceptional powers would be required in this period, but they were to be few, and the most controversial ones were to be as short-lived as possible.

This was what constitutional lawyers Francisco Campos and Carlos Medeiros da Silva were told after Costa e Silva called them to the War Ministry and asked them to write an Ato Institucional—an Institutional Act, which would temporarily amend the constitution.[1] The lawyers rolled up their sleeves at the War Minister's tables and drafted the Ato during the course of one long, warm day. Professor Francisco Campos, who had created the authoritarian constitution of 1937, wrote the prologue and one or two articles of the Ato Institucional of 1964; Carlos Medeiros da Silva wrote the rest of the articles. These translated into legal phraseology the wishes of Costa e Silva and Castelo Branco.

During the consideration of the draft by the Military High Command and the Justice Minister, "hard liners" clashed with those who held a more moderate view.

The "hard liners" included Admiral Rademaker and Dr. Gama e Silva, who was Minister of Justice and of Education. Gama e Silva was preparing to have troops close down the University of Brasília and expel those who had turned the university into what he has called "a Communist hotbed." He favored closing down Congress and instituting a drastic cleanup to put Brazil into a condition that he felt would allow it later to renew democratic ways fully. Rademaker believed that

[1] Francisco Campos, interview, Rio de Janeiro, December 14, 1965.

the Revolutionary High Command should maintain control for at least a month and take strong steps, such as throwing out about half the federal congressmen and three or four Supreme Court justices. Costa e Silva had the final word, however, and these "hard line" views did not prevail.

Francisco Campos' prologue is a message to the nation explaining the need of the Ato Institucional, and the right and the responsibility of the commanders-in-chief of the three branches of the armed forces to issue it. A government that had "deliberately sought to bolshevize the country" had been toppled by the revolution, which now alone had the right to dictate rules that would give the new government the power necessary for acting on behalf of the nation.

These rules called for the election of a President and Vice-President by Congress within two days of the April 9 signing of the Ato Institucional. In the case of this election, the Ato decreed that no one was ineligible, thus settling a dispute about the legality of the Castelo Branco candidacy. (Already former Justice Minister Vicente Ráo had stated that the constitutional provision about chiefs of staff having to leave their posts three months before elections applied only in the case of direct elections by the people.)

All the articles of the Ato were to expire on January 31, 1966, with the installation of the President and Vice-President elected by popular vote on October 3, 1965, as called for by the 1946 constitution.[2]

The main provisions affected congressional procedure and the fate of individuals who were felt to have made the revolution necessary. Legislative projects submitted to Congress by the President were to become law if not acted on within thirty days. Budgets submitted by the President were not to be increased by Congress.

For a period of six months the new rulers were to be able to dismiss persons from their posts regardless of what the laws or the constitution might say about tenure rights. "In the interest of peace and the national

[2] A Second Institutional Act (Ato Institucional), issued by President Castelo Branco and his cabinet in October 1965, modified arrangements established by the Institutional Act of April 1964. It postponed the presidential and vice-presidential elections until October 1966 and made them indirect elections (by Congress). It extended Castelo Branco's term until March 15, 1967. It ended the political parties that had existed until October 1965.

honor," the signers of the Ato could suspend the political rights of individuals for ten years and could cancel the mandates of federal, state, or municipal legislators. When the new President took office to succeed Mazzilli, these powers were to be transferred for him to use in accordance with recommendations of the National Security Council. However, after a period of sixty days had passed, no new names were to be added to the list of those who had lost their political rights.[3]

Rademaker had proposed that the cancellation of political rights be for fifteen years. This had helped get the final wording to say ten years —a compromise suggested by Gama e Silva—instead of the five years stipulated in the original draft of the Ato.[4]

The Ato Institucional, signed by the three military ministers on April 9 at a ceremony at the War Ministry, was condemned by a part of the press. Rio's *Correio da Manhã* declared that Congress had been made into "a mere consultive assembly of the Military Junta." Lawyer Heráclito Sobral Pinto stated that the military ministers had not been delegated by the Brazilian people to act as they had and were only shielded by their weapons.

"Hard liners" also had faults to find with the Ato. Some of them felt that it would be best to have the Comando Revolucionário (the military ministers) name the new President and Vice-President, thus avoiding the necessity of dealing with politicians of the PSD. Rademaker condemned the arrangement, which assured the vice-presidency for Alkmim.

Rademaker's list of persons to be deprived of their political rights included the names of the three "leftist" Supreme Court Justices about whom there was now much discussion. But neither they, nor numerous well-known PSD politicians on Rademaker's list, were affected when the final decisions were made.

Immediately after signing the Ato Institucional, the military ministers announced that they were depriving Goulart, Quadros, and Luís Carlos Prestes of their political rights for ten years. Then three PTB

---

[3] The Second Institutional Act (of October 27, 1965) again allowed the cancellation of the political rights of individuals.

[4] August Hamann Rademaker Grünewald, interview, Rio de Janeiro, December 13, 1965; Luís Antônio Gama e Silva, interview, São Paulo, November 18, 1966.

congressmen were seized by the police in Brasília. This led Kubitschek to warn against "radicalization."

On April 11, the federal legislators gathered in Brasília to elect Castelo Branco and Alkmim. Since Dutra and Kruel had withdrawn as presidential candidates, Castelo Branco very nearly received the unanimous vote that it was felt would augur well for the forthcoming administration. It took two ballots for Alkmim to overcome Auro de Moura Andrade's bid for the vice-presidency. Some of the new "revolutionaries" were not enthusiastic about Alkmim, who had been closely associated with Kubitschek in the past. João Agripino, disappointed because the UDN had supported Alkmim in the voting, declared that in his opinion the Vice-President-elect did not represent the hopes of the revolution.

Forty legislators (thirty-nine congressmen and one senator) were not allowed to participate in the election because on April 10 "the Supreme Command of the Revolution" had declared their mandates ended and had placed them on the list of one hundred whose political rights were taken away for a decade.

This list included former Goulart cabinet ministers Abelardo Jurema, Paulo de Tarso, Almino Afonso, Amauri Silva, Celso Furtado, Wilson Fadul, and João Pinheiro Neto. Governor Miguel Arrais and Guanabara's Vice-Governor Elói Dutra were also named, and presidential intimates like Darci Ribeiro, Raul Riff, and Samuel Wainer were among "the first one hundred." So were Congressmen Brizola, Bocaiuva Cunha, Francisco Julião, Neiva Moreira, Max da Costa Santos, Marco Antônio Coelho, Roland Corbisier, José Aparecido de Oliveira, and Benedito Cerqueira. Among the military personnel listed were Marshal Osvino Ferreira Alves, Cabo José Anselmo (of the Sailor's Association), and Antônio Garcia Filho, the sergeant who had been elected to Congress. Also included were numerous labor leaders, such as Osvaldo Pacheco, Clodsmidt Riani, Dante Pelacani, Roberto Morena, Rafael Martineli, Melo Bastos, and Hércules Correia.[5]

---

[5] A full list of "the first one hundred" is given in *Correio da Manhã*, April 11, 1964. It included Luís Carlos Prestes and ex-Presidents Quadros and Goulart.

General Costa e Silva (who was displeased with some aspects of his past relations with Quadros) was particularly insistent that Quadros be deprived of his political rights.

The victims could neither defend themselves nor make appeals; nor were they told what the charges were.

Another list was published on April 14. After Castelo Branco and Alkmim were inaugurated on April 15, additional lists appeared, bringing to nearly three hundred the number of those who lost their political rights under the Ato Institucional of April 9.[6] The new names included some of the military figures of the Goulart regime: Admirals Pedro Paulo de Araújo Suzano and Cândido Aragão, and Generals Argemiro Assis Brasil, Euriale de Jesus Zerbini, and Luís Tavares da Cunha Melo; also General Nelson Werneck Sodré, ISEB's Marxist historian. Yet the number affected by the Ato Institucional was a fraction of the number recommended by military and civilian "hard liners."

The greatest suspense surrounded the future of Kubitschek. It was known that the National Security Council, whose secretary was General Ernesto Geisel, was studying the case of the former President. Kubitschek, worried about growing talk of those old issues, the origin of his "personal fortune" and "deals" with Communists, asked Senator Moura Andrade to have a full investigation made. In a letter to lawyer Sobral Pinto, Kubitschek maintained that his accusers, "unable to point to these imaginary assets in Brazil," were stating that the "fictitious fortune" was deposited abroad and thus were freeing themselves of the problem of proving their statements.

On May 25 Kubitschek addressed a note to the Brazilian people declaring that the people had already judged him and were eager to do so again at the first opportunity. His foes, he asserted, sought to eliminate "not only a candidate but also the democratic regime itself." War Minister Costa e Silva (the only Mazzilli military minister to be retained by Castelo Branco) likened Kubitschek's language and tone to that used by Goulart in his speech to the sergeants at the Automobile Club. Kubitschek replied that he could see no similarity. Costa e Silva retorted that Kubitschek was acting in desperation.

Kubitschek appeared in Brasília to defend himself in what he knew

---

[6] See Ruy Mesquita and Gilles Lapouge, *31/3,* letter of Ruy Mesquita, p. 23. Mesquita says that, under the Ato Institucional of April 9, 1964, exactly 299 persons lost their political rights for ten years, among them 5 governors, 11 mayors, 51 federal congressmen, 2 senators, and 46 military officers.

was his last Senate speech. "The workings of the Ato Institucional are such that those who are threatened are not given access to the accusatory dossiers. Thus the revolutionaries of Brazil turn against the most sacred conquests of the law. I do not know exactly what they accuse me of. I only pick up rumors and mutterings of old stories already disproved and disparaged by irrefutable replies. Now the nation lives under the effects of terror, and here I express my solidarity with those who are suffering from the processes of inquisition, which recall the dramatic moments through which humanity has passed. . . . I know that in this Brazilian land tyrannies do not last. That we are a human nation, inspired by the spirit of justice. . . . I repeat, the blow which they wish to deal to my person, as former Head of State, will strike the democratic life, the free will of the people. . . . This act is an act of usurpation and not an act of punishment. They cancel much more than my political rights; they cancel the political rights of Brazil!"[7]

On the evening of June 8, just within the sixty-day period that began with the signing of the Ato Institucional, it was announced that President Castelo Branco, considering the recommendation of the National Security Council, was canceling Kubitschek's political rights for ten years. Five days later the former President left with his family for Europe.

[7] Mário Victor, *Cinco Anos que Abalaram o Brasil: de Jânio Quadros ao Marechal Castelo Branco*, pp. 585–586.

LACERDA, who had assailed past Presidents, was soon assailing President Castelo Branco.

Late in 1966 Lacerda and Kubitschek smilingly shook hands in Lisbon, Portugal. Their reconciliation took place after Marshal Costa e Silva had become President-elect, the result of another indirect election by Congress—as specified by a far-reaching Second Institutional Act. The world learned that Kubitschek and Lacerda were setting aside their past "divergences" and pledging themselves to work together in a Frente Ampla (Broad Front) to oust those who, Lacerda said, had "betrayed" the revolution of 1964.

Past differences between Lacerda and Goulart—a feature of the 1954–1964 decade—were overlooked after Lacerda flew to Montevideo in September 1967 to call on Goulart. Lacerda made the trip, he said, in order to find out whether "every man has within himself enough patriotism and worthiness to set aside personal resentments and ideological divergences in favor of a union for the nation and the people."[1] In Montevideo Goulart joined the Frente Ampla amidst handshakes and manifestations of good will between him and Lacerda.

This meeting gave Brizola, also in Uruguay, another opportunity to attack his brother-in-law. He announced that Goulart's understanding with Lacerda did not surprise him, and he added that, "due to the same lack of principles, Goulart lost his authority as President and was deposed with surprising facility. Lacerda, in my opinion, continues the same person he always was. The sacrifice of President Getúlio Vargas and his farewell message cannot be forgotten so easily."[2]

[1] Carlos Lacerda, "Porque Encontrei Jango," *Fatos & Fotos,* VII, no. 349 (October 7, 1967), p. 15.
[2] *Jornal do Brasil,* September 26, 1967.

NOTES ABOUT THE ELECTORATE, THE LEGAL POLITICAL
PARTIES, AND THE COMMUNIST PARTY OF BRAZIL

1. A word about the electorate

The 1946 constitution made voting a requirement as well as a right of
those who were eligible. With certain exceptions, all who were over eighteen
years of age were eligible. The exceptions included soldiers, sailors, noncommissioned military officers, and illiterates.

Before he fell from office, Goulart was advocating—as one of his reforms
—that illiteracy no longer be a reason for denying an individual the right to
vote. The proposed reform would have increased the electorate in some regions more than in others. In particular, the electorate in the Northeast
would have been greatly enlarged. Brazil's rural population majority[1] would
have attained a voting majority, which it did not have under the 1946 constitution. The rural population contained a larger percentage of those who
had not reached voting age; of greater importance, the rural population was
high in illiteracy.

Brazil's estimated total population in 1962 was 75 million. About half
had not reached voting age; and about 47 per cent of Brazil's population of
voting age was illiterate, leaving a voting potential of 18.5 million, or one
voter per four inhabitants.

[1] The 1960 census shows a population of 70.2 million, broken down into 31.6
million "urban" and 38.6 million "rural" inhabitants. The so-called urban population
was living in over 6,500 cities, towns, and villages, of which about 5,000 had less
than 2,000 inhabitants each. If the 3.5 million inhabitants living in villages of less
than 2,000 are considered as rural, then only 40 per cent of Brazil's population—instead of 45 per cent—was urban in 1960. The statistics used here are based on the
census definition of rural and urban.

State or Territory	Area (1000 Km²)	% of Brazil	1962 Estimated Population (thousands)	% of Brazil	1962 Estimated Electoral Potential (thousands)	% of Brazil
Acre	153	1.8	171	0.2	30.6	0.2
Amazonas	1564	18.4	768	1.0	169.1	0.9
Pará	1251	14.7	1647	2.2	397.3	2.1
Rondônia	243	2.9	80	0.1	20.4	0.1
Rio Branco	230	2.7	32	....	6.7	....
Amapá	140	1.6	77	0.1	17.1	0.1
NORTH	3581	42.1	2775	3.7	641.2	3.4
Maranhão	329	3.9	2718	3.6	321.5	1.8
Piauí	251	2.9	1306	1.7	170.1	0.9
Ceará	151	1.8	3472	4.6	547.0	3.0
R. G. Norte	53	0.6	1195	1.6	176.0	1.1
Paraíba	56	0.7	2080	2.8	298.5	1.6
Pernambuco	98	1.2	4292	5.7	753.7	4.0
Alagoas	28	0.3	1307	1.7	156.1	0.8
F. Noronha	....	....	2	....	1.0	....
NORTHEAST	966	11.4	16372	21.6	2423.9	13.2
Sergipe	22	0.3	784	1.0	121.8	0.6
Bahia	561	6.6	6234	8.3	1052.3	5.7
M. Gerais	583	6.8	10242	13.7	2231.2	12.0
E. Santo	50	0.6	1263	1.7	288.8	1.5
Rio de J.	43	0.5	3667	4.9	1093.3	5.9
Guanabara	1	....	3517	4.7	1714.0	9.2
EAST	1260	14.8	25707	34.3	6501.4	34.9
São Paulo	248	2.9	13868	18.5	4735.3	25.5
Paraná	200	2.3	4905	6.5	1210.3	6.5
S. Catarina	96	1.1	2282	3.0	606.1	3.3
R. G. Sul	282	3.3	5731	7.6	1828.3	9.8
SOUTH	826	9.6	26786	35.7	8380.0	45.1
Mato Grosso	1231	14.5	1013	1.4	220.7	1.2
Goiás	642	7.5	2140	2.9	358.5	1.9
Brasília	6	0.1	160	0.2	59.1	0.3
CENTER-WEST	1879	22.1	3313	4.5	638.3	3.4
BRAZIL	8512	100.0	74953	100.0	18584.8	100.0

ESTIMATED LITERACY RATE (%)

	"rural"	"urban"	overall
North	35	73	51
Northeast	20	55	35
East	30	73	54
South	47	79	66
Center-west	31	63	44

Source of Table (above and opposite): "Análise Socio-Político-Eleitoral," unpublished manuscript prepared by Escritório Técnico Paulo de Assis Ribeiro.

Of this voting potential of 18.5 million, 13 million were classified as "urban" (living in cities, towns, and villages) and only 5.5 million were "rural." The cities, towns, and villages were providing one potential voter per 2.7 inhabitants, compared with one per 7.2 inhabitants in "rural" areas.[2]

Twenty-five per cent of Brazil's population was found to be residing in 45 municipalities, which included all cities of over 100,000 and also included all the capitals (state, territorial, and national). This 25 per cent of the population (in 0.3 per cent of Brazil's area) furnished 43 per cent of the nation's voting potential.

The political parties—of which there were thirteen—could also take into consideration the wide variance of voting potential in different regions. To cite two extremes: the "rural" areas in the Northeast were found to have one potential voter per 11.6 inhabitants whereas the "urban" sectors of Brazil's four southern states offered one per 2.4 inhabitants. This meant that, in 1962, of the 11 million inhabitants living in "rural" areas in the Northeast, only 900,000 could vote, whereas of the 14 million living in "urban" areas in the south, 6 million could vote. This disparity was due in part to the larger percentage, in the southern "urban" areas, of those who had reached the voting age. Above all it was due to a 20 per cent literacy rate attributed to the Northeast "rural" areas compared with a 79 per cent literacy rate attributed to the southern "urban" areas.

[2] These voting potential figures, and those which follow, are from "Análise Sócio-Político-Eleitoral" (unpublished manuscript prepared by Escritório Técnico Paulo de Assis Ribeiro).

2. Note about the legal political parties

Most of the thirteen parties came into existence in 1945 as the Vargas dictatorship prepared to bow out before the wave of political democracy which accompanied the military failure of the totalitarian nations. These parties were either for or against the record of Vargas' "short period of fifteen years" (1930–1945).

Under the inspiration of Vargas himself, two parties were founded. They became two of the "big three" that operated from 1945 until 1965, when all existing parties were ended. These two, the Partido Social Democrático (PSD) and the Partido Trabalhista Brasileiro (PTB) reflected different forces that Vargas had built up. The PSD was the party of political figures who had held posts in the federal government and had administered the states and territories on behalf of the dictatorship. The PTB emphasized the social legislation of the Vargas years and attracted workers who had benefited from it or who could expect to benefit from a continuation of a pro-labor policy. By arranging for the organization of the PTB, Vargas cut into the strength of the Communist Party of Brazil, which, finding itself legal in 1945, busily sought converts.

Vargas' foes, hoping to win the December 1945 elections, created the União Democrática Nacional (UDN) to bring together all the anti-Getulistas. The UDN, like the Vargas-inspired PSD and PTB, has been one of the three large national parties. Its spirit has been described as one of opposition. It stressed its antidictatorship and anticorruption principles.

The common dislike felt by the early UDN members for the pre-1945 Vargas record did not mean that they could all work together happily. Not long after the UDN was organized, numerous other anti-Getulista parties came into being. Some of them, like the Partido Republicano (PR) and Partido Libertador (PL), carried on political organizations that had been abolished by Vargas in December 1937. The adepts of Plínio Salgado, whose green-shirted Integralistas had marched for "God, Country, and Family" in the 1930's until Vargas stopped them, founded the Partido de Representação Popular (PRP). A Christian Democratic Party (Partido Democrata Cristão–PDC) was organized. In 1946, when national parties were required to have a membership of at least fifty-thousand voters, some very small ones were swallowed up by the Partido Social Progressista (PSP); this was "the party of Ademar de Barros," whom Vargas had fired five years earlier from his post of running the important state of São Paulo.

The anti-Vargas Socialists remained for a while as the "Democratic Left" of the UDN, but in 1947 they separated in order to found their own party, the Partido Socialista Brasileiro (PSB).

In 1945 and 1946 three small *trabalhista* (labor) parties, all seeking to imitate the Vargas-founded PTB, came into being. After some name-changing they became known as the Partido Trabalhista Nacional, Partido Rural Trabalhista, and Partido Social Trabalhista (PTN, PRT, PST). A fourth, the Movimento Trabalhista Renovador (MTR) was established in 1961 when a PTB leader broke with Goulart. Leaders, often with a PTB background, have gone from one to another of these small *trabalhista* parties.

The strength of the small parties was apt to be limited to areas in which their leaders were influential. Thus the Partido Republicano functioned mostly in Minas Gerais, home state of its president, and the Partido Libertador mostly in the southernmost state of Rio Grande do Sul, home state of its president. Nine of the twenty-three federal *deputados* elected in 1962 by the Partido Social Progressista, were from São Paulo, home of PSP President Ademar de Barros.

Of the thirteen parties, only the PSD, UDN, and PTB had a very wide geographic distribution of strength. In 1962 these three elected 320 of the 409 *deputados* (congressmen) to the federal Chamber of Deputies. (The PSD elected 119, the UDN 97, and the PTB 104). Each of these three parties had federal representatives from most of Brazil's twenty-five political subdivisions (twenty-two states and three territories). The fourth largest party—Ademar de Barros' PSP—elected twenty-three representatives from nine states or territories. Each of the remaining nine parties elected *deputados* from only a handful of states—no more than six states and commonly about half that number.[3]

The programs offered by the thirteen parties were in most cases vague. In some cases—like that of the Partido Socialista Brasileiro, advocate of socializing all means of production—they were clear. However, the electorate gave little attention to the programs, and the parties frequently overlooked the purposes that were expressed when they were being established.

With so many parties in the field, all sorts of alliances took place at times of local and national elections. Particularly in the case of local elections, these alliances indicated that party labels stood for little. One of the numerous alliances for electoral purposes was that in the north between

[3] Statistics in this paragraph are from Institute for the Comparative Study of Political Systems, *Brazil: Election Factbook*, no. 2 (September 1965). This very complete factbook contains a wealth of information about voters, political personalities and organizations, electoral laws, and election outcomes.

the anti-Getulista UDN and the Getulista PTB (frequently accused of corruption by the UDN).

The Communist Party of Brazil, after being declared illegal in 1947, sold its support to those who would buy it, and there were many who would. It also arranged to have Communists run as candidates of other parties. The Partido Socialista Brasileiro was a favorite vehicle for Communist candidates.

Splits took place within parties. In the PSD a "dissident wing" was keen on cooperating with the UDN at a time when the "orthodox wing" opposed the idea.

None of this much troubled the electorate, with its interest in personalities so much greater than its interest in rather meaningless party labels. Still, under some circumstances the use of a party machine could be of much help to a candidate. Particularly in the backlands at times of congressional elections, the "barranca colonels"—as in the past—could deliver votes that they controlled for reasons not connected with political personalities or issues.

The Second Institutional Act, issued by President Castelo Branco and his cabinet in October 1965, ended the political parties that had existed until then. A two-party system was established.

3. Notes about the Communist Party of Brazil

In July 1922, three months after its formation, the Partido Comunista do Brasil (PCB) was declared illegal. Except for the first eight months in 1927, it continued to have an illegal status until 1945.

Throughout most of the 1920's PCB leaders—former Anarchists who now gave their allegiance to Moscow's Third International—struggled against Brazilian authorities and worked to establish cells in factories. Although half of the new adherents usually dropped out quickly, membership was raised from several hundred to approximately one thousand in 1928.

Communist publications aroused much interest. A Communist Youth Movement attracted about 250, mostly in Rio (then the federal capital). The Party tried to be a political factor by participating in an "electoral united front" in the Rio area: two Communists were elected to the Rio municipal council in 1928.

As the 1920's came to a close, the PCB was afflicted by internal dissensions and by extremely sectarian directives from Moscow. Some left the PCB to support Trotsky, who had lost out to Stalin in the Soviet Union.

Brazilian authorities, concerned with tension caused by the 1930 presidential election, cracked down on the PCB.

When Vargas came to power with the revolution of October 1930, the PCB had only a few hundred members. Its directing Central Committee (CC), harassed by the Rio police, moved to São Paulo. The Paulista authorities, shortly before undertaking an unsuccessful rebellion against Vargas in 1932, arrested all CC members. For a while the PCB was without leadership.

Liberties provided by the 1934 constitution allowed strikes to occur and made it easier for Party militants to operate. Communists, Socialists, and labor leaders often battled against the strongly anti-Communist Integralistas, who paraded and saluted in green shirts. The Communists saw the Integralista movement as part of a world-wide Nazi-Fascist build-up.

After the German Communist Party had been defeated by the Nazis, the Communist Third International (Comintern) pushed for Popular Fronts. The Popular Front in Brazil took the form of the Aliança Nacional Libertadora (ANL). Early in 1935 the ANL came forth with an "anti-imperialist" program calling for the end of payments on Brazil's foreign debt, nationalization of all "imperialistic companies," and the distribution of large landholdings to those who worked the land. The ANL attracted many who did not know that it was Communist-inspired.

Carlos Lacerda, a twenty-one–year-old student enthusiastic about the program of the ANL, nominated Luís Carlos Prestes to be its honorary president. Prestes, known as the "Cavalier of Hope" after leading a band of revolutionary fighters in the Brazilian interior in the mid-1920's, had a large popular following. In April 1935 he secretly returned to Brazil, coming from the Soviet Union where he had spent the early 1930's doing political work with members of the Comintern's Executive Committee.

Prestes, with the help of some prominent international Communists, was to lead a national anti-imperialist revolution in Brazil. This revolution, scheduled to be staged by workers, soldiers, and the "anti-imperialist bourgeoisie," was to give Brazil a "popular national revolutionary government" with Comrade Prestes at its head. The government was later to transform itself into "the democratic dictatorship of the workers and peasants in the form of soviets."

In July 1935, after Prestes sought to encourage "the idea of assault" in "the conscience of the great masses," the Vargas regime closed the ANL. But the work of Prestes brought several thousand members to the PCB.

The plans for a coordinated uprising were known in detail by the Vargas government, which had agents posing as Communist planners. Rebels in the Northeast started the uprising ahead of schedule in November 1935. A few days later, just as the bloody rebellion in Recife was being quelled, some Rio Communists in the military carried out Prestes' orders and participated in two uprisings. They were unsuccessful—handicapped because they lacked support in military and civilian circles and because the authorities knew their plans.

Throughout the late 1930's the government jailed thousands of Communists and alleged Communists. In March 1936 Prestes was captured in Rio, shortly after he had ordered the assassination of sixteen-year-old Elza Fernandes, who was suspected of informing the police about her Communist companions. Some Brazilian Communists left Brazil, and later a few of them made their way to Spain to participate in the fighting against Franco.

The PCB, with two or three thousand members, was again without leadership after the jailing of its Central Committee in May 1940. Six months later Prestes' seventeen-year jail sentence (handed down in 1937) was extended an additional thirty years because of his role in Elza Fernandes' assassination.

With Brazil's declaration of war against the Axis (at the side of the Soviet Union) in August 1942, and with the dissolution of the Comintern in 1943, conditions changed for Brazilian Communists. A few, the "liquidationists," proposed that the PCB made sense no longer, the class struggle having disappeared. Many Communists enthusiastically joined such groups as the Society of the Friends of America, which wanted democracy (instead of Vargas) in Brazil. These Communists said that it was more important to fight "fascism" in Brazil than abroad.

Reorganization of the PCB in 1943 was taken over by a group led by Diógenes de Arruda Câmara. This group got the support of Prestes ("South America's most famous political prisoner"), and both it and Prestes argued for collaboration with the Vargas government for the sake of the war effort against fascism in Europe.

Prestes, freed in April 1945 in a climate of amnesty and goodwill toward Russia, backed the pro-Vargas wing of Brazilian Communism. While reorganizing the Party—about to become legal—the martyred and somewhat mythical "Cavalier of Hope" toured Brazil attracting many thousands to the PCB. At the same time President Vargas was calling on the workers to join the PTB.

In the elections of December 1945—following the military coup that overthrew Vargas—the PCB did quite well. Its presidential candidate, non-Communist Iedo Fiuza, received 570,000 votes, almost 10 per cent of the total. Prestes was handsomely elected senator from the Federal District. To the national Chamber of Deputies, the PCB elected 14 out of a total of 286 *deputados*.

By the end of 1945 the PCB had roughly 60,000 members. A year later its membership had risen to its peak, about 150,000. Then it fell on difficult days. The Cold War was early reflected in Brazil in the bad relations between the PCB and the government of Marshal Eurico Gaspar Dutra (1946–1951). Communists had long been horrified by Dutra and his generals, and Dutra and his generals had long been horrified by Communists. Prestes declared that if Brazil should join any imperialist nation in war against the Soviet Union, the PCB would back the latter. Following the publication of scathing remarks about the Dutra regime in *The Literary Gazette* of the Soviet Union, the Dutra administration broke the recently established diplomatic relations between Brazil and the U.S.S.R.

In Brazil the PCB was declared illegal, and its members were thrown out of their legislative seats. Prison sentences against Prestes and some of his followers forced them underground. Prestes, in hiding, issued violent manifestos calling for the overthrow of Dutra, "the puppet of the Yankee imperialists." During the presidential race of 1950 Prestes condemned all three candidates, including Vargas (the "tyrant landowner"), who won.

With Prestes in hiding, the Party—its membership down to about sixty thousand—was administered in a dictatorial manner by Diógenes de Arruda Câmara. Arruda Câmara, an admirer of Stalin (whom he sought to imitate) faithfully followed the instructions of the Communist Party of the Soviet Union (CPSU).

Returning from the Nineteenth Congress of the CPSU (October 1952), Arruda Câmara revealed a new PCB program, which he proudly described as having been drawn up by Stalin. Its main point was that Communist fire was to be concentrated against United States imperialism and not against other imperialisms. Prestes adhered to the new line. Soon after Stalin's death (March 1953), he published a piece of Party "self-criticism" calling for a turn from the "erroneous" sectarianism of the previous five years.

Early in 1954, as the PCB prepared for its Fourth Party Congress, Brazilian Communist leaders were saying that all Brazilian anti-imperialists should unite to fight the Yankees and their "servile instrument," the Vargas government. Although peace had come to Korea, the "North American imperialists" were pictured as seeking to turn the Brazilian people into cannon fodder in a war of aggression. The Vargas regime was described as a government of national treason, preparing for war.

With his suicide on August 24, 1954, Vargas suddenly became a hero of the PCB, which rushed instructions to its followers to make the most of his farewell letter and to attack the United States Embassy and consulates. At the PCB's Fourth Party Congress in Santos in November 1954, a paper from Prestes said that "the deposition of Vargas and his replacement by the vilest lackeys of the United States war provokers was carried out under the inspiration of, and by the direct order of, the North American ambassador in Rio." A purpose, Prestes added, had been to allow Standard Oil to take over Brazilian petroleum.[4]

In the 1955 presidential election the PCB gave effective support to the so-called Getulista slate: Juscelino Kubitschek for President and Jango Goulart for Vice-President. Prestes, pleased with the victorious outcome, stated that "the study, assimilation, and application of the experiences of the CPSU are the bases of the successes of the PCB."[5]

During Kubitschek's presidency (1956–1961) great changes occurred in the PCB because of repercussions from Khrushchev's de-Stalinization speech (February 1956) and because of a court decision (March 1958) dismissing the charges that had kept Prestes and others in hiding.

Khrushchev's accusations against Stalin were used against Arruda Câmara and his "directing nucleus." Opponents of the "personality cult"—calling themselves "renovators" and gleefully advocating the democratization of the PCB—engaged in an unprecedented free-for-all at Central Committee meetings and in the Communist press. With the Hungarian upheaval under way, they heaped abuse on the Communist Party of the Soviet Union.

In his "gag letter" of November 1956, Prestes called for the end of this sort of freedom. He said that "attacks against the Soviet Union and the CPSU are inadmissable in our ranks." The so-called renovators were distressed soon afterward when the party's press organs were invaded by PCB members who stuck by Arruda Câmara's "directing nucleus."

In 1957, after columns in *Voz Operária* and *Imprensa Popular* ranted against the "renovators," leading "renovators" quit the Party. Partly be-

---

[4] Luiz Carlos Prestes, "Informe de Balanço do Comitê Central do Brasil," *Problemas*, no. 64 (December 1954–February 1955), pp. 47–103.

[5] *Noticias de Hoje*, São Paulo, December 6, 1955, transcribed from *Democracia Popular*, no. 48.

cause of these resignations, and partly because of the upheaval that had taken place after the news from Hungary, there was a great exodus from the PCB. The membership is said to have fallen from around fifty-five thousand to around thirty thousand.

Prestes gave his backing to a new group, which had been careful during the internal fight and which now blamed the "directing nucleus" for all of the trouble. Prestes and the new group—known as the Bahia Group— secured control from Arruda Câmara and his followers in July 1957. Arruda Câmara issued a "self-criticism."

In March 1958 Prestes and his new associates attacked the "grave errors of the past: errors of dogmatic and sectarian character." The PCB went far to the "right," calling for a peaceful path and a "nationalist and democratic united front," which was not to overthrow the government. "The Brazilian bourgeoisie becomes more and more aware of the exploitation exercised by the North American monopolies."

Prestes praised the work of Kubitschek's Finance Minister, José Maria Alkmin; and he sped around Brazil, getting badly needed funds by selling PCB support to candidates in the 1958 congressional and gubernatorial elections. He suggested that an alliance with Plínio Salgado's PRP was a possibility, but the old leader of the Integralista "Green Shirts" expressed his lack of interest.

Prestes' backing of Ademar de Barros, who was running for the governorship of São Paulo, led to the resignation of several Central Committee members. Communist youths, walking out of the Party in São Paulo, said that the "PCB's electoral agreements lack any kind of class content."

While Prestes defended the inclusion of large landholders in the anti-imperialist front ("they are struggling against the high prices of du Pont's chemicals"), members of the ousted "directing nucleus" assailed his "opportunism."

These critics, men like Maurício Grabois, João Amazonas, and Pedro Pomar, failed to win control of the Central Committee at the Fifth Party Congress in 1960. The closing session of the Congress, held in a Rio auditorium, attracted two thousand. Labor leaders and representatives of the PTB were at the speakers' table to hear Prestes praise Cuba and declare that the day would come when Goulart would be able to appear in a public square to sign a pact of action with the Communists.

Seeking legality for the PCB, Prestes and his followers in August 1961 issued some new statutes that made no mention of Marxism; they changed the Party name from the more international Partido Comunista do Brasil to Partido Comunista Brasileiro.

The fallen Grabois, Amazonas, and Pomar pointed out that such changes could only be made by a Party Congress. They took the former Party name, Partido Comunista do Brasil (PC do B), and associated its cause with the violent line of Red China. Since the PCB's monthly publication, *A Classe Operária,* had been registered in Grabois' name, the PC do B took it over also. But this China-line party, which praised Stalin and attacked the Soviet Union, did not attract many followers.

SOURCES OF MATERIAL,
GLOSSARY, *and* INDEX

SOURCES OF MATERIAL

Information was obtained from conversations and written works such as those mentioned below. Spellings of titles and authors' names are those appearing on the title pages of the works cited.

Ação Democrática. Monthly publication of Instituto Brasileiro de Ação Democrática (IBAD), 1959–1963.

Afonso, Almino. Interviews, Santiago, Chile, June 26 and 28, 1967.

Aleixo, Pedro. Interview, Brasília, October 14, 1965.

Alkmim, José Maria. Interview, Brasília, October 15, 1965.

Almeida, Fernando H. Mendes de, ed. *Constituições do Brasil.* 4th ed. São Paulo: Edição Saraiva, 1963.

Almeida, Pedro Geraldo de. Interview, Rio de Janeiro, November 4, 1965.

Alves, Marcio Moreira. *Torturas e Torturados.* 2nd ed. Rio de Janeiro: Emprêsa Journalística P. N., 1967.

——. Interview, Rio de Janeiro, November 11, 1967.

Amorim, Paulo Henrique. "Sua Excelência, O Pelego." *Realidade,* II, no. 24 (March 1968).

Análise e Perspectiva Econômica (APEC). Brazilian Fortnightly Economic Letter. Rio de Janeiro: APEC Editôra, July 20, 1962–May 13, 1964.

——. *A Economia Brasileira e Suas Perspectivas.* Rio de Janeiro: APEC Editôra. Annual issues of May 1963 and May 1964.

Andrada, José Bonifácio Lafaiete de. Interview, Brasília, October 19, 1965.

Andrade, Antônio Ribeiro de. Interviews, São Paulo, November 15, 1966; November 25, 1967.

Andrade, Auro Soares de Moura. Interview, Brasília, October 21, 1965.

Apolônio, Luís. Interviews, São Paulo, November 18, 1966; November 7, 1967.

Aragão, Augusto César Moniz de. "O Seu Castigo é Decompor-se Vivo." Declaration in *O Globo,* August 29, 1967.

Aragão, Raimundo Moniz de. Interviews, Rio de Janeiro, November 4, 1965; October 11, 1966.

Arraes, Miguel. *O Povo no Poder*. (Speech given in São Paulo May 22, 1963). São Paulo: Editôra Fulgor, 1963.

————. *Palavra de Arraes*. Rio de Janeiro: Editôra Civilização Brasileira, c. 1965.

Arruda, Ângelo Simões. Interviews, São Paulo, November 16 and December 3, 1965.

Ayres Filho, Paulo. Interview, São Paulo, November 23, 1965.

Bailey, Norman A., ed. *Latin America: Politics, Economics, and Hemispheric Security*. The Center for Strategic Studies. New York: Frederick A. Praeger, Publisher, 1965.

Baker, Herbert W. Interviews, Rio de Janeiro, October 11, 1966; October 6, 1967.

————, *et al*. "Labor Directory: Brazil." Mimeographed report (91 pages). Rio de Janeiro, American Embassy, 1968.

Baklanoff, Eric N., ed. *New Perspectives of Brazil*. Nashville: Vanderbilt University Press, 1966.

Baldessarini, Hugo. Letter in *O Estado de S. Paulo*, dateline Rio de Janeiro, April 21, 1956.

Bandeira, Luís Alberto Moniz. *O 24 de Agôsto de Jânio Quadros*. Rio de Janeiro: Editôra Melso, 1961.

————. *O Caminho da Revolução Brasileira*. Rio de Janeiro: Editôra Melso, n.d.

Barata, Júlio. Interview, Rio de Janeiro, December 16, 1965.

Barbosa, Gustavo Simões. Interview, Rio de Janeiro, December 16, 1967.

Barreto, Lêda. *Julião—Nordeste—Revolução*. Rio de Janeiro: Editôra Civilização Brasileira, 1963.

Barros, Ademar de. "Pró Brasília Fiant Eximia! Discurso do Governador Adhemar de Barros, na Concentração Democrática do Dia 22 de Junho de 1963." (Mimeographed.)

————. Interview, São Paulo, December 1, 1965.

Barros, Adirson de. *Ascensão e Queda de Miguel Arraes*. Rio de Janeiro: Editôra Equador, 1965.

————. "Por Que Jango Caiu." *O Cruzeiro* (Extra), April 10, 1964.

Barturem, Padre José. Interview, Salvador, October 14, 1967.

Basbaum, Leoncio. *História Sincera da Republica, Vol. IV: de Jânio Quadros a Costa e Silva (1961–1967)*. São Paulo: Editôra Fulgor, 1968.

————. Interviews, São Paulo, November 16, 1966; November 5 and 24, 1967.

Bastos, Amélia Molina and other officers of the Campanha da Mulher pela Democracia (CAMDE). Interview, Rio de Janeiro, December 13, 1965.

Bastos, Joaquim Justino Alves. *Encontro com o Tempo.* Pôrto Alegre: Editôra Globo, 1965.

Batista, Ernesto de Melo. Interviews, Rio de Janeiro, December 18, 1965; October 13 and 29, 1966; December 4, 1967.

Bemis, George W. *From Crisis to Revolution: Monthly Case Studies.* Los Angeles: School of Public Administration, University of Southern California, 1964.

Berle, Adolf A. Interview, Austin, March 8, 1963.

Bezerra, Gregório. *Eu, Gregório Bezerra, Acuso!* n.p., 1967.

————. Interview, Recife, October 24, 1967.

Biblioteca da Câmara dos Deputados. "Bibliografia sôbre a Revolução de 31 de Março." *Boletim da Biblioteca da Câmara dos Deputados,* 13, no. 2 (July–December 1964), 499–514.

Biblioteca do Exército. *A Revolução de 31 de Março: 2º Aniversário.* Rio de Janeiro: Biblioteca do Exército, 1966.

Boone, William T. Report regarding Lacerda's television speech of April 1, 1964.

Borer, Cecil. Interview, Rio de Janeiro, October 7, 1966.

Borer, Charles. Interviews, Rio de Janeiro, October 5, 1966; October 6, 1967.

Borges, Gustavo. "Operação Salame. Coronel Gustavo Borges Conta para 'O Cruzeiro' a História Secreta da Revolução." *O Cruzeiro,* May 30, 1964.

Borges, Mauro. *O Golpe em Goiás: História de uma Grande Traição.* Rio de Janeiro: Editôra Civilização Brasileira, 1965.

Botto, Carlos Penna. "A Façanha do Tamandaré." *Manchete,* no. 188 (November 24, 1955).

————. Interviews, Rio de Janeiro, October 27, 1965; October 3, 1966; December 10, 1967.

Braga, Cláudio. Interview, Montevideo, November 16, 1967.

Braga, Nei. Interview, Rio de Janeiro, December 21, 1965.

Brancante, Eldino F. Interviews, São Paulo, November 23 and 24, 1965; December 3, 1965; November 19 and 20, 1967.

Brancante, Maria Helena. "Coube-me a Honrosa Delegação de Saudar o General-de-Divisão Sebastião Dalyzio Menna Barreto." Paper presented at meeting of the Instituto Histórico e Geográfico de São Paulo, June 5, 1965. (8 typewritten pages.)

Branco, Carlos Castello. "O Dia Seguinte." *Realidade*, II, no. 20 (November 1967).

Branco, Humberto de Alencar Castello. "Solução Dada ao Inquérito Policial Militar . . . acusações levantadas contra os Capitães José Carlos Santos Júnior e Creso Cardoso da Cunha Coimbra." Belém, February 16, 1960. (7 typewritten pages.)

Brandini, Roberto. Interview, São Paulo, November 24, 1965.

Brasil, Urgente. Weekly newspaper. Editôra Veritas, São Paulo, issues for 1963.

Brazil Herald. Brazil's only English-language daily newspaper.

Brito, Antônio Ferreira de Oliveira. Interview, Brasília, October 20, 1965.

Brito, Felix Pacheco Raimundo de. Interview, Rio de Janeiro, December 14, 1965.

Brizola, Leonel. *Organização dos "Grupos de Onze Companheiros" ou "Comandos Nacionalistas."* Rio de Janeiro, 1963. (11-page brochure.)

————. Interviews, Pôrto Alegre, February 3, 1962; Atlántida, Uruguay, November 14, 1967.

Bulhões, Otávio Gouveia de. Interview, Rio de Janeiro, November 8, 1965.

Cabral, Carlos Castilho. *Tempos de Jânio e Outros Tempos.* Rio de Janeiro: Editôra Civilização Brasileira, 1962.

Cadernos do Nosso Tempo. Journal of Instituto Brasileiro de Economia, Sociologia, e Política (IBESP), Rio de Janeiro. 5 issues, 1953–1956.

Café Filho, João. *Do Sindicato ao Catete.* 2 vols. Rio de Janeiro: Livraria José Olympio, 1966.

————. Interviews, Rio de Janeiro, October 8 and December 20, 1965.

Callado, Antônio. *Tempo de Arraes: Padres e Comunistas na Revolução sem Violência.* 4th ed. Rio de Janeiro: José Alvaro, 1965.

Calmon, João. Interview, Rio de Janeiro, November 9, 1965.

Câmara, Hélder. *Revolução Dentro da Paz.* 2nd ed. Rio de Janeiro: Editôra Sabiá Ltda., 1968.

Campista, Ari. Interviews, Rio de Janeiro, October 4, 9, and 23, 1968.

Campos, Francisco. Interview, Rio de Janeiro, December 14, 1965.

Campos, Milton Soares de. Interview, Brasília, October 21, 1965.

Campos, Renato Carneiro. *Igreja, Política e Região.* Recife: Instituto Joaquim Nabuco de Pesquisas, 1967.

Campos, Roberto. Interviews, Rio de Janeiro, October 28 and December 1, 1966.

Canavó Filho, José. Statements to José Stacchini, *O Estado de S. Paulo*, June 13, 20, and 27, 1965.

Caó, Epitácio. *Carreirista da Traição.* 2nd ed. n.p.: Gernasa, 1964.

Capanema, Gustavo. Interview, Brasília, October 23, 1965.

Cardoso, Adauto Lúcio. Interview, Rio de Janeiro, December 15, 1965.

Carneiro, Glauco. "Forte de Copacabana Não Foi Tomado" (based on interview with César Montagna de Souza). *O Cruzeiro*, April 25, 1964.

―――. *História das Revoluções Brasileiras*, II (1930–1964). Preface and Comments by Osvaldo Torres Galvão. Rio de Janeiro: Edições O Cruzeiro, 1965.

Caruso, João. Interview, Uruguay, November 14, 1967.

Carvalho, Ferdinando de. Interviews, Rio de Janeiro, October 11, 1966; Curitiba, November 10, 1967.

Castro, Moacir Werneck de. Interview, Rio de Janeiro, December 2, 1967.

Castro, Viriato de. *Espada x Vassoura: Marechal Lott.* São Paulo: Palácio do Livro, 1959.

―――. *O Ex-Leão de São Manoel: Adhemar.* São Paulo: Palácio do Livro, 1960.

―――. *O Fenômeno Jânio Quadros.* São Paulo: Palácio do Livro, 1959.

Cavalcanti, Artur de Lima. Interviews, Recife, October 24 and 26, 1967.

Cavalcanti, Caio de Lima. Interviews, Rio de Janeiro, October 28, 1965; October 22, 1967.

Cavalcanti, Deocleciano de Holanda. Interview, Rio de Janeiro, December 18, 1968.

Cavalcanti, José Costa. Interview, Brasília, October 15, 1965.

Cavalcanti, Natalício Tenório. Interview, Caxias, Rio de Janeiro, December 7, 1968.

Cavalcanti, Paulo. Interview, Recife, October 25, 1967.

Cavalcanti, Sandra. Interview, Rio de Janeiro, October 21, 1966.

Cavalcanti, Themístocles Brandão. *Pareceres do Consultor Geral da República*, II (July–November 1955). Rio de Janeiro: Editôra A. Coelho Filho, 1956.

―――. Interview, Rio de Janeiro, October 8, 1965.

"O CGT: Império da Corrupção." *O Cruzeiro*, May 16, 1964.

Chaves, Sebastião. Interviews, São Paulo, November 20 and 22, 1967.

Cid, Pedro Vilela. Interview, Natal, October 18, 1968.

Coelho, Nilo de Souza. Interview, Brasília, October 15, 1965; Recife, October 27, 1967.

Comunismo no Brasil, O. 4 vols. Inquérito Policial Militar No. 709. Rio de Janeiro: Biblioteca do Exército, 1966–1967.

Cony, Carlos Heitor. *O Ato e o Fato: Crônicas Políticas.* 4th ed. Rio de Janeiro: Editôra Civilização Brasileira, 1964.

Corbisier, Roland. *Formação e Problema da Cultura Brasileira.* Rio de Janeiro: Instituto Superior de Estudos Brasileiros, 1960.

———. Interview, Rio de Janeiro, October 25, 1966.

Corrêa, Oscar Dias. Interviews, Brasília, October 18 and 22, 1965.

Correio da Manhã. Rio de Janeiro daily newspaper.

Correio Paulistano. São Paulo daily newspaper.

Costa, Edgard. *Os Grandes Julgamentos do Supremo Tribunal Federal,* III (1947–1955). Rio de Janeiro: Editôra Civilização Brasileira, 1964.

———. *A Legislação Eleitoral Brasileira: Histórico, Comentários e Sugestões.* n.p.: Departamento de Imprensa Nacional, 1964.

Costa, Joffre Gomes da. *Marechal Henrique Lott.* Rio de Janeiro: n.p., 1960.

Crespo, Padre Paulo. Interview, Recife, October 16, 1968.

Cruzeiro, O. Rio de Janeiro weekly magazine. Issues of 1955–1964. Also Extra Edition (Edição Histórica da Revolução) of April 10, 1964.

Cunha, Luís Fernando Bocaiuva. Interviews, Rio de Janeiro, December 5 and 18, 1968.

Cunha, Vasco Leitão da. Interview, Washington, June 24, 1966.

Dantas, Francisco San Tiago. *Idéias e Rumos para a Revolução Brasileira.* Rio de Janeiro: Livraria José Olympio, 1963.

Dantas, João Ribeiro. Interview, Rio de Janeiro, December 20, 1965.

Denys, Odílio. "Denis Conta Tudo." Separata da Entrevista Concedida pelo Mal. Odylio Denis à Revista *Fatos & Fotos,* May 2, 1964.

———. Interviews, Rio de Janeiro, December 14, 1965; November 29, 1966.

D'Horta, Oscar Pedroso. "As Rosas e as Pedras do Caminho de Lacerda." *Manchete,* August 12, 1967.

Diário do Congresso Nacional.

Diário de Notícias. Rio de Janeiro daily newspaper.

Dimas Filho, Nelson. *Costa e Silva: o Homem e o Líder.* Rio de Janeiro: Edições O Cruzeiro, 1966.

Dines, Alberto, *et al. Os Idos de Março e a Queda em Abril.* 2nd ed. Rio de Janeiro: José Alvaro, 1964.

Dória, Seixas. *Eu, Réu Sem Crime.* 3rd ed. Rio de Janeiro: Editôra Equador, n.d.

Dos Passos, John. *Brazil on the Move*. Garden City: Doubleday & Company, 1963.

Duarte, Paulo. Interviews, São Paulo, November 23 and 29, 1965; November 12, 1966.

Dubnic, Vladimir Reisky de. *Political Trends in Brazil*. Washington, D.C.: Public Affairs Press, 1968.

Dunne, George H. "Happening in São Paulo." *America*, September 23, 1967.

Dutra, Eloy. *IBAD: Sigla de Corrupção*. Rio de Janeiro: Editôra Civilização Brasileira, 1963.

Dutra, Eurico Gaspar. "Minha Vida Não Me Pertence" (statements to Mário de Moraes). *O Cruzeiro*, April 25, 1964.

Estado de S. Paulo, O. São Paulo daily newspaper.

Estatuto do Trabalhador Rural. Recife: Edição da Federação dos Trabalhadores de Pernambuco, 1963.

Estudos Sociais. Rio de Janeiro Communist journal. Nineteen issues appeared, 1958–1964.

Etcheverry, João. Interview, Rio de Janeiro, October 3, 1968.

Fadul, Wilson. Interview, Rio de Janeiro, November 1, 1967.

Fairbairn, Arnoldo Hasselmann. Interview, Rio de Janeiro, December 6, 1965.

Falcão, Armando. "Denúncia ao Povo Brasileiro." (Pamphlet transcribing declarations made to *Jornal do Brasil* and *O Estado de S. Paulo,* November 21, 1963.)

———. *Réus do Futuro*. Rio de Janeiro: O Cruzeiro, S. A., 1962.

———. Interviews, Rio de Janeiro, November 30, 1966; Tucson, May 19, 1968; Rio de Janeiro, October 6 and December 18, 1968.

Falconieri da Cunha, Olímpio. Interview, Rio de Janeiro, November 10, 1965.

Fatos & Fotos. Rio de Janeiro weekly magazine. Issues of 1963–1967. Also Extra edition (A Grande Rebelião) of April 4, 1964.

Federação das Associações Rurais do Estado de São Paulo. Mimeographed bulletin with observations about project of State Law No. 154 of March 30, 1960. São Paulo, May, 1960.

Fernal, Petrônio. Interview, Brasília, October 19, 1965.

Fernandes, Hélio. "Doze Heróis da Grande Vitória." *Tribuna da Imprensa*, April 3, 1964.

Ferraz, Otávio Marcondes. Interview, São Paulo, August 9, 1963.

Ferreira, Oliveiros S. *As Fôrças Armadas e o Desafio da Revolução*. Rio de Janeiro: Edições GRD, 1964.

Figueiredo, João Batista Leopoldo de. Interview, São Paulo, November 26, 1965.

Fischlowitz, Estanislau. Memorandum, August 1966.

Fleury, Heber Perillo. Interview, São Paulo, November 24, 1965.

Folha do Norte. Belém newspaper.

Franco, Afonso Arinos de Melo. *A Escalada: Memórias*. Rio de Janeiro: Livraria José Olympio, 1965.

————. *Planalto: Memórias*. Rio de Janeiro: Livraria José Olympio, 1968.

————. Interviews, Brasília, October 14 and 16, 1965; Rio de Janeiro, November 4, 1966; December 15, 1967.

————, and Raul Pilla. *Presidencialismo ou Parlamentarismo*. Rio de Janeiro: Livraria José Olympio, 1958.

————. SEE ALSO Quadros, Jânio.

Freire, Paulo. Interview, Maipú, Chile, June 28, 1967.

Fundo de Ação Social. Circular letter, 1962; statement of October 18, 1965 (São Paulo).

Furtado, Celso. *Um Projeto para o Brasil*. 4th ed. Rio de Janeiro: Editôra Saga S. A., 1968.

Gallotti, Luís. Interview, Rio de Janeiro, December 13, 1965.

Galvão, Flávio. Interview, São Paulo, November 24, 1965.

Gama, José Santos Saldanha da. Interview, Rio de Janeiro, October 24, 1966.

Garcez, Lucas Nogueira. Interview, São Paulo, November 22, 1965.

Gazeta, A. São Paulo daily newspaper.

Globo, O. Rio de Janeiro daily newspaper.

Godinho, Padre Antônio de Oliveira. Interview, São Paulo, November 21, 1965.

————. Translation (into Portuguese) of *Encíclica Mater et Magistra*. Sorocaba, São Paulo: Cadernos da Faculdade de Filosofia, Ciências e Letras de Sorocaba, 1962.

Gomieri, Onofre Valentin. *Jânio Quadros o Insaciavel de Poder*. n.p.: Editôra e Distribuidora São Paulo–Rio, 1960.

Gordon, Lincoln. Conversation, Rio de Janeiro, December 18, 1965; interview, Washington, D.C., January 17, 1969.

Goulart, João. *Desenvolvimento e Independência: Discursos, 1961*. Brasília: n.p., 1962.

————. Interview, Montevideo, November 17, 1967.

Goulart, Maurício. Interview, São José do Rio Prêto, São Paulo, November 19, 1968.

Guedes, Carlos Luís. "Gen. Guedes Relata o Comêco do Movimento." *Correio da Manhã*, April 3, 1964.

———. Interview, São Paulo, November 18, 1965.

Guimarães, Napoleão Alencastro. Interview, Rio de Janeiro, October 8, 1965.

Gudin, Eugênio. *Análise de Problemas Brasileiros, 1958–1964*. Rio de Janeiro: Livraria Agir Editôra, 1965.

Hall, Clarence W. "The Country That Saved Itself." *The Reader's Digest*, November 1964.

Halperin, Ernst. "Peking and the Latin American Communists." *The China Quarterly*, no. 29 (January–March 1967).

Harding, Timothy F. "Revolution Tomorrow: The Failure of the Left in Brazil." *Studies on the Left*, IV, no. 4 (Fall 1964).

Heck, Sílvio. "Depoimento sôbre Renúncia de Jânio 'Estarrece' Heck" (declaration). *Jornal do Brasil*, November 2, 1967.

———. Interview, Rio de Janeiro, December 13, 1965.

Henrique, João. *Organização Agrária sem Comunismo*. 2nd ed. São Paulo: Editôra Ave-Maria, 1966.

Herrera, Heitor A. Interviews, Rio de Janeiro, November 29 and December 7, 1965.

Hirschman, Albert O. *Journeys toward Progress*. New York: The Twentieth-Century Fund, 1963.

Honsi, Alberto. Interview, Brasília, October 19, 1965.

Horowitz, Irving Louis. *Revolution in Brazil: Politics and Society in a Developing Nation*. New York: E. T. Dutton & Co., Inc., 1964.

Huber, Gilberto. Interview, Rio de Janeiro, November 29, 1965.

Imprensa Popular. Communist daily newspaper. Rio de Janeiro, 1955, 1956, 1957.

Institute for the Comparative Study of Political Systems. *Brazil: Election Factbook*, no. 2. Washington, D.C.: n.p., September 1965. (Major contributors: Charles Daugherty, James Rowe, and Ronald Schneider.)

Instituto Brasileiro de Ação Democrática. *Recomendações sobre Reforma Agrária*. Rio de Janeiro: Edição do IBAD, 1961.

Instituto Brasileiro de Relações Internacionais. "A Compra das Concessionárias de Energia Elétrica." Parts I and II. *Revista Brasileira de Política Internacional*, VIII, nos. 30, 31, and 32 (June, September, and December 1965).

Jaguaribe, Hélio. "As Eleições de 62." *Tempo Brasileiro,* I, no. 2 (December 1962).

——. *Desenvolvimento Econômica e Desenvolvimento Político.* Rio de Janeiro: Editôra Fundo de Cultura S. A., 1962.

——. *O Nacionalismo na Atualidade Brasileira.* Rio de Janeiro: Instituto Superior de Estudos Brasileiros, 1958.

Jorge, Jerônimo. "Os Serviços Secretos Prepararam a Revolta de Abril." *O Estado de S. Paulo,* April 12, 1964.

Jorge, Salomão. *A Vida do Marechal Lott: Com a Visão Panorâmica da Obra Monumental do Presidente Juscelino Kubitschek de Oliveira.* São Paulo: Gráfica e Editôra Edigraf, 1960.

Jornal, O. Rio de Janeiro daily newspaper.

Jornal do Brasil. Rio de Janeiro daily newspaper. (See especially "UNE Acaba 27 Anos depois de Surgir Combatendo a Ditadura," November 8, 1964.)

Jornal do Commercio. Rio de Janeiro daily newspaper.

Julião, Francisco. *Até Quarta, Isabela!* Rio de Janeiro: Editôra Civilização Brasileira, n.d.

——. *Que São as Ligas Camponesas?* Rio de Janeiro: Editôra Civilização Brasileira, 1962.

Jurema, Abelardo. *Sexta-Feira, 13: Os Últimos Dias do Govêrno João Goulart.* 2nd ed. Rio de Janeiro: Edições O Cruzeiro, 1964.

Kelly, José Eduardo do Prado. Interview, Rio de Janeiro, October 8, 1965.

Krieger, Daniel. Interview, Brasília, October 13, 1965.

Kruel, Amauri. Interviews, São Paulo, November 15 and 30, 1965; Guanabara, October 21, 1967.

Lacerda, Carlos. *O Caminho da Liberdade.* 2nd ed. Rio de Janeiro: Graf. Ouvidor, 1957.

——. *Crítica e Autocrítica.* Rio de Janeiro: Editôra Nova Fronteira, 1966.

——. "Porque Encontrei Jango." *Fatos & Fotos,* VII, no. 349 (October 7, 1967).

——. "Rosas e Pedras do Meu Caminho." *Manchete,* chaps. 10, 11, and 12, nos. 791–793 (June 17 and 24, and July 1, 1967).

——. Interview, Rio de Janeiro, October 11, 1967.

Lacerda, Flávio Suplici de. Interview, Brasília, October 16, 1965.

Lago, Mário. *1º de Abril: Estórias para a História.* Rio de Janeiro: Editôra Civilização Brasileira, 1964.

Lameirão, José Chaves. Declaration at 24th Criminal Court, Guanabara State, re Processo No. 9899 ("Movimento de Aragarças"), May 8, 1961. (3 typewritten pages.) Copies in files of Luís Mendes de Morais Neto and in Latin American Collection, The University of Texas, Austin, Texas.

Lapouge, Gilles and Ruy Mesquita. *31/3*. São Paulo: Anhambi, 1964.

Leal, Vitór Nunes. Interview, Brasília, October 22, 1965.

Lee, Fernando. Interview, São Paulo, November 22, 1965.

Leeds, Anthony. "Brazil and the Myth of Francisco Julião." In *Politics of Change in Latin America,* ed. by Joseph Maier and Richard W. Weatherhead. New York: Frederick A. Praeger, 1964.

Leite, Cleantho de Paiva. Interviews, Santiago, Chile, June 27 and 28, 1967.

Levy, Herbert V. *Liberdade e Justiça Social*. 2nd ed. São Paulo: Livraria Martins, 1962.

———. "Por Que a Reforma da Constituição?" (Speech in Congress, May 29, 1963.)

———. Interviews, São Paulo, August 9, 1963; November 15, 1965; Brasília, October 20, 1965.

Liebof, Jack. Interviews, São Paulo, November 9 and 10, 1966; November 9, 1967.

Lima, Afonso de Albuquerque. Interviews, Rio de Janeiro, September 12, 1963; November 9, 1965; October 8, 1966; December 5, 1967; October 10, 1968.

Lima, Francisco Negrão de. Interview, Rio de Janeiro, December 20, 1966.

Lima, Hermes. *Idéias e Figuras*. Rio de Janeiro: Ministério da Educacão e Cultura, 1957.

———. Interview, Brasília, October 17, 1965; São Paulo, November 21, 1968.

Lima Sobrinho, Alexandre José Barbosa. Interview, Rio de Janeiro, October 11, 1967.

Lodygensky, Wladimir. Interviews, Brasília, October 21 and 22, 1965; São Paulo, November 16, 1965.

Lopes, Lucas. Interviews, Rio de Janeiro, October 30, 1965; October 4, 1966.

Lott, Henrique Baptista Duffles Teixeira. "Depoimento de Lott." *Manchete,* November 19, 1955.

———. Interview, Rio de Janeiro, August 27, 1963.

Loureiro Júnior, José. *O Golpe de Novembro e Outros Discursos*. Rio de Janeiro: Livraria Clássica Brasileira, 1957.

————. *Parlamentarismo e Presidencialismo.* São Paulo: Editôra Revista dos Tribunais, 1962.

————. Interviews, Brasília, October 14, 1965; São Paulo, November 16, 1965.

Luz, Carlos. Speech in Chamber of Deputies, November 14, 1955. Given in Bento Munhoz da Rocha, *Radiografia de Novembro*, pp. 133–154.

————. "Carlos Luz Presta Seu Depoimento para a História" (interview given to Arlindo Silva). *O Cruzeiro*, December 3, 1955.

Macarini, Paulo. Interview, Brasília, October 21, 1965.

Machado, F. Zenha. *Os Últimos Dias do Govêrno de Vargas.* Rio de Janeiro: Editôra Lux Ltda., 1955.

Maciel Júnior, Luís. Interview, São Paulo, November 24, 1965.

Magaldi, Antônio Pereira. Interview, São Paulo, November 18, 1968.

Magalhães, Gualter Maria Menezes de. Interview (aboard *Tamandaré*), Rio de Janeiro, December 6, 1965.

Magalhães, Ivo. Interview, Montevideo, November 16, 1967.

Magalhães, Juraci. Interview, Brasília, October 21, 1965.

Maghenzani, Hélcio. Interview, São Paulo, November 14, 1968.

Maia Neto, João Cândido. *Brasil—Guerra-Quente na América Latina.* Rio de Janeiro: Editôra Civilização Brasileira, 1965.

————. *Coluna por Um.* 2nd ed. Rio de Janeiro: Edições Gernasa, n.d.

————. Interview, Montevideo, November 16, 1967.

Maier, Joseph and Richard W. Weatherhead, eds. *Politics of Change in Latin America.* New York: Frederick A. Praeger.

Manchete. Rio de Janeiro weekly magazine. Issues of 1955–1964. Also Edição Histórica (April 1964) and Suplemento Especial (sponsored by Cia. Siderúrgica Nacional, Cia. Vale do Rio Doce, Petrobrás and Eletrobrás): "O que Jango ja fez," (1963).

Maquis. Rio de Janeiro anti-Communist weekly magazine. Issues of 1961 and 1962.

Marcondes, J. V. Freitas. *Radiografia da Liderança Sindical Paulista.* São Paulo: Instituto Cultural do Trabalho, 1964.

Marinha do Brasil. *Cruzador Tamandaré.* n.p., n.d.

Marroquim, Murilo. "Ação do IV Exército Contra Arraes." *O Cruzeiro*, April 25, 1964.

Marshall, Andrew. *Brazil.* New York: Walker and Company, 1966.

Martineli, Osneli. Interview, Rio de Janeiro, October 12, 1966.

Martins, Antônio Navas. Interview, São Paulo, November 22, 1968.

Matias, Rodrigues. *Marcha da Família com Deus pela Liberdade: Um Ato de Fé numa Hora de Trevas.* São Paulo: Empresa Gráfica Tietê, 1964.

Maurel Filho, Emílio. Interview, Rio de Janeiro, October 11, 1965.

Mazzilli, Ranieri. Interview, Rio de Janeiro, December 12, 1965.

Meireles, João Carlos de Souza. Interviews, São Paulo, November 20 and 22, 1967.

Melo, Humberto. Interview, Rio de Janeiro, November 30, 1967.

Melo, Márcio de Souza e. Interview, Rio de Janeiro, December 17, 1965.

Melo Filho, Murilo. "Mamede." *O Cruzeiro,* December 25, 1965.

Melo, Nelson de. Interview, Rio de Janeiro, October 28, 1965.

Mesquita Filho, Júlio de. Interview, São Paulo, November 20, 1965.

Mesquita, Ruy. Interview, São Paulo, December 2, 1965.

―――, and Gilles Lapouge. *31/3.* São Paulo: Anhambi, 1964.

Meyer, Celso. Interview, Rio de Janeiro, December 12, 1967.

Mikhailov, Syrgei. Interview, Rio de Janeiro, October 25, 1966.

Moniz, Edmundo. *O Golpe de Abril.* Rio de Janeiro: Editôra Civilização Brasileira, 1965.

Montoro, André Franco. *Salário-Família: Promoção Humana do Trabalhador.* Rio de Janeiro: Livraria Agir, 1963.

―――. Interview, São Paulo, November 29, 1965.

Morais Neto, Luís Mendes de. Declaration at 24th Criminal Court, Guanabara State, re Processo No. 9899 ("Movimento de Aragarças"), January 26, 1960. (6 typewritten pages.)

―――. Interviews, Rio de Janeiro, October 19 and November 25, 1966 (at which Dr. Mendes de Morais Neto provided complete collection of documents on the Aragarças rebellion).

Morais Neto, Prudente de. Interviews, Rio de Janeiro, August 31, 1963; October 6, 1965; December 13, 1966; October 20, 1967.

Morel, Edmar. *O Golpe Começou em Washington.* Rio de Janeiro: Editôra Civilização Brasileira, 1965.

Morrison, de Lesseps S. *Latin American Mission.* New York: Simon and Schuster, 1965.

Moss, Gabriel Grün. "Grum Moss Aponta Engôdo na Versão de Jânio Quadros" (declaration). *Jornal do Brasil,* November 7, 1967.

―――. Interviews, Rio de Janeiro, December 12, 1965; December 4, 1968.

Moura, Arthur S. Interview, Rio de Janeiro, January 7, 1968.

Mourão Filho, Olímpio. Interviews, Rio de Janeiro, October 9, 1965; November 29, 1966.

Movimento de Educação de Base. *Viver E Lutar: 2º Livro de Leitura Para Adultos.* n.p.: MEB, October, 1963.

Müller, Filinto. Interview, Brasília, October 15, 1965.

Mundo Ilustrado. Rio de Janeiro weekly. Issues of 1954 and 1959.

Muniz, Antônio Guedes. Interview, Rio de Janeiro, December 7, 1965.

Nasser, David. "Caiu a República dos Compadres." *O Cruzeiro,* December 3, 1955.

————. *João sem Mêdo.* Rio de Janeiro: Edições O Cruzeiro, 1965.

Nazario, Joaquim Pinto. Interview, São Paulo, November 14, 1968.

Neves, Tancredo. Interview, Rio de Janeiro, October 7, 1965.

Nogueira, José Bonifácio Coutinho. Interview, São Paulo, November 22, 1965.

Notícias de Hoje. Communist daily newspaper. São Paulo. Issues of 1955 and 1956.

Novos Rumos. Communist weekly newspaper. Rio de Janeiro. Issues of 1959–1964.

Nunes, Janari Gentil. Interview, Brasília, October 18, 1965.

Oliveira, Croaci Cavalheiro de. Interview, Brasília, October 19, 1965.

Oliveira, João Adil de. Interview, Rio de Janeiro, December 20, 1965.

Oliveira, Mário Lopes de. Interview, Rio de Janeiro, October 31, 1968.

Pacheco, Sigefredo. Interview, Brasília, October 16, 1965.

Padilha, Raimundo Delmiriano. Interview, Brasília, October 13, 1965.

Paiva, Glycon de. "Petrobrás como Banco da Subversão Nacional e Escola Prática de Corrupção." *Jornal do Brasil,* February 16, 1964.

Partido Comunista Brasileiro. "Teses Para Discussão." Special supplement of *Novos Rumos,* March 27–April 2, 1964.

Pearson, Neale J. *Small Farmer and Worker Pressure Groups in Brazil.* Ann Arbor, Michigan: University Microfilms, 1968.

Pedreira, Fernando. *Março 31: Civis e Militares no Processo da Crise Brasileira.* Rio de Janeiro: José Alvaro, 1964.

Peixoto, Alzira Vargas do Amaral. "A Vida de Getúlio Conforme Narração ao Jornalista Raul Giudicelli." Rio de Janeiro *Fátos & Fotos* magazine series, June 15, 1963, to Chap. 13 on October 5, 1963.

Peixoto, Ernâni do Amaral. Interview, Brasília, October 15, 1965.

Pelacani, Dante. Interview, São Paulo, November 24, 1968.

Penido, Osvaldo M. Interviews, Rio de Janeiro, September 6, 1963; October 5, 1965; October 10, 1967.

Pequenho, Syndulpho de Azevedo. Interview, Rio de Janeiro, October 28, 1968.

Peralva, Osvaldo. *O Retrato*. Pôrto Alegre: Editôra Globo, 1962.

———. Interviews, Rio de Janeiro, September 14, 1963; October 5, 1967.

Pereira, J. *Bilhetinhos de Jânio*. 2nd ed. São Paulo: Editôra e Distribuidora Musa, 1959.

Pieruccetti, Oswaldo. Letter of January 18, 1968 to J.W.F.D.

Pilla, Raul. Interview, Brasília, October 13, 1965.

———, and Afonso Arinos de Melo Franco. *Presidencialismo ou Parlamentarismo*. Rio de Janeiro: Livraria José Olympio, 1958.

Pinheiro, Edward Catete. Interview, Brasília, October 13, 1965.

Pinheiro Neto, João. *A Ilusão Monetarista*. Rio de Janeiro: Editôra Forense, 1968.

———. Interview, Rio de Janeiro, October 8, 1968.

Pinna, Gerson de. Interview, Rio de Janeiro, October 14, 1966.

Pinto, José de Magalhães. Interview, Rio de Janeiro, December 5, 1967.

Pinto, Olavo Bilac. *Guerra Revolucionária*. Rio de Janeiro: Editôra Forense, 1964.

———. Interview, Brasília, October 14, 1965.

PN (Política & Negócios). Weekly magazine. Rio de Janeiro. Issues of 1961.

Poerner, Arthur José. *O Poder Jovem: História da Participação Política dos Estudantes Brasileiros*. Rio de Janeiro: Editôra Civilização Brasileira, 1968.

Poland, Haroldo Cecil. Interview, Rio de Janeiro, December 9, 1965.

Porro, Alessandro. "Porque Êle É um Cassado." *Realidade*, August 1967.

Prado Júnior, Caio. Interviews, São Paulo, November 17, 1965; November 9, 1966.

Prado, Sálvio de Almeida. Interview, São Paulo, November 18, 1965.

Prestes, Luiz Carlos. "Informe de Balanço do Comitê Central do Brasil." *Problemas*, no. 64 (December 1954–February 1955).

———. *Os Comunistas e o Govêrno Jânio Quadros*. Rio de Janeiro: Editôra Aliança do Brasil Ltda., 1961.

———. *Por Que os Comunistas Apóiam Lott e Jango*. Rio de Janeiro: Editorial Vitória, 1960.

Previati, Olavo. Interview, Rio de Janeiro, December 18, 1968.

Primeiro Exército, Comando da 4a Região Militar, 4a Divisão da Infantaria e Guarnição de Juiz de Fora, Ajudância Geral. *Relatório da Revolução Democrática Iniciada pela 4a RM e 4a DI em 31 de Março de 1964*. Special Bulletin, Juiz de Fora, May 9, 1964.

Problemas: Revista Mensal de Cultura Política. Communist monthly. Issues 60–73 (August 1954–June 1956).

Pupo Neto, Trajano. Interview, São Paulo, November 25, 1965.

Quadros, Eloá. Press statement of August 26, 1961 (as reported in *O Estado de S. Paulo*).

Quadros, Jânio. "Brazil's New Foreign Policy." *Foreign Affairs*, 40, no. 1 (October 1961).

—————, *Mensagem ao Congresso Nacional Remetida pelo Presidente da República na Abertura da Sessão Legislativa de 1961*. Brasília: Departamento de Imprensa Nacional, 1961.

—————, and Afonso Arinos de Melo Franco. *História do Povo Brasileiro*. 2nd ed. Vol. 6. São Paulo: J. Quadros Editôres Culturais S. A., 1968.

—————, and Afonso Arinos de Mello Franco. "O Porquê da Renúncia." *Realidade,* II, no. 20 (November 1967).

Rabello, Ophelina. *A Rede Sindical Paulista: Tentativa de Caracterização*. São Paulo: Instituto Cultural do Trabalho, 1965.

Rabelo, Genival. "O Inquérito." *PN (Política & Negócios)*, XXII, no. 498 (October 7, 1961).

Rademaker Grünewald, Augusto Hamann. Interview, Rio de Janeiro, December 15, 1965.

Ramos, Guerreiro. *Mito e Verdade da Revolução Brasileira*. Rio de Janeiro: Zahar Editôres, 1963.

Ramos, João Batista. Interviews, Brasília, October 18 and 20, 1965.

Ramos, Mário Braga. Interview, Brasília, October 19, 1965.

Ramos, Plínio de Abreu. *Brasil, 11 de Novembro*. São Paulo: Editôra Fulgor, 1960.

Ramos, Rodrigo Otávio Jordão. Interviews, Rio de Janeiro, November 11, 1965; Recife, October 24, 1967.

Razão, A. Weekly newspaper published in São Paulo. Nos. 32–52 (March–August 1952).

Realidade. São Paulo monthly magazine.

"A Rebelião de Aragarças." *Mundo Ilustrado*, Rio de Janeiro, December 12 and 19, 1959.

Reifschneider, Telmo Becker. Interview (aboard *Tamandaré*), Rio de Janeiro, December 6, 1965.

Reis, Levi Aarão. Interviews, Rio de Janeiro, December 13 and 15, 1965; October 13, 1966.

Riani, Clodsmidt. Interview, Juiz de Fora, November 2, 1968.

Ribeiro, Darci. Interview, Montevideo, November 13, 1967.

Ribeiro, Paulo de Assis. "Análise Sócio-Político-Eleitoral." Unpublished manuscript prepared shortly before Goulart's fall.

Riff, Raul. Interviews, Rio de Janeiro, October 2 and 9, and December 5, 1968.

Rocha, Anísio. "Libelo contra a Infiltração Comunista no Atual Govêrno." (Speech in Chamber of Deputies.)

Rocha, Bento Munhoz da. *Radiografia de Novembro.* 2nd ed. Rio de Janeiro: Editôra Civilização Brasileira, 1961.

————. Interview, Curitiba, November 28, 1965.

Rocha, Francisco Brochado da. *Mensagem ao Congresso Nacional Remetida pelo Presidente do Conselho de Ministros, Solicitando Delegação de Poderes para Legislar.* Brasília: Departmento de Imprensa Nacional, 1962.

Rodrigues, Nelson. *Memórias.* Rio de Janeiro: Edições Correio da Manhã, 1967.

Rotta, José. Interview, São Paulo, November 30, 1965.

Rowe, James W. "The 'Revolution' and the 'System': Notes on Brazilian Politics," *American University Field Staff Reports,* XII, nos. 3, 4, 5 (July and August 1966).

Sá, Gilberto Crockatt de. Interviews, Rio de Janeiro, October 9 and 11, 1967; December 12 and 17, 1968.

Sá, Mem de. *O Problema da Remessa de Lucros.* Rio de Janeiro: Associação Comercial da Guanabara, 1962.

Salgado, Plínio. Interview, Brasília, October 14, 1965.

Sampaio, Hélio Garnier. Interview, Rio de Janeiro, October 24, 1966.

Sanders, Thomas G. "Brazil's Catholic Left." *America,* November 18, 1967.

Santos, Rui. Interview, Brasília, October 15, 1965.

Santos, Waltrudes. Interviews, Rio de Janeiro, September 30 and October 25, 1968.

São Paulo State, Secretaria da Segurança Pública, Departamento de Ordem Política e Social. *Relatório: Inquérito Instaurado contra Luiz Carlos Prestes e Outros por Ocasião da Revolução de Março de 1964.* São Paulo: Serviço Gráfico da Secretaria da Segurança Pública, 1964.

Sarmento, Siseno. Interview, São Paulo, November 21, 1967.

Sátiro e Souza, Ernâni Aires. Interview, Brasília, October 22, 1965.

Schenberg, Mário. Interview, São Paulo, November 14, 1966.

Siekman, Philip. "When Executives Turned Revolutionaries." *Fortune,* September 1964.

Silva, Antônio Carlos Pacheco e. *A Guerra Subversiva em Marcha.* São Paulo: Centro das Indústrias do Estado de São Paulo, 1961.

————. Interview, São Paulo, November 20, 1967.

Silva, Arlindo. "As Cartas Secretas dos Generais a Brizola." *O Cruzeiro,* August 15, 1964.

Silva, Evandro Lins e. Interview, Brasília, October 17, 1965.

Silva, Golberi do Couto e. Interviews, Rio de Janeiro, December 8, 1965; October 4, 1966.

Silva, Luís Antônio Gama e. Interview, São Paulo, November 18, 1966.

Silva Filho, Leonides Alves da. Interview, Recife, October 14, 1968.

Silveira, Paulo. Interview, Rio de Janeiro, December 17, 1968.

Silveira, Regina Figueiredo and other officers of the União Cívica Feminina. Interview, São Paulo, November 24, 1965.

Simonsen, Mário Henrique. *A Experiência Inflacionária no Brasil.* Guanabara: Instituto de Pesquisas e Estudos Sociais (IPÊS), 1964.

Skidmore, Thomas E. *Politics in Brazil, 1930–1964: An Experiment in Democracy.* New York: Oxford University Press, 1967.

Soares, Irineu de Macedo. Interview, Rio de Janeiro, November 1, 1966.

Sodré, Nelson Werneck. *A História da Imprensa no Brasil.* Rio de Janeiro: Editôra Civilização Brasileira, 1966.

———. *História Militar do Brasil.* Rio de Janeiro: Editôra Civilização Brasileira, 1965.

———. Interview, Rio de Janeiro, December 9, 1967.

Souza, J. J. Moscardo de. Interview, New York, September 22, 1968.

Spinelli, Mário. "A Marcha da Coluna Meira Matos," n.d. (A publication on one sheet.)

Stacchini, José. [Articles on José Canavó Filho.] *O Estado de S. Paulo,* June 13, 20 and 27, 1965.

———. *Março 64: Mobilização da Audácia.* São Paulo: Companhia Editôra Nacional, 1965.

Sussekind, Arnaldo. Interviews, Rio de Janeiro, October 26, 1965; December 19, 1967.

Tarso, Paulo de. "Explicação Inicial." May 1963. Introduction to the publication of two of his speeches in Congress.

———. Interviews, Santiago, Chile, June 26 and 27, 1967.

Távora, Araken. *Brasil, 1º de Abril.* 2nd ed. Rio de Janeiro: Bruno Buccini, 1964.

Távora, Juarez. "Entrevistado por Arnaldo Nogueira; Programa 'Falando Francamente'—T. V. Tupi—Rio, 22 de Novembro de 1956." (Typewritten.)

———. "Esclarecimento Prestados pelo Marechal Juarez Távora, á Margem da Escolha do Marechal Castelo Branco para a Presidência da República em Abril de 1964." Rio de Janeiro, October 12, 1966. (Type-written for J.W.F.D.) Full text given in Leoncio Basbaum, *História Sincera da República,* IV, 135–137.

————. "Esquema de Ação para Tentar Dirimir a Atual Crise Político-Militar." Rio de Janeiro, March 1956. (Typewritten memorandum.)

————. "Porque Desisti de Ser Candidato em 4 de Abril Findo." 1955. (Typewritten memorandum.)

————. "Pronunciamento de Juarez sobre os Acontecimentos Político-Militares." In *Diário de Notícias, O Jornal,* and other newspapers, November 22, 1956.

————. Interviews, Rio de Janeiro, October 5, 1966; October 20, and November 27, 1967.

Teixeira, Francisco. Interview, Rio de Janeiro, November 28, 1967.

Tejo, Limeira. *Jango: Debate sôbre a Crise dos Nossos Tempos.* Rio de Janeiro: Editorial Andes, 1957.

Telles, Jover. *O Movimento Sindical no Brasil.* Rio de Janeiro: Editorial Vitória Limitada, 1962.

Therry, Leonard D. "Dominant Power Components in the Brazilian University Student Movement Prior to April 1964." *Journal of Inter-American Studies,* VII, no. 1 (January 1965).

Torres, João Camillo de Oliveira. *Cartilha do Parlamentarismo.* Belo Horizonte: Editôra Itatiaia, 1962.

Tribuna da Imprensa. Rio de Janeiro daily newspaper.

Tuma, Nicolau. Interview, Brasília, October 14, 1965.

Última Hora. Daily newspaper. Use was made of São Paulo and Rio de Janeiro editions.

U. S. Congress. Senate. Hearing before the Subcommittee to Investigate the Administration of the Internal Security Act and Other Internal Security Laws of the Committee on the Judiciary, 88th Cong., 1st sess., October 2, 1963. *Documentation of Communist Penetration in Latin America,* U. S. Government Printing Office, 1964 (Appendix II) and 1965 (Appendix I and Testimony of Jules Dubois).

Valadares, Benedito. Interview, Brasília, October 21, 1965.

Vale, Edmundo Jordão Amorim do. Interviews, Rio de Janeiro, September 7, 1963; November 10, 1965.

Vampré, Waldeck Lisboa. Interview, Rio de Janeiro, October 13, 1966.

Veliz, Claudio, ed. *The Politics of Conformity in Latin America.* London, New York, Toronto: Oxford University Press, 1967.

Vellozo, Sérgio Luiz Rocha. Interview, Rio de Janeiro, October 8, 1968.

Veloso, Haroldo. Interviews, Marietta, Georgia, January 6–7, 1966.

Veloso, Padre Pedro. Interviews, Rio de Janeiro, December 9, 1965; October 18, 1966.

Vereker, Anthony. Letters to J. W. F. D.; interview, Rio de Janeiro, December 6, 1965.

Victor, Mário. *Cinco Anos que Abalaram o Brasil: de Jânio Quadros ao Marechal Castelo Branco.* Rio de Janeiro: Editôra Civilização Brasileira, 1965.

Vig, Norman. "The Communist Party of Brazil." Seminar Report, Columbia University, February 1963.

Walters, Vernon. Interviews, Rio de Janeiro, November 3, 1965; December 19, 1966.

Weatherhead, Richard W. See Maier, Joseph.

Werneck, Luís. Interview, São Paulo, November 24, 1965.

Ação Católica: Catholic Action. In the early 1950's Ação Católica established such Catholic Youth organizations as JEC, JOC, and JUC.

Ação Popular (AP): Popular Action. Established in 1962 by former leaders of JUC. Played important role in UNE (National Union of Students).

AID: Agency for International Development (USAID).

Alvorada Palace: presidential residence in Brasília (the capital of Brazil beginning in April 1960).

AMFORP: American and Foreign Power Company.

AP: SEE Ação Popular.

Ato Institucional: Institutional Act, modifying the constitution.

aventura: hazardous enterprise, or risky venture.

barranca colonel (*coronel de barranca*): a political boss in the interior who could count on electors to vote as he asked, often in return for favors. These colonels (*coroneis*) would negotiate with candidates for elective political office. The term was used by Almino Afonso, congressman from Amazonas, but was not generally used throughout Brazil.

bilhetinhos: short notes.

Brazilian Anti-Communist Crusade. SEE Cruzada Brasileira Anticomunista.

brigadeiro: brigadier. High Air Force rank.

brizoletas: term sometimes used in referring to small denominational notes used as local currency and issued by the state government of Rio Grande do Sul—of which Leonel Brizola was governor—during the political-military crisis of August–September 1961.

cabo: corporal.

câmara: chamber.

Câmara dos Deputados: Chamber of Deputies (House of Representatives).

CAMDE: Campanha da Mulher pela Democracia (Women's Campaign for Democracy). Rio de Janeiro (Guanabara) anti-Communist organization.

Campos Elísios Palace: palace of governorship of São Paulo.

Carioca: pertaining to, or native of, the city of Rio de Janeiro.

Casa Civil: civilian staff of the presidential office.

Casa Militar: military household; the military staff of the presidential office.

Catete Palace: presidential palace in the city of Rio, now a museum.

CBTC: See Confederação Brasileira dos Trabalhadores Cristãos.

cédula oficial: official ballot.

cédula única: single ballot.

CGG: See Comando Geral de Greve.

CGT: See Comando Geral dos Trabalhadores. See also Comando de Greve dos Trabalhadores.

Círculos Operários: Worker Circles, formed by Catholic leaders of the Confederação Brasiliera dos Trabalhadores Cristãos.

Clube da Lanterna: Lantern Club, in which Lacerda was influential. It issued strong pronouncements against the post-Vargas Getulistas and was closed down by Kubitschek's military ministers in November 1956.

CNTC: Confederação Nacional dos Trabalhadores no Comércio (National Confederation of Workers in Commerce). An official labor confederation.

CNTI: Confederação Nacional dos Trabalhadores na Indústria (National Confederation of Workers in Industry). An official labor confederation.

CNTTMFA: Confederação Nacional dos Trabalhadores nos Transportes Marítimos, Fluviais, e Aéreos (National Confederation of Workers in Maritime, River, and Air Transport). An official labor confederation.

CNTTT: Confederação Nacional dos Trabalhadores no Transporte Terrestre (National Confederation of Land Transport Workers). An official labor confederation.

Comando de Greve dos Trabalhadores (CGT): Workers' Strike Command, of August–September 1961. An unofficial labor organization.

Comando Geral de Greve (CGG): General Strike Command. An unofficial labor organization. After calling two general strikes in 1962, it called itself the Comando Geral dos Trabalhadores (q.v.).

Comando Geral dos Trabalhadores (CGT): General Command of Workers. Not official.

comício: meeting; rally.

Comissão Nacional de Sindicalização Rural: National Commission for Rural Syndicalization, established late in 1962 by the Labor Ministry and SUPRA to promote the formation of rural *sindicatos*.

concentração: concentration; gathering of people.

confederação: confederation. In the officially sponsored arrangement, a confederation is made up of participating employee or employer federations.

Confederação Brasileira dos Trabalhadores Cristãos (CBTC): Brazilian Confederation of Christian Workers. Catholic, not Far Left, and not part of government's official arrangement.

conselho: board.

Constitutionalist Revolution: unsuccessful revolution of 1932 against Vargas and the Provisional Government (1930–1934) he headed. The revolutionaries, located almost exclusively in São Paulo, maintained that the dictatorial Provisional Government (which had taken over Brazil after the 1930 revolution) did not intend to arrange for Brazil to have elections and a constitution.

CONTAG: Confederação Nacional dos Trabalhadores na Agricultura (National Confederation of Workers in Agriculture). An official labor confederation, established in December 1963.

CONTEC: Confederação Nacional dos Trabalhadores nos Estabelecimentos de Crédito (National Confederation of Workers in Credit Establishments). An official labor confederation.

CPOS: Comissão Permanente de Organizações Sindicais (Permanent Commission of Union Organizations). A Guanabara unofficial council of industrial labor leaders, established during Kubitschek's government by Ari Campista and Communists. Communists took control and Campista left.

CPSU: Communist Party of the Soviet Union.

Cruzada Brasileira Anticomunista. Brazilian Anti-Communist Crusade. An organization, largely civilian, established in 1952 and headed by Admiral Carlos Pena Bôto. It enjoyed considerable press support until 1957. At its height it had, according to Pena Bôto, about 10,000 dues-paying supporters, but it is much smaller today.

Cruzada Democrática: Democratic Crusade. An anti-Communist group of military officers, which was victorious in the Military Club election of May 1952.

cruzeiro: Brazilian unit of currency. In 1955 about 75 cruzeiros could purchase one dollar. The cruzeiro steadily declined in value so that at the end of March 1964 it took 1840 cruzeiros to purchase one dollar.

CUTAL: Central Única de Trabajadores de América Latina (Single Center of Workers of Latin America). Communist-controlled Latin American labor organization.

Democratic Crusade. SEE Cruzada Democrática.

deputado: congressman or assemblyman.

diminuição moral: loss of status.

discurso bomba: speech made to provoke a great reaction.

dispositivo: backing, support, arrangement, layout. *dispositivo militar*: military backing. *dispositivo sindical:* backing by organized labor.

EMFA: Estado Maior das Fôrças Armadas (The Armed Forces General Staff).

enrolar: to roll up or wrap up.

entreguista: term used to speak of a Brazilian said to be working to turn Brazil or Brazil's assets over to foreigners.

Escola Superior de Guerra: National War College.

FAB: Fôrça Aérea Brasileira. Brazilian Air Force.

favela: slum.

federação: federation. In the officially sponsored arrangement, a federation is made up of participating *sindicatos* (unions or employers' groups). The American Embassy in Rio de Janeiro advises that "Five or more unions may band together to form a federation. Three or more federations (which are usually organized on a state-wide or interstate basis) may band together to form a national confederation" (see H. W. Baker *et al.,* "Labor Directory: Brazil," p. 20).

Fôrça Pública: São Paulo state police force.

Forum Sindical de Debates de Santos: Syndical Forum of Discussions of Santos. Far Left labor organization. Not official.

frente: front.

Frente de Mobilização Popular: Popular Mobilization Front. Far Left front.

Frente de Renovação Nacional: Front of National Renovation, supporting Juarez Távora and Milton Campos for President and Vice-President in 1955.

Frente Parlamentar Nacionalista (FPN): Nationalist Parliamentary Front.

frente popular: popular front.

Fundo de Ação Social. São Paulo anti-Communist organization established by businessmen associated with foreign firms.

Gaúcho: pertaining to, or native of, Rio Grande do Sul (southernmost state).

gerencialismo (from *gerenciar*—to manage): a word coined by Ademar de Barros to denote the efficient management he proposed to put into practice if elected President of Brazil.

Getulista: connected with Getúlio Vargas or with his followers.

golpe: coup.

golpista: favoring a coup.

Green Shirt: SEE Integralista.

Grupo Compacto: Compact Group. PTB supporters of a nationalist and leftist bloodless revolution.

Grupo da Sorbonne: group of officers connected with the Escola Superior de Guerra (National War College).

Grupos de Onze Companheiros: Groups of Eleven Companions, organized by Brizola.

Guanabara Palace: Once a presidential palace in Rio de Janeiro, this became the office of the governor of Guanabara in 1960. In that year the federal capital was moved from Rio de Janeiro to Brasília, and the old federal district (including the city of Rio de Janeiro) became the state of Guanabara.

Guarda Civil: city police force.

horário duplo: a workday with specified hours in the morning and in the afternoon and with time off for lunch. This differed from the *horário corrido,* according to which the employee would work without a lunch break. The *horário corrido,* sometimes consisting of six hours for government workers, often allowed such a worker to hold also a job with another employer.

IBAD: Instituto Brasileiro de Ação Democrática (Brazilian Institute of Democratic Action). Anti-Communist organization, well known for supporting electoral candidates who opposed the Far Left.

ICFTU: International Confederation of Free Trade Unions.

Ilha das Cobras: Island of the Snakes. Just off the Navy Ministry in Rio, it has naval installations.

impedimento: impediment.

impedir: to impede. SEE *votação de impedimento.*

IMF: International Monetary Fund.

impôsto sindical: tax on all wage and salary earners (established by the Provisional Government [1930–1934] of Vargas at one day's pay per year) for supporting the official setup of syndicates, federations, and confederations.

Integralista: pertaining to Ação Integralista Brasileira, a nationalist political party of the 1930's, whose members marched and saluted in green shirts on behalf of "God, Country, and Family." Its "national chief" was Plínio Salgado.

Instituto Cultural do Trabalho (ICT): Cultural Institute of Labor. São Paulo anti-Communist organization for training labor leaders throughout Brazil.

intervenção: intervention. The federal government, on numerous occasions during the twentieth century, found reasons for declaring state governments ended and for appointing *interventores* to run the states on behalf of the federal government. Similarly, the federal government has, at times, "intervened" in labor unions.

IPÊS: Instituto de Pesquisas e Estudos Sociais (Institute of Social Research and Studies). Anti-Communist organization established by businessmen.

ISEB: Instituto Superior de Estudos Brasileiros (Higher Institute of Brazilian Studies). Nationalistic; government-supported.

Janguista: connected with Jango Goulart.

Janista: connected with Jânio Quadros.

JEC: Juventude Estudantil Católica (Catholic Student Youth). This organization played an important role in secondary school student organizations and in UBES.

JOC: Juventude Operária Católica (Catholic Working Youth).

JUC: Juventude Universitária Católica (Catholic University Youth). This organization played an important role in the UNE until 1962, when some JUC leaders helped form Ação Popular; thereafter Ação Popular played that role among university youths.

Laranjeiras Palace: Presidential palace in the city of Rio, used by the presidency before and after the transfer of the federal capital to Brasília.

legalidade: legality.

Liga Feminina Nacionalista da Guanabara: Women's Nationalist League of Guanabara.

ligas camponesas: peasant leagues.

MEB: Movimento de Educação de Base (Basic Education Movement). Established by bishops, with Education Ministry assistance, to use radio in advancing basic education. Also used primers to reduce illiteracy.

memorial: memorandum.

Mineiro: pertaining to, or native of, state of Minas Gerais.

MMC: Movimento Militar Constitucionalista (Constitutionalist Military Movement). Supported the inauguration of Kubitschek and Goulart after the 1955 election.

MNPT: Movimento Nacional Popular Trabalhista (National Popular Labor Movement). Communist-controlled organization backing Kubitschek for President and Goulart for Vice-President in 1955.

Movimento Nacionalista Feminino: Women's Nationalist Movement.

Movimento Sindical da Guanabara: Union Movement of Guanabara. Unofficial labor leader group, in Communist hands in the early 1960's.

MSD: Movimento Sindical Democrático (Democratic Syndical Movement). Anti-Communist labor organization. Not official.

NOVACAP: Companhia Urbanizadora da Nova Capital. Urbanizing Company of the New Capital.

Operação Limpeza: Operation Cleanup.

ORIT: Organización Regional Interamericana de Trabajadores (Inter-American Regional Organization of Workers). Non-Communist.

PAC: Pacto de Ação Conjunta (Pact of United Action). Unofficial labor organization.

Pacto de Unidade e Ação (PUA): Pact of Unity and Action. Far Left labor organization. Not official. Originally a group of maritime and railroad workers who went on strike during Kubitschek's presidency.

Palácio da Liberdade: Liberty Palace. Palace of the governor of the state of Minas Gerais.

Paulista: pertaining to, or native of, São Paulo.

PCB: Until 1961: Partido Comunista do Brasil (Communist Party of Brazil). After 1961: Partido Comunista Brasileiro (Brazilian Communist Party). Headed by Luís Carlos Prestes and affiliated with Moscow.

PDC: Partido Democrata Cristão (Christian Democratic Party). Political party.

Petrobrás: Petróleo Brasileiro, S.A. Brazilian government petroleum company, with monopoly on petroleum extraction.

PL: Partido Libertador (Liberator Party). Small political party (in which Raul Pilla was influential) originally established in the state of Rio Grande do Sul in the 1920's.

Planalto Palace: presidential office in Brasília, the capital of Brazil beginning in April 1960.

POLOP: Política Operária. Marxist revolutionary organization active in UNE.

PR: Partido Republicano (Republican Party). Political party in which Artur Bernardes and his son were influential.

PRP: Partido de Representação Popular (Party of Popular Representation).

Political party in which Plínio Salgado (former Integralista Green Shirt leader) was influential.

PSB: Partido Socialista Brasileiro (Brazilian Socialist Party). Political party.

PSD: Partido Social Democrático (Social Democratic Party). Political party established in 1945 at the suggestion of Getúlio Vargas.

PSP: Partido Social Progressista (Social Progressive Party). Political party in which Ademar de Barros was influential.

PTB: Partido Trabalhista Brasileiro (Brazilian Labor Party). Political party established in 1945 at the suggestion of Getúlio Vargas.

PUA: SEE Pacto de Unidade e Ação.

República Sindicalista: Syndicalist Republic. Said to be a republic run by labor unions.

sindicato: syndicate. Labor union or employers' group. To become official these have to be approved by the Labor Ministry.

Sociedade Rural Brasileira: Brazilian Rural Society. Represented landowners.

SUDENE: Superintendência do Desenvolvimento do Nordeste (Superintendency for the Development of the Northeast). Government entity.

SUMOC: Superintendência da Moeda e do Crédito (Superintendency of Money and Credit). Government entity.

SUPRA: Superintendência de Política Agrária (Superintendency of Agrarian Policy). Government entity.

tenente: lieutenant. Used to denote an Army officer who participated in the movements that resulted in the revolutions of 1922, 1924–1927, and 1930.

Tiradentes Palace: meeting place of federal Chamber of Deputies in Rio, before federal capital was moved to Brasília (1960).

Tribuna da Imprensa: Rio daily newspaper, managed for years by Carlos Lacerda.

Tribunal Superior Eleitoral: Superior Electoral Tribunal. Top court in the electoral justice system.

UBES: União Brasileira dos Estudantes Secundários (Brazilian Union of Secondary School Students). Secondary school students' official organization.

UCF: SEE União Cívica Feminina.

UDN: União Democrática Nacional (National Democratic Union). Political party organized in 1945 to oppose Getúlio Vargas.

ULTAB: União dos Lavradores e Trabalhadores Agrícolas do Brasil (Union of Farm Hands and Agricultural Workers of Brazil). Communist body for organizing peasants.

Ultima Hora: pro-Vargas and pro-Goulart daily newspaper, managed by Samuel Wainer.

UNE: União Nacional dos Estudantes (National Union of Students). Official organization of university students.

União Cívica Feminina (UCF): Women's Civic Union. São Paulo anti-Communist organization.

UST: União Sindical dos Trabalhadores (Syndical Union of Workers). Not official. Active in 1963, and said to have been leftist, pro-Goulart, and independent of Communist labor leaders.

VARIG: S. A. Emprêsa de Viação Aérea Riograndense. The oldest commercial airline in Brazil, founded in 1927.

votação de impedimento: vote taken in the Chamber of Deputies and the Senate to support the motion that the President or Acting President of Brazil found himself impeded—prevented by the force of circumstances —from governing, and that he should therefore be replaced by the next-in-line.

Voz da Legalidade: Voice of Legality. Radio program of Brizola.